ACKNOWLEDGMENTS

Laubach Literacy International wishes to thank Winifred Seely Myers Love for her generous gift to *The Frank C. Laubach Heritage Collection* in honor of the Seely Family and in loving memory of Effa Seely (Mrs. Frank) Laubach.

Laubach Literacy International also gratefully acknowledges the support of The Chatlos Foundation and the following persons whose generous gifts assisted in the publication of *The Frank C. Laubach Heritage Collection*:

Dorothy M. Ballard
Louise H. Bashore
Todd & Lucile Brownlee
William H. Foland in loving memory of his wife, Mary Beth Foland
Marie E. Foust & Amon L. Stauffer
Sylvia N. Furtick
Ida & Hunter Goodrich in loving memory of Nina H. Goodrich
   & Julie V. Heal
John & Louise Hawkins
Walter Kline Hillmer & Walter Knox Hillmer
   in loving memory of Mary E. Hillmer
William S. Lewis
Edna M. Schmidt
Bertha Henry Taylor

THE HERITAGE COLLECTION

FRANK C. LAUBACH

Man of Prayer

*Selected writings
of a world missionary*

Introduction by
Karen R. Norton

Laubach Literacy International
Syracuse, New York

ISBN 0-88336-580-4

Copyright © 1990 by Laubach Literacy International, Syracuse, New York

    All rights reserved. No portion of this book may be reproduced without written permission from Laubach Literacy International.

    This collection was published to preserve the main body of Frank C. Laubach's written works. The three volumes: *Man of Prayer*, *Teacher* and *Man of Justice and Peace*, share his thoughts and describe his tireless efforts along the many paths he walked toward his vision of a better world.

    The written works selected for this collection are out of print, as are the many other books, booklets and pamphlets written by Frank C. Laubach. By necessity, many of the books selected have not been reprinted in their entirety. Original versions of Frank C. Laubach's written works may be available through the public library system, or may be studied in the Frank C. Laubach reading room at Laubach Literacy International in Syracuse, New York.

    The four book collection may be purchased from:

New Readers Press, publishing division
of Laubach Literacy International
1320 Jamesville Avenue, Box 131
Syracuse, New York 13210

Contents

INTRODUCTION   1

Part 1. Letters by a Modern Mystic   17

Part 2. Learning the Vocabulary of God   49

Part 3. You Are My Friends
    Christ Is the World's Hope   115
    Christ in Our Midst Today   122
    Christ Pursuing Us   129
    Christ Speaks to Us All   139
    You Must Be Born Again   142
    How His Love Enlarges Us   149
    Working with Him   159
    The Rewards of His Friendship   167
    Christ's Friendship Is Its Own Reward   178
    Mystical Experiences   186

Part 4. Game with Minutes   191

Part 5. Prayer: The Mightiest Force in the World
    Pray for World Leaders   213
    Pray for the Church   218
    How Prayer Helps God   223
    Prayer Experiments   230
    Christ—The Answer   242
    Our Appalling Power   252

Part 6. Channels of Spiritual Power
    The Only Way Out   261
    Becoming Sons of God   267
    Christ Opens the Way   273
    God the Bridge Builder   279
    Saints Get Blocked, Too!   283
    How to Be a River   290

God Speaks   298
How We Can Help God   311
How We Can Save the World   319

Part 7. Two Articles on Prayer
Meditation on The Lord's Prayer   325
What Kind of Prayer Abides?   327

Introduction

By Karen R. Norton

The Formative Years

Frank Laubach was born in Benton, Pennsylvania in 1884 and grew to young manhood amidst the values and security of late nineteenth-century, small-town America. His life was shaped by the example of his parents' charity toward neighbors and by participation in the religious activities that were so central to town life. He described his youthful commitment at the altar of the Benton Methodist Church as one of the high points of his life.

When he was about 16, Laubach began to take seriously a call to the ordained ministry. After three years of school teaching and five years of higher education, he enrolled jointly in Union Theological Seminary and Columbia University in New York City. The Seminary's scholarly approach to biblical studies challenged Laubach's faith and raised questions he resolved — 15 years later — through direct knowledge of God.

At Union, Harry Emerson Fosdick and others introduced him to "higher criticism," an historical and linguisitic approach to biblical studies that demonstrates that the Old Testament and Gospels are a compendium of oral and written reports woven together by editors, who also added their own interpretations. In this view, the Bible is, at least in part, a record of people's struggle to understand God.

Walter Rauschenbusch, the theologian of the "social gospel," was immensely popular while he was in theological school. Laubach named him as a primary theological influence. Rauschenbusch pastored a New York City church near "Hell's Kitchen," where he discovered that a religion focused on individual piety and salvation was thoroughly inadequate in addressing the suffering he saw every day. He spent the rest of his life developing a theological context for Christian social activism. Rauschenbusch also cultivated a deep personal spirituality, and he published both theological and devotional works. Laubach's life was to mirror Rauschenbusch's work in many ways.

In 1914 while he was completing his Ph.D in sociology, Laubach, 30, was commissioned a missionary by the Congregational Church. He and his wife, Effa, were sent to Lanao, the northwest province of the Philippine Island of Mindanao. Lanao was occupied by American troops, who were trying to keep peace among the Islamic Maranao people. Laubach had longed for just such a challenge — to serve where the need was great and conditions difficult. But the Maranao people did not welcome a Christian missionary, and the climate was so volatile that American officers advised him to leave.

During the next fifteen years, he organized churches, helped establish Union Theological Seminary in Manila, served for a year as Dean of the School of Education at the University of Manila, wrote two books about the Philippines, and traveled extensively in the United States to interpret the Philippine mission.

About 1925 Laubach's active and seemingly successful career fell apart. The Board of Trustees of Union Theological Seminary decided to establish a separate adminstration for its growing college in Manila, which prepared young Filipinos for seminary. Laubach, a member of the Board, wanted the new position of president of the college. Out of chivalry, he voted for his opponent and lost the presidency by one vote.

Laubach was disappointed and bitter. For the next two years an onslaught of illnesses left him a semi-invalid. When he finally realized that his own attitude was affecting his health, he determined that he needed a richer devotional life and closer contact with the God he was called to serve. He tried to call God to mind at least once every quarter hour, but the discipline did not take root.

Finally restored to health after an extended furlough in the United States, Laubach was offered the opportunity for which he had waited. Tensions had eased in Lanao, and his mission board invited him to return.

When he arrived in Lanao on December 1, 1929, Laubach was bursting with plans for the Maranao people. But his plans were not their plans, and he was rebuffed. Once again Laubach was faced with failure, and the chasm between his high ambitions and the reality of his situation deepened his sense of defeat. For more than a decade he had been convinced that the Philippines would become a light for the Orient. For twenty years he had felt a distinct call to a "large needy work, larger than I am and needing just me," but the nature of that work had never been clear.

To add to his discouragement, Laubach was deeply lonely. He and his wife, Effa, had already lost three children to malaria. Because there were no health services available in Lanao, Effa and their only surviving child remained at Baguio, 900 miles to the north.

In despair, Laubach with his dog, Tip, sought the solitude of Signal Hill, overlooking Lake Lanao. From the depths of his anguish he appealed for the companionship of God. As Laubach recalled:

> Tip had his nose up under my arm and was trying to lick the tears off my cheeks. My lips began to move and it seemed to me that God was speaking.

"My child," my lips said, "you have failed because you do not really love these Moros (Maranaos). You feel superior to them because you are white. If you can forget you are an American and think only how I love them, they will respond."

I answered back to the sunset, "God, I don't know whether you spoke to me through my lips, but if you did, it was the truth. My plans have all gone to pieces. Drive me out of myself and come and take possession of me and think thy thoughts in my mind."

My lips spoke to me again: "If you want the Moros to be fair to your religion, be fair to theirs. Study their Koran with them."

I went down the hill and told some panditas (priests) that I wanted to study their Koran. The next day they crowded into my little cottage, each with a Koran under his arm. They were bent upon making a Moslem out of me! So we went to work with great zeal.[1]

Laubach returned to Signal Hill every evening, seeking God's guidance and companionship. He felt like a pioneer in two efforts at once. He was developing a literacy campaign in the Maranao language, and it was warmly received. But in his spiritual explorations, he felt very alone, out of step with his colleagues and the theological tradition of which he was a part. The challenges he received from others mirrored his own doubts about the truth of his inner experience. In a letter to his father, he recorded a conversation with a staff member of his mission board.

"Miss _____ had raised the question which had come to me a thousand times whether I had a right to separate my family for any cause. "But," I had replied, "it is certain to me that it is God's will and that I must be here. Then she had replied, "Men sometimes think that it is the will of God when it is their own selfish desires. I think it is horrible for you to be separated from your family for four months. Men like you ought never to marry...."

I went home to a dreadful night. For if I could not trust the voice of God in my own soul, if what I thought was God was really some subtle selfishness which I myself could not fathom, then the very universe had cracked asunder for me. If this was not God, who had given me such wondrous hours of fellowship and comfort when I was lonesome, I could not help doubting all religion. The night was poisoned hell, and I arose haggard and sick.

Then when I saw Miss _____ I showed her the article I had written about the wonderful way God is walking ahead of me here preparing the way. She replied, "American educated people will not take any stock in that. God is not bothering with such trivial things. He is too lofty for trifles. What you thought was God was really your own quickness to see and appropriate opportunities....Americans will like what you write better if you do not tell them that God is going around interfering with nature for your benefit."[2]

This challenge gave Laubach the opportunity he needed to conquer his own doubts. He quickly resolved to continue the spiritual experiment that lasted a lifetime. It was a strenuous journey, and he continued to challenge himself, seeking moment by moment to do God's will. His faith gradually grew to a simple, profound, and radiant trust.

Theological Perspectives

Mysticism

> It is as much our duty to live in the beauty of the presence of God on some mount of transfiguration until we become white with Christ as it is for us to go down where they grope, and grovel, and groan, and lift them to new life.[3]

Laubach continued to feel isolated and set apart in his spiritual explorations, and he read voraciously to find confirmation, companionship, and self-understanding. His most immediate sources of inspiration were the saints and mystics of the Catholic Church. He was particularly drawn to the writings of St. Theresa, a sixteenth-century Spanish nun, one of a school of Carmelite mystics. St. Theresa described seven stages of the inner journey, which culminates, through periods of intense ecstacy and anguish, in peaceful union with Christ.

None of Laubach's reading, however, was a substitute for direct, unmediated communion with God. He rigorously cultivated an attitude of openness and regularly awoke at 4:00 a.m., concentrating intensely to create the inner quiet needed to hear God. In the early years, the experience was often ecstatic and transforming, and sometimes painful as he acknowledged the tremendous waste of his earlier "unled life" and his failure to respond to the loving presence that had always been at hand.

Laubach was sensitive to the popular view that mysticism is an esoteric, passive, or cloistered activity. Thus his definition of mysticism was simple and inclusive: "Everybody is a mystic if he believes that God answers back when he prays." Millions of people have had mystical experiences; the difference between these millions and the classical mystics is only a matter of sustained effort.

Over time the mystic grows more deeply aware of the presence of the God who dwells within. But Laubach insisted that the mystical experience is not validated by the intensity of the emotion that accompanies it. It is "not spiritual chills and fevers but abiding faith." Above all the experience of God will meet one acid test: If it is genuine, the mystic will want to work with God to visit the sick, feed the hungry, and give hope to the oppressed.

Laubach knew that he could not capture the mystical experience in words or logic, and he referred repeatedly to the barrier his education erected against intimate friendship with God. He considered his theological education an obstacle not because it was "wrong" but because it was partial; it appealed to his mind, but not to his heart. It did not fire or transform his whole person. But Laubach did not reject the role of thinking in the spiritual life, and his theological training shaped the experience of the God he was seeking.

The Nature of God

> I obey no man-made orthodoxy. The one thing of which you can always be sure when you hear a statement about me is — "God is more than that."[4]

Laubach believed that the idea of God is always evolving. God comes to each stage of culture in the form that culture can understand. Thus the "light of Christ" is present in all religions, no matter how primitive or sophisticated.

In his early years, Laubach saw great potential for bridging divisions between people through devotion to the one God found in all religions. It seemed to him "that people of all sects may try this constant fellowship with God. Even those of other religions like Islam may do so. And why not the Hindus? An inner circle which cannot interfere with or antagonize any sect could grow up...and do away with a great deal of hypocrisy which now exists."[5]

Because of this stance, Laubach sought to identify and adopt the truth he saw in non-Christian faiths. The influence of Hinduism and Islam was particularly apparent in his understanding of the nature of God. Hinduism taught him of God's immanence. Islam taught him the centrality of the will of God and the futility of presuming to coax God to change the universal laws God has established.

Laubach was awed by God the Creator. In the laws of evolution he saw the blueprint of creation, a vast, on-going process reaching toward completion. But he was even more awed by the opportunity God gives to human beings. Despite their weakness and insignificance as measured against the scale of the universe, God invites people to participate in finishing the creation.

Laubach's primary focus was on this intimate God, the God who has chosen to need co-creators. He described a God who enjoys and needs love and prayer and who waits for those who will accept the invitation to work on behalf of the creation.

From those who accept the invitation, God demands all — a full-hearted obedience and surrender. In Laubach's view, "obedience" is not the mark of slavery but a means of discovering the deep correspondence between God and humanity. When men and women live out of this correspondence, they willingly and eagerly desire to do God's will.

Though people cannot begin to know God's total plan, God is amazingly immanent and accessible to the sincere seeker. Laubach found God at all times, in all places, and under all conditions. "Everything is bathed in God. I swim in God as a fish in the sea. Every object is my idol to remind me of God."[6]

Jesus

> Jesus was strongly on the side of the poor.[7]

The sharpest distinction Laubach made between God and the Son of God is that God can never be described or understood. Jesus, on the other hand, is deeply appealing and always available to the human heart, and Laubach sought to make him a brotherly companion.

Jesus is the Son of God because of his minute-by-minute obedience to God. Jesus continually asks God, "What, Father, do you want me to do?" His constant communication and immediate response becomes communion, and through this oneness, Jesus reveals God's nature. Jesus shows God's tenderness, compassion, and willingness to suffer on behalf of creation. He forever removes the fear that God is the judge and policeman of the universe. Jesus accepts and even welcomes human imperfections, for they are his opportunity to pour out transforming love.

Jesus is not an idea or an abstraction but a magnetically beautiful person who loves compellingly and can be loved in return. Everyone hungers to love and be loved, and it is this deep longing that draws Jesus into the human heart. Some of the greatest mystics have the deepest human passions, and these, Laubach wrote, can be lavished on Jesus. Jesus can be loved without restraint, with utter abandon.

Jesus' love and companionship empower his followers to emulate his example, and Laubach emphasized three aspects of this example to which all people are invited to aspire. The first is Jesus' constant communion with God. From this communion flows his unceasing service to humanity. Jesus seeks the hungry, the broken, and the sick, and loves the unlovely, not for what they are but for what they can become. If people seeking Jesus' companionship through prayer feel spiritually dry, Laubach said, it is probably because Jesus is at work in a slum or a prison waiting for them to catch up.

Laubach was well aware that the way of Jesus is often at odds with organized religion. Religious people, he observed, are often snobbish, desiring to associate only with what is beautiful. Jesus, however, ate with the outcast. His standard for choosing friends is the depth of their need — not how much they can offer but how much they can receive. Followers of Jesus must practice this standard of friendship just as surely as they pray.

The crucifixion is the ultimate mark of Jesus' devotion to humanity. He experienced human suffering on the cross, and, through his identification with all who are in need, he continues to suffer. Men and women understand the injustice of Jesus' death on the cross, Laubach believed, and through deep companionship with Jesus, they can also learn to recognize the great social evils that help cause the suffering of those with whom he identifies. Social injustice, Laubach wrote, is camouflaged, so ingrained that it is taken for granted. A deep friendship with Jesus is a "color card" for identifying these institutional wrongs.

Laubach also saw in Jesus' obedience unto death an example for contemporary men and women. He warned that giving up self-interest also means giving up self protection. One may be cheated, robbed, or beaten. Followers of Jesus may also be called to die in the cause of justice. If so, they will experience the full mystery of suffering love.[8]

The Role of Humanity

> God has set millions of little gods free on this earth to create whatever we think about. We are "Sons of God" with a vengance.[9]

In Laubach's view it is entirely possible for people to build the Kingdom of God on earth — provided it is built in partnership with God. They can be co-creators with God, participants in the creative process that began with the creation of the universe.

God has put no limits on human freedom; the human race is free to do what it will, free even to destroy itself in war. The root cause of this danger, Laubach held, is that individuals and nations alike are guided by self-interest and greed.

Laubach believed in social and political reform, but he also believed that reform tends to follow rather than lead public morality. If reform is not widely accepted, it is only a staying action. Lasting change can only be brought about by a radical transformation of human nature. Then earth can be "annexed to heaven."

The perfection of humanity is a dangerous concept, however. Again and again Laubach wrote that men and women can grow toward perfection but never achieve it.

Prayer Discipline

> Any method, absolutely any method, is your method if you find it opens the doors toward heaven and helps you gain close contact with God. And it is not your method, no matter who does it, if it does not succeed in doing that.[10]

Laubach defined prayer as any effort or activity that fosters the awareness of God's presence. Prayer is the simple recognition that God is present at all times, under all conditions and through all people. Prayer may be answered by a wordless sense of the Presence. Or the answer may be more specific — a deed to be done or an attitude that must change.

Cultivating openness to the universal Presence, however, takes time. Laubach advised the beginner to start slowly and work toward spending an hour or two a day in prayer. When it is sustained for years, the practice of prayer will become as natural as eating or sleeping.

Novices must pray out of the deepest desires of their hearts; otherwise, prayer does not involve the whole person. But the heart's desires will expand over time to include God's concerns for the world. This prayer "helps God" and builds toward the profound companionship Laubach valued above all.

Laubach was certain that boring prayer was useless, for he discovered in God constant surprise and continuous adventure. If he found a new approach to prayer uninteresting, he discarded it. His own favorite techniques were humming the Methodist hymns he'd learned as a child, practicing two-way conversations with God, and constant reading of the scriptures.

Laubach's prayer techniques engage the senses of sight, sound, smell and touch. Some include physical movement. Writing, talking out loud, gazing at a picture or photograph, or reading a book to God are all helpful forms of prayer. Prayers do not need to be long and elaborate. Simply whispering "Jesus" to oneself during daily activities or holding in mind the image of Christ and the object of the prayer can be very effective.

Intercessory prayer — prayer on behalf of individuals and nations — was at the center of Laubach's prayer discipline. But Laubach redefined intercession. Instead of pleading with God to intercede on behalf of a person or situation, Laubach interceded with people by directing the power of his prayer toward opening their minds and hearts to God's will for them.

Through constant practice Laubach welded prayer and action into one. He carried the needs of the world into the heart of his solitary prayer, and he disciplined himself to find God in every detail of a life filled with constant activity. After twenty-five years of practicing the presence of God, he wrote that there is very little distinction between prayer and action. They are nearly simultaneous: "We cannot keep Him unless we give Him away."[11]

Prayer often suggests deeds to be done, and Laubach advised keeping a notebook handy to record the ideas that occur during prayer. But prayer is four-fifths of the deed because God helps to identify the most appropriate action, guides in its implementation, and releases energy to bring the deed to completion. Through prayer, God becomes a full partner in the action.

All the prayer techniques Laubach suggested, however, are only a beginning. They are but a knock on a door opening to a great adventure that depends only on God. Ultimately, prayer becomes a simple trust and a simple following, for in the end "there is nothing we can do excepting to throw ourselves open to God."

Discernment

> All that we need in this great venture...is courage and faith: courage in our own natural powers of inquiry, and faith that every question has its own appropriate answer.[12]

During the 1940s, when Laubach led prayer workshops throughout America, his listeners wanted to know how prayer is to be tested. How do we distinguish between what is of God and what is only wishful thinking? If we think we hear God speaking, how do we know it is not just auto-suggestion?

Laubach responded that scripture, observation, and experimentation are all means of validating the human experience of God. But the primary validation is that the experience will always be accompanied by a burning desire to serve others.

Laubach had studied the Bible for twenty years before he met God directly, and he knew the Bible was no substitute for the experience. Afterwards he read the scriptures, and particularly the Gospels, with new eyes. Their value was in exposing him, again and again, to the life and works of the One he knew first-hand.

The generation Laubach addressed had been shaken by an approach to biblical scholarship that teaches that much of the gospel record of the life of Jesus is not fact but theology. Who, then, is Jesus, and where is he to be found? Laubach cites the example of Albert Schweitzer, who

> accepting the 'higher criticism,' finds little solid ground for knowing the historical Jesus, and believes that if we are to know Him at all we must know Him by trying to follow His way of love and learning by experience what the eternal Christ will do to us when we follow Him. Schweitzer is trying that experiment with Christ in his Africa mission.[13]

Laubach was convinced that all people are as capable as Schweitzer of discovering, through their own experiments, the truth of the living God. He believed that science and spirituality are compatible, and that in time, science would even discover research methods that would give prayer a scientific basis.

Laubach told prospective prayer practitioners that it is not necessary to believe in order to begin the experiment. They need only make a sincere effort and observe the results. Any reasonable thought or course of action is God's voice. Anything that leads people from wrongdoing or enkindles selfless love is God's call.

In the absence of commonly accepted "laws of prayer," he recommended that prayer practitioners keep a log of their prayer experiences and share them with others to uncover the commonalities. People who pray for others are urged to observe the impact on strangers for whom they pray.

A growing inner knowledge of God, developed over years of practicing the presence, is another standard against which to test answers to prayer. Is the answer to prayer consistent with other experiences of God? Is there a growing delight in God's companionship? If so, Laubach said, progress is being made.

Laubach settled for himself the question of discernment in the early years of his prayer experiences on Signal Hill. Weighing the consequences of belief and unbelief on his life, he chose to believe. His own struggle with discernment was replaced with a simple trust: God speaks and I listen. I speak and God listens.

Evangelism

> Those people in the Christian Church who think that they only will be saved for their orthodoxy, while the rest of us go to hell, do not know they are carrying into their religion the Pharisee's selfish desire to triumph over others.[14]

Laubach respected all religious traditions he encountered, finding great value in native religions, as well as the major religions of the world. At the same time, he was a harsh critic of Christianity and individual Christians. Laubach noted that Communism promised exactly what Christians should be doing: enabling men and women to rise above desperate poverty. The problem with Christianity was that

> we were not earnest enough about saving the world; we were obsessed by making money. We Christians today must therefore confess our responsibility for the failure of the world....What is the matter with our Christianity? We have watered down the high summons of Jesus until it sounds like a lazy, good natured, but utterly selfish philosophy of 'mind your own business'.[15]

Laubach understood the person and message of Jesus to be the most profound revelation of God. He emphasized, especially in his later years, that the world would be safe, the hungry fed, the naked clothed only by a radical transformation of human nature into the likeness of Christ. Hence, the whole world needed evangelization, including those Christian churches that promoted a "kind of half adherence, which is not a total surrender of all we have, but is merely conformity to the codes of respectability."[16]

Laubach's work with the Maranao people was launched when God directed him to study the Koran. While some members of Laubach's sponsoring mission board were distressed to learn of his Christian mysticism, others were distressed to learn that he had worshipped with the Maranaos in their mosque. Few of the Maranaos became Christian and Laubach knew that being Christian in name was worthless. Far better to be Islamic or Hindu in affiliation, while living the message of Jesus, as did some of the Maranao people and as did Gandhi.

The most effective evangelism, Laubach wrote, is by example. Christian missionaries do not need verbal "propaganda" if they respond to the needs of those around them. They must serve all people, not just those who are already Christian, as some of the missionary educators in India were doing.

Laubach said, however, that to follow the demanding ethic of Jesus one needed to know Jesus and be empowered by his companionship. So he shared the story of Jesus whenever it was appropriate.

> You people who cannot read and write are blind to what is in books. The educated people own all the land and have all the money, because they see the secrets in books which you cannot see. Jesus does not want you to be blind and hungry. He wants you to see. He wants you to have plenty of food and clothing for your children.[17]

Laubach offered this message of justice and human dignity to encourage the desperately poor in the struggle to improve their own lot. It could be the first step in developing what Laubach called religion, "not doctrine or faith, primarily, but primarily the directed will," through which God could pour out world-transforming love.

Man and Mystic: The Legacy

> So if anybody were to ask me how to find God I should say at once, hunt out the deepest need you can find and forget all about your own comfort while you try to meet that need. Talk to God about it, and—he will be there. You will know it.[18]

Frank Laubach achieved national recognition as a man of prayer and international recognition as a teacher of millions. He expanded the definition of "mystic" by fusing prayer with worldly action and bringing the needs of the world to the center of prayer.

During his lifetime, hundreds of thousands of his books were sold to spiritually hungry Americans. *Prayer: The Mightiest Force in the World* and *Channels of Spiritual Power* each sold more than 200,000 copies. *Letters by a Modern Mystic* has been reprinted more than twenty times.

In the popular religious press, reviewers commented on Laubach's simple, direct style and religious philosophy. Professional theologians had more difficulty with his works. One of them wrote that *You Are My Friends* would offend the sophisticated and the rational, "but to the humble, child-like seeker for Christ there breathes through this whole book a spirit of power, of faith, of enviably constant intimacy with the Saviour....What is it in our lives which makes us shun emotional commitment and communication?"[19] Other reviewers said that though Laubach wrote "graphically and beautifully," some readers might be uncomfortable with the personal experience the books contained.

Laubach was always very modest about the self revelation in his writings. He never thought of his mystical experiences as guidelines for others. He considered them his deepest and best experiences and offered them in the hope that others would share with him in return. There is a strange and unhelpful conspiracy of silence, he said, about what is best and most meaningful in us.

Those who heard Laubach speak or knew him personally were captivated by his radiance. Norman Vincent Peale wrote,

> While sitting in the pulpit of the Marble Collegiate Church, I happened to notice a man sitting rather far back in the sanctuary, which was filled with people. The light from one of the windows was falling on his face, which was in profile. I was struck with the extraordinary saintliness of this face, but I did not recognize the man. I only recall that the thought crossed my mind that here was a person not known to me, who truly had the light of God on his face. Suddenly he turned his head, and in the full view I saw that it was Frank Laubach. I feel that I was granted an unusual penetrative insight into the beautiful soul of this great man.[20]

Others were moved by Laubach's deep calm, which spoke to them of "the quiet rhythms of heaven." Some were struck by the power of his presence, even though no words were exchanged. Others remember one-to-one conversations, the intensity of Laubach's listening, and the value he placed on their personhood and their plans.

But the result of Laubach's prayer life was more than radiant being; it was also energetic doing. He worked to the end of his life creating literacy materials, helping to organize educational programs, and telling audiences across America of the needs of the silent billion. He traveled to 103 countries to help organize literacy programs in cooperation with mission programs, governments, and businesses. In railroad stations, on shipboard, in the backseats of cars he balanced his typewriter on his lap to write books and articles intended to unite spiritually hungry Americans with their starving brothers and sisters abroad.

Laubach expected never to cease working on behalf of the wounded world. He joked that if heaven was only a choir of harps, he'd prefer to remain earthbound, taking harp lessons. In more solemn moments, he was still haunted by the gulf between his ambition and his deeds. Very late in life, he commented:

> I am the world's chief failure. Babies come faster than literacy. My chief message...has been that we must adopt compassionate service, but today this nation believes more in naked power than ever in our history. We must bridge the vast chasm between the rich who grow richer and the poor who grow hungrier...but the chasm grows wider every year. But I am not dead yet, and I shall kick while life remains.[21]

If Frank Laubach was dissatisfied with his accomplishments, however, he was peaceful in the knowledge that God was calling others to complete the task. With energy, verve, and enthusiasm he told his listeners until the day he died: You are capable. You can save the world.

Laubach's Writings

Frank Laubach published fifteen books and pamphlets and numerous articles on prayer and other religious topics. The works printed in this volume contain the central themes of his written record. They are presented in chronological order. *Letters By A Modern Mystic*, *Learning the Vocabulary of God*, and *Game with Minutes* are printed in their entirety. *You Are My Friends*, *Prayer: the Mightiest Force in the World*, and *Channels of Spiritual Power* are excerpted. Two articles are also included.

The first three books in this volume are infused with the passion, ecstacy, and wonder of Laubach's direct experience with God. *Letters By A Modern Mystic* and *Learning the Vocabulary of God* record his struggle and success in practicing the presence of God. *You Are My Friends*, though not a daily journal, grew out of the author's passionate friendship with Jesus. In the remaining works in this volume Laubach describes how and why to pray.

In all of these works Laubach wanted to inspire his readers to launch their own spiritual expeditions and to share the profound joy that filled his own life. Laubach's works are straightforward and enlivened with poetic metaphor, anecdote, and scripture. His images are often compelling, always down to earth, and sometimes startling.

Frank Laubach called his writings only a rough map of one man's spiritual journey. In recounting his adventures, he did not want followers but fellow explorers in the unknown continent of prayer.

ENDNOTES

Notes in the introduction refer to these editions of the works of Frank C. Laubach.

Channels of Spiritual Power. Westwood, NJ: Fleming H. Revell, 1954.

Forty Years with the Silent Billion. Old Tappan, NJ: Fleming H. Revell, 1970.

Game with Minutes. St. Paul: Macalester Park, 1953.

How to Teach One and Win One for Christ. Grand Rapids, Michigan: Zondervan, 1964.

Learning the Vocabulary of God. Nashville: Upper Room, 1956.

Letters by a Modern Mystic. Syracuse: New Readers Press, 1979.

Prayer: The Mightiest Force in the World. New York: Fleming H. Revell, 1946.

You Are My Friends. Syracuse: New Readers Press, 1969.

1. *Forty Years with the Silent Billion*, pp. 26–27.
2. Laubach to father, March 9, 1930. The Laubach Collection, Syracuse University Archives, Box #1, File #4.
3. *Letters by a Modern Mystic*, p. 35.
4. *Learning the Vocabulary of God*, pp. 69–70.
5. Laubach to father, April 8, 1930. The Laubach Collection, Box #1, File #4.
6. *Learning the Vocabulary of God*, p. 12.
7. *You Are My Friends*, p. 6.
8. *Channels of Spiritual Power*, p. 64.
9. *Prayer: The Mightiest Force in the World*, p. 88.
10. *Channels of Spiritual Power*, p. 95.
11. Ibid., p. 133.
12. *You Are My Friends*, p. 17..
13. Laubach, "Solid Rock for Shaking Faith," n.d. The Laubach Collection, Box #113, File #4.
14. *Channels of Spiritual Power*, p. 106..
15. Ibid., p. 180.
16. *You Are My Friends*, p. 53.
17. *How to Teach One and Win One for Christ*, p. 36.

18. *Letters by a Modern Mystic*, p. 46.
19. N.F.S. Ferre, "*You Are My Friends*, by Frank C. Laubach," *Andover Newton Bulletin* (June, 1942).
20. Norman Vincent Peale quoted in David E. Mason, *Frank C. Laubach, Teacher of Millions* (Minneapolis: Dennison, 1967), p. 299.
21. Mason, *Frank C. Laubach, Teacher of Millions*, pp. 308–9.

Part 1

Letters by a Modern Mystic

Letters by a Modern Mystic

This volume is composed of excerpts from letters written during the two years following Frank Laubach's mystical and transforming experience on Signal Hill in the Philippines. Laubach's original letters contain descriptions of the two unknown continents he was exploring: the developing adult literacy effort and the practice of prayer.

The letters were first published in Laubach's hometown newspaper, *The Argus*. Missionary Constance Padwick of Cairo, Egypt later excerpted those portions of the letters describing Laubach's prayer experiments, mimeographed them, and circulated them to fellow missionaries. Padwick's collection was first published in America in 1937. It has been reprinted more than twenty times.

Windows open outward   January 3, 1930

To be able to look backward and say, "This, this has been the finest year of my life"—that is glorious! But anticipation! To be able to look ahead and say, "The present year can and shall be better!"—that is more glorious!

If we said such things about our achievements, we would be consummate egotists. But if we are speaking of God's kindness, and we speak truly, we are but grateful. And this is what I do witness. I have done nothing but open windows—God has done all the rest. There have been few if any conspicuous achievements. There has been a succession of marvelous experiences of the friendship of God. I feel, as I look back over the year, that it would have been impossible to have held much more without breaking with sheer joy. It was the lonesomest year, in some ways the hardest year, of my life, but the most gloriously full of voices from heaven.

And it closed very beautifully. The young men and girls of Silliman were gathered for a watch night service. We were resolving new high resolves until nearly twelve o'clock.

As for me I resolved that I would succeed better this year with my experiment of filling every minute full of the thought of God than I succeeded last year.

And I added another resolve—to be as wide open toward people and their need, as I am toward God. Windows open outward as well as upward! Windows especially open downward where people need most!

Conscious listening to
the inner voice   January 20, 1930

Living in the atmosphere of Islam is proving—thus far—a tremendous spiritual stimulus. Mohammed is helping me. I have no more intention of giving up Christianity and becoming a Mohammedan than I had twenty years ago, but I find myself richer for the Islamic experience of God.

Islam stresses the will of God. It is supreme. We cannot alter any of His mighty decrees. To try to do so means annihilation. Submission is the first and last duty of man.

That is exactly what I have been needing in my Christian life. Although I have been a minister and missionary for fifteen years, I have not lived the entire day of every day in minute by minute effort to follow the will of God. Two years ago a profound dissatisfaction led me to begin trying to line up my actions with the will of God about every fifteen minutes or every half hour. Other people to whom I confessed this intention said it was impossible. I judge from what I have heard that few people are really trying even that. But this year I have started out trying to live all my waking moments in conscious listening, to the inner voice, asking without ceasing, "What, Father, do you desire said? What, Father, do you desire this minute?"

It is clear that this is exactly what Jesus was doing all day every day. But it is not what His followers have been doing in very large numbers.

Open your soul and entertain the glory of God   **January 26, 1930**

You who will read these letters will know that I am here exploring two lands which for me are new. One of them is within my own soul, the other is in the soul of the Moros.

For the past few days I have been experimenting in a more complete surrender than ever before. I am taking by deliberate act of will, enough time from each hour to give God much thought. Yesterday and today I have made a new adventure, which is not easy to express. I am feeling God in each movement, by an act of will—willing that He shall direct these fingers that now strike this typewriter—willing that He shall pour through my steps as I walk—willing that He shall direct my words as I speak, and my very jaws as I eat!

You will object to this intense introspection. Do not try it, unless you feel dissatisfied with your own relationship with God, but at least allow me to realize all the leadership of God I can. I am disgusted with the pettiness and futility of my unled self. If the way out is not more perfect slavery to God than what is the way out? Paul speaks of our liberty in Christ. I am trying to be utterly free from everybody, free from my own self, but completely enslaved to the will of God every moment of this day.

We used to sing a song in the church in Benton which I liked, but which I never really practiced until now. It runs:

> "Moment by moment I'm kept in His love;
> Moment by moment I've life from above;
> Looking to Jesus till glory doth shine;
> Moment by moment, O Lord, I am Thine."

It is exactly that "moment by moment," every waking moment, surrender, responsiveness, obedience, sensitiveness, pliability, "lost in His love," that I now have the mind-bent to explore with all my might. It means two burning passions: First, to be like Jesus. Second, to respond to God as a violin responds to the bow of the master.

In defense of my opening my soul and laying it bare to the public gaze in this fashion, I may say that it seems to me that we really seldom do anybody much good excepting as we share the deepest experiences of our souls in this way. It is not the fashion to tell your inmost thoughts, but there are many wrong fashions, and concealment of the best in us is wrong. I disapprove of the usual practice of talking "small talk" whenever we meet, and holding a veil over our souls. If we are so impoverished that we have nothing to reveal but small talk, then we need to struggle for more richness of soul. As for me I am convinced that this spiritual pilgrimage which I am making is infinitely worthwhile, the most important thing I know of to talk about. And talk I shall while there is anybody to listen. And I hunger—O how I hunger! for others to tell me their soul adventures.

Outside the window, as I completed the last page, has been one of the most splendorous sunsets I have ever seen. And these words came singing through my soul, "Looking to Jesus 'till glory doth shine!" Glory had been shining all across the sky until everything was crimson. Even the paper on which I was writing became red with the reflection from the roseate sky. It was the reflection of my own soul where God had today been painting his wonderful visions. Is not this marvelous sky a parable! Open your soul and entertain the glory of God and after a while that glory will be reflected in the world about you and in the very clouds above your head.

Only one thing now   **January 29, 1930**

I feel simply carried along each hour, doing my part in a plan which is far beyond myself. This sense of cooperation with God in little things is what so astonishes me, for I never have felt it this way before. I need something, and turn round to find it waiting for me. I must work, to be sure, but there is God working along with me. To know this gives a sense of security and assurance for the future which is also new to my life. I seem to have to make sure of only one thing now, and every other thing "takes care of itself," or I prefer to say what is more true, God takes care of all the rest. My part is to live this hour in continuous inner conversation with God and in perfect responsiveness to His will. To make this hour gloriously rich. This seems to be all I need think about.

A lever to lift the world   **February 9, 1930**

I feel sure now that our thoughts flow around the world even when we do not express them. So I mean to make a contribution with my thoughts every hour. I am making a strenuous effort of will to concentrate upon people, those in my presence and those out of sight in order to send to them my thoughts of Christ. I propose to think as hard of God as I can when in crowds, in the confidence that really dynamic thought will influence many others.

Perhaps you have begun to suspect what tremendous dynamite lies hidden in this idea. If the Christian people, the really Christian people of the world began to comprehend the power of thought, they could use it as a lever to lift the world! If people realize that telepathy is a fact—though as yet not reduced to law—that ought to be the signal for a tremendous movement among Christian people to keep their thoughts right, to make them helpful every hour from morning to night. We may yet attempt to make the world over by the sheer force of good thoughts!

Undiscovered continents of spiritual living   March 1, 1930

The sense of being led by an unseen hand which takes mine while another hand reaches ahead and prepares the way, grows upon me daily. I do not need to strain at all to find opportunity. It piles in upon me as the waves roll over the beach, and yet there is time to do something about each opportunity.

Perhaps a man who has been an ordained minister since 1914 ought to be ashamed to confess that he never before felt the joy of complete hourly, minute by minute—now what shall I call it?—more than surrender. I had that before. More than listening to God. I tried that before. I cannot find the word that will mean to you or to me what I am now experiencing. It is a will act. I compel my mind to open straight out toward God. I wait and listen with determined sensitiveness. I fix my attention there, and sometimes it requires a long time early in the morning to attain that mental state. I determine not to get out of bed until that mind-set, that concentration upon God, is settled. It also requires determination to keep it there, for I feel as though the words and thoughts of others near me were constantly exerting a drag backward or sidewise. But for the most part recently I have not lost sight of this purpose for long and have soon come back to it. After awhile, perhaps, it will become a habit, and the sense of effort will grow less.

But why do I constantly harp upon this inner experience? Because I feel convinced that for me and for you who read there lies ahead undiscovered continents of spiritual living compared with which we are infants in arms.

And I must witness that people outside are treating me differently. Obstacles which I once would have regarded as insurmountable are melting away like a mirage. People are becoming friendly who suspected or neglected me. I feel, I feel like one who has had his violin out of tune with the orchestra and at last is in harmony with the music of the universe.

As for me, I never lived, I was half dead, I was a rotting tree, until I reached the place where I wholly, with utter honesty, resolved and then re-resolved that I would find God's will, and I would do that will though every fiber in me said no, and I would win the battle in my thoughts. It was as though some deep artesian well had been struck in my soul or souls and strength came forth. I do not claim success even for a day yet, in my mind, not complete success all day but some days are close to success, and every day is tingling with the joy of a glorious discovery. That thing is eternal. That thing is undefeatable. You and I shall soon blow away from our bodies. Money, praise, poverty, opposition, these make no difference, for they will all alike be forgotten in a thousand years, but this spirit which comes to a mind set upon continuous surrender, this spirit is timeless life.

Boundless joy broken loose   March 9, 1930

For the first time in my life I know what I must do off in lonesome Lanao. I know why God left this aching void, for Himself to fill. Off on this mountain I must do three things:

1. I must pursue this voyage of discovery in quest of God's will. I must because the world needs me to do it.

2. I must plunge into mighty experiments in intercessory prayer, to test my hypothesis that God needs my help to do His will for others, and that my prayer releases His power. I must be His channel, for the world needs me.

3. I must confront these Moros with a divine love which will speak Christ to them though I never use His name. They must see God in me, and I must see God in them. Not to change the name of their religion, but to take their hand and say, "Come, let us look for God."

A few days ago as we came on the priests, they were praying, in one boat with thirty-five Moros, many of whom called to me to join. So I held out my hands and prayed with them, and as earnestly as any of them. One of them said "He is Islam," and I replied, "A friend of Islam."

My teacher, Dato Pambaya, told me this week that a good Muslim ought to utter the sacred word for God every time he begins to do anything, to sleep, or walk, or work, or even turn around. A good Muslim would fill his life with God. I fear there are few good Muslims.

But so would a real Christlike Christian speak to God every time he did anything—and I fear there are few good Christians.

What right then have I or any other person to come here and change the name of these people from Muslim to Christian, unless I lead them to a life fuller of God than they have now? Clearly, clearly, my job here is not to go to the town plaza and make proselytes, it is to live wrapped in God, trembling to

His thoughts, burning with His passion. And, my loved one, that is the best gift you can give to your own town.

I look up at this page and it is not red hot as my soul is now. It is black ink. It ought to be written with the red ribbon. You will not see the tears that are falling on this typewriter, tears of a boundless joy broken loose.

The most wonderful discovery that has ever come to me is that I do not have to wait until some future time for the glorious hour. I need not sing, "Oh that will be glory for me—" and wait for any grave. This hour can be heaven. Any hour for any body can be as rich as God! For do you not see that God is trying experiments with human lives. That is why there are so many of them. He has one billion seven hundred million experiments going around the world at this moment. And His questions is, "How far will this man and that woman allow me to carry this hour?" This Sunday afternoon at three o'clock He was asking it of us all. I do not know what the rest of you said, but as for me, I asked, "God, how wonderful dost Thou wish this hour alone with Thee to be?" And God answered convincingly:

"It can be as wonderful as any hour that any human being has ever lived. For I who pushed life up through the protozoan and the tiny grass, and the fish and the bird and the dog and the gorilla and the man, and who am reaching out toward divine sons, I have not become satisfied yet. I am not only willing to make this hour marvelous. I am in travail to set you akindle with the Christ-thing which has no name. How fully can you surrender and not be afraid?"

And I answered:

"Fill my mind with Thy mind to the last crevice. Catch me up in Thine arms and make this hour as terribly glorious as any human being ever lived, if Thou wilt.

"And God, I scarce see how one could live if his heart held more than mine has had from Thee these past two hours."

Will they last? Ah, that is the question I must not ask. I shall just live this hour on until it is full, then step into the next hour. Neither tomorrow matters, nor yesterday. Every now is an eternity if it is full of God.

But how "practical" is this for the average man? It seems to me now that yonder plowman could be like Calixto Sanidad, when he was a lonesome and mistreated plowboy, "with my eyes on the furrow, and my hands on the lines, but my thoughts on God." The carpenter could be as full of God as was Christ when he drove nails. The millions at looms and lathes could make the hours glorious. Some hour spent by some night watchman might be the most glorious ever lived on earth. God is not through yet. He is breaking through and I think the poor have less callousness for Him to overcome as a rule than have the rich.

On the other hand the rich man has the wonderful opportunity of paying a sacrifice which will cut his heart almost out. If he seeks the place where his wealth is needed most, then throws all he has into that cause and then throws himself into the cause with his money, as Jesus asked the rich young ruler to do, his money will at that moment be transmuted into the golden threads of heaven. Maybe there is another way, but to me there seems only a blank wall for wealthy men save through the doorway I have entered, a sacrifice that hurts and hurts and—behind Calvary, God!

Outside the sky is alight with golden sunset. To me that is God, working on the sky, as He has worked so wonderfully this afternoon within me.

**Meeting God soul to soul
and face to face** March 15, 1930

If these letters are to be given a name I think it must be "The Story of a Re-conversion," for something of this sort is still in progress. This week a new and to me marvelous experience has come out of my loneliness. I have been so desperately lonesome that it was unbearable save by talking with God. And so every waking moment of the week I have been looking toward Him, with perhaps the exception of an hour or two.

Last Thursday night I was listening to a phonograph in Lumbatan and allowing my heart to commune, when something broke within me, and I longed not only to lift my own will up and give it completely to God, but also to lift all the wills in the world up and offer them all in utter surrender to His will. To feel this great longing as I felt it then with all my being, to desire to put one's shoulder under all the world's hunger and need, and to carry it all to God, is not this the highest longing one can ever feel? Probably not, but it is the climax of my spiritual experience to this date. God, be the thought within my brain, and be the thought in every brain in the world, so that no thought save the thoughts of God shall take birth in any human mind. And this will be heaven!

How infinitely richer this direct firsthand grasping of God Himself is, than the old method which I used and recommended for years, the reading of endless devotional books. Almost it seems to me now that the very Bible cannot be read as a substitute for meeting God soul to soul and face to face. And yet, how was this new closeness achieved? Ah, I know now that it was by cutting the very heart of my heart and by suffering. Somebody was telling me this week that nobody can make a violin speak the last depths of human longing until that soul has been made tender by some great anguish. I do not say it is the only way to the heart of God, but I must witness that it has opened an inner shrine for me which I never entered before.

Can we think His thoughts all the time?
March 23, 1930

You and you and you and I do experience fine fresh contact with God sometimes, and do carry out His will sometimes. One question now to be put to the test is this: Can we have that contact with God all the time? All the time awake, fall asleep in His arms, and awaken in His presence, can we attain that? Can we do His will all the time? Can we think His thoughts all the time?

Or are there periods when business, and pleasures, and crowding companions must necessarily push God out of our thoughts? "Of course, that is self-evident. If one thinks of God all the time, he will never get anything else done." So I thought too, until now, but I am changing my view. We can keep two things in mind at once. Indeed we cannot keep one thing in mind more than half a second. Mind is a flowing something. It oscillates. Concentration is merely the continuous return to the same problem from a million angles. We do not think of one thing. We always think of the relationship of at least two things, and more often of three or more things simultaneously. So my problem is this: Can I bring God back in my mind-flow every few seconds so that God shall always be in my mind as an after image, shall always be one of the elements in every concept and percept?

I choose to make the rest of my life an experiment in answering this question.

Someone may be saying that this introspection and this struggle to achieve God-consciousness is abnormal and perilous. I am going to take the risks, for somebody ought to do it, in this day when psychological experimentation has given a fresh approach to our spiritual problems. If our religious premises are correct at all then this oneness with God is the most normal condition one can have. It is what made Christ, Christ. It is what St. Augustine meant when he said "Thou has made us for Thyself, and our souls are restless until they find their rest in Thee."

I do not invite anybody else to follow this arduous path. I wish many might. We need to know so much which one man alone cannot answer. For example:

"Can a laboring man successfully attain this continuous surrender to God? Can a man working at a machine pray for people all day long, talk with God all day long, and at the same time do his task efficiently?"

"Can a merchant do business, can an accountant keep books, ceaselessly surrendered to God?"

"Can a mother wash dishes, care for the babies, continuously talking to God?"

"Can a politician keep in a state of continuous contact with God, and not lose the following of the crowds?"

"Can little children be taught to talk and listen to God inwardly all day long, and what is the effect upon them?"

Briefly, is this a thing which the entire human race might conceivably aspire to achieve? Do we really mean what we say when we repeat "the highest end of man is to find God and to do his will" all the time?

If you are like myself this has been pretty strong diet this afternoon. It may even prove discouraging. So I will put something simpler and more attainable:

"Any hour of any day may be made perfect by merely choosing. It is perfect if one looks toward God that entire hour, waiting for his leadership all through the hour and trying hard to do every tiny thing exactly as God wishes it done, as perfectly as possible. No emotions are necessary. Just the doing of God's will perfectly makes the hour a perfect one. And the results of that one perfect hour, I believe, will echo down through eternity."

The possession of God has caught me up   April 18, 1930

I have tasted a thrill in fellowship with God which has made anything discordant with God disgusting. This afternoon the possession of God has caught me up with such sheer joy that I thought I never had known anything like it. God was so close and so amazingly lovely that I felt like melting all over with a strange blissful contentment. Having had this experience, which comes to me now several times a week, the thrill of filth repels me, for I know its power to drag me from God. And after an hour of close friendship with God my soul feels clean, as new fallen snow.

Everywhere people are beautiful—or at least they have a beautiful side...On the boat from Manila last week was a painted woman, alone. I spoke to her because she was lonesome. Three of the ship's officers nearby tittered as though they thought a scandal was brewing, so I talked loud enough for them to hear. I told her I was looking for God. As naturally as a preacher she replied, "God is everywhere around us and in us if we only open our eyes. All the world is beautiful if we have eyes to see the beauty, for the world is packed with God." "Thank you for that," I said, "I love it! What are you going to Cebu for?" "To put on my special act. You see I dance before seven mirrors. Nobody else, so far as I know, in the world, has just this act. I am traveling alone, making my own engagements, for it is too expensive to have a property man. I was treated wonderfully well through India, wonderfully well!" I liked the way she pronounced that word, and the memories which lingered in her tired eyes. "And many people in Manila wrote me lovely letters, asking me to come back. Oh the world is full of good people, full of good people." When the dinner bell rang I said, "I am going about the world trying to find wonderful hours, and I shall remember this as one of them."

Incessant submission to God has proven extremely difficult April 19, 1930

This conscious, incessant submission to God has proven extremely difficult, and I have surrendered for the past few days. And today and yesterday I saw evidences of the result. In an effort to be witty I have said biting things which have hurt the feelings of others, and have been short and impatient. I tremble, for I have told at least one of these men of this experiment, and he will think this is the result. It is very dangerous to tell people, and yet, I must tell and I must start over now and succeed. This philosophy that one can begin all over instantly at any moment, is proving of great help.

If this record of a soul struggle to find God is to be complete it must not omit the story of difficulty and failure. I have not succeeded very well so far. This week, for example, has not been one of the finest in my life, though it has been above the average. I have to make a greater effort next week. I have undertaken something which, at my age at least, is hard, harder than I had anticipated. But I resolve not to give up the effort.

Yet strain does not seem to do good. At this moment I feel something "let go" inside, and lo, God is here! It is a heart melting "here-ness," a lovely whispering of father to child, and the reason I did not have it before, was because I failed to let go.

And back of that failure there was something else. A crowd of people arrived who, when they are in a crowd, wish to talk or think nothing of religion. I fear I have not wanted some of them to think me religious for fear I might cease to be interesting.

Fellowship with God is something one dare not cover, for it smothers to death. It is like a tender infant or a delicate little plant, for a long nurturing is the price of having it, while it vanishes in a second of time, the very moment indeed, one's eye ceases to be "single." One cannot worship God and Mammon for the reason that God slips out and is gone as soon as we try to seat some other unworthy affection beside Him. The other idol stays and

God vanishes. Not because God is "a jealous God" but because sincerity and insincerity are contradictions and cannot both exist at the same time in the same place.

Open toward God and wide awake — April 22, 1930

The "experiment" is interesting, although I am not very successful, thus far. The idea of God slips out of my sight for I suppose two thirds of every day, thus far. This morning I started out fresh, by finding a rich experience of God in the sunrise. Then I tried to let Him control my hands while I was shaving and dressing and eating breakfast. Now I am trying to let God control my hands as I pound the typewriter keys. If I could keep this morning up I should have a far higher average today than I have had for some time.

This afternoon as I look at the people teeming about me, and then think of God's point of view, I feel that this mighty stretch of time in which He has been pushing men upward is to continue for many more millions of years. We are yet to become what the spiritual giants have been and more than many of them were. Here the selection favors those who keep themselves wide open toward God and wide awake. Our possibilities are perhaps not limitless, but they are at least infinitely above our present possibilities of imagination.

There is nothing that we can do excepting to throw ourselves open to God. There is, there must be, so much more in Him than He can give us, because we are so sleepy and because our capacity is so pitifully small. It ought to be tremendously helpful to be able to acquire the habit of reaching out strongly after God's thoughts, and to ask, "God what have you to put into my mind now if only I can be large enough?" That waiting, eager attitude ought to give God the chance he needs. I am finding every day that the best of the five or six ways in which I try to keep contact with God is for me to wait for His thoughts, to ask Him to speak.

It is working — May 14, 1930

Oh, this thing of keeping in constant touch with God, of making Him the object of my thought and the companion of my conversations, is the most amazing thing I ever ran across. It is working. I cannot do it even half of a day—not yet, but I believe I shall be doing it some day for the entire day. It is a matter of acquiring a new habit of thought. Now I like God's presence so much that when for a half hour or so He slips out of mind—as He does many times a day—I feel as though I had deserted Him, and as though I had lost something very precious in my life.

Souls dead to God look sadly out of hungry eyes

May 24, 1930

This has been a week of wonders. God is at work everywhere preparing the way for His work in Lanao. I shall tell you some of the wonders presently. But just at this moment you must hear more of this sacred evening. The day had been rich but strenuous, so I climbed "Signal Hill" back of my house talking and listening to God all the way up, all the way back, all the lovely half hour on the top. And God talked back! I let my tongue go loose and from it there flowed poetry far more beautiful than any I ever composed. It flowed without pausing and without ever a failing syllable for a half hour. I listened astonished and full of joy and gratitude. I wanted a dictaphone for I knew that I should not be able to remember it—and now I cannot. "Why," someone may ask, "did God waste His poetry on you alone, when you could not carry it home." You will have to ask God that question. I only know He did and I am happy in the memory.

Below me lay the rice fields and as I looked across them I heard my tongue saying aloud, "Child, just as the rice needs the sunshine every day, and could not grow if it had sun only once a week or one hour a day, so you need me all day of every day. People over all the world are withering because they are open toward God only rarely. Every waking minute is not too much."

A few months ago I was trying to write a chapter on the "discovering of God." Now that I have discovered Him I find that it is a continuous discovery. Every day is rich with new aspects of Him and His working. As one makes new discoveries about his friends by being with them, so one discovers the "individuality" of God if one entertains Him continuously. One thing I have seen this week is that God loves beauty. Everything He makes is lovely. The clouds, the tumbling river, the waving lake, the soaring eagle, the slender blade of grass, the whispering of the wind, the fluttering butterfly, this graceful transparent nameless child of the lake which clings to my window for an hour and vanishes for ever. Beautiful craft of God! And I know that He makes my thought-life beautiful when I am open all the day to Him. If I throw these mind-windows apart and say "God, what shall we think of now?" He answers always in some graceful, tender dream. And I know that God is love hungry, for He is constantly pointing me to some dull, dead soul which He has never reached and wistfully urges me to help Him reach that stolid, tight shut mind. Oh God, how I long to help You with these Moros. And with these Americans! And with these Filipinos! All day I see souls dead to God look sadly out of hungry eyes. I want them to know my discovery! That any minute can be paradise, that any place can be heaven! That any man can have God! That every man does have God the moment he speaks to God, or listens for Him!

As I analyze myself I find several things happening to me as a result of these two months of strenuous effort to keep God in mind every minute. This concentration upon God is strenuous, but everything else has ceased to be so. I think more clearly, I forget less frequently. Things which I did with a strain before, I now do easily and with no effort whatever. I worry about nothing, and lose no sleep. I walk on air a good part of the time. Even the mirror reveals a new light in my eyes and face. I no longer feel in a hurry about anything. Everything goes right. Each minute I meet calmly as though it were not important. Nothing can go wrong excepting one thing. That is that God may slip from my mind if I do not keep on my guard. If He is there, the universe is with me. My task is simple and clear.

And I witness to the way in which the world reacts. Take Lanao and the Moros for illustration. Their responsiveness is to me a continuous source of amazement. I do nothing that I can see excepting to pray for them, and to walk among them thinking of God. They know I am a Protestant. Yet two of the leading Moslem priests have gone around the province telling everybody that I would help the people to know God.

One new lesson   **June 1, 1930**

Inwardly this has been a very uneven week. As a whole, my end of the experiment has been failure for most of the week. My physical condition and too many distractions have proven too much for me, and God has not been in the center of my mind for one-fifth of the time, or perhaps one-tenth. But today has been a wonderful day, and some of yesterday was wonderful. The week with its failures and successes has taught me one new lesson. It is this: "I must talk about God, or I cannot keep Him in my mind. I must give Him away in order to have Him." That is the law of the spirit world. What one gives one has, what one keeps to oneself one loses.

Do you suppose that through all eternity the price we will need to pay for keeping God will be that we must endlessly be giving Him away?

Begin to build heaven   **June 3, 1930**

This experiment which I am trying is the most strenuous discipline which any man ever attempted. I am not succeeding in keeping God in my mind very many hours of the day, and from the point of view of experiment number one I should have to record a pretty high percentage of failure. But the other experiment—what happens when I do succeed—is so successful that it makes up for the failure of number one. God does work a change. The moment I turn to Him it is like turning on an electric current which I feel through my whole being. I find also that the effort to keep God in my mind does something to my mind which every mind needs to have done to it. I am given something difficult enough to keep my mind with a keen edge. The constant temptation of every man is to allow his mind to grow old and lose its edge. I feel that I am perhaps more lazy mentally than the average person, and I require the very mental discipline which this constant effort affords.

So my answer to my two questions to date would be

1. "Can it be done all the time?" Hardly.

2. "Does the effort help?" Tremendously. Nothing I have ever found proves such a tonic to mind and body.

Are you building sacred palaces for yourself? I meant to write "places" to be sure, but I think I shall leave the word "palaces" for that is what any house becomes when it is sacred. The most important discovery of my whole life is that one can take a little rough cabin and transform it into a palace just by flooding it with thoughts of God. When one has spent many months in a little house like this in daily thoughts about God, the very entering of the house, the very sight of it as one approaches, starts associations which set the heart tingling and the mind flowing. I have come to the point where I must have my house, in order to write the best letters or think the richest thoughts.

So in this sense one man after the other builds his own heaven or his hell. It does not matter where one is, one can at once begin to build heaven, by thoughts which one thinks while in that place.... I have learned the secret of heaven building—anywhere.

This morning I read awhile about the tremendous consecration with which the scientists are studying the finest details about the sun, in an effort to find how to predict the weather, and to know how to use its power. And I feel that not yet have I thrown myself into the crucible of this experiment of mind with all the abandon of the successful scientist. We have heard the saying "All a man's failures are inside himself." And I am willing to confess that as yet I have not "striven unto blood" to win this battle. What I want to prove is that the thing can be done by all people under all conditions, but I have not proven it yet. This much I do see—what an incredibly high thing Jesus did.

A great lonesome hunger comes over me at this moment for someone who has passed through the same long, long channels of hope, and aspiration, and despair, and failure, to whom I can talk tonight. And yet—there is no such person. As we grow older all our paths diverge, and in all the world I suppose I could find nobody who could wholly understand me excepting God—and neither can you! Ah, God, what a new nearness this brings for Thee and me, to realize that Thou alone canst understand me, for Thou alone knowest all! Thou art no longer a stranger, God! Thou art the only being in the universe who is not partly a stranger! I invite others inside but they cannot come all the way. Thou art all the way inside with me—here—and every time I forget and push Thee out, Thou art eager to return! Ah, God, I mean to struggle tonight and tomorrow as never before, not once to dismiss Thee. For when I lose Thee for an hour I lose and the world loses more than we can know. The thing Thou wouldst do can only be done when Thou hast full swing all the time.

I looked at people with a love God gave   June 15, 1930

I walk out in the street full of Moros, and if my soul is as full of God as it sometimes is, I see what happens as I look into their eyes and pray for them. No man need try to persuade me that God does not reach them, for I see the thing happen, and now I know that every person we ever meet is God's opportunity, if only, if only we were not so much of the time shut off from God.

Last Monday was the most completely successful day of my life to date so far as giving my day in complete and continuous surrender to God is concerned—though I shall hope for far better days—and I remember how as I looked at people with a love God gave, they looked back and acted as though they wanted to go with me. I felt then that for a day I saw a little of that marvelous pull that Jesus had as He walked along the road day after day "God-intoxicated" and radiant with the endless communion of His soul with God.

As simple as opening and closing a swinging door   June 22, 1930

I have just returned from a walk alone, a walk so wonderful that I feel like reducing it to a universal rule, that all people ought to take a walk every evening all alone where they can talk aloud without being heard by anyone, and that during this entire walk they all ought to talk with God, allowing Him to use their tongues to talk back—and letting God do most of the talking.

For this seems to be the very thing for which I have been feeling all these weeks. You have followed my experiment and have seen many confessions of daily failure, as I tried to keep God in mind in the second person. Well, today has not been a failure. The thought of God has drifted out occasionally but not for long. But this day has been a different day from any other of my life, for I have not tried to pray in the sense of talking to God but I have let God do the talking with my tongue or in my inner life when my tongue was silent. It has been as simple as opening and closing a swinging door. And without any of the old strain the whole day passed beautifully with God saying wonderful things to me.

The reality all about you is greater than the imperfect symbols of things which you have in words July 2, 1930

The newest experiment, and at present the most thrilling, is letting God talk through my own tongue and through my own fingers on the typewriter.

I have been letting my tongue talk on Signal Hill behind my house and then have come home and written on the typewriter all I could remember of it. Here is one sample:

"I speak to you, not through your tongue only, but also through everything which you see in nature through the beauty of this sunset, through the little Moro boy who stands beside you without understanding what you are saying, and who wonders what you are looking at in the clouds. If I do not speak to you in words at times, it is because the reality all about you is greater than the imperfect symbols of things which you have in words. It is not necessary for your tongue to speak, nor even for any definite thoughts to light your mind, for I myself am infinitely more important for you than anything I can give you—even than the most brilliant thoughts. So when thoughts do come, welcome them, and when they do not flow freely simply rest back and love, and grant me the shared joy of being loved by you. For I, too, by my very nature, am hungry with an insatiable hunger for the love of all of you, just as your love reaches out at your highest moments to all the people about you. So child, I, even I, God, whom people have foolishly feared and flattered for my gifts, I want love and friendship more than I want groveling subjects. So while we love each other, child, my share is as keen as yours."

I have written in this letter what my tongue said as I let it speak, not because I wish to recommend any of the above as prophetic, but simply because I think it may prove helpful to those who have been dissatisfied with their own contact with God and who may find this a helpful practice in making contacts with God. Day after day I find this very helpful in little intimate personal ways, which would have no value for others.

I am well aware of the probability of criticism because it is "mysticism"—as though any man could be a believer in Jesus without believing in "mysticism"!—or because many people think that the days of direct contact with God, or at least words from God, stopped with the closing of the New Testament. But then what a stupid world this would be if one never did anything different for fear of criticism!

**This is what all life can have
if you are willing** July 9, 1930

Never did I so feel the need of a silent typewriter as at this moment, for every stroke clashes with the marvelous silence of the hills tonight. I am still under the spell of that hush and of that sunset. In all my life I have never seen a sight so beautiful as Lanao tonight...I suppose there have been equally beautiful scenes since the world was created, but not more beautiful for me. For it adequately reflected the passion of love which I feel toward the Lanao people as I look and pray from the hill.

And as I talked and tasted the sweetness of the luscious light, and told God that this was for me the masterpiece of His creation, He told me through my own voice:

"Ah, child, this is but the symbol of beauties, and wonders which I mean to give you when you are willing and ready. I must give them, I will give them, if only you will climb your spiritual hill and open your soul eyes and look. This is what all life can have if you are willing. I ache with longings which poor little people cannot even suspect, to open up wider and ever wider universes of glory to you all."

If asked my chief difficulty in meeting these Moros, I should have to reply, "No chief difficulty excepting to keep ready spiritually." And I wonder whether here is not the only serious difficulty anywhere. This year I am readier than I have ever been before, and perhaps this is why people seem readier also.

**"Important duties" which keep us
from helping little people are not
duties but sins** August 21, 1930

I shall be forty-six in two weeks. I no longer have the sense that life is all before me, as I had a few years ago. Some of it is behind—and a miserable poor past it is, so far below what I had dreamed that I dare not even think of it. Nor dare I think much of the future. This present, if it is full of God, is the only refuge I have from poisonous disappointment and even almost rebellion against God. Here is this book of Reinhold Niebuhr, a man who seems to pour out wonderful thought as easily as one pours coffee. Why could not the rest of the world, including of course myself, be gifted like he is? And so many of the people here, and everywhere seem to have more cramped lives and hopeless minds even than I have. I have been trying to teach a boy to read this afternoon, but his mind seems to be like pouring water into a mosquito net. He could not pronounce "i" without forgetting "a." What a tragedy to live in the world he lives in. I felt a warm love for the boy, and he felt it, for his eyes were moist as he told me he had neither father nor mother. At times when one looks out upon life all one sees are wrecks, and in upon life, too—wrecks! Ah, God, what is all this wreckage for?

I sat leaning upon my typewriter for a long while after that sentence, for a voice began to talk to me. "The wreckage is the birthpangs of love." And when I wanted to put my arm around that dirty, cross-eyed orphan Moro with his stupid brain, I was proving that...

As I sit over in that old building day after day patiently toiling with one man or boy to teach him the alphabet, and so hold him to a larger world, I often wonder whether this work is becoming to a man of my age. But when that same man fondly runs his fingers through my hair and looks his love while he says "Mapia bapa"—good uncle—I know that a little love is created. If this entire universe is a desperate attempt of love to incarnate itself, then "important duties" which keep us from helping little people are not duties but sins—or am I all the while trying to justify my own failure?

Home from a wonderful hour with God in the sunset. Oh, those colors, those awful piles of clouds, those misty mysteries, those silent changes across the sky. If one could only forget oneself entirely and enjoy the universe—but some of us are too selfish to wipe ourselves out of the picture. We are deep sea fish. They say there are fish under the ocean which are under such pressure that they dare not come near the surface or they perish. We are just that sort of fish, for we dare not venture far above the bottom of the atmosphere-ocean, or we die. We are not fish, we are worms on the bottom, for we cannot even swim in our ocean. And we are as little mentally as we are physically, and as tied to the bottom. Poor worms! And I suppose that this self pity on this page is an excellent illustration of our littleness. When I feel like blaming God, then at that moment I show the real ugliness of my selfishness—for I know perfectly well that I should be quite complacent about all the innumerable creatures below man, and about all the innumerable creatures who are barely man, about the creatures who are robbed of their manhood by other selfish creatures like myself, I should not blame God for all these if I had all I wanted.

Here I was engaging in the most glorious action of all human and of all superhuman life—I was communing with the very God of the universe Himself. He was showing me His very heart, even the angels can do no more than this. I forgot that my being choked down against the bottom of an ocean like an octopus, and like an octopus in disposition, too, makes no difference at all. A prison or a dungeon makes no difference if one is with God. We preach and profess that as true, and it is true, but upon my word I do not see many people who seem to have experienced it. I am exactly like these Moro women and children. "Bapa," they say, "may I have this?" If I say "Yes," they forget to take it, but if I say "No," they beg me for it.

The beauty of immense need September 2, 1930

Tip and I and God were together tonight on Signal Hill. Oh, God, let me put on paper the glory that was there. The sunset was not more beautiful that at other times, but God said more in it. I suppose it was because I was trying to make this first day of my forty-sixth year high. And that I suppose is why all of us have some high days and some low ones. God is always awaiting the chance to give us high days. We so seldom are in deep earnest about giving Him His chance.

But the effort to say this colossal thing throws me into despair. It cannot be said, can it even be hinted at? There were black clouds which swiftly turned crimson and pale yellow. Now those black clouds are shooting out their fiery tongues through the darkness.

Far off in the middle of the lake a long perfect waterspout stood like a colossal pillar from the clouds to the splashing water. It was the first perfect waterspout that I have seen from sea to sky. Above my head those black, angry clouds turned into glorious gold, from the hidden sun. But it was not this that made the evening wonderful. God was speaking.

I patted Tip's head as he nestled up under my arm, and told him:

"We are two tiny insects in the midst of this terrifying universe. I know a little more than you do, you nice, black dog, but not much more. Compared with that gigantic Being who wheels these awful spheres of fire through the sky I am as near nothing as you are. I know as little about God as you know about me, perhaps ten thousand times less. And perhaps you are wiser than I, for you are contented to be patted on the head and to hunt for fleas, while I am impatient to break loose into the universe. I thought, Tip, when I was younger, that Kant was wrong when he said the three greatest moral demands as God, freedom, and immortality, but now I believe he was incredibly right. My soul at forty-six demands immortality as much as it demands God. And it demands freedom from this prison we call the world and the flesh as much as it demands immortality."

Then out of the skies there came a silent voice, "Your black clouds give the sun its chance. It is surprise, it is escape from darkness to light that makes life so rich. Your prison is also your paint box from which all the beauty you know is pouring. Lanao, where you now sit, is one of the most beautiful creations in all the reaches of space. And here you have the privilege of opening eyes to see beauty, which otherwise would not see. It is selfish of you to desire to escape, until you can take humanity with you. You are not Christlike until you demand that even after you die, your soul shall stay and help others come through to the larger life. I almost fear that my nightly visions, much as I love to give them to you, are making you more selfish, more hungry to get, less eager to give. The most beautiful thing in the universe for you is Lanao stretching around this lake at your feet, for it contains the beauty of immense need. You must awaken hunger there, for until they hunger they cannot be fed."

Oh, tonight I so hunger to be able to tell what else happened. But that other thing was all emotion, a painfully sweet stretching forth of arms skyward to receive and Lanao-ward to give.

Symbolizing the truth   September 21, 1930

Our search for God through narrow straits has brought a sudden revelation, like an explorer who has just come out upon a limitless sea. It is not any particularly new idea but a new feeling, which came almost of itself. Today God seems to me to be just behind everything. I feel Him there. He is just under my hand, just under the typewriter, just behind this desk, just inside the file, just inside the camera.

One of these Moro fairy tales has the fairies standing behind every rock looking at the hero. That is how I feel about God today. Of course this is only a way of symbolizing the truth that God is invisible and that He is everywhere. I cannot imagine seeing the invisible, but I can imagine God hiding Himself behind everything in sight.

For a lonesome man there is something infinitely homey and conforting in feeling God so close, so everywhere! Nowhere one turns is away from friendship, for God is smiling there.

It is difficult to convey to another the joy of having broken into the new sea of realizing God's "here-ness." This morning our theme was "Jesus' view of prayer." It seemed so wonderfully true that just the privilege of fellowship with God is infinitely more than anything that God could give. When He gives Himself He is giving more than anything else in the universe.

There is no defeat
unless one loses God
September 22, 1930

We have got to saturate ourselves with the rainbows and the sunset marvels in order to radiate them. It is as much our duty to live in the beauty of the presence of God on some mount of transfiguration until we become white with Christ as it is for us to go down where they grope, and grovel, and groan, and lift them to new life. After all, the deepest truth is that the Christlike life is glorious, undefeatably glorious. There is no defeat unless one loses God, and then all is defeat though it be housed in castles and buried in fortunes.

Joy in endless giving
October 7, 1930

It is that spirit of greed which Jesus said God hated more than any other. It is so diametrically opposite to the spirit of God. For God forever lavishes His gifts upon the good and bad alike, and finds all His joy in endless giving.

You see, I feel deeply about us all. Beside Jesus the whole lot of us are so contemptible. I do not see how God stomachs us at all. But God is like Jesus, and like Jesus, He will not give up until we, too, are like Jesus.

Worries have faded away
October 12, 1930

How I wish, wish, wish that a dozen or more persons who are trying the experiment of holding God endlessly in mind would all write their experiences so that each would know what the other was finding as a result! The results, I think, would astound the world. At least the results of my own effort are astounding to me.

Worries have faded away like ugly clouds and my soul rests in the sunshine of perpetual peace. I can lie down anywhere in this universe bathed around by my own Father's Spirit. The very universe has come to seem so homey! I know only a little more about it than before, but that little is all! It is vibrant with the electric ecstacy of God! I know what it means to be "God-intoxicated."

How fine of these Moro boys to come and lean on one's knee, or run their fingers through one's hair—or rub the bald spots and ask why they are so! They know that we love them, but they do not realize what a gulf—at least historically—separates us. If they did, would they be so affectionate? If they knew all, if they knew the love of God in all its wondrous fervor they would!

And to think that less than a year ago we were writing about "the most difficult place under the American flag, if not in the world!"

No, New York City is the most difficult place in the world, for in New York they demand ability, unusual ability, while here in Lanao, they demand only love—unusual love. And the love of God may be had for the receiving.

The pathway of true intuition   October 15, 1930

Has God ever struck you as the great stirrer up? One thing He seems to have determined is that we shall not fall asleep. We make or discover paradises for ourselves, and these paradises begin to lull us into sleepy satisfaction. Then God comes with His awakening hand, takes us by the shoulders and gives us a thorough awakening.

And God knows we need it. If our destiny is to grow on and on and on, into some far more beautiful creatures than we are now, with more of the ideals of Christ, that means that we need to have the shells broken quite frequently so that we can grow.

My confidence that this earth is but a brief school grows into certainty as my fellowship with God grows more tender. As a discipline this world is admirable.

Jesus and Buddha had almost the same message about this life. Buddha said, "Abolish all desire." Jesus said, "Fix not your desires upon this earth, but lay up all the desires you can for a fuller life, which begins within you now, and is endless." Many people seek other escapes. Some in prodigious work, some in reckless play, some in drugs, some in insanity—for insanity is but an escape from pitiless, crushing failure. But I wish to tell all the world that needs a better way, that God on Signal Hill satisfies, and sends through me a glow of glory which makes me sure that this is the pathway of true intuition.

The beauty of sacrifice is the final word in beauty   December 6, 1930

Sometimes one feels that there is a discord between the cross and beauty. But there really cannot be, for God is found best through those two doorways. This grey-blue rolling water tinged with whitecaps, hemmed with distant green hills and crowned with colored clouds and baby-blue sky reveals God's love of beauty—and God is so lavish with His paintbrush in the tropics. He is lavish everywhere if one only has eyes to see Him at work.

But when one comes to personality, one demands more than a pretty face or even a soul that sings for joy. There is in the universe a higher kind of beauty. It is the beauty of sacrifice, of giving up for others, of suffering for others. A woman has not reached her highest beauty until she lays down her ease and chooses pain for bearing and nursing her child. A man has not found his highest beauty until his brow is tinged with care for some cause he loves more than himself. The beauty of sacrifice is the final word in beauty.

The only doorway to the very heart of God
February 6, 1931

Tonight, lonesome and half ill with a cold, I am learning from experience that there is a deep peace that grows out of illness and loneliness and a sense of failure. These things do drive me up my hill to God, and then there comes into my soul through the very tears a comfort which is so much better than laughter. It is "the peace of God that passeth all understanding" unless one has it. God cannot get close when everything is delightful. He seems to need these darker hours, these empty-hearted-hours to mean the most to people. You and I have known that over the coffin. We have known it when we parted and our hearts were sore. We have known it when we lay in bed helpless. Is this a deep truth in the very heart of nature? We sing,

"Nearer, my God, to Thee, nearer to Thee!
E'en though it be a cross that lifteth me."

Is the cross the only doorway to the very heart of God?

We are what we are now
February 10, 1931

If there is any contribution that I have to make to the world that will live, surely it must be my experience of God on Signal Hill. This afternoon I climbed my way to the top weighted with a sense of remorse. Everything wrong that I have done in twenty years came back and made me feel like a dreadful sinner. I told God about it, but do not intend to write any confessions here. We are so eager to judge people by their past, and it is not fair. We are what we are now, not an hour ago, and what we are planning, not what we are vainly trying to forget.

As I stood on the top very much inclined to let the tears break out of my eyes, my tongue stopped talking to God and began talking from God to me.

"Ah, little child, I have hurt you tonight, and now I feel sorry with you. All you have confessed is true, but I love you still. I love you for coming here and telling me about it. I love you for hungering after me. I love you for being willing to be better. That is all I ask of people. Ah, I have wanted to do so much for you as soon as you would allow it. Now, with a sore and lonesome heart you are ready. And after this torture I must pull you close to my heart, tiny little one."

And into my heart there stole another new love for God I never knew so strongly before. I felt like saying:

"God, I do not know Thee nor this universe nor my own self. Everything becomes more mysterious the longer I think about it. But I thank Thee that Jesus showed us that Thou art burning, yearning, eager to do more for us than Thou canst. Thou art like those plowmen who must break the soil and tear it apart before seeds will grow. Thou hast plowed my heart tonight until it is tender and ready for something to grow. I thank Thee, God, I thank Thee, because I could not have felt thine healing hand if the pain had not been so acute.

"God, how can we reconcile this need of pain with our effort to abolish all misery?"

The answer seemed convincing to me:

"If you abolish the physical suffering of the world, there will still be disappointed love, yearnings which cannot be satisfied, which will leave hearts bleeding even as they do today. Mansions have as many burning hearts as do poor houses. The things which drag men down to grossness and incessant selfishness must be wiped out. Then hearts will become sore over infinitely larger things than selfish needs. They will learn to bleed for a world with the hearts of Jesus." There will be more suffering than today, for only love knows how to suffer divinely. But the meanness of suffering for one's own selfish disappointments will be gone, and we will see a magnificence and sublimity in suffering that will make us glad.

Why do we not always hear Thy voice? February 25, 1931

As I lay on the warm earth on Signal Hill last night I asked God the question:

"Why is it that Thou dost allow us on this earth to do nearly all the talking? Why do we not always hear Thy voice, since Thou art so much wiser than we are?"

Instantly back came the answer. I could see it, from beginning to end, in a second, though it may require more than a minute to write it down. So many of these thoughts from God are hurled at me in an instant like that:

"When you are teaching the Moros to read, your art is to say as little as you can and leave them to say as much as they will. That is why I leave you to do and say as much as you can, while I say little. You learn by doing, even when you make mistakes and correct them. You are to be sons and daughters of God, and now you are taking the first feeble steps of infants. Every step you take alone is infinitely more important than you now imagine, because the thing I am preparing you for exceeds all your imagination. So the talking you do to me is essential. The talking others do to you, when they are trying to talk up to your expectations is more important than the talks you give to them. This is the best way to act: Talk a great deal to me. Let others talk a great deal to you, appreciating everything fine they say and neglecting their mistakes."

How much of this glory can one carry into business?   March 3, 1931

Oh, if we only let God have His full chance He will break our hearts with the glory of His revelation. That is the privilege which the preacher can have above others. It is his business to look into the very face of God until he aches with bliss. And that is how I feel this morning after two hours of wonderful thinking with God. And now on this "mount of transfiguration" I do not want ever to leave. I want to keep this lovely aching heart forever. But that would not be Christlike. I must now carry all I can of Him across the river to the Moro school. There are figures and there are salaries to be considered, for it is the end of the month. How much of this glory can one carry into business?

It's a choice, and I choose Christ   April 5, 1931

We see ourselves on trial with Jesus. He could walk into the jaws of death to do His blessed work for others. He could dare to speak out against wrong and take the consequences. He could receive floggings, could allow men to spit in His face, could endure the agony of thorns in His head, could be taunted without a word or even a thought of anger, could think of His mother while writhing on the cross, could cry, "Father, forgive them, for they know not what they do." I have read books which said that these words were evidently imaginary for nobody could say anything when suffering the excruciating torture of hanging by nails. But Jesus was such an "impossible" person more than once in His life. This scene fits into His whole character. True, nobody else can think of others when suffering like that, but Jesus was better than the rest of us. Tragedy, magnificent horror! The best man who ever lived dying because He was too good to run away.

That would have driven humanity more deeply into despair. They might or might not have remembered Jesus. I think they would have tried to forget Him. For humanity wants to believe that God is good, and the crucifixion portrays God forsaking the finest example of loyalty we can find. God was betraying His staunchest defender. That cross alone is horrible. The God who would allow the drama to stop there would be a monster or dead. "My God, why...?"

So we cannot believe in a good God unless we have Easter. It is a difficult story to believe, because we have had nothing else quite like it before or since. But it is only the difficulty of believing the unprecedented. On the other hand to doubt it is far more difficult. I must either rule out the whole story of the life of Jesus or else rule out any intelligence or heart from the universe. And if I do that my troubles are far more than intellectual—they become moral. I cannot actually sacrifice myself for others, at least not to death, for, noble as it may sound, it is folly. The act of Jesus becomes not only rash and useless but misleading to the rest of mankind.

> "How is it proved? It isn't proved, you fool! It can't be proved. How can you prove a victory before it's won? How can you prove a man who leads to be your leader worth following unless you follow to the death, and out beyond mere death, which is not anything but Satan's lie upon eternal life...And you? You want to argue. Well, I won't. It's a choice, and I choose Christ."—Studdert Kennedy.

That last sentence is the crux of the whole matter, it is a choice, and while choosing Christ brings mystery, rejecting Him brings despair.

A continuous silent conversation of heart to heart with God   September 28, 1931

The fashion today is to place God in court and give Him a trial. We have had such a lust for "debunking" every good and useful man in history that even God cannot escape. It is one of the unfortunate by products of the quest for truth, plus an unlovely hunger in humanity for scandal. It is a species of jealousy. We dislike to believe that anybody else is quite as good as we are, not even God.

As for me, I choose to stop following this current, to stop posing as the judge of the universe. If it brought any good results I might continue, but to date it has carried me out into the desert and left me there. The books one reads also end on the desert.

I choose another road for myself. I choose to look at people through God, using God as my glasses, colored with His love for them.

Last year, as you know, I decided to try to keep God in mind all the time. That was rather easy for a lonesome man in a strange land. It has always been easier for the shepherds, and the monks, and anchorites than for people surrounded by crowds.

But today it is an altogether different thing. I am no longer lonesome. The hours of the day from dawn to bedtime are spent in the presence of others. Either this new situation will crowd God out or I must take Him into it all. I must learn a continuous silent conversation of heart to heart with God while looking into other eyes and listening to other voices. If I decide to do this it is far more difficult than the thing I was doing before.

Yet if this experiment is to have any value for busy people it must be worked under exactly these conditions of high pressure and throngs of people.

There is only one way to do it. God must share my thoughts of Moro grammar, and Moro epics, and type, and teaching people to read, and talking over the latest excitement with my family as we read the newspapers. So I am resolved to let nothing, nothing, stop me from this effort save sheer fatigue that stops all thought.

One need not tell God everything about the people for whom one prays. Holding them one by one steadily before the mind and willing that God may have His will with them is the best, for God knows better than we what our friends need, yet our prayer releases His power, we know not how.

I propose to make a strenuous effort of the will to concentrate upon each person I meet alone and to send him my thought of God. I propose to think as hard of the will of God as I can when in crowds. Thus I hope to prove by experimentation what this will accomplish toward making a better world.

This afternoon has brought a wonderful experience, all inside my own mind. I closed my eyes to pray and the faces of those before me, then those in the houses near by, then those down the line, and across the river, and down the highway to the next town, and the next, and the next, then in concentric circles around the lake, and over the mountains to the coast, then across the sea to the north, then over the wide ocean to California, then across America to the people whom I know, then over to Europe to the people whom I have met there, then to the Near East where my missionary friends live, then to India where I have other friends, to others in China, and to the multitudes who are suffering the dreadful pangs of cold and starvation—around the world in less than a minute, and for a time the whole of my soul seemed to be lit up with a divine light as it held the world up to God!

I cannot get God by holding Him off at arm's length like a photograph, but by leaning forward intently as one would respond to one's lover. Love so insatiable as the love of God can never be satisfied until we respond to the limit. Nor will He be satisfied until His aching arms receive my neighbors, too, and all the surging multitudes of the world, all of us together responding to Him and to one another.

A gentle pressure of the will   September 28, 1931

When one has struck some wonderful blessing that all mankind has a right to know about, no custom or false modesty should prevent him from telling it, even though it may mean the unbarring of his soul to the public gaze.

I have found such a way of life. I ask nobody else to live it, or even to try it. I only witness that it is wonderful, it is indeed heaven on earth. And it is very simple, so simple that any child could practice it. Just to pray inwardly for everybody one meets, and to keep on all day without stopping, even when doing other work of every kind.

This simple practice requires only a gentle pressure of the will, not more than a person can exert easily. It grows easier as the habit becomes fixed.

Yet it transforms life into heaven. Everybody takes on a new richness, and all the world seems tinted with glory. I do not of course know what others think of me, but the joy which I have within cannot be described. If there never were any other reward than that, it would more than justify the practice to me.

Today I have noticed that when I forget other people I become fatigued rather quickly. When I am reminded of my purpose and start again holding people, seen and unseen, before God, a new exhilaration comes to me, and all the fatigue vanishes.

Deepening discovery   October 11, 1931

Knowing God better and better is an achievement of friendship. "When two persons fall in love there may be such a strong feeling of fellowship, such a delight in the friend's presence, that one may lose oneself in the deepening discovery of another person." The self and the person loved become equally real.

There are, therefore, three questions which we may ask: "Do you believe in God?" That is not getting very far. "The devils believe and tremble." Second, "Are you acquainted with God?" We are acquainted with people with whom we have had some business dealings. Third, "Is God your friend?" or putting this another way, "Do you love God?"

It is this third stage that is really vital. How is it to be achieved? Precisely as any friendship is achieved. By doing things together. The depth and intensity of the friendship will depend upon variety and extent of the things we do and enjoy together. Will the friendship be constant? That again depends upon the permanence of our common interests, and upon whether or not our interests grow into ever widening circles, so that we do not stagnate. The highest friendship demands growth. "It must be progressive as life itself is progressive." Friends must walk together; they cannot long stand still together, for that means death to friendship and to life.

Friendship with God is the friendship of child with parent. As an ideal son grows daily into closer relationship with his father, so we may grow into closer love with God by widening into His interests, and thinking His thoughts and sharing His enterprises.

Far more than any other device of God to create love was the cross where the lovingest person the world has known hangs loving through all His pain. That cross has become the symbol of religion and of love for a third of the world because it touches the deepest depths of human love.

All I have said is mere words, until one sets out helping God right wrongs, helping God help the helpless, loving and talking it over with God. Then there comes a great sense of the close up, warm intimate heart of reality. God simply creeps in and you know He is here in your heart. He has become your friend by working along with you.

So if anybody were to ask me how to find God I should say at once, hunt out the deepest need you can find and forget all about your own comfort while you try to meet that need. Talk to God about it, and—He will be there. You will know it.

**Learn to hold God
by the hand and rest**   January 2, 1932

In school a teacher lays out work for his pupils. I resolve to accept each situation of this year as God's layout for that hour, and never to lament that it is a very commonplace or disappointing task. One can pour something divine into every situation.

One of the mental characteristics against which I have rebelled most is the frequency of my "blank spells" when I cannot think of anything worth writing, and sometimes cannot remember names. Henceforth I resolve to regard these as God's signal that I am to stop and listen. Sometimes you want to talk to your son, and sometimes you want to hold him tight in silence. God is that way with us, He wants to hold still with us in silence.

Here is something we can share with all the people in the world. They cannot all be brilliant or rich or beautiful. They cannot all even dream beautiful dreams like God gives some of us. They cannot all enjoy music. Their hearts do not all burn with love. But everybody can learn to hold God by the hand and rest. And when God is ready to speak the fresh thoughts of heaven will flow in like a crystal spring. Everybody rests at the end of the day, what a world gain if everybody could rest in the waiting arms of the Father, and listen until He whispers.

Part 2

Learning the Vocabulary of God

Learning the Vocabulary of God

This prayer diary was written in 1937 while Laubach was conducting literacy campaigns in India and Africa. Laubach was still headquartered in Lanao, but news of his pioneering adult literacy programs brought invitations to assist in developing literacy programs all over the world.

The diary, addressed to God, is a vehicle for the dialogue with God that had been a daily practice for Laubach since 1930. It records Laubach's step-by-step effort to practice the presence of God in the midst of daily affairs, whether preparing literacy lessons, meeting with the Indian poet, Tagore, or being tempted to hide his deepest convictions from other passengers aboard a ship between India and Africa.

First published in 1956, this volume was also published in 1964 under the title *Frank Laubach's Prayer Diary*.

Preface

One supreme problem for each man is how to live each day nobly, how to make the most out of the day so that no gap or chasm will yawn between the real and the ideal, as it does yawn in the low days of most men. We can help one another, can we not, by revealing how we are struggling to make our days sublime? We sin against one another, do we not, when we conceal our best under a plea of shyness or reticense? The chief inspirations in our lives are the examples of earnest, striving men and women, are they not—Paul, Thomas a Kempis, Stanley Jones, Sherwood Eddy, John Mott, who in turn drew from the perfect life of Christ?

Ask God, "How can I do the most for the world?" and will He not answer, "Live the most Christlike life you can, and let me see it"?

As a father who entertains high hopes for his son, I pass on this diary of my struggles for the noble life to you, my son Bob, and to any other sons who may, by chance, see what I have written here.

The Salutation of the Dawn
Listen to the Exhortation of the Dawn!
Look to this day!
For it is Life, the very Life of Life.
In its brief course lie all the
Verities and Realities of your Existence:
    The Bliss of Growth,
    The Glory of Action,
    The Splendor of Beauty:
For yesterday is but a Dream,
And To-morrow is only a Vision:
But to-day well-lived makes
Every Yesterday a Dream of Happiness,
And every To-morrow a Vision of Hope.
Look well, therefore, to this day.
Such is the Salutation of the Dawn!

—From the Sanskrit

January, 1937

Nagpur [India]   Friday 1

God, I want to give You every minute of this year. I shall try to keep You in mind every moment of my waking hours. I shall try to let my hand write what You direct. I shall try to let You be the speaker and direct every word. I shall try to let You direct my acts. I shall try to learn Your language as it was taught by Jesus and all others through whom You speak—in beauty and singing birds and cool breezes, in radiant Christlike faces, in sacrifices and in tears. It will cost not only much, but everything that conflicts with this resolve.

Nagpur   Saturday 2

God, since every minute this year is to be directed by You, I must learn Your language. I must study Your full vocabulary. What I hear and see and feel today that would have been meaningless yesterday must now reveal Your meaning. A pain in my left arm and occasionally over my heart are Your voice saying that there are no minutes to be wasted away from You.

I am surprised at miracles which seem already to be happening. Meeting with Agatha Harrison and Mrs. Carl Heath seems to be a miracle. They will introduce me to the women's organizations of India and to the Indian Congress through Nehru.

"Take heed how ye hear."

Raipur   Sunday 3

God, waiting for this motor to start, surrounded by people who are waiting for motors and talking in an unknown tongue, what are You saying? If I try to hear You in all this sound and color, I am as bewildered as when I try to understand these men and women speaking Hindi. Perhaps I shall one day understand both You and them. In all this crowd I found only one interpreter to tell me how much to pay. Do I need an interpreter for Your language? O Christ, Your lovely words, Your lovely deeds are not beyond my understanding. And when I think of You, Your love begins to burn in my heart. I must be like You, seeking need and trying to help every minute. I have tried in vain to know why need exists. But this I know and it is enough: that I must seek need, and love and help.

Baroda Bazaar   **Monday 4**

God, if You rule every movement, You will be inside my eyes directing them. The eyes are the windows of the soul. If You are in my eyes, men will see You there and call You Love. Then my life will be love with a picture of Christ in the center; Christ bearing a cross and wearing thorns, and with anguish in His heart. That love will bless everybody and harm nobody.

As my hostess read the Bible and prayed, I heard You speaking this morning. She was the channel broadcasting Your words. I shall try to listen for Your speaking through the language of men, especially men who are trying to do Your will.

Baroda Bazaar   **Tuesday 5**

God, teach me how to hold on to You when thronged by people who are interested in other subjects more than in You. Help me today to increase my knowledge of Your vocabulary. As we have to learn a few words each day, what will these new words be today? Over three hundred and thirty million who cannot read are calling for help. Need is Your language, is a word from You. How to approach this problem is baffling. Unsolved problems are Your language, for in them You are our schoolmaster training us to be Your children. I thank You for the call to share a real need with You. You teach by the project method!

Baroda Bazaar   **Wednesday 6**

God, this prayer calendar says, "We sometimes fail because we imagine God is not interested in the little things. We are bidden to take everything to God." That would mean every movement of the hand. I have found, of late, that I write better if I ask You to flow through my hand. I have found that if I pray when I have lost something, You usually guide me straight to it. Not always, but I think whenever necessary.

This seeking to learn Your vocabulary seems to be the clue! Every hour is new evidence that You are trying to speak. This morning the prayer calendar asked, "How many messages have you had from God?" That was a message from God! You speak from the pages of books.

Baroda Bazaar   **Thursday 7**

God, this going in search of Your vocabulary promises to open a whole world of new vision. I have a little book in my pocket to record Your words as they come to me all day long, just as I might learn any language. Yesterday I heard You speak and saw You write in conscience, pain, loneliness, the breeze, a woven mat. These said, "Cooperate with God." A half-naked child, the blue heaven, a slow carabao, memories of early life (the past is Your voice); my dead friends, especially my father who passed over last year but seems to be here; poor eyes, failures, dreams, two mottoes on the walls, the silence, piano music, the radio, rippling water, a radiant smile of love—these, too, are words God spoke.

Baroda Bazaar Friday 8

God, we often open doors and find we have stepped into heaven. Last night I asked the Koenigs for piano music because I had heard the children playing. Mr. and Mrs. Koenig played Beethoven's *Fifth Symphony* as I had never heard it before. Every note was Your music for me. We find You by opening the right doors.

Evidently this experiment in keeping You every moment in mind is not new. The prayer calendar this morning says: "We ought, in the secret of our hearts, to be communing with God, our Father, all day long, hearing His voice, asking His guidance." As we advance in acquaintance with God, we shall have more of the spirit of little children—putting all our trust in Him.

Calcutta Saturday 9

God, this attempt to keep my will bent toward Your will is integrating me. Here in this Calcutta station, I feel new power such as I have not had for many years. The task to which You have called me is as hard to accomplish as scaling Mount Everest, but You can accomplish it if I can keep my will attuned to Your will. My task is a simple one, after all. It is just to guard this will. Religion seems to me today to be not doctrine or faith, primarily, but primarily the directed will. That is my task, to hold my will to the current of power, and let You sweep through endlessly.

Santiniketan Sunday 10

God, Your mind is superior to mine in one tremendous particular: You will never forget me, or any other, because You can think of countless billions of subjects at the same instant. I try to keep You in mind every second, but I can think of only one set of things in an instant. My effort results in a succession of spasmodic starts with You and wanderings into other thoughts which leave You out. Perhaps I may need to keep a score based upon how frequently I come back to You for direction. It does make me feel at home to return to You and whisper "Father" in your ear every minute. This titanic task You led me to attack calls out will and a surging sense of power. We must lift heavy weights if we are to become strong.

Santiniketan   **Monday 11**

God, what is a man's best gift to mankind? To be beautiful of soul and then let people see into your soul—this is what I learned as I looked upon the face of Rabindranath Tagore and listened to him tell of his school and his ideals. His beautiful face reminded me of Moses. I tried to think of You every moment and to let You look through my eyes. His long, friendly response leads me to believe he saw You.

I must talk to others about You more than I have done. I can neither help them nor discover their deepest best unless I reveal this fellowship with You to everybody. To meet You every minute of every day to share You with others is to live a full life. What new miracle will enrich this day?

Santiniketan   **Tuesday 12**

God, last night in the clear, dry air of India I saw the sun for the first time. Behind the western trees it was a terrible, immense circle of fiery flame one hundred thousand miles across. It blinded and fascinated me. So far away! And yet it seemed just over the edge of the world. Then I studied the stars and saw for the first time the vast difference in distance between Venus and some star near by. That sky full of those stupendous fiery furies like our sun! And for You all these dizzy distances are but spans of the hand. My Earth is but a speck and I less than an electron. Yet among the electrons You are at home as easily as along the mighty reaches of the universe, and at home in whatever may be beyond. After all, I cannot comprehend You. But if You are love, I can relax and not fear for today or eternity. All mighty!

Calcutta   **Wednesday 13**

This search for the vocabulary of God gives new meaning to many Bible verses. Open before me are the words of Luke 8:18 and 21: "Take heed therefore how ye hear" and "My mother and my brethren are these which hear the word of God, and do it." "Hear God and do it" is the center of this year's effort to hear and do, every instant of my waking day. To hear and do perfectly would be like Jesus. It would mean purity in the deep recesses of thought. I witness to any person who may read this spiritual diary that I am astonished at the rich new inspiration which now floods my mind with fresh glorious vision from Heaven. I wrote a chapter yesterday on learning the vocabulary of God. Will it become a book, dear Father?

Calcutta   **Thursday 14**

God, this Testament confirms my quest of Your words. I open it at random: "He that hath ears...hear." "Hear ye him." So life becomes simply—to hear Your words and do them, moment after moment, one minute at a time. I cannot see far ahead; the details fade as I look far. But that is what faith is for, to keep away worry for the future. "Thy faith hath saved thee" from the future. One minute at a time—this one—listening, saying "Guide my fingers, God, across this page. Guide my thoughts, God, through my brain. Set my love on fire for India's needy multitudes, for the half of the world to whom You have called me." "If ye abide in me." Help me today not to lose the contact even for one minute. My light shines only when the switch is on. Help me not to break this glorious connection, ever.

Calcutta   **Friday 15**

God, how often you speak to us from the pages of the Gospels. "Why do ye not understand my speech?" asks Christ on this morning's page. This morning I seemed to catch a glimpse of the meaning of idols in history, and even today. Sometimes they were used by men who, like myself, fought their own wandering minds in a vain effort not to lose You in the midst of insistent noisy, fascinating distractions. This Testament is a help. A crucifix may help many. A rosary holds the wavering mind. Religious statues and pictures of saints looking heavenward help all of us. An image is useful when it helps us fix the mind fast to God. It is wrong when it makes God small or limited. God is in an idol because He is also everywhere. "In hell...thou art there."

The escape from idolatry for India is not to stop idolatry, but to help those who worship idols to see God within and beneath all things. Walt Whitman and Wordsworth knew this. So! everything is bathed in God. I swim in God as a fish in the sea. Every object is my idol to remind me of God. So my mind cannot escape! "Thou art there, there, there...."

Asansol   **Saturday 16**

God, how wonderfully we do find when we seek. We find what we seek—and always more! If we seek the best, it is better than we had supposed the best could be. We open doors expecting to find more than we expect. It is always good—plus or bad—plus.

God, help me to welcome each day as a game with circumstances, to conquer the obstacles which rise like fog to shut You out. They call out new strength of will and so develop that strength. Teach me, God, to try hardest when I want to try least. Make me hottest in soul when the environment is coldest, for their sakes who are cold. When in Rome, may I be unlike the Romans most!

Buxar V. P., India — Sunday 17

God, thank You for being my friend when there is no other friend in sight. Thank You for speaking through my voice and telling me that my new life close up to You makes You very happy. So much makes You sad. How my own past must have saddened You. But now Your joy adds to mine. Thank You for the burning axle that led me to stop at Buxar to start the speakers of Bhojpuri toward a new hope. Thank You that when I am sleepy, I can just rest back in trust upon Your breast. I thank You for looking at me through the gentle, dark eyes of that modest Indian girl. Now, for one hour I shall try not to let You escape from my thought for a second.

Allahabad — Monday 18

God, I have felt Your hand leading today. You have not failed me once in the moments of testing. My job of not forgetting You at all has been imperfect, though better than some other days. Your part of coming to meet my need has been perfect. You, whom we call King, are the most faithful slave of us all, giving air, the sun, food, everything endlessly, love never growing lax. We forget. You never forget, night or day, with the burden of the universe on Your shoulders. At once my King and my Servant, working for and in us, managing our very alimentary canals. I look at a great man or a great cathedral and tremble. Help me to have Your courage.

En route Allahabad to Jubbulpore — Tuesday 19

God, that group of women weeping as they say farewell to their man reveals the love they hold for him. Are You that love? Are You the love in me this morning that makes me pray for Bob and feel such eager longing to fold the big boy in my arms and help him in his struggles? If You are as I am in Your eagerness for Your children, why does not Your heart break? If I loved these millions as I love Bob, I should go mad with frustrated longings. Even with my weak love I want to weep for them. Yet You, who never sleeps and can never forget one suffering, despairing, fearing, desperate creature for a single second, have the courage to love and suffer the pain of the whole world. You are eternally on Your Cross.

Jubbulpore — Wednesday 20

God, this day is packed with important contacts. Speak every word my tongue utters for me. Walk in my mind and think Your thoughts there. Burn in my heart. Direct my eyes. Dwell, love in me all day.

Dwell, too, God, in everyone of us and among us all as we seek Your mind and Your heart concerning literacy and India's need. Set our souls on fire today in this conference so that we may never lose courage again. Not the flare of a sheet of paper—but burn like the eternal sun in our hearts. Then illiteracy will melt away and Christ will rule.

Train Leaving Jubbulpore — Thursday 21

God, I leave this conference in thanksgiving, believing it was beyond all comparison the best literacy conference we have ever had. Every hour was lived in prayer, and every hour You were present, working to bring Your will to pass, because we gave You a clear channel through which to work. As those delegates go home, God, hold them to their high resolves. You can use my earnest prayer tonight to hold them. So now I pray and will pray tomorrow. Thank you for something inside that aches, God, with intense feeling. It is the way You love India and care for these millions until Your great heart aches!

Railway Station, Allahabad — Friday 22

If continuous communion with You, God, is possible for all people under all conditions, it must be possible here in this station with people talking all around me. But it requires a greater effort of the will to concentrate upon You when around me are men who show no evidence of giving You a thought, and when the injustice of master and cringing slave stands out so hideously. God, teach me to love these poor creatures underneath not this moment only. Teach me to have Thine own undying fire and to transmute that fire into a program that will emancipate because it is planned and led by You. As I think down through India, here, God, is a prayer for all who seek Your mind and who long to free slaves.

Mainpuri **Saturday 23**

God, thank You for contacts with other earnest souls, for those who poured out the best of life for You when they received little praise from other men. God, as I talked to those new Christians from the depressed classes today, saw their dull faces and felt how far they seemed to have to go, I could realize a little of all the discouragement You must feel for all of us. But how You must glory in these sacrificial souls who live in tents and try to bring new thoughts of You to the outcastes. God, use my prayer to send them new courage—the world's real heroes! And, O God, take my prayer to help break the deadening indifference and hopelessness of the oppressed millions here.

There Big Ben struck from London over Mr. Lawrence's radio. Was that Your voice, God, from London?

En route to Agra **Sunday 24**

He said, "Where is your faith?" We all feel amazed at Jesus and try to give Him praise. What God seeks is not praise, but growth into the likeness of Christ, into the achievements of Christ. Any fear that we cannot be like Him, even when we ask God, is what Jesus rebuked and rebukes yet, because we are to become strong, not to apologize for failing all our lives. Astonishment does not please Jesus, for He is not a slight-of-hand performer but fearlessly real. "They being afraid wondered." We do that in the presence of illness or of nature's disasters. We cringe like slaves; we do not stand unafraid like some. In three consecutive pages of Luke, Jesus shows us how to command wind, waves, devils, and death. We are making many Christians in India. We do not seem to be making many miracle working Christians like Sadhu Sundar Sing. We preach and practice a weak Christianity.

"Be not afraid! Be strong in…the power of his might." A flabby Christian too weak to conquer self, afraid of other people—this curses our age.

Agar **Monday 25**

God, I thank You for having let me see the Taj Mahal by moonlight, like one of the "many mansions" of heaven descended to earth! Those white fleecy clouds which reached from the fairy dome to heaven were like a net which had just let it down and set it in the moonlight. Perfection in perfect marble! And You are calling us to make such perfection of all this world. No, not that perfection built on oppression. But perfection of love as harmonious and lovely as the moonlight dream. We begin where we are masters, inside ourselves. We look at Jesus, the Taj Mahal of Spirit. We listen every second while Your still voice directs the building of a Taj Mahal within, built on love—listening and serving.

Agar   **Tuesday 26**

God, to be under Your will in every act, in every thought—that is my dead-earnest purpose! I grit my teeth tight, for this purpose demands will! I fight to keep my thoughts out of bypaths where You are not leading.

Shall we write a book together about literacy in India? A joint authorship of God and F.L.? The thought came from You this morning, I agree! We will begin to collect our material and lay out our outline when this page is finished. Keep me from doubting or vacillating. Keep me driving with You until that work is completed. First, I have this Testament to read. "Her sins, which are many, are forgiven; for she loved much." "Thy sins are forgiven." God, I do love much, and so Your words mean me, too.

Near Moga   **Wednesday 27**

God, after a sleepless night, I open my eyes, laughing, for we are together! Sleep is not necessary. Disturbances like that man coughing below me all night are good for character if I do not let them keep me from You. If every annoyance can be made to remind me to turn and grip Your hand and ask You, "What are You saying through this vexation?" then I can turn life's rough spots into Your vocabulary. If I can do that perfectly, nothing can defeat my soul. It will all be on the credit side of the ledger.

> "Then welcome each rebuff
> That turns earth's smoothness rough."

And yet—with the immense task before me—I had no right to lie there permitting myself to be exposed to his cough. I ought to have moved for India's sake.

Lahore [Pakistan]   **Thursday 28**

God, unusually lonesome so far as the world is concerned because I am entirely among strangers who are little interested in me and less in my work, I laugh, wholly at ease. This is Your work and You have sent me here…

March, 1937

Godhra [India]   Wednesday 3
Romans 3

    God, it is very difficult to keep out thoughts which cannot stay in the same mind with Thee. Perhaps that fight, too, is very good for me. Perhaps it is the link of understanding with everybody around me. Sex fancies surge up from the depths of our nature. That is how this morning begins. But I welcome it as a challenge to overcome these enemies of fellowship. I must, I can, I shall overwhelm them today. Here is my will, God, make it triumphant within. If this is possible for people on sick beds, it must be possible for me.

    Thus I see that the best gift I have for others is to succeed in this spiritual adventure. "Sail on and on and on!" especially when I do not want to!

En route Allahabad   Thursday 4
Romans 4

    God, I see what is the real curse of our race—so few do love their neighbors as themselves. So few will sacrifice self-interest to bless all. So few will give themselves to the task of aiding others. Outside this window I see mile after mile of dry land which would blossom if it had two things—water and freedom from oppressive owners. Sun pumps could be used to draw the water from the earth. But somebody objects that the glass to make sun pumps is expensive. Why expensive? Why could not the immense abundance of sand be used to make this glass in great, cheap quantities? It could, but men do not yet care enough.

    Or we could teach all India to read if we adopted a simple alphabet. Why do people not do it? Because those who read do not really care for those who are illiterate. It would be so easy, but indifference makes it so impossible.

Allahabad   Friday 5
Romans 5

    God, was it my thought of Thee that led the boy in the train to say, "How to find everlasting life is the question." How glad I am that my own personal experience arose to my lips to answer him. What a good illustration of the fact that we need to be full every instant and then just pour out what we have without strain or posing. This morning, as I came from the train and prayed for all the people on the street, I felt new energy surge into me. What it does to all of them to receive that instant prayer I may never know. What it does for me is electrical. It drives out fatigue and thrills one with eager power. How curious one's mind feels thus encircling others. Is Jesus like that?

Allahabad   Saturday 6
Romans 6

God, thank Thee for the freshness of discovery, which lends zest to every day, when I listen to Thy voice and wait until Thou leadest. Thank Thee that it has proved right to venture so far on faith. Thank Thee for the way literacy lessons came into being this morning so much better than I had expected. Thank Thee for this splendid group of cooperators who are working so eagerly with me. Thank Thee for the new doors which keep opening for this crusade against illiteracy. Help me, oh, help keep the door open toward Thee and the door closed toward sin in any of its forms. Thine, all Thine, nothing but Thine, walking through the doors Thou dost open, obeying instantly!

Allahabad   Sunday 7
Romans 7

Before me lies Streeter's *The God Who Speaks*. If Thou dost speak to one, Thou dost speak to all. If Thou dost speak ever, Thou dost speak always. If Thou dost speak anywhere, Thou dost speak everywhere. And I may listen for Thee to speak in the *Bhagavad-Gita*, where we read:

"I am the taste in the water. I am the light in sun and moon, sound in the ether, manhood in men.

"The pure scent in air am I, and the light in fire; the life in all born beings am I.

"I am victory, resolution, the Goodness of those possessed by the Goodness-mood."

Surely Thou canst and dost speak through every good for anything may become and does become Thine instrument.

Allahabad   Monday 8
Romans 8

God, thank Thee for yesterday's vision of the Mass Movement. I pray for those men with their white turbans and for those women. God bless that young secretary of the Chamar caste who sought the guidance of Smith. God bless those twenty or more who were baptized. God bless us as we seek to prepare easy ways for them to learn to read.

What a wonderful minute by minute demonstration life is that the one thing needful is to be led by Thee in every decision, in every word.

I felt, God, as if I was fighting confused and clashing thought currents yesterday. Help, God, that all those missionaries may be completely surrendered and not one prove a hindrance, but all prove a great blessing.

Allahabad   **Tuesday 9**
Romans 9

God, thank Thee for the quite wonderful way in which the Hindi and Urdu characters have arranged themselves for learning purposes. It seems a miracle that they should so easily find this arrangement, as though they had been planned for this from eternity. Thank Thee for the way in which my brain works over these ideas and never lets them go until they are perfect. This has surely come from Thee when my windows were open toward Thee. Since I have found by many experiences of the past that new insights were given daily whenever I opened the door to Thee, God, now I am open and eager for fresh revelation.

Allahabad   **Wednesday 10**
Romans 10

God, thank Thee for giving me a new approach this morning as I awoke. It broke upon my consciousness after I had said: "God, Thou knowest the full answer to our question." Then the perfect answer came!

How I do want to succeed in keeping Thee in my thought every second. How I do want to make all thought a process of consulting with Thee, for I always get surprises when I am open Theeward and am always barren when I forget Thee. Teach me how to carry everything and every thought to Thee so that at last I will not seek thoughts apart from Thyself, but always take Thee along.

Allahabad   **Thursday 11**
Romans 11

God, how marvelously Thou hast broken open this Urdu Dihate set of lessons today. But of all today's miracles, the greatest is this: To know that I find Thee best when I work listening, not when I am still or meditative or even on my knees in prayer, but when I work listening and cooperating.

Thank Thee, too, that the habit of constant conversation grows easier each day. I really do believe all thought can be conversations with Thee. And what is this strange new sense of knowing answers instead of being baffled, a sense of intellectual miracles happening. O God, I am so glad to see that our real battles are all in the mind. Outward acts of sin are outcroppings of inner disease. Outward acts of kindness are also outcroppings of fellowship.

Allahabad   **Friday 12**
Romans 12

God, what a wonderful chapter is Romans 12: Be transformed in mind...the perfect will of God.... Let love be without hypocrisy...condescend to men of low estate...avenge not yourselves... If thine enemy hunger, feed him...overcome evil with good.

Paul has passed over this land I am now exploring.

Weatherhead in his book, *The Transforming Friendship*, finds fellowship with Thee far easier than I find it. He just lets go, believes, and finds it simple. He thinks will is not a factor, that resolutions make no difference or at least fail. "Just leave the door to God ajar," he says. Yes, but I have to put the shoulder of my will against that door and keep it open by grim determination. My mind gives me trouble. If Weatherhead had as much sin in his past life as I have had, would it be so easy?

Allahabad   **Saturday 13**
Romans 13

God, as I was looking at the food before me and trying to see Thee in it, I lifted it to my lips. Then I realized that I would be eating Thee in that food. Whenever we take any food, Thou art there. I have been seeking to hear Thee and see Thee, but not until now to taste Thee in food, or smell Thee in flowers.

God, help me to keep my head as new, wonderful doors open, like this all-Hindi Revision Committee of the Congress has done.

Dost Thou really suffer from disappointment at our failures? We in this world cannot have the highest type of character unless we suffer for this world. Does the Cross reveal Thy character, God?

Allahabad   Sunday 14
Romans 14

    God, what a wonderful week of work with Thee this good week has been. How marvelously Thou hast kindled my mind to break into new effort. And now, as I am about to leave, here is a prayer for the men who are to continue on with experiments. I pray for Ralla Ram, for he knows the secret now, and for all these other loyal persons. Help them to follow the search for Thine answers. As I face this committee on the final revision of the Hindi alphabet, God, accomplish Thy will through me. God, is McGavren right and Miss Chapman and Hivali? Are the Christians the only people Thou desirest to learn to read? I do so want to please Thee. But are not all the people of India Thy children? And if we stop serving them, can we reveal Christ?

Allahabad   **Monday 15**
I Corinthians I

    Yesterday was to me a series of miracles. The young man who followed me home to tell about his loneliness of soul, the unexpected eagerness of Kaka Kalilkar for a reformed spelling as complete as I was seeking, the eagerness with which he adopted the idea of printing a paper in this simple script, so easy that it could be learned in a day, the couple who asked me to have dinner and who shared with me their spiritual longings—all these things verified my faith. But here, now, is a new day. What fresh miracles will it produce? The real question is, "What dost Thou desire done each minute?" I must not worry about surprises but only about perfect, full obedience.

En route to Bombay   **Tuesday 16**
I Corinthians 2

    God, I thank Thee that the Hindi lessons were completed for the printer. I am glad for the young man who spent an hour sharing his problem about the future. Glad you led me into the Remington offices. Now, God, I face the very important choice of alternatives as to alphabet. Shall I try to introduce my own facial alphabet, or the reformed alphabet which Kaka Kalilkar approved, or labor on with the alphabets now in existence? I am at this extremely important turning of the road. Thou knowest the answer. Give me both faith and the mind open heavenward to hear Thy voice so that there may be no regrets. Prepare the leaders of India to accept what Thou dost desire. The utterly simple alphabet seems very hard to promote, but not for Thee, God, is it?

Bombay   Wednesday 17
I Corinthians 3

God, as I looked at huge Venus, and the inconceivably distant stars, as I gazed through the trees at the awful sun as it set far over the plain, and realized something of its fiery immensity, I remembered that these are mere toys in Thy hands. Thou art everywhere all the time. Then this is my universe too. And when I have done all of this job Thou desirest me to do on earth, I will tackle other jobs with Thee across these mighty reaches. With Thee are an innumerable host of Thy friends. But, God, make my heart tender in eagerness that people all about me in Bombay, in India, in all this world, may share Thee, too. God, should my prayer be more purposive? Are there critical issues that need my prayer at this moment? Does it matter?

Bombay   Thursday 18
I Corinthians 4

God, more important than having constant fellowship, is to do Thy desire. Can I tire Thee out with my small chatter as I tired the bishop yesterday? My constant listening is Thy desire, and my speaking only as Thou dost dictate. What world-need dost Thou desire me to share now in prayer? These depressed classes? Thank Thee for opening the door in this wonderful, unexpected manner to Ambedkar. Yet, what I should do is ask Thee to prepare him and me for the interview. And I do ask Thee for us both, for it may affect all India.

I look at the globe that is set in the picture frame they presented me in Allahabad and pray for Mexico, Camargo, Sanchez, Neff; for Africa and those I am so soon to see there.

Bombay   Friday 19
I Corinthians 5

God, help that no physical weakness may cause me to fail to do all Thou art planning for today. These new letters came today like an answer, especially from Mrs. Stuhaan who tells of her mystical experiences. We need to cover the world with a mighty network of prayer partners, for it is a big world and the factors opposing Thee are terribly strong.

This is the evening of a lonely, discouraging day. Ambedkar wants the government to do the experimenting, and thinks the new government ought to be approached. Perhaps, but, God—no, this cannot be defeat! This lonely, discouraging day will but help me to sympathize with the millions upon millions upon millions who are discouraged, and will help me to long harder to help and help and help. Some new step has always come out of this kind of discouragement. It will again.

Sholapur   Saturday 20
I Corinthians 6

God, yesterday I failed to keep close to Thee for hours, and wondered why I could not conquer fever and heat. Today, too, has not been very constant. The tremendous heat is my excuse. But who wants excuses! This, God, is an opportunity to find what obstacles can be overcome. Paul said that nothing can separate us. Can heat? As I try to find improvements for Marathi, God, give me Thy wisdom for their sakes. The lessons must be made easy; in this heat no great effort of the illiterates is possible. Help me, God, to find a way to make it very easy. Thy way, exactly. Thy way, God. All Thy way. Not more than Thy way, not less.

Sholapur   Sunday 21, Palm Sunday
I Corinthians 7

After reading in Garland's *Forty Years of Psychic Research* last night, I wonder, God, what immense unseen realities remain to be discovered. But, after all, in all that unseen there are two personalities so infinitely above the rest that I do well to confine my quest to Thee, God, and to Jesus, leaving the others until I step across. But if my grand old father or some others there are helping, and if Thou dost desire me to know it, I am willing. Help me all day, all minutes of today, to keep in Thy close presence, to keep listening, on this still Sabbath morning, to Thy voices, all Thy voices from a thousand directions, inner and outer.

Sholapur   Monday 22
I Corinthians 8

God, this discipline of the mind not to forget Thee is very, very much the hardest thing I ever tried. I am finding this little globe my best help. It helps me follow Thy thoughts for all men.

This effort must be more than just keeping Thee in mind, something more than constant listening. It must be letting Thee think Thy world thoughts in my mind all day long. Some of those thoughts are close by, some of them far away, wherever the great need happens to be. My thoughts leap to Spain, where hatred has broken loose at its worst. God, I pray for Spain, and I pray that Thy will may be accomplished there. God, can we not find any way to peace and justice? Must justice lie beyond another war? God, I pray for the West. Canst Thou save her from destruction?

Sholapur   **Tuesday 23**
I Corinthians 9

Lord, we need more reincarnations of Thy perfect love like the Christ. Is that the goal every Christian ought to make his own? The question seems to answer itself. But how, God, can all these little Christians succeed when those who have the best opportunity find it so hard? I see only two things: first, constant outpourings of Thy Holy Spirit; second, the doctrine of ever fresh beginnings. We may forgetfully sink for an hour, but we may also start over at any moment.

But we have not tapped Thy reservoir. That is our real trouble. Thou hast the invisible dust in Thy hands, and not a star or a speck of star dust is out of Thy vision. Thy power to see us through our little problems is limitless. We need only to have connections all the time with Thee.

Sholapur   **Wednesday 24**
I Corinthians 10

God, what marvellous wisdom Paul reveals when he says: "I buffet my body and bring it into bondage." Let him that thinketh he standeth take heed lest he fall. There hath no temptation taken you but such as man can bear: but God...will with the temptation make also the way of escape.... Let no man seek his own, but each his neighbor's good.... Give no occasion of stumbling, either to Jews, or to Greeks, or to the church of God: even as I also please all men in all things, not seeking mine own profit...that they may be saved."

What, God, would be for me the highest, utmost possibility for this minute? Shall my thoughts enmesh with Thine as Thou dost play over the earth?

Sholapur   Thursday 25
I Corinthians 11

God, I thank Thee that this new method is attracting so many illiterates and enabling them to teach one another. I thank Thee for the letters from Godhra and Allahabad and Jubbulpore, giving me courage to believe that at last we are on the right track for the languages of India and for students to teach one another. It is Thy gift to India.

Help me not to slump now, but to do better in keeping close to Thee than I did the first quarter. This has been far the best three months of my life. I have learned by experience how true it is that I need only keep close every minute and Thou wilt do the rest. So, God, may I be closer to Thee and more constantly closer.

Poona   Friday 26, Good Friday
I Corinthians 12

John, in chapters 13 through 19, tells about Thursday night and Friday of the Crucifixion. Alone in this railroad station I hear the echo of that sacred tragedy. Anything I am that is worth being at all, that would be worth perpetuating at all, comes from that sweet sufferer. The moment I allow myself to cut loose from Thee, O Christ of God, I become despicable and my will divides against itself. When my will clings to Thy will, miracles happen. I have seen miracles happening since January. Thou art the vine; this branch and these millions of branches wither except when we abide in Thee. Deeper yet, O Christ, deeper, deeper, yet into Thy broken heart let me bury my will, that from Thy heart I may draw the power of Pentecost. Help me stay. Help me abide. Nothing else in the world matters but that: the power to stay deep in Thy broken heart.

Bombay   Saturday 27
I Corinthians 13

God, for the marvellous way Thou didst open up doors in Poona yesterday, I simply sit openmouthed in amazement. For Mr. Bhagwat, that greathearted Brahman; for Mr. Kellock; and Director of Education Grieve, and his fine support. Thou art ahead and will again open all the doors today as Thou dost desire, so that my hopes for Urdu may be realized—our hopes, Father! God, give that other splendid Brahman, Kulkarane in Sholapur, Thy blessing and make him a power. Did I miss an opportunity last night by not listening every moment while with Grieve? Make today a listening day, a day of guidance all day.

May I perfectly illustrate in spirit today Paul's marvelous thirteenth chapter of I Corinthians.

Bombay   Sunday 28, Easter Sunday
I Corinthians 14

Father, just home from Easter morning service, I seem amazed at new discoveries in the world of Spirit. Last night I saw how nearly every person in that church moved, acted as though he saw the vision of Christ, as I tried to help Christ become visible and audible, to help Him plead with each one to give everything, every thought, every minute. Thou art always here. Dost Thou need me to be a medium to help Thee to become visible and audible? The answer seems to be "yes"! Christ, the invisible may be visible, may speak when He can use my mysterious body powers which psychic research seems to prove exist. O Christ, if Thou canst use me, use anything, everything I have!

Bombay   Monday 29
I Corinthians 15

God, experience proves that a minute with Thee always brings fruit, often wonderful fruit; experience proves that a minute apart from Thee is wasted or full of thoughts of malice or vice. Abide in me as the branch abides in the vine. It abides all the time, every moment. Before me is an electric plug. The moment I disconnect the cord, the light goes out. What I got the last minute does not help. I may still be a little warm, but I am no longer a light. "Apart from me ye can do nothing"—say nothing, be nothing, help nothing. So I must keep plugged in every second. Hard but essential. Think Thy thoughts, God, here all day—Thine, not mine.

Bombay   Tuesday 30
I Corinthians 16

My child, this world of the spirit into which you are venturing is as much vaster than the earth you have known, as the fourth dimension is vaster than the third or the third than the second. But beyond the fourth lies the fifth and on and on and on. So you must not expect to know the laws of the Spirit until you first face a vast number of facts hard to relate. Those who have seen it and spoken have seen only small fragments. The Apocalypse,

Swedenborg, George Fox, Mary Baker Eddy, the spiritualists, the mystics, see in part and do not tell enough to make you able to state the laws of the Unseen. But keep on after discoveries that will exceed anything that hath entered the mind of man.

S.S. Tairea, Bombay **Wednesday 31**
II Corinthians 1

Father, there is so much self that obtrudes and makes people unwilling to hear what I have to say about Thee. Perhaps, too, it is my voice or appearance. Perhaps as my wrinkles deepen more people will turn away toward youth. Then nothing can save excepting that Thou wilt fill more and more of the void until at last it is all Thyself. Alone on this ship, as the gong tells visitors to leave and as the gangplank descends, help, O help, make these lovely days perfectly Thine. Let us see what can happen to all the passengers if I keep open to Thee and to them the whole long voyage. I leave India with her racial and religious prejudices to enter Africa which is fuller of racial hatred and wrong. O pure Love, possess me as I try to help Africa's tragic missions. (3:00 P.M.)

April, 1937

S. S. Tairea, en route to Porbandar　　　　　　　　　　　Thursday 1
II Corinthians 2

God, we can melt away the prejudices and hatred and walls that curse the human race everywhere, only by showing our freedom from these mean little minds. Christ, Thou hast revealed God as love. All over the face of the earth, in every religion, we see other aspects of God. Many are true, and some but partially true, and all too small. The whole universe is too small to reveal more than a minute fraction of God, for infinite time and God only know what fourth, fifth, nth dimensions there may be! So, Christ, Thy love should open us all to seek new light from all religions, not close us to everybody else as though we already had it all. We have a key—but we must use Christ as a key to unlock all truth to all men, not to lock ourselves from people of other faiths.

S. S. Tairea　　　　　　　　　　　　　　　　　　　　　　　Friday 2
II Corinthians 3:3
Conscious of God, 25%; Willful Refusal, None

God, for some days, at least, I shall try to give my daily mark on two points, for there have been too many mediocre days this past month. I shall mark first what percentage of the day I was conscious of Thee. Next I shall mark whether my will rebelled against what I believed to be Thy will during the whole day. Perhaps this sense of being marked will keep me at my task.

Then help, Lord, that to see anybody will be to pray! To hear anybody, as these children talking, that boy crying, may be to pray! Help me in this English ship not to expect snobbery but friendliness, and when they hold me off, may I not be sensitive. May I bless the crew, the passengers with whom I shall work on Gujarati and Kanarese. How would Jesus act on this ship?

S. S. Tairea　　　　　　　　　　　　　　　　　　　　　　Saturday 3
II Corinthians 3
Conscious, 50%; Refusal, None

God, yesterday was fairly close, yet only about one fourth of the time was I conscious of Thee. Why so small? The passengers are not religious (excuse number one!). But they do not know that I am religious. It has not seemed natural to talk about it to them. Perhaps this is my lesson: To have God I must give Him at every opportunity. Then the building of Gujarati charts drew my thought from Thee nearly every minute. Let me try it today with Thee. The preparation of material for the India report also pushed Thee out. I did remember Thee during much of the ping-pong. Thus far this morning it has been over 90 per cent. "Ye are...an epistle of Christ...written not with ink, but with the Spirit of the living God." "Ye are...known and read of all men."

In this game with minutes we must define our rules: Any thought of God, Christ, religion, helping others, spiritually communing with nature, planning a better world, lovingly talking or praying for others, counts as good if the inner thought of God comes and goes each minute.

S. S. Tairea   Sunday 4
II Corinthians 4
Conscious, 75%; Refusal, a Little

God, what a marvellous chapter! And three months ago I would have passed it without comment! "We have...renounced the hidden things of shame not walking in craftiness, nor handling the world of God deceitfully." Just what does this utterness of surrender mean! And as I see the closing in of physical life, I begin to appreciate II Corinthians 4:7-10. "I believed, and therefore did I speak." God help me to break through this habit of concealment which curses my life.

"Though our outward man is decaying, yet our inward man is renewed day by day. For our light affliction...worketh...." Have I not learned that! "We look not at the things which are seen, but at the things which are not seen...eternal." One must live to the utmost in order to appreciate Paul. I add singing prayers to the list of ways to hold God in mind, or whistling them, or humming them.

S. S. Tairea   Monday 5
II Corinthians 5
Conscious, 80%; Surrender, Almost Perfect

God, it is going to be very difficult to write these percentages truthfully. Somebody may read this diary and call me a weakling. But if, as Paul says, "We must all appear before the judgment seat of Christ," I had better face chagrin now. Paul would say, "You could have made yesterday a full 100%." Then why, having started on a rare height, did I will to read murder tales and "Indiscreet Confessions"? It does seem true that the pendulum, swung beyond normal, swings back. How to prevent that back swing? How to prevent it today all day? I must tackle each minute and be its master, each hour and make it as magnificent as possible. But, God, I am afraid of those grand words. I know too many such words that ended nowhere.

S. S. Tairea   Tuesday 6
II Corinthians 6
Conscious 25%; Surrender, 50%

"Having nothing, and yet possessing all things....for we are a temple of the living God; even as God had said, I will dwell in them, and walk in them."

When Paul was in the ship en route to Rome, he took possession of it. When Jesus lay asleep in the boat in Galilee, He awoke to take possession of it. As I learn all the possibilities of life, I shall take possession of the ships on which I ride. I shall not again ride in a ship and let circumstances rule me. God dwelling in me. I shall make circumstances do His full will. I shall find a way through defenses which people throw around themselves. I shall try to the full to find what prayer can accomplish while talking and playing with people. Help me keep this purpose fixed.

S. S. Tairea   Wednesday 7
II Corinthians 7
Conscious, 75%; Surrender, 100%

As I sat devoutly at the morning mass yesterday, I wondered whether the wise, old Roman Catholic Church did not perhaps work a real miracle at the Eucharist after all. Do they help Thee, Christ, to materialize for some of those present? Does faith make it possible for Thee to be present, and canst Thou thus make Thyself more real to the worshipers because of a full church? And does the semidarkness with candles prove a better environment that a bright light would be?

Yesterday, Lord, I saw how an experiment in prayer may be tried by athletes! I tried to put my arm in Thy control and my playing improved so much that instead of losing, I won. I tried to put my opponent's arm under Thy control and believe he did better. We humans have not begun to suspect what a field for useful scientific research prayer is!

S. S. Tairea   Thursday 8
II Corinthians 8
Conscious, 75%; Surrender, 100%

God, last night we crossed the equator. We saw nothing, felt nothing, save the laughter of merrymakers. Yet the equator is a fact in Thy mind and in our minds. And I begged Thee to help me cross an equator of the soul, out of weakness into integration and constant strength, to make this day and the future 100% days in surrender. All of them!

God, that crimson, blood-smeared sunset over Africa was Thy call, and I listened to it for half an hour. Africa needs us. God, we have a key to Christ, to hope, to justice. O God, I fear my weak self! Do not let me ever lose that glorious vision!

Thou, Lord, dost talk, and art talking now! This beautiful "Salutation of the Dawn" is Thy eager voice. "Look to this day, for it is life. Today well lived makes every yesterday a dream of happiness...." How happy yesterday leaves me this morning! And an ancient Sanskrit writer knew that!

S. S. Tairea   Friday 9
II Corinthians 9

God is opening doors! This good Bishop who read the International Review of Missions article and told me he strongly backed me. He said that Africa has a hundred million less people than formerly, that forced labor was the reason, and that he would speak with the Fathers at Mombasa and see what could be done. What can be done? What can be done for the darkest, bloodiest, saddest spot in all the world, so near Abyssinia where six thousand more were massacred a few days ago? My stomach is sick, my heart breaks, I cannot see through these tears. O spirit of Livingstone, can I help the land you opened and where you perished? This Colonel said, "The Africans are the most gentlemanly, courteous, likeable men on earth." And we whites are often beasts! God, help me to help Julia Kellersberger and all other burning hearts to help Thee help helpless Africa.

Train to Nairobi, Kenya, [Africa]   Saturday 10
II Corinthians 10

God, on this immense and almost uninhabited plain will one day dwell millions of happy people, in a world where they will know how to treat one another like brothers. Will this color line persist? Or will we plan for the children who are to come regardless of their color, realizing that we must not only serve men today but also serve the unborn. Would not the idea of planned babies be in line with the spirit of Jesus? Does it make any difference, after all, what color of skin the heirs of the earth possess? To be even a little like Thee, it is necessary not only to think of the whole world but also of the future, to plan for tomorrow, to dream with H. G. Wells of the perfect world that is to come, and we help Thee bring it into Africa. Here is a marvelous opening for lovers of men.

Jeanes School, Nairobi Sunday 11
II Corinthians 11

God, I love these Africans, with their friendly, happy dispositions and their willingness to help! What a contrast to the selfishness one finds on the trains in India! How much freer from snobbery than whites! As Thou art looking down upon this human family, if Thou wert to whisper in my ear the people Thou lovest most, would they be the blacks? No, for skins are not black nor white to Thee, races are not races to Thee. Nor dost Thou love men for what they are, but rather for that vision of what they can be and will be when they surrender and allow miracles to happen minute by minute. Help, God, that today I may take the whole roof off my soul and let Thee pack every corner with love every minute of today. Then I shall fit into Thy plan for Africa. Eyes, fingers, tongue, thoughts guided by the Voice of Silence.

Kenya, en route to Kisumu Monday 12
II Corinthians 12

God, these primitive faces, people clothed in rags, and low grass huts of the stone age, surrounded by British homes crowd time's awful reach into the same hour. Those dirty clothes full of holes are so like the parts of civilization these people get—its dirt, and its rags, the tatters of our civilization.

I hope that a thousand years hence people will look back and see how primitive our souls are. Our Mussolinis, our hypocritical rich, pretending to believe in Christ! We have just passed a lovely home established by some Englishman, with a delightful green arbor. Is that his contribution to Africa? Then with me is Archdeacon Owen giving himself for Africa—is his gift not the realer?

God, how the women of the world need light! especially these Kikuyu women with their distorted ears and their painful burdens.

Kisumu, Lake Victoria, Kenya Tuesday 13
II Corinthians 13

Lord, will Lake Victoria, with this thirty-mile-wide plain, one day be the site of a mighty civilization? What frightful crimes have stained these shores—and all shores where men have ever lived—the veil of the past may conceal. But, God, how canst Thou and I actively, purposefully help those who are consciously or unconsciously preparing the way for tomorrow? Can soul-force help Thee and these Africans about the Lake? Wilt Thou dream

Thy dreams with and in me for this continent? The British government seems to be doing better than I had hoped. Direct my act and thought so that all Thy will may come to pass tomorrow or tonight. My soul goes out to the Kellersbergers as they pray and toil for Christ in the Congo. May my fire re-enkindle their fire.

Kisumu Hotel, Lake Victoria, Kenya   **Wednesday 14**
Galatians 1

God, thank Thee for the violin and piano music which took hold of me with resistless power and demanded that I should come back to a new level. Thank Thee for the sense of power that swept like a wave around the guests in this hotel, for the purpose to help all of them, for the grip of Thy plan for the future of Lake Victoria. May the imprint of this purpose drive deep into the hearts of us all. Thou hast spoken straight out of the unseen to us all and across all Africa and around the whole world. Thank Thee for the power to help Thee ride into the secret places of men's hearts on the wings of music, for the tremendous power of silent self-giving. God, how can we weak things keep on this plane?

Maseno, Lake Victoria, Kenya   **Thursday 15**
Galatians 2

God, what a future can belong to these magnificent black Dhuluo boys and the others in this school! How reverent they were! What power in that deep-toned "Amen" from 150 throats!

Back in their homes, their mothers and fathers are ignorant but eager to learn. Help us tomorrow to find a way so that this campaign may sweep like an epidemic through all Africa, a beneficent epidemic of release and hope, and the smile of Christ!

And now, God, as we undertake this first African language, have Thy perfect way, so that we may go straight and true to Thy will. We do our best and highest for Africa only if Thou art the author and finisher. I yield all—fingers, thoughts, love, lips—to Thee.

Maseno, Lake Victoria, Kenya   **Friday 16**
Galatians 3

God, I have found by unhappy experiences that unless I talk to others about this experiment, my day is a failure. Is that a law of this spiritual adventure? If I do not set the pace, if I do not create the atmosphere, I become a mere victim of conditions. My environment makes me, but I choose the environment. This Testament, this "Fellowship of Silence," this "Great Souls at Prayer," this "Devotional Diary," this book "Awake"—these are my morning teachers because I attend their school. And this "Fourfold Sacrament" is like a gentle angel hand across my brow, like the soft notes of a faint violin, like the heartaches of those who love. This "Sacrament of Work" is Thee speaking.

> Lord, teach us to love,
> Teach us to love in perfection,
> Obeying Thine own great command
> That we love one another even as Christ loved us.

Thank Thee, Father, for this morning which leaves me feeling melted all over with Christ-love.

Maseno, Lake Victoria   **Saturday 17**
Galatians 4

God, thank Thee for St. Patrick's "lorica", or hymn, speaking across thirteen centuries:

> "I arise today
> Through God's strength to pilot me:
> God's might to uphold me,
> God's wisdom to guide me,
> God's eye to look before me,
> God's ear to hear me,
> God's word to speak for me,
> God's hand to guard me....
>
> "Christ with me, Christ before me, Christ behind me,
> Christ in me, Christ beneath me, Christ above me,
> Christ on my right, Christ on my left,
> Christ when I lie down, Christ when I sit down, Christ when I arise.
> Christ in the heart of every man who thinks of me,
> Christ in the mouth of every one who speaks of me,
> Christ in every eye that sees me,
> Christ in every ear that hears me.
>
> "I arise today
> Through a mighty strength, the invocation of the Trinity."

Maseno   **Sunday 18**
Galatians 5

"The fruit of the Spirit is love, joy, peace, longsuffering, gentleness, goodness, faith, meekness, temperance." Paul speaks of "Faith which worketh by love." He says, "...by love serve one another."

"Father,
Dear Father,
My soul reaches up once more to Thee,
For Thy morning Kiss.
Because Thou, Father God, art Ruler and Lover in one."

What use of this day will wreathe Thy lips with happy smiles, Father, and make Thee give me a kiss of good night with the words, "Well done"? How loving, how large must my thought be? Only one simple task—to keep the window wide open, to try to keep consciously obedient to Thy voice—and Thou wilt tell all the rest.

Kima, Lake Victoria, Kenya   **Monday 19**
Galatians 6

Thank Thee, Father, for the wonderful committee that pushed these lessons today. For women like Mrs. Ludwig and Mrs. Hull to throw their whole souls into preparing pictures.

As the radio in the next room reaches across to England and all the world, so let our prayers for the world reach around to every part of the world. What new era are the radio and the airplane and perhaps television ushering in? Is this the day when walls between nations will crumble and a world brotherhood will begin? God, where are those who are ready to join Thee and one another in drawing men into a loving, united brotherhood?

Kima   **Tuesday 20**
Ephesians 1

Among these real, practical, unpretentious people my heart longs to be real. May I not try to be superior but to be simple and dependable and honest. Here the rawest of raw material is being brought into touch with Christ.

Thank Thee for the gratitude of these fine folk, for the excellent progress our lessons made, for the miracle that sent me here where they need and want my help. My heart thrills at beholding Thy hand ever over the horizon. It was Thy hand that sent me into the heart of Africa, and wonderful results will burst upon this country. God, speak comfort to the lonely heart of this missionary who buried wife and three babies here.

Kisumu, Lake Victoria   Wednesday 21
Ephesians 2

For the first time this year, God, I have been compelled to write this diary a day late. But it is far better to have lived as I have lately than to write about living. What utterness of consecration, what simplicity, what love of the Negroes, what practical common sense, in this mission of the church of God! For the chapel crowded with black faces hiding Thy children, for their music, for putting the right message on my lips—Father, thank Thee.

God, for all the millions of mind-darkened people around this great lake basin, I pray. For these Bunyore people and these Dhuluo people for whom we made language lessons, I pray. For the missionaries, for their cooperation, I pray, that "they may be one."

En route from Kisumu   Thursday 22
Ephesians 3

God, to build the new habit in my mind requires a gentle and nearly constant pressure of the will. Teach me to apply this pressure more continuously and with more effectiveness in praying for others, for Thou dost desire us to be powerful as well as clean. "That ye may be strengthened with power through his Spirit in the inward man"—power to see souls behind faces, power to pray for those I see outside this car window, power to ooze into or push into the inner souls of others with my prayer and carry Thee with me all the way to the center. Last night, as I prayed hard for those Kima students, I felt that they felt that outreach. Does some emulation reach people? I not only dare, I must find out, now that this possible channel of working for Christ has revealed itself. "Power through his spirit." Help me not to look at these half-naked savages as curiosities but with eager desire to help Thee reach them.

En route to Kikuyu   Friday 23
Ephesians 4

God, what stupendous conceptions are packed in Paul's letter! What a soul Paul had, what penetration into this world of Spirit which I begin to explore! Only one was ahead of him as he passed on into the land no human being had ever before explored. "The mystery, which for all ages hath been hid in God." "Christ Jesus...in whom we have boldness and access in confidence." Paul, daring to go on alone, away from the childhood in which all men were, and nearly all men still are—pressing on "unto a fullgrown man, unto the measure of the stature of the fullness of Christ." "For the perfecting of the saints...." "...be renewed in the spirit of your mind, and put on the new man.... Let all bitterness and wrath, and anger, and clamor, and railing be put away from you, be ye kind one to another, tenderhearted, forgiving each other, even as God also in Christ forgave you." That sick little Jew with that Titan soul!

Kikuyu   **Saturday 24**
Ephesians 5

God, how like a game life is! Why not call it a game with minutes? Under all sorts of handicaps which must be faced and overcome, I have one goal to reach, filling that minute with useful fellowship with Thee, and with service directed by Thee. This morning, with eyes aching, my game is to win through as though there were no handicaps.

Thank Thee for those sleepless hours which I used to try to send the picture of Christ to people near and far around the world. I must grow in this power to help others to contact with Thee, and such growth will come only from exercise. Thou dost need us to be effective as well as devoted.

Alliance School, Kikuyu   **Sunday 25**
Ephesians 6

God, thank Thee for making the gentle pressure of the will change this morning's atmosphere, so that a church service changed from cold to warm. I must learn that will and thought can change the world, and I must teach other Christians to use that mighty, gentle power.

An idea that the sun pump will some day be a boon to the human race takes hold of me. Is it a vision I share with Thee? If it is, then give me perseverance to see it through.

Thank Thee for the mind-bent that broke into an empty conversation today and made it of permanent value to us all. Thank Thee for this wonderful letter from a prayer partner.

Four things are immensely right: Prayer every minute, prayer for others, this prayer partnership, this literacy effort.

Kikuyu   **Monday 26**
Philippians 1

"Let your life be worthy of Christ, with one soul striving for the faith." This living on the highest plane is a matter of constant choice of the highest thing to think or see or do at each moment. Often when I turn toward the highest my brain is blank. Then I can say, "Father I am empty, waiting to be filled, listening for Thee to speak." Nothing is higher than listening to God, unless it be suffering with others and for others. To go through a black hospital without suffering acutely is an indication of low sympathy and lack of love. Measure your Christlikeness by your capacity to share other people's pain and to have an overwhelming desire to relieve.

Alliance School, Kikuyu   **Tuesday 27**
Philippians 2

My child, when you pray to me of your own little troubles and doubts, your prayer is pretty thin and small. When you reach out to help other people by offering yourself as a channel for me, your prayer becomes at once large and noble. You need not pray about your own personal affairs at all, for I will provide for those. Pray for others! Make your whole day a prayer for others. Think of them one by one, and try to help them to a rich contact with me. Your effort to bring the picture of Christ into their minds was good. I will day by day teach you endless ways to make this priceless voyage of discovery in a little-known land of the Spirit. Put a gentle but continuous pressure on your will to do this. When reading, put your will effort into those of whom you read. When talking, pour your prayer into those to whom you speak and of whom you speak. Thus you will learn what Christ-love in all its fullness and irresistable power is, a terrific, outreaching love-will.

Alliance School, Kikuyu   **Wednesday 28**
Philippians 3

"Not that I had already obtained or am already made perfect...but one thing I do, forgetting the things which are behind, and stretching forward...I press toward the goal...the high calling of God in Christ Jesus." Was it the high price Paul paid or pain he endured that whipped up his passion for Christ? Can any man conquer the dulling effect of comfort?

Last night I saw one new advance in this experiment with Thee. I saw that the best way to pray for others is to say: "Christ show me where Thou art seeking entrance in vain so that I may add my prayer and help Thee enter." The faces floated before my eyes. Thank Thee when sleepless hours come that give me time to pray for many.

Thank Thee for the soul hunger in the missionaries here, the soul hunger which came to meet mine at last night's meeting. This is new evidence that this road will help other Christians.

Alliance School, Kikuyu Thursday 29
Philippians 4

"My son, I have seen races slowly emerge from savagery to some degree of kindliness as centuries rolled by. England is better now than in the fierce days of the invaders. And I can wait while out of this racial wrong some better race emerges in Africa. I wait, but this betterment does not happen by accident. I wait for men and women who will surrender their lives wholly and eagerly, who will ache with eager longing to bless Africa, who will be consuming fires, zealously self-giving. There are such men and women now, and each one pushes Africa upward toward her better day.

"But what of the millions who have lived and are living with no opportunity to know the higher life?" you are asking. If you learn to see just around you, you will know that life stretches on and on, with ample ages in which to fulfill what these brief days lack. All of you are but gurgling infants as yet, all of you."

Alliance School, Kikuyu Friday 30
Colossians 1

Today, Father, closes the four most glorious months of my life. With what conviction of experience I can now urge youth to try to have glorious years! As I look back over this uneven life, there is much I want to hide forever in the crimson flood of Christ's blood. But the high years are sources of joy: The year when Tommy Ash led me to the Methodist altar; the year in Perkiomen; the year in Spring Street; the years when I wandered over America speaking; the first year in Lanao (Philippines); last year in America; but far above them all these four months! We are stepping into a new world hand in hand, and sailing with thrilling eagerness toward unknown shores.

Not where one is most significant, but the direction and speed with which one is going. I know that the best gift I have for the world is to help men discover this new continent of the Spirit, to discover it for them and beckon them to come.

At fifty-two nothing I ever did is worth preserving except the high aspirations. They are my "treasures in heaven." God, help me to continue that gentle but incessant pressure of the will "on and on and on"!

May, 1937

En route Nairobi to Mombasa   **Saturday 1**
Colossians 2

God, two lessons came out of this day. Last night, because my hosts served sherry, I assumed they would not be interested in the realm of the spirit. Then I saw in their library Nikolai Berdiaev's *Freedom and the Spirit*, and today told them a little. "How perfectly thrilling!" exclaimed one of them. Lesson 1: I must hide what I have from nobody.

These grand people, Mr., Mrs., and Miss Grieve, to whom I told all during my week with them, came all the way to Nairobi to see me off, and by their looks and words proved (Lesson 2) that friendship is far, far best when we share our deepest highest best selves with one another. I cannot forget the hand grips of others who attended the Tuesday night prayer meeting, and said they could never express their gratitude. God, help me to love to share with strangers.

In front of a Barroom, Mombasa   **Sunday 2**
Colossians 3

God, how strange to be writing this in a town where I have no friends, in a hotel outside the barroom window, Sunday morning, and not to feel alone, "For thou art with me." I try to see Thy sweet face on this chair in front of me. I try to help Thee step into the mind of the chauffeur in that car; and he turns to look, as nearly all people do now. So here I am manufacturing my atmosphere with nothing but my Testament and this diary to help me help Thee change my environment. We must be masters in every situation in order to win this constant war. I am amazed at the way that chauffeur glues his eyes on me, and the bartender comes out to look. Here and in places like this are where Christ needs help most. The Salvation Army is tremendously right. The rest of us confuse fastidious snobbery with religion and become Pharisees, thanking God that we are not as that bartender. So we say we "fight" sin by avoiding sinners, while Jesus was a friend of sinners and ate with them. He sought incessantly to help others; we seek merely to save ourselves.

S. S. Chantilly, Mombasa to Zanzibar　　　　　　　　　　　　**Monday 3**
Colossians 4

"Perfect and complete in all the will of God." "Continue steadfastly in prayer,...praying for us also, that God may open unto us a door for the word, to speak the mystery of Christ."

Another even more strange situation today is the one on this French ship. Almost all passengers are unable to speak English, and I speak such poor French that they would dislike talking with me. A perfect chance to try what sheer, steadfast prayer can do! So I will today try to help Thee reach into the heart of each passenger I meet. Can we make a real advance in this prayer art today? There are two things with which we deal—power to press through and pure quality of our message when we do get through. The latter is something Thou only canst give. So my simple task is to listen and follow. The channel is wide open from Thee to them all day long! Come, Spirit, and rush through and out like a reversed waterspout! Downward and outward....

Zanzibar, English Club House　　　　　　　　　　　　**Tuesday 4**
I Thessalonians 1

God, the laboratory of each day's experience teaches two lessons and proves them valid. First, when a man is speaking with me, pouring out his long story, he has opened his mind to me, he is tuned in; and while I listen I can be sending back to his mind my silent prayers for God to enter. All over the world are people anxious to talk to us. Let them tell it! and call it God's opportunity. Second, I am like an oarsman rowing against a current. My will-pressure must be gentle but constant, to listen to God, to pray for others incessantly, to look at people as souls and not as clothes, or bodies, or even minds. The moment the pressure on the oar ceases, I drift, and downward.... "Let go and let God" does not fit my experience. "Take hold and keep hold of God" is what it feels like to me. There is a will-act, and I can feel the spiritual muscles growing from rowing!

Zanzibar　　　　　　　　　　　　**Wednesday 5**
I Thessalonians 2

God, Thou dost never fail us. This morning I listened and prayed, while this committee did the work, and Thou didst guide us. What resulted must have seemed like magic to that committee. It did also to me!

As I reread those glorious letters from my prayer regiment, I realized that we make our own heaven! We build it, and then inhabit it. Rather, we plant it like a mustard seed; and Thou givest the crop. I planted ideas which came from Thee, and all these people have given the good thoughts back with interest. Why must one wait until he is fifty-two to learn that what a man sows he shall reap? Why cannot youth know that without first sowing hell?

Zanzibar   Thursday 6
I Thessalonians 3

Sure as life, God, Thou art at work! Daily I see Thy hand! Out from the library shelves stood *Raymond* by Oliver Lodge, *Human Personality* by F. W. H. Myers, *The Vital Message* of Conan Doyle, and Barrett's *On the Threshold of the Unseen*. My voyage of spiritual discovery must not ignore those amazing findings.

But they are not to deflect me from my course, which is straight toward Thee. They may encourage and suggest but not retard or confuse. It is simple now, when my will must simply be pressed toward Thee, endlessly and gently toward Thee!

And this wonderful third chapter of Thessalonians is Thy voice. It contains a mighty will, a mighty love, a mighty loyalty, and mighty courage in persecution.

Zanzibar   Friday 7
I Thessalonians 4

God, I stand today on the edge of another form of intercessory prayer and hesitate whether to follow a path so unusual. Last night, when wakeful, I closed my eyes in the darkness and took a journey with my mind to some of my friends, imagined myself walking into their homes, shaking hands and then saying, "I have come to say: The Spirit of Jesus floods your minds and your hearts." Then I said farewell and came back to Zanzibar. Is it right? If it helps people to a fuller experience of Christ, it is necessary as well as right to use any door God opens. Is this the new experience Thou hast opened through Lodge and Barrett? I must try before I know whether it is fruitful and really reaches others. I will begin systematically with a notebook.

Zanzibar   Saturday 8
I Thessalonians 5

God, You do step out of the pages of books into our minds! What a succession of wonderful visions You gave me just now from this letter of Paul's! His words shoot into me like bullets, every sentence a bull's eye.

You are speaking from the pages of Sir Oliver Lodge, "Christ was a planetary manifestation of Deity, the highest and simplest to man, a revelation in the only form accessible to man, a revelation in the full-bodied form of humanity." Jesus enables us to trust God—God's pity, His love, His friendliness, His compassion, His eager desire to help men—so that in Christ I need fear neither man nor devil nor death itself. Death—a new adventurous voyage of discovery.

But, God, You do not step forth from books unless we seek books where You are to be found. The detective story I read yesterday was a sheer waste of time.

Zanzibar   **Sunday 9**

God, to whom I write on this page, is there any truth in the words of this Sama-Veda? "If thou sayest, 'I know Him in part,' thou deceivest thyself, for not to be wholly ignorant of Him is not to know Him. He who believes that he does not know Him is he that does know Him."

"My child, this is both true and false. They who believe they finally know my secret are very foolish. They who, like the materialists of your day, make silly little denials about me are caught in pure ignorance and will appear as ridiculous to men a century hence as Butler does to you now.

"But, though you cannot know all while on that plane, you can speak and I will hear, you can hear and I will speak, you can follow and I will lead, you can obey and I will direct. But if you refuse, my heart aches, for I know how yours must ache before you return to me. You are crossing the stage of eternity as I venture upon an experiment in free wills, and those who prove that I can trust them with Sonship shall one day know all."

Zanzibar   **Monday 10**
II Thessalonians 1

God, I seem to be discovering with dizzy speed how wide this spiritual Universe may prove to be. Thou art placing before me books which exceed all I had dreamed I might see. Maeterlinck's *The Great Secret* collects with convincing power the new scientific evidence of the spiritual world. Then these three volumes of Swedenborg, *Heaven and Hell, The Divine Love and Wisdom, The Divine Providence*, seem to be saying exactly what these modern books seem to tell of the unseen, though Swedenborg lived two centuries ago. Help me with unbiased, fearless mind to "weigh and consider" evidence from whatever source, for, like my race and age, I have been dogmatic, narrow, and proud of my blindness. What a little man, in what a big universe! How sure on what meager evidence! Teach me to be open-minded and quietly humble—but burning up with passion to help others!

Zanzibar Tuesday 11
II Thessalonians 2, 3

Overwhelmed by the sense of Thy stupendously immense power and size and wisdom, as these books truthfully remind me, and of my own stupid, blundering, frail little soul and body, I am ashamed of the way I have so often approached Thee. Why are we so weak, why these clouds in our memories and thoughts? But then I hear You reply:

"My little one, I never felt hurt at your familiar way of coming to me. It is neglect that grieves me, because you cut yourself off from wisdom and love. I want you to be at perfect ease anywhere, through your trust in me.

"But as for weakness, you mortals have all the powers I dare give you. See what Western men do with chemistry! Suppose I gave you the secret of atomic energy now. I must permit the far more worthy secrets of the soul to be known to a few—the rest would use them to ruin the world. So telepathy is guarded by love, and only they who love can use it."

Coronation of George VI, Residency, Zanzibar Wednesday 12
I Timothy 1

God, as the British Empire crowns its new king today, what a surging of varied and often disharmonious emotions pulsate in millions of breasts. Thank Thee for the mighty emotions and the sense of world vision Thou gavest me during that service this morning, when my thought reached out and gripped this floating ball called earth and I willed unity, love, Christ for every nation and color. Did all the people in that church, did all the British Empire, did all the world feel that vibration? Now while the British Isles are alive with the great day, I sit here and try to help Thee reach through this excitement to men's hearts. Use me to change Mussolini! Use me to reach Spain. Use me to reach Hitler and set him right! Shall I journey to them in thought and try to talk to them for Thee? I will try! (12:00 noon)

Zanzibar Thursday 13
I Timothy 2

God, if Jesus sat here permitting Thee to write, what wouldst Thou say? What dost Thou desire done today? Thank Thee for permitting me to share in opening the new door through Mrs. Johnson's Moslem Girls school. Thank Thee that they needed an interpreter, because I had a chance to pray after each sentence. Thank Thee for the incredible way in which doors have flung open here for Hindus, Arabs, Africans. For those three hundred who came last night, show me how most effectively to pray for them, and for the women in that girls school, and for the Indian teachers, and the African teachers. I shall try to listen carefully so that Thou canst reveal the best possible method of teaching Swahili. Thank Thee for new vistas I just begin to see. May all Thy will, all Thy love—work today, all the minutes.

En route to Dar es Salaam   **Friday 14**
I Timothy 3

God, for this privilege of sharing the dreams of a young doctor and planning for a better world, I thank Thee. Help me, God, to become freer from boasting about America and to feel only for Thee each minute. I often slump so badly below the ideal when in conversation with others, and talk too much, not waiting until Thou hast said Thy mind. Was this list of world needs Thy list of needs: cooperative societies, planetary mindedness, openness toward the Spirit, the zest for discovery in every important direction—was that enough?

My thought returns to that committee of Arabs who responded so wonderfully this morning. I think ahead to Dar es Salaam, and want all, all, all Thy will, only Thy will done while there. All, only.

New Africa Hotel, Dar es Salaam   **Saturday 15**

God, our silver wedding day and ten thousand miles apart. If this had been two years ago, how desperately lonely I should have felt. But Effa and I are not apart. I can send my soul to her and she hers to me. Soul is all that has permanent significance. And Thou art working through me this morning. My soul has stepped forth to bear Thy picture, Christ, Thy love-will to all the people in this hotel, to all the voices I heard outside, to scores who floated into my memory across the globe. And I am astonished to find that there is not a trace of loneliness this morning; space does not exist for the soul that knows how to leap and reach! Tongue and pen become secondary, for thoughts fly anywhere with more than light's swiftness. The world belongs only to those who hold it in their arms and pray for it. Government titles are delusions.

Dar es Salaam Hotel   **Sunday 16**
I Timothy 4

God, in this voyage of discovery in the world of Spirit some amazing surprise awaits around nearly every corner. "The laying on of hands" really does something if it be true that our souls are radioactive. There is truth in the Roman Catholic doctrine of apostolic succession. The Roman Catholics are wrong when they say theirs is the only succession—as negatives are more often false than true.

From now onward I shall search for some secret wrapped in every superstition and in every religion that grips men's hearts. They meet or offer to meet some human need. Paul might have meant me instead of Timothy when he said, "Meditate upon these things; give thyself wholly to them; that thy profiting may appear to all." "Be thou an example of the believers." Wholly—that is what I need more of Thy help to achieve. In the tired hours of the afternoon "our souls grow weary." Help this day to be wholly at its best conquering this hotel atmosphere—wholly! Make me ready for miracles today!

Dar es Salaam, the Dar es Salaam Club   **Monday 17**
I Timothy 5

God, a great many pious thoughts protrude from my consciousness like rocks sticking out of the ocean, but they are not the highest, the last highest, are they? They are not the thoughts in Thy mind. May I ask Thee to think in my mind?

"To grant that fully, my child, would be for you to think all my infinitely countless thoughts at once. You are not safe for that, are you? The universe would be in peril if you possessed that much power before your will is perfect. And when your will becomes perfect, you will ask me that all these Africans, all these Europeans may also share all my thoughts. You will not ask more for yourself than you do for everybody. And you are far from that in your daily practice."

God, save me from being dragged even further toward unconscious snobbery by the luxuries of this club and the attentions of officials. Do something to save me for everybody. Thou hast done it, for even now I can reach the arms of my soul around every soul in the world!

Dar es Salaam Club Tuesday 18
I Timothy 6

Marvelously close, God, help me to keep thinking of Thee all day today, as love crowding gently as the ether, warm as the sunlight, into every nook and cranny of my thoughts, words, looks, acts—love pressing in, and oozing out, floating like perfume out to others.

> "O Love that wilt not let me go,
> I rest my weary soul in Thee;
> I give thee back the life I owe,
> That in Thine ocean depths its flow
> May richer, fuller be."

"My child, this makes me happy. Now let love flow out to my world of needy people all about you. Despise not one of the least. Do not see color or clothes, just souls and my children. Do not hear titles or languages, just hear me speak through them. I call from behind every eye, I float upon every wave of speech and song and sigh. See me in people, for I seek to make them grow in Christlike love."

Dar es Salaam Wednesday 19
II Timothy 1

Father, here is my willing hand to be directed across the page by Thee. Here is my brain; walk through it and put its thoughts in order after Thine own love-will. I wait unwilling to write save as I am sure Thou art directing.

"My child, hold up to this high effort all day long. As you reached upward and outward yesterday morning and evening, learn habitually to keep that outreach for everybody whom you meet or think of every minute. Do not surrender to your tired feelings, for this outreach-upreach does not exhaust you. It can be the constant state of mind. Yes, you may read the books written on clairvoyance and witchcraft, but not much, for your fellowship with me directly is the pearl of great price. So saturate your spirit in me."

Dar es Salaam Thursday 20
II Timothy 2

God, my education is only just beginning this year. Indeed, it may not advance far in this life. We humans stand on the edge of a vast unknown and are wise only when we realize how little we know, as *Ether and Reality* by Oliver Lodge reminds us. We may spend eternity learning....

This couple, Mr. and Mrs. Dowd, who were married today at such a mature age will need Thee, Lord. Did they not need me and did I not fail them? I should have found a chance to help them. Help me, God, to press every last drop out of each opportunity to help people, and not to yield to the habit of running away from people. Make me always sensitive to the need of others, keen to sense the carefully hidden need!

I will pray for them now, 9:30 p.m.

Father, Thou art planning and working. Thank Thee for the success of the Swahili charts today, astonishing all of us.

Dar es Salaam   **Friday 21**
II Timothy 3

Dear, dear Father God, pour in and through and out over the world; begin this early hour and continue until these eyes close in sleep after a glorious day of serving as Thy roadway into men's souls. I almost gasped at the amazing wisdom packed into this third chapter of Timothy and at the power with which it set my own soul electric! Are these words of Aldous Huxley true or false: "The perfect height cannot be lived on, only visited—the soul cannot always feel what it feels sometimes—ecstatic states are rare—man has one hour of ecstasy in every hundred." Perhaps true of him and those he knows but certainly not of this year, Lord. The curve is up and down many hours nearly every day—up last night as Thou didst speak through the cool, silent southern stars and the crosses in the sky. Up this sweet morning—O Father, how I love!

Dar es Salaam Club   **Saturday 22**
II Timothy 4

Sitting in the church alone for a long while trying to give Thee out to many people, I wanted to become that way habitually, so that to see a man would be more than to pray; it would be to give him my soul filled with Thee, O Christ. Can I become that way to the English with their insufferable snobbery? Can I ignore it? Can Love and I draw a circle to take them in and to understand them and to give my soul to them full of Christ? That is a good test! "The common" people are easy to love and help. Give me love enough even for snobs!

This second letter of Paul to Timothy brings tears. Poor, wonderful Paul! "The time of my departure is come," "All that are in Asia turned away from me," "Hymenaeus and Philetus...have erred," "Demas forsook me," "Alexander...did me much evil," "Only Luke is with me." He wants

Timothy to "come shortly." O Paul, you tasted the same desertion Christ experienced! It is necessary to be "made perfect through suffering." All of us must, sooner or later.

Dar es Salaam Club — Sunday 23
Titus I

Father, am I not learning that the best way to pray for people is to go and sit near them and pray while there? Perhaps holding their letters or photos in my hand is as effective. This experiment which I began May 8 with letters and photos, recording the hour when I pray, may answer this question.

Looking at Johnson's African pictures last night, with the growling lions devouring a zebra and the shrieking baboons fighting monkeys, then pondering upon "the still small voice of the spirit," I see that the soul must grow out of coarse, cruel, dumbness and numbness, like that of a rhinoceros, into the sensitive acuteness of the violinist scarce touching his high note. The soul must become like the mystic who hears the whisper of the Spirit.

Dar es Salaam, German Pension — Monday 24
Titus II

God, if like the radio, I am succeeding in sending out thoughts to other minds, the real question is what my mind tells other minds. The radio is a great invention, but that music yonder across the street is not worth broadcasting. Every wave of prayer from my mind must say, "Love, sacrifice, Christ, truth, loyalty, faith, beauty of soul, growth toward perfection, surrender, let the spirit of Christ flood your soul, live in the presence of God, help and help and help...." I want the power of broadcasting to grow only when the message is purely and perfectly what Thou dost desire.

Thank Thee for the growing eagerness of the Africans and the ease with which they are learning to read and write. What kindly, lovable souls these Africans are!

Dar es Salaam, German Pension — Tuesday 25
Titus 3

Father, lonely, surrounded by noise and folly, I need Thee today. It is an opportunity to try putting more pressure on the will upward toward Thee and outward toward others. Here is a situation to challenge my strength of purpose. A challenge to make the life lived close to Thee joyously attractive to these others! When they speak only German, help me to speak the silent language of Christ. Nothing about self—all about Thee throughout the meal.

As I walked homeward this afternoon through the native section, after teaching in the school, I saw another truth; Thou art ever eager to reach out Thine arms and enfold those who are lonesome, the aged whom we all forget, the poor, the obscure little people, when they plead to Thee. The ugly, those with nothing to attract, can nestle in Thine arms.

How often we say this!

Thank Thee for the pain that makes me experience it—with Christ. I could not have known it at the Club. How blind, how blind we are!

Dar es Salaam, German Pension   **Wednesday 26**
Philemon

Father, thank Thee for the sleepless hours of last night when I could pray so intensely for so many people. If the collisions of countless electrons produce waves in ether, if our nerves are minute broadcasting tubes, then does the conflict between the will to sleep and a rebellious excitement start waves around the world? Can we sublimate all kinds of mental crises into powerful broadcasts about Thee? Minds touch other minds far away when emotions are working intensely, as in accidents, approaching death and danger, more frequently than at any other time. Must feelings be stirred to reach far? Perhaps so, we do not yet know; but we do know they work that way thousands of times. Thank Thee for every cut, for every hour of loneliness, for every sense of horror, for every struggle of temptation that stirs me deeply, if it also helps me to be Thy radio station to many souls. Anything, Lord, but do not let my soul sleep!

Dar es Salaam, German Pension   **Thursday 27**
Hebrews 1

Father, at this large meeting this morning Thou didst prove once more that when I call upon Thee, Thou art always quick to respond. Thank Thee for the privilege of seeing such progress and so much interest, and for leading the way to the best lessons we have ever made. Help, O help me to stay very, very, very close this whole week.

Were those six men just emerging from illiteracy the nearest to Thy heart in all that gathering? God, does Thy heart ache as mine does at thought of the multitudes of little people who have no hope, who are driven to vice as their only source of emotion, for poor stupid girls who see no other way to a life of variety and attention than vice. What a frightful, hideous sin the "righteous" commit in not affording innocent doorways to a more abundant life! And we think we can be "sinless" by staying away from the victims of our neglect!

Dar es Salaam, German Pension — Friday 28
Hebrews 2

Father, tired but very happy at the complete success of this African journey, I feel glad tonight at the gratitude and eagerness of the Africans. I am glad to learn afresh that the most rewarding work in the world is to help those whom everybody else forgets. In this town where a line cuts first and second class officials apart, I am glad that I have drifted among "the poorest, lowliest and lost," for almost all of us whites are climbers shouldering or glaring out of our way the very people who need us most. Thank Thee tonight that I never was and never can be a "social success," for, weak thing that I am, I too would doubtless have cut those who need me most—the forgotten, the poverty-stricken, the colored brothers of Thy world and mine, and I would have lost this joy!

British Residency, Zanzibar — Saturday 29
Hebrews 3

God, those three whom I know to be immoral in Dar es Salaam, whom I so wanted to help, and yet whom I left without a word concerning Thee, worry me tonight. Perhaps, if I had reached some more prayerful state, they would have listened. Perhaps my life spoke more than I realized. I think I felt the awakening of their consciences. Is it cruel to make them miserable in those circumstances unless I help them out of their bondage? No, for the end of this life is not happiness found by putting the conscience to sleep. And my prayer can follow them. O love that will not let them go, use my prayer for them.

Thank Thee for these Arabs with whom I am seeking the ideal way of teaching Arabic, and may Thine arms be around us as we work together and get Thy full will accomplished.

British Residency, Zanzibar — Sunday 30
Hebrews 4

God, the perfection of sainthood lies along one stern hazardous road: complete mastery of one's body; constant effort to improve environment; complete, perfect obedience to the will of God; slave of the Highest, master of the lower. That will mean loving all things lower, not for what they are yet, but for what they may become and for what I may, by love and service, help them to become. Help me to be afraid of no man no matter how strong or antagonistic, but to walk into his mind with my thoughts, carrying the cross of Christ at the heart of my thoughts, and demanding that he surrender to Christ. Tighten up this new habit that I so feebly have tried to cultivate. Starting over now, help me to carry Christ to every soul I meet or think of—Christ, aggressively, tenderly, eagerly, lovingly, irresistably and constantly. I do not want to forget! nor make a half success.

British Residency, Zanzibar Monday 31
Hebrews 5

How astonishing is this gospel! The maker of worlds put wee, two-legged creatures on a tiny planet of a second rate sun, put in those wee creatures souls, set these souls free, and then began gently to knock at the doors of their hearts begging them to open and let Him come in and do them greater good! Every second He sustains their lives, sees to the very center—yet cannot enter the inner soul until we open the door. He came and clothed Himself in flesh to woo our affection. He let men torture and crucify His body, He suffered and suffers when men refuse to let Him enlarge and glorify them. This amazing story is just a little beyond our comprehension, and yet we grasp enough of it at times—at those moments when our souls hunger and thirst—enough of it to fling ourselves weeping into Thine open arms, as I do now, O incomprehensible, incredible Love!

June, 1937

On Ship at Mombasa, S. S. Takliwa Tuesday 1
Hebrews 6

Father, as we press on unto perfection, how can we master situations? How can I learn to hold Thee in mind when, like last night and this morning, I am in a cabin with two other men, or in a dining room talking with people? It should be easier on this ship half full of passengers.

What would perfection mean? Perfect poise, smooth nerves, perfect control of one's thoughts, perfect mastery of every situation, perfect wide-openness upward to Thee. We need hours of solitude for this discipline. Then, if the human race is to achieve this perfection, there must be fewer people, no crowding, wide parks for solitary wandering, spots where men can talk aloud to Thee. This "pressing on toward perfection" is not perfect until we press for world perfection.

S. S. Takliwa Wednesday 2
Hebrews 7

As I turn my back upon Africa, where two months of eager exploring in Dhuluo, Olinyore, Kikuyu, and Swahili brought such fine results, my prayer shall haunt the men and places I have seen. God, do keep dear friends in Maseno, Kima, Jeanes School, Alliance, the Italian priests, the directors, the inspector, those Africans with their hearts aching with mine to help their people; and in Zanzibar the Principal, the director, those fine Africans, the Arabs, the Indians, the Jeanes teacher, the Catholic priest, the governor, all of whom have taken some of my heart; in Dar es Salaam, the director and his wife, those fine African leaders, those men and women whom we taught, the teachers of Central School, the great-souled editor of Mamba Leo, the Germans whom I could not reach—and back of them that mighty pitiful, hopeful continent—God, God, God.

"My boy, thank you for sharing Africa with me in your burdened heart."

S. S. Takliwa Thursday 3
Hebrews 9

As conversation turned on death yesterday, it set my thoughts upon that adventure. If scientific inquiry does, as I believe, support belief in the survival of the soul, if psychic research does bear out the hope that we shall sail forth upon a new, glorious voyage of discovery, then we need to publish all that evidence to help people everywhere. We all need to learn to look forward to that new "awakening from this sleep called life" with keen zest! If I can feel then as I do now, I think I shall step into the next life with positive, impatient eagerness when God has done what He can do with me here. We will not stop working through all eternity. My mother, father, children, Garrett Edwards, Warren Siegfried are still working—especially, I think, my fine dad.

S. S. Takliwa   Friday 4
Hebrews 10

God, what was the meaning of that vision last night when I saw a finished gilded or golden inscription—was that a rift in the clouds that told some of Thy story? I cannot remember it now, though I saw enough in a second to fill this page. It was something like this:

"I come to each stage of culture in the form that stage can understand. To the neolithic man I came in neolithic form...." I cannot recall the beautiful words you used to describe all cultures. That tablet must still lie in my memory, and will return when you wish. Did the Koran look like that to Mohammed? Dare I ask such questions? "Yes! That was what the tablet meant. Just that. Be not bound by another man's conception of orthodoxy. I am breaking through to humanity wherever, whenever, however men say 'come,' and I obey no man-made orthodoxy. The one thing of which you can always be sure when you hear a statement about me is—'God is more than that.'"

Seychelles Islands, S. S. Takliwa   Saturday 5
Hebrews 11

This eleventh chapter of Hebrews made me catch my breath with the sheer loftiness of its glory. It broke upon me after ten chapters which meant but little. Was it my limitation that brought no responsive fire? Must one experience the great heights in order to understand them? I have lived so much of this chapter! "Being warned of God concerning things not seen as yet...." "When he was called, obeyed...and he went out, not knowing whither he went. By faith he became a sojourner in the land of promise." "They were strangers and pilgrims on the earth....now they desire a better country....choosing rather to share ill treatment...than to enjoy the pleasures of sin....he endured, as seeing him who is invisible....that apart from us they should not be made perfect." Does the past still need us for its perfecting? Yes! And let me rise above this heat, this strange environment, and live up to that goal! Now!

S. S. Takliwa   **Sunday 6**
Hebrews 12

"Our God is a consuming fire." How honestly do I face that side of Thy nature, God? I have tried to forget all but Thy love and patience because I have fallen so far short of Thy Will. "God dealeth with you as with sons." He chasteneth us "that we may be partakers of his holiness." I have forgotten the "consuming fire" and remembered only Thy "redeeming fire." Ah, my son, read on! "Removing...those things that are shaken,...that those things which are not shaken may remain." The spirit cannot be destroyed; it can only be purified. What looks like destruction of life from your present point of view is burning out the dross, and preserving the gold. The things that are seen melt away like the waves outside your porthole. The things not seen are eternal. "Let us also, seeing...lay aside every weight, and the sin which doth so easily beset us."

S. S. Takliwa   **Monday 7**
Hebrews 13

Father, when we come heartbroken to Thee, art Thou as I was when this dear little girl came and wept in my arms because she had said "damn." We are all so like that ten-year-old dear. We hear others and imitate them and then cry our eyes out. And didst Thou smile in Thy heart as I kissed her cheek and felt a glad pain with her?

"And to communicate forget not." God, I see that the pathway toward being "perfect in every good work to do His will" must be the entrance of every door that helps me speak to others. I refused to try to heal that cripple when the Voice said "heal him." I refused to lead the service on my own initiative. I want to stop refusing. I said I was lonesome because a half dozen English people on board are snobs. But this ship is full of Indians and others who need me. God help me to follow the voice into second class and into steerage. Down there they think I am the snob!

S. S. Takliwa   **Tuesday 8**
James 1

Again, the drinking and dancing on the deck has set loose profound depths of intensity which I have sublimated by prayer for friends until my eyes in the mirror blazed black and penetrating. I begin to realize how we need temptation, loneliness, disappointment, pain, failure or some tragedy to draw out these latent powers which otherwise lie dormant. Then, when these conditions are around, we need to know how to harness them for Thee and for our fellow men. Perhaps this year is telling me how to capitalize my difficulties. "Count it all joy...when ye fall into manifold temptations.... that ye may be perfect and entire, lacking in nothing." How far, how far I have yet to go! But Thou, O Christ, are standing far up yonder beckoning and smiling. Even Thou wast enkindled with incredible power by the conflict with Thine enemies and by Thy suffering. It is the way to soul-power. "E'en though it be a cross—Nearer, my God, to Thee!"

S. S. Takliwa   Wednesday 9
James 2

Father, here is my hand. With a sluggish brain I shall let Thee speak through me to this paper if it is Thy will. Where would Jesus wander, what would He do if He were on this ship? Would He remain on first class deck? Surely He would visit the whole ship, giving His benediction as He passed along. They would not need to understand His words, for His love would reach out like a halo and people would feel, as well as see His smile. I gave Thee my hand to write this. Now, Father, here are my feet to walk where Jesus would go, where Jesus will go in me. Here are my lips, here my heart, my love, to be made beautifully Christlike by Thine own Self. And now, if love is pure and unselfish and tender—Christ-filled—we, Thou in me, will make our tour of the other classes.

S. S. Takliwa   Thursday 10
James 3

When I am in touch with Thee, fruits begin to appear at once as they did yesterday when I had re-surrendered everything. And when I am not consciously and wholly yielded, then appears resentment at English snobbery. All the while the really important factor was my own unlikeness to the warmhearted Christ. Looking back to my college days and since, I now believe all my social failures have been failures to possess enough of the love of Christ, failures to abide every moment in the vine. "Apart from me ye can do nothing." That is no pious platitude—it is a grim key to failure. I have been so hideously selfish and touchy and divided and weak away from Thee that I do not want to forget to make every minute a new surrender. Here is my will. Do not let me have it back, I hate that ugly, separated self. Apart from Thee self rots!

S. S. Takliwa   Friday 11
James 4
Conscious 80%

    This week had almost passed when I had such an unusual opportunity to concentrate upon Thee. Yet only one day was over 70%. And Thou knowest how almost fiercely earnest I was yesterday morning! And I know the reason—I have kept it a secret. The two who saw this diary last week helped me greatly. I thought nobody on the ship this week would understand. That was fear and lack of faith. This I have learned at least—I cannot keep my secret. Somebody on this ship must share it today. Perhaps showing this diary to people must from today onward become a part of the experiment. Praying for people is not enough. I cannot keep Thee. I cannot keep surrendered to Thee except when I am giving Thee away. But now, to whom? Father, lead me.

Arrived 7:00 A.M., Bombay Harbor (India)   Saturday 12
James 5

    Thank Thee for the response of that sailor to this diary, for the responses of all three to whom I have given it, and for the wonderful way in which the whole day changed. I have learned that I cannot go about praying for people or trying to keep Thee in mind when I am not doing all I can to help, to share, to teach, and to lift. Piety cannot be a substitute for works and for witness. Thank Thee that sharing this book has thus far proven a blessing to those who received it and to me who shared it. Now, as I go ashore, help me, O help me, God, to step through every door toward which Thy finger points. Take these four faculties that matter most—my eyes to look for need, my ears, my tongue, my brain. Spirit Christ melt into me from head to foot—love!

C.M.S. Building, Proctor Rd., Bombay   Sunday 13
I Peter 1

    Thank Thee, Father, for the wonderful letters that came yesterday. The past still lives and speaks to the present, through letters as well as through memories. We are building day by day an invisible temple. All of those past days are bricks in the temple. Those events do make us what we are today. I feel like shouting to the whole world this morning: "Watch today very jealously. It will rise again to bless or curse you." Youth does not know this, does not know how true are the words of Jesus. "Nothing is hidden that shall not be revealed." Perhaps the judgment day may consist of exhibiting that temple built by our past to the hosts of heaven to make them praise or shudder! No, that cannot be, for evil must not enter heaven. But the perfect Christ will help us finish our perfect temple.

C.M.S. Building, Bombay   Monday 14
I Peter 2

Tomorrow, Father, begins the last fifteen days of this, the most earnest and glorious six months of my life. Yet not one day has been a complete success. Even had I remembered Thee a whole day, there would have been heights beyond of perfect surrender, perfect subjection of ugly, little self, perfect thinking only Thy thoughts, perfect loving service of others, perfect disdain of color or caste or education, so that I should go out on the street overflowing with Christ-love, exhaling it as the "dama de noche" fills the air with her fragrance. Those Himalayas of the Spirit-life help me realize what a mean, low person I am—and these all about me. But we can rise! We are rising! God, let us get our teeth into this day and see what we can do with it. No forgetting! No fearing! No refusing! No yielding to heat or tired feelings! Just a day full of "Yes, Lord, yes!"

Girls School, Sholapur   Tuesday 15
I Peter 3
Conscious 75%

Life is to fill these white pages for fifteen more days. There aches in my breast a painful longing to write wonderful days in this and in the higher book of Life. Be present, be Master each ticking second! Every thought toward Thee or, better still, from Thee every moment.

These six months have taught me how I must make an environment that constantly reminds me. This little crucifix, a gift of gratitude, and my thinking of Jesus in an empty chair beside me, are good reminders. Praying for an hour yesterday for all in the car was a great help. My telling my secret to others made yesterday one of the sweetest days of my life. I must tell it on every occasion.

Thank Thee for Margaret Sangster's *Little Letters to God*. She knows the secret! Thank Thee that such a soaring soul can get into secular journals. We can never overcome evil by denunciations. We must flood the world with glory drawn out of God's own heart, and make it irresistible!

Home of Rev. F.C. Sackett, Wednesday 16
Secunderabad, Hyderabad State
I Peter 4
Conscious 95%

This day, a higher percentage than any before it, is so rich I could write pages! What enabled me to keep Thee in mind all day? First, praying for these thousands whom I passed. Second, telling Mr. Sackett about my experiment at the very first opportunity. Third, reading *The Disciple Whom Jesus Loved* by Lofthouse. Fourth, talking aloud to and from God. Fifth, a resolute "No" to books and scenes that might break the endless contact with God. Sixth, a picture of Christ on this wall. Seventh, Mr. Sackett bringing me two books, *Letters of Samuel Rutherford*, and *Quiet Hours* by Fulsford. How strikingly those for whom I prayed in the bus responded today! Is my spirit perhaps becoming incandescent when Thy full current is on? When they turned and looked, should I have spoken? "The perfect Father and the perfect Son, each of them revealed in the other, while into that relation the human race is intended itself to enter." That, says Lofthouse, is the thing no other religion ever thought of. Into that relationship we are invited. What glowing glory feeds my soul!

Home of Rev. F.C. Sackett, Thursday 17
Secunderabad, also Medak
I Peter 5

Father God, direct this mind and these fingers. The interest shown by the servants in Sholapur proves these little globes of the world to be fine for opening the subject. Thank Thee for the miracles of today—the miracle that brought me far out to this rural station of Medak, among lovely Christians and prepared this marvelous committee to drop all other work and join in preparing the new Telugu lessons; for the amazing progress made in one day, for the growing ease with which it was possible today to witness.

Here, Father, is an earnest prayer for the illiterate men and women who studied today. May this begin the life of glory in Christ for them, and for all the depressed multitudes joining the church. May surrender be complete, their souls undying fires of devotion, their minds wide with Thy world vision! (7:00 A.M.)

Medak, Hyderabad State   Friday 18
II Peter 1

Dear God, telling others about my experiments in practicing Thy presence, is the best of all aids to success. Would this new upsurging of power have come at all without the pouring out of all I had last night? "Go ye into all the world, and preach the gospel to every creature," for you increase by sharing and lose when you refuse. What folly this fear has been all these many past lost years! Teach us followers round Thy little world to be afraid of neither man nor devil, but to be afraid of one thing only, refusal to take every chance to tell it, tell what matters more to us and them than all the world besides. Make us quick to see open doors, quick to enter them, and tenderly loving with a gentle, considerate, imaginative, selfless ability to share with others. (7:30 A.M.)

Medak   Saturday 19
II Peter 2

This miracle of being led here where they all so need help, of seeing this committee formed without previous notice, the finest committee we ever had, of seeing fifteen excellent lessons in Telugu emerge in two days, with duplicate copies of each, takes one's breath.

The sight of that magnificent Medak Cathedral, the finest Christian church in India, out on these plains, symbol of the permanence of Christ in India, built by all the poor people's money and loving labor, is another miracle. God help Indian people to pack the walls and atmosphere of that cathedral with the glory of perfect surrender. Make it Thy Spirit clothed in cement and stone! Here, God, take all of me You can use and use me to help that church to exhale Christ!

En route to Bangalore, Mysore   Sunday 20
II Peter 3
Conscious 85%

For this book of Kerr's, *The Vision of God*, I thank Thee, Father, because it contains some nuggets of pure gold. "Unbroken, personal intercourse with the Divine is the end for which man was created; a foretaste of this experience is possible even in this life." "For final self-forgetfulness, the whole attention of the soul must be centered upon the most absorbing, the most inspiring and the most perfect of objects." Final self-forgetfulness—is that necessary for perfection? Perhaps. But self-forgetfulness is not attained by severe self-discipline. It will be a fact when Thou hast come to absorb all our thoughts, when every thought is from Thee or to Thee. So let us begin instantly! Now, what is Thy voice saying, as Thou speakest in a million ways? "Witness, My Child, tell the one story all the world needs to know. Tell everybody everywhere without a moment of hesitation."

Bangalore   Monday 21
I John 1

God, my conscience troubles me; too many situations have defeated me. I am afraid of people. Yesterday I thought I could find no way to begin speaking of Thee to those men on the train. High above me Himalayas of character show me how far down I still am. The very fact that this worries me, while all about are so many thousands who probably have not yet even begun to try, shows how low I am. This is not self-forgetfulness. Please, please, God, do Thy thinking here, Thy world thinking, as Thou art lovingly brooding over Thy two billion souls. What, God, would be a good way to open the question of Christ? Is this not a major problem for timid Christians? We cannot stop after praying for people, for if we pray only, we soon cease to do even that. There must be a fine balance of prayer and service and witnessing.

Bangalore, Missionary Rest Home   Tuesday 22
I John 2

God, bless the old people who look back upon their best days with wistful longings. Help them to understand that even ninety-one years is but infancy for the soul, and to look ahead with eager expectancy to the more glorious adventure that lies ahead.

As one hears of the collapse of the Church Union plans in India and the onward sweep of the Oxford Groups, does it mean, God, that perhaps these old shells are too cold, too hollow to matter much, and that a new outpouring of Thy spirit can flow only with a new fullness of surrender? If so, then perhaps such vital movements as the Oxford Groups may put Thy spirit into the present churches, for where Thou art, O Christ, there is the church.

Bangalore, Missionary Rest Home   Wednesday 23
I John 3

More miracles! until one expects them daily. That the director should appear one minute after I called, that he should find such an excellent aid at his side to help, that this Methodist Normal should be eager to aid and so swift, that the drawing master should be so competent, that Miss Swift should be able to call the missionaries so quickly, and many other happy facts reveal Thy hand working, Father. And this marvelous chapter, tenderly exclaiming, "Behold what manner of love the Father hath bestowed upon us, that we should be called sons of God.... Beloved, now are we children of God.... we shall be like him.... And every one that hath this hope set on him purifieth himself.... Hereby know we love because he laid down his life for us: and we ought to lay down our lives.... Let us not love in word, neither with the tongue; but in deed and in truth." There is the trouble with our age—we did not practice what we professed; then we doubted, supposing our faith to be false because we were false to our faith.

Madras, Railroad Station   **Thursday 24**
1 John 4

Enough to write a book this morning! This supremely glorious chapter four of First John: "God is love." "Let us love one another:...every one that loveth is begotten of God." "He that abideth in love abideth in God.... There is no fear in love: but perfect love casteth out fear...he that feareth is not made perfect in love."

For that splendid gathering of missionaries and their sympathetic interest, thank Thee, and for those two ardent Oxford Groupers who took me to dinner and poured out their radiant witness of how utter surrender had changed them and changed the prostitutes whom they are rescuing. They are right; a really transformed world must well up out of a transformed humanity. The Oxford Groupers have gone to the heart of reality as few others have. They seem like old friends.

Madras Y.W.C.A.   **Friday 25**
I John 5

As thousands of people watch the Dionne Quintuplets from behind special glass windows, seeing the children but unseen by them, perhaps we, too, are "surrounded by a great cloud of witnesses" who see through a one-way screen what we do and what we think. Are they watching—father, mother, children, Mayor Phillips? How the list suddenly swells! Are they looking through the one-way window as we play our game with minutes? We must play it as though sixty-thousand unseen rooters wanted us to win, would be wounded, as love only can be wounded, when we fail. Perfect abiding in His arms and minute by minute obedience to His will is the goal. Thank Thee, Father, for Cecil Rose's *When Man Listens*. These Oxford Groupers have taken in earnest three simple fundamentals—God has a plan, God speaks, man must listen and obey anything God says.

Madras Y.W.C.A.   Saturday 26
II John

This book, *Testament of Man*, in which Arthur Stanley tries to illustrate the spiritual experiences of all ages, shows that spiritual threadbareness is the characteristic of this age. The book deliberately omits a wealth of glorious experiences that could fill ten volumes, while this New Testament speaks from every page rich glorious spiritual food for the soul. And this *When Man Listens* glows with Thy Spirit. We need fresh, daring spiritual discoveries, whole continents of them, and we need them terribly. We need a new wideness, a world-wideness. When men will to see God only through the narrow slit science may offer, they see nothing but an "oblong blur."

Thank Thee, Father, for the grave of Annie Besant, and that speaking sunset, and the whispering trees, and that lovely shadow on the water haunted with seekers after Thee.

Train to Trichinopoly,   Sunday 27
En route to Colombo (Ceylon)
III John

I see clearly that we can accomplish what we are and not more. Opportunities come and go so swiftly that we must seize them instantly or never. Thank Thee, Father, for the high plane struck in the first moment and sustained in Madras, where so much depended upon that first moment. That high level leaves a pure, sweet taste in the mouth of one's memory. But in retrospect I see how that a nobler I might have entered doors I did not then see. Thank Thee, dear Lord, for all the precious friendships in Christ which spread over India and Africa. Today it seems to me the only sure supporters of literacy are those tied to my soul by Thee. And those who know the most about my aspiration seem closest even though they have not revealed themselves to me as I have to them. We must get into one another's souls and find the hidden best. We must learn to make everlasting friendships—in three days, or even one!

Colombo, S.S. Potsdam												Monday 28
Jude

Guidance yesterday and today did work as the Groupers said it would. Thank Thee, Father, for the way contact with them has put an edge on my conscience about witnessing. Why did it seem so hard and hopeless to witness to that circus man and prize fighter last night, until he himself opened the subject of religion? Why did he do that twice? Make my witness stronger, surer. Perhaps it does not require much talk if it is accompanied by prayer. Thank Thee that he showed his great gratitude for the Oxford Group book. And how Thou hast guided this forenoon: to the newspaper, the Y.M.C.A., the director, the principal of the Training School, and other places. Thank Thee for leading me back to Effa—make me a constant joy and uplift for her.

S.S. Potsdam												Tuesday 29
Revelation 1
Conscious 80%

As I looked into the mirror over this desk, I did not see a face at all like the dear dreams that have flooded my mind. There are no ugly wrinkles like that on the forehead of my soul. One's face keeps dragging behind all the perplexities and strains and clashing desires of a lifetime, and also the long lifetime of that mysterious call that came up for a million years and passed to me through my parents. That mirror does not tell the truth about my soul today. And when I walk this deck, I do not see souls as they are or will become, but only distortions dragged up from the past. Help me, Father, to see their future and help it to become true! Here is another wistful prayer for India, where I have seen Thee working so many miracles. It is sweet to share the eager longings which fill Thy breast for India, and the breasts of thousands of Christ-filled Christian missionaries. God use me to send them new joy.

S.S. Potsdam												Wednesday 30
Revelation 2

The last morning of the best six months inwardly and outwardly of my life, up to this time, finds me, Father, appreciating the Oxford Groups. We are running on parallel lines. To be a Grouper I should not need to change at all in seeking Thy guidance, or in writing a diary! I shall have to struggle harder for absolute perfection in purity, honesty, unselfishness, and love. Could I find a trusted friend and tell everything in my past—could I? That would be a humiliation. But was it not exactly what St. Augustine's *Confessions* tells all the world? God, I am willing when Thou commandest; but Thou wilt desire me to help him who hears, not harm him. The Group is ahead of me also in witnessing, and I shall need to carry that burden closer to my heart. But do I not have something to contribute from these six months: (1) the game of keeping Thee in mind every second, (2) praying for every person I meet or think of, (3) learning Thy language, and so understanding what Thou art saying every moment. These are some of the lessons and rewards of the past six months of struggle and glory.

A Final Word

The 1937 diary was a daily record of an effort to hear God's instructions, minute by minute, and to carry them out in a new, creative field which was far beyond my own abilities. I am sure God did through us what none of us who worked together could have done alone and without Him. The foundations were being laid for a literacy program which has since spread far over the world.

All of us had the sense of being caught up in a purpose we only dimly understood. Everywhere we were under a strange excitement. I am sure there are periods when God needs us for important purposes, and keeps pushing us and calling us and helping us to reach His goal. We did not realize in 1937 what stupendous changes were taking place and were yet to take place in the world. Looking back, one can now see that universal literacy is necessary for the world that is now emerging. God was using us to help prepare illiterate men to read His Word. The Bible is the most important Word that God has ever recorded. Nearly two thirds of the world could not read that Bible in 1937. Today it looks as if education will, indeed, become universal.

How much of that strange, wonderful experience of God's help was due to the fact that He needed us to help Him? How much of it was due to our own earnest, spiritual quest? I really do not know. I think God gave us that passionate hunger to do His will as well as that wonderful fulfillment. When one has an intensely earnest desire to carry out the will of God, God can then get His messages through and His work accomplished.

Of course, if this is true at all, it is enormously important. It is of all truths the most needed by a floundering, groping world. Everybody wants to improve himself or his position in life, but most individuals are trying to do it alone. They soon discover that they cannot lift themselves by their own boot straps. Yet they do not know how to reach up and grasp the hand of God.

Spiritual discoveries are not like discoveries in the physical world. We may all observe an experiment in physics or chemistry, but we cannot look into the mind of another person and see the secret and infinitely complicated thoughts which come and go. All we can do is to describe to one another what goes on within ourselves. This is why those who are undertaking spiritual pilgrimages ought to keep daily diaries and make them available to one another, especially if they make exciting discoveries.

I am sometimes asked whether I continued the spiritual voyage recorded in *Letters of a Modern Mystic* and in this book, *Learning the Vocabulary of God*; and if so, what were the results. The answer is that I never stopped—and I now suspect that you and I shall never cease taking voyages and making discoveries through all eternity. My explorations down through the years have followed a large variety of directions, almost every direction on the compass. I find that in 1942 I was fascinated with the question, How to listen? Here are some memos from that period:

Luke 8:21   **Saturday, July 4, 1942**

God, there are two ways to listen to Thee. One is passive, like those who enjoy an opera—with emotion but no action. The other way is active—when we are alert to receive our orders from Thee and to obey. Then we offer not only our heart and mind but also our strength to Thee. Both ways are right when we use them at the right time. Frequently when we are passively listening, Thou dost send a message about something we must do. Then we must do at once what Thou commandest. I resolve to listen much more and to rush around in nervous futility much less.

John 14:15–18   **Sunday, July 5**

God, wisdom and knowledge come to those who listen to You. Those who "wait upon the Lord" are opening their lives to the very fountain source of all wisdom. We who are trying this way of getting knowledge find that our listening hours are rich with inspiring things to write or say or do. Only when we hold our ears close to Your lips do we have this sense of a sudden invasion of a divine idea.

God, you talk to us through our best thoughts. Lovely ideas are your whispers, even though we may never suspect that they come from You. I am sure that every step forward in my life came as an idea while I was looking up with the eyes of my soul, waiting to be "stirred by the invisible."

As the years passed, I have found that obedience to God's voice is even more difficult than hearing Him speak. I find in my 1950 diaries scores of pages on how to make obedience absolute. I was having more trouble with a rebellious will than a deaf ear. It became clear to me then that even Jesus Himself earned the complete confidence of the Father, so that all things could be entrusted to Him, by total, constant, unwavering, glad, instantaneous obedience. Jesus says: My meat is to do the will of Him that sent me." John quotes Jesus as saying: "If any man willeth to do his will he shall know." Jesus knew perfectly because He was perfectly willing to know. One could not know if one were not willing to obey; the moment the willingness was perfect, the answer would be there. That is what I believed in 1950. But I am not so sure today that this is the last word.

Many people down through the centuries have believed that they were absolutely right, but today we are convinced that they were absolutely wrong. The world is full of such people, who are convinced, but wrong. Indeed, I suspect that by this time next century people will say that we are all wrong in our dependence upon military force. We try to force our convictions upon men who try to force their convictions upon us. One of the chief causes of disputes and war is that men have such deep convictions that they fight and kill men with equally deep convictions—all of them sure that they are right!

How shall we prevent ourselves from holding wrong convictions? One way is to seek the advice of many people of quite diverse opinions. That may help us to face all the facts. But then everybody may be wrong! Often whole nations are.

If, as we believe, Christ is the way, the truth and the life, then one way for us to see with a clear eye is to saturate ourselves day after day in Christ and His teaching, to walk with Him across the pages of the four gospels until we instantly and instinctively look at every question from His viewpoint. Then His word that bears on every question will leap to our lips.

The other way is to consult Christ; to talk directly to Him. I heard Roland Brown tell a dream he had had. He saw that his mind was far larger than the confines of his skull. Indeed, it was a vast room. There was a knock at the door of his mind. He opened the door, and there stood Jesus.

"Come in. You are welcome," said Roland.

"I cannot come in," said Jesus, "unless I can sit on the throne of your mind and become your King."

"Come in and take the throne, and be my King forever," said Roland.

Then Jesus came in and sat upon the throne and directed Roland's life and thoughts and will.

Instead of thinking by ourselves, it is a fascinating adventure for you and me to try whether we can acquire the fixed habit of looking to the King on the throne of our minds to supply every thought and to initiate every act.

Talking everything over with the King and accepting His decisions is a wonderfully exhilarating, relaxing happy way to live. He ceases to be like a King and becomes a warm, close, affectionate brother, as He was to His disciples.

Jesus said, "My mother and my brethren are these who hear the word of God, and do it."

Part 3

You Are My Friends

You Are My Friends

While not a prayer diary, *You Are My Friends* is infused with the passion of the personal companionship Frank Laubach shared with Jesus. This focus differentiates the book from the previous volumes in which the mystical focus was theocentric, or God-centered.

Laubach felt that God is beyond comprehension but the person and deeds of Jesus are perfectly understandable. It is also quite clear that the life of Jesus is the example toward which each person is to aspire. The excerpts that follow contain Laubach's reflections on the loving companionship of Jesus and how to incorporate Jesus' viewpoint into one's own life.

The basis for this book, first published in the United States in 1942, was sixty-four page tracts printed in Lanao and distributed among the Maranao people in the late 1930s.

Christ Is the World's Hope

We can make a paradise out of our whole world any time we choose. We have the scientific knowledge; we need make no new discoveries. There is more than enough genius in production, an abundance of raw materials and more manpower than we know what to do with. More than enough of everything to build a paradise! Of everything save—love. We need only live the command of Jesus "Love thy neighbor as thyself" and all of us within thirty years shall have ample. This does not refer to a few favored countries but to the entire planet. Indeed it is impossible for a few favored countries alone to have plenty. What we have we must share.

We are prevented from making an Eden out of earth only because we love ourselves more than we love our neighbors. What is in our hearts is reflected in our behavior. Thus we try to accumulate more things than others while they accumulate more things than we; each becomes envious of the other. Greed and resentment develop, cause the petty village quarrels and the devastating world wars. Our own selfishness is "enemy number one." To be sure, there is unselfish generosity in our natures, much of it, but it is yet too weak to overcome the self-seeking instinct.

If fifty horse power pushes a car east while sixty horse power pushes the car west the car will go west by the law of "the resultant of forces." The resultant of spiritual forces are pushing our world toward hell, because we take care of ourselves primarily. Now all you need to reverse the direction of that car is to add twenty horse power eastward. And all we need to push our world upward is not perfection; it is to release greater quantities of loving cooperation until it outweighs our selfishness. We have been predominantly selfish, and all we need is to put the weight on the other side and become habitually cooperative.

Chemistry affords a useful illustration. If two liquids or gases refuse to unite, a third one called a "catalyzer" is thrown in, and in its presence the first two substances suddenly fall in love and join hands to produce something new. Our civilization needs a "catalyzer" to make us love one another more, so we will reverse our present tragic madness. And we know where that catalyzer is to be found—Jesus Christ. Men need to become more like Jesus Christ until the cohesive power of love leads us to work together for the welfare of all humanity.

We love a person more than an abstraction

If, therefore, we wish the world to adopt the principles of Jesus, we must help the world to fall in love with him.

Most of us find that codes of ethics, or beautiful mottoes, or firm resolves have little more power to hold us than though we clung to a cloud. In this respect St. Paul was one of us. He tried to obey the Jewish law, but it did not have enough holding power to keep him from falling. He cried, "I do not do the good things that I want to do."

But when Paul surrendered his heart to Jesus Christ he found what has been called the "explosive power of a great affection." His tremendous love for Christ took away all taste for the evils he had previously liked. "I count all things but loss for the excellency of the knowledge of Christ Jesus my Lord: for whom I have suffered the loss of all things, and do count them rubbish, that I may win Christ."

Christ transforms multitudes today

Jesus has the same power today that he had in the days of his flesh to enter the hearts of men and to drive out devils. This is no new truth and it is no guess. It is one of the best attested facts in the world. Millions of people of every race and continent have felt his magnetic charm lift them out of sin and despair. What he said about himself is true: "I, if I be lifted up from the earth, will draw all men unto me." That he has this mighty lifting power each of us may easily prove for himself. To feel that lift we need only touch him as iron touches a magnet.

He not only lifts, but he surprises, for he leads us to more wonderful experiences than the soul can find in any other direction. It is like an ascent in an airplane, while the horizon seems to grow ever wider. When Benjamin Franklin sent his kite into the sky and drew sparks from thunderclouds, he little dreamed what a marvelous new world of discovery awaited inventors in the realm of electricity. It turns out this way when you begin to explore the friendship of Jesus: you penetrate further and further into a glorious new world of discovery. I do not know where this progressive discovery will end. Probably nobody has found that end in this world, for it reaches over the boundaries into eternity; probably it really begins in eternity. But multitudes have followed this way far enough to turn around and call back with enthusiasm: "Look, all you friends who are seeking love. This road satisfies and opens into fresh rich experiences. Try it!"

We follow first and know later

"But," you may ask, "how much must I believe about Jesus in order to try cultivating his friendship?" All you need do is to agree that he is worth following; and then you follow, just as the disciples did. Consider how little they knew about Jesus at the beginning; they knew far less than we know. They saw an interesting and magnetic personality; they decided to walk with him and see what he would do. After they had followed him for a few months their hearts felt a tremendous love and their minds reached a tremendous truth.

If you agree that when we sit at the feet of a beautiful person we absorb some of his fine qualities, if you agree that Jesus was beautiful, then, "that is all you know and all you need to know" at the outset. It was enough for the disciples. It is enough for us. Like them we shall learn gradually by our own experience.

He is so lovely that you can begin by resolving as Richard Watson Gilder puts it:

> If Jesus Christ is a man
> And only a man—I say
> That of all mankind I will cleave to him
> And to him I will cleave always.
>
> If Jesus Christ is a god
> And the only God—I swear
> I will follow him through Heaven and Hell
> And the earth and the sea and the air.

If some doubting Thomas refuses to try Christ unless he can first solve his intellectual difficulties, he is neither like the disciples nor like modern scientific investigators. Chemists do not refuse to begin experiments until they have had their questions answered; if they did, they would never discover anything.

Following him across the Gospels

What most men think they know about Jesus is half mistaken, because they have not carefully studied his life story. We must watch him walking across the pages of the New Testament. We must ask him what interested him most and what were the things which he rejected. This is no short task though it is a happy one. We find that even after we have practically memorized all Jesus ever did or said, new flashes of insight keep coming at every new reading.

After reading the Gospels many times as a whole some of us have found it stimulating to read each Gospel slowly and to change the word "Jesus" to "I," so as to make the accounts read like an autobiography. We did that in our church in the Philippines, and after that we read the Gospels through again, trying to realize that Jesus was with us, and changing "Jesus" and "He" to "you"—speaking to him. We had a picture of Jesus before us. Reading in that way made him very real.

It is helpful to do the reading in a circle of two or more, and to have a regular hour each day. Even though the Gospels are finished quickly, this method of reading them makes us want to go over them again and again. Thus we learn to know Jesus as a real person. He grows upon us, so to speak, as we see more and more of the charm that he had for the men and women who followed him in Galilee long ago. After a few such readings we feel his warmth as his love touches our famished hearts. Soon the dead words of the narrative seem to throb with life. Jesus becomes for us a living comfort and a very tender friend. More than any dogma and more than any cold intellectual truth, the Christ of the Gospels satisfies our hunger for somebody we can love and adore.

His passion was people

As we become better acquainted with him we see that he was primarily interested in people and in their problems. He was passionately fond of helping those in need. He saw deep needs that others failed to see. He was called the greatest Physician because he healed everything and everybody he touched. He could not endure seeing men suffer. As you read in the Gospel of Mark of his cures, piling high upon one another, you feel there was in him a love hot enough to burn out disease. To this day people healed in the name of Jesus—and there are many of them—say they feel a warm glow pass through their bodies when the disease goes. His love literally burns out disease.

He pitied hungry people and fed them. His heart was with the naked, the imprisoned, and every lonesome stranger. He hugged babes to his breast, as he exclaimed: "Suffer the little children to come unto me... for of such is the kingdom of God."

He liked a wholesome good time, because he loved to make other people happy. At every invitation he attended feasts and wedding parties. He always went where somebody might need him, and never avoided anybody for the sake of appearances. You could count on him never to let you down. On the last terrible day his disciples fled, but he walked straight to the cross, walked out to Calvary to save those who had deserted him. His love was like that!

He demanded justice

He was strongly on the side of the poor and rather terrifying in his denunciation of the rich who kept their abundance away from those in need. "Blessed are you who are poor," he said, "for the Kingdom of God is yours.... But alas for you who are rich, for you have had your comfort." It was not the mere possession of wealth that he condemned. What he denounced was the fact that rich men could be hard enough to be unwilling to use their wealth for the alleviation of the sufferings of others. The rich man who hoarded and took his ease Jesus said was a fool: "This night shall thy soul be required of thee." Matthew said he would pay back everybody he had ever robbed, and give half of what he had to feed the poor. This pleased Jesus, for the disciple had caught the spirit of the master who taught that it was "more blessed to give than to receive."

He had lived in a carpenter's home for thirty years, and was a friend of labor. He means just what he said when he cried: "Come unto me, all ye that labor and are heavy laden, and I will give you rest." Fishermen were his bosom companions.

A genius as a friendmaker

As a friendmaker Jesus was a genius. Read his life until you become saturated with it, and you will realize how warm was his affection for those near him. When he looked at men with his tenderly loving eyes and said, "Come with me," they found him irresistible. They left their work and families and followed him without a thought of pay, to the very end of his life. They hung on his words of sympathy and watched his deeds of mercy with an ever-rising affection. Every word and deed of his was to make them love him more, as though with a thousand unseen threads he were knitting his soul to theirs. We can see their hardness melting before his love, like butter over a fire. He made himself the king of their hearts.

His twelve closest friends followed him with ever increasing awe as they watched his strange unearthly self-giving love in constant action. Every minute of the day they saw him lifting his eyes to his Father asking: "Father, whom can I help, now? Who needs me next? Whom can I heal, or console, or encourage, or save, or transform?" Every minute of the day he was helping somebody, from the time he awoke in the morning until he closed his eyes at night.

Words cannot convey the love which played back and forth like unseen electric impulses between the heart of Jesus and those of his friends. It was a love that sighed, and longed and pitied and hungered. The disciples reached a point where they could not endure being out of his sight. To be near him was life. To be away from him was to be out in the lonesome cold. Here was love pure as a mountain stream. It set a new high for love's possibilities among friends. His warmest adorers followed him when the rest had fled. The chief concern of his life seemed to be to make a little circle understand what friendship can really be, to help them to see that heaven itself is nothing more than perfect friendship.

See him rising from the last supper with his friends about him, as he takes a towel and washes their feet. John leans back against his breast and the beloved disciple hears every word and remembers it all his days:

"I have called you friends," Jesus is telling them; "for all things that I have heard of my Father I have made known unto you.... As I have loved you, you must also love one another." And later on he told them:

"I am not going to leave you friendless. I am coming back to you. In a little while the world will not see me any more, but you will still see me, because I shall live on, and you will live on too. When that day comes you will know that I am in union with my Father and you are with me and I am with you.... Whoever loves me will be loved by my Father."

Over and over he repeated, "Anyone who loves me will observe my teaching, and my Father will love him and we will come to him and live with him." In all history there is nothing with which to compare this tender farewell of Jesus. John heard it and recorded it for us. They are words of infinite love crushed from the heart of divine tragedy.

His hunger for friendship is revealed, strangely, for the very man who was to betray him. While they were eating, Jesus was greatly moved and said solemnly: "I tell you, it is one of you who will betray me." He was tender to Judas even at that moment and he gave him his love with the bread which he dipped into the broth for him. There never was such an amazing illustration of "loving your enemies." Judas felt the strong pull of that love to the last; when he knew that Jesus was dead, the thought of that betrayed love drove him mad, and made him kill himself.

When Calvary held Jesus on a cross, the distracted disciples crept off into hiding and wanted to die. He who was their joy and their reason for living, had ceased to live, and they were numb with loneliness and anguish.

When he said "If I be lifted up (on the cross) I will draw all men unto me," he saw the redeeming qualities in human nature—our capacity to suffer with innocent suffering, our indignation at injustice, our gratitude to one who suffers in our behalf. We have in us an instinct which cannot but protest against pure innocence being treated as he was treated and outraged for us.

It is that sad act of self-giving that makes it so easy for us to love Christ with complete abandon. The Old Testament command, "Love the Lord thy God with all thine heart, and with all thy soul, with all thy might," was seldom obeyed because one cannot, as unreservedly as that, love by command. We can love only as totally as we are commanded when his love from the cross draws it out of us. Christ from the cross touches to the quick all the most intense emotions human nature knows—pity, gratitude, love, sorrow, joy, horror, grief, shame, penitence, release, ecstasy, surrender, loyalty.

Christ In Our Midst Today

The death of the friend whom we love more than all the rest of the world leaves a dull and paralyzing anguish. The greater the love the greater the grief. If Jesus had remained dead the memory of such a lovable friend, with such high ideals and such a heroic end, could have left only deep despair.

But Jesus rose from the dead and was seen alive by the disciples. He appeared and disappeared again and again so that they knew he was there with them every minute. "Lo, I am with you always," he said, "even unto the end of the world." This was the fact which lifted the disciples out of hopelessness into a sudden overwhelming ecstasy, into a sense of victory and a feeling of resistless power. When they were sure that he lived, they were undefeatable. Nothing could frighten them, certainly not mere death!

"O death, where is thy sting?" wrote Paul as he faced death. "O grave, where is thy victory? Thanks be to God, which giveth us the victory through our Lord Jesus Christ."

This, I believe, is the crucial fact on which the fate of Christianity depends. If Christ did not rise from the dead he was a deluded idealist, mistaken at the point of his most vital belief, and the validity of all his other contentions would be open to doubt. Real friendship with him would be impossible, at least for most of us. We could only say: "He was such a wonderful friend," as we might say of Socrates or Marcus Aurelius. But Jesus is alive, an invisible person, more alive than you and I are. This is the reason why he can be—and pleads with us to allow him to be—our friend now.

But how can you who doubt it become sure? You may well ask that question with trembling eagerness, for it is the all-important question. You may seek the answer by examining historical evidence. You have Peter's testimony: "We have not followed cunningly devised fables... but were eyewitnesses." (II Peter 1:16) You have the testimony of Paul who said that the resurrection of Christ was the question for which he was on trial in Jerusalem: "It is for my hope of the resurrection that I am called in question." He stated the issue perfectly: "If Christ be not risen, our faith is vain, we are of all men most miserable," and then went on to say:

"But Christ is risen from the dead... He was buried... He rose again the third day... He was seen of Cephas, then of the twelve. After that, he was seen of above five hundred brethren at once, of whom the greater part remain unto this present, but some have fallen asleep. After that, he was seen of James; then of all the apostles." This is what Paul wrote to his new church in Corinth some twenty years after the resurrection. If Jesus had not risen and had not been seen, there would have been no early Church, there would have been no St. Paul, there would be no Church today.

But in our day a great many people hold the question of Christ's resurrection in abeyance. They doubt whether the records are genuine, or they wonder whether the appearances were mass hallucination, wishful thinking of men hypnotized by grief and despair. They take comfort in the assurance that Jesus is at least an immortal influence, as George Eliot hoped to become in her *Choir Invisible*, one of those "immortal dead who live again in lives made better by their presence." They try to suspend judgment, hoping that scientific methods applied to Biblical criticism may finally settle the question whether Jesus really rose and is alive today.

Unfortunately higher criticism holds out no hope of giving us much more historical proof than we now possess. We have nearly all the evidence that we can ever hope to find through archaeological discoveries, and over this evidence the world's best minds have worked as they have worked over no other evidence in history. Their steady perseverance has strengthened the circumstantial testimony for his resurrection, but it is still possible for doubters to reject it if they wish to follow a nineteenth-century habit of "deflating heroes" and of doubting everything until "science" proves it.

How to be sure he lives

After all, how ridiculous it is to try, by authenticating his resurrection papers, to prove that Jesus is alive! Waiting for archaeologists to dig up more evidence about ancient history is the wrong way to prove that a person is alive. Multitudes of people are living today who have no birth certificates. The only proof we need that they were born is that we know them and see their works. Even if our friends are in some distant part of the world, so that we cannot go to see them, we have ways to make sure that they are alive. I had never until recently seen the President of the United States, but I had not earlier doubted his living.

A gentleman from Philadelphia wrote to me in the Philippines, "I have read a book of yours, and want to be your friend." I did not write back, "Send me your birth certificate, a sworn statement that you really wrote this letter, and proof that you have not died during the month required for the letter to reach the Philippines." That would have been "scientific" to be sure, but there was another and better way. I answered his letter. He proved to be not only alive, but a rare blessing. He has opened up whole new vistas of life for me as a result of our new friendship.

This is the best way, and I think the only final way, to be sure that Jesus Christ is really alive today. We get in touch with him. We accept the invitation which is published in the Bible, "Come unto me... you are my friends." We try him as a friend. In the years that follow he becomes not only a friend but incomparably the most blessed personality that ever influenced our lives. That fact is an unspeakably important truth. We know he rose because we have felt him at work in us. The writer of a popular song struck it exactly, "You ask me how I know he lives. He lives within my heart."

When you were in college you were unable to pass judgment upon a manual of experiments in physics or chemistry until you had tried those experiments yourself. That is true of the invisible Christ. The only way to prove him is to try experiments with him. The only laboratory you have for experiments of the spirit is your own soul. The attitude of many of us to Christ is like that of the silly youth who races across the campus of a college and announces to his playmates: "I've gone through college and there is nothing in it but swell girls and football players." Casually reading the Gospels is like that boy going across the campus. To cultivate his friendship is to enter the classroom and the laboratory. We cannot know until we do that. And we who have welcomed him into the soul "know that he is and that he rewards all them that come unto him."

Because Christ is alive and here, a wonderfully intimate friendship is possible for us now. At this very moment I have that delightful experience of his friendship as I write. You may have it as you read. Indeed to millions of us there have come such intimate and wonderful visitations that we venture to tell them to those only who are able to appreciate them. All over the world the glories of Pentecost appear and reappear. We could not have these if Jesus were only a memory of one who died two thousand years ago.

There were years of my life when I thought that Jesus was a good man who had in his due time died. While I admired him, I could not enjoy him as a friend, nor could I accept him as a mighty power to direct my life. During that period he was to me an admirable idealist but a man mistaken in his hopes; a man too good for this heartless universe. Without a living Christ to love, I found only a cold, dead, heartless God. Now that I know that Christ lives and responds, he is my Master and the Master of the universe. He transforms my views of God and of the universe and of my own life. He turned gloom into joy. With this risen Christ who emerged from the tomb we are becoming friends in this book. And if you doubt, the way to be sure is to try. You will have intimate experiences piling up into overwhelming conviction. You will not only know him but you will be in love with him.

The laboratory is your soul

In this effort to reach Christ as a friend, do not allow yourself to be discouraged by what are called "psychologies of religion" or "philosophies of religion," written by men who have not entered the laboratories of their own souls to test Christ's friendship. On the theme of this book no man can speak with authority unless he himself has made the test in his own life and in his own problems. We have too often set up as "authorities" men who are simply blind leaders of the blind. One of the most famous of those philosophers of religion will pardon me, I hope, if I quote what he said sadly to me: "I would give anything in the world to have the experience of Christ that you have." Speaking from the depths of my heart I gave him the only possible answer. "You will never find it along the pathway of pure intellect," I said. "It is revealed unto babes."

Love and faith are the two eyes by which we can see Christ. "This is the victory that overcometh the world, even our faith." The faith that ensures victory is the faith to try for yourself within the laboratory of your own soul. Doubt is the very opposite of that faith, its contradiction, its negation. Doubt paralyzes action. Faith engenders courage. All that we need in this great venture for Christ's friendship is courage and faith: courage in our own natural powers of inquiry, and faith in the principle that every question has its own appropriate answer. That is the faith of the research worker in the field of experimental science. It is also the faith demanded of him who would explore the possibilities of the friendship of Christ.

He is here now

But someone may ask: "Where is Christ now?"

On this question there seems to be a contradiction between Matthew and Mark. The last verse in Matthew quotes Jesus as saying: "I will always be with you, to the very close of age." But Mark says: "The Lord Jesus was caught up into heaven and took his seat at God's right hand." How could Jesus be in some far-off heaven and at the same time be with us? Some people say that Christ is gone and that only his Holy Spirit remains here to represent him. But there is another answer. If Jesus is seated "at God's right hand," where is God's right hand? The majestic 139th Psalm says that God's hand is here, is indeed holding us!

> Thou hast beset me behind and before, and laid thine hand upon me...
> Whither shall I go from thy spirit? or whither shall I flee from thy presence?
> If I ascend up into heaven, thou art there; if I make my bed in hell, behold, thou art there.
> If I take the wings of the morning, and dwell in the uttermost parts of the sea;
> Even there shall thy hand lead me, and thy right hand shall hold me.

If, as this Psalm says, God's right hand is holding us, and if Jesus is beside God's right hand, then Jesus is close, his hand is on us! Where Jesus is, there is heaven; so heaven must be at our elbows!

The science of physics has helped us realize that there is a world about us which we neither see nor hear. Countless millions of electromagnetic waves are carrying music through our bodies every instant, but only those hear the music who possess receiving instruments and are tuned in. Our eyes can see only a narrow band of these waves which throb about us and in us. All those longer and shorter than the special wave lengths of our eyes are unseen, and until a few years ago were wholly unsuspected. When we consider the spores, microbes, bacteria, molecules, atoms in and about us, we realize that our eyes never see a millionth part of the "physical world." Who can guess what spiritual realm may exist unseen before our eyes? If we discover that the spirit world is unseen and yet is all about us, we need feel no surprise.

Paul told the Athenians that God is "not far from every one of us: for in him we live, and move, and have our being." So it isn't orthodox to place Christ far away in the sky! If we knew how to take one step in the right direction we should be in Heaven. God, Jesus, and Heaven are that near!

If Christ is here, where is he? He said, "Where two or three are gathered together in my name, there am I in the midst of them." We may think of him as sitting in a chair beside us, or as standing by our side, with his hand on our shoulders: "Thou has laid thine hand upon me." St. Patrick could feel Christ above, below, in front, behind, beside, and inside like a great enveloping halo. St. Paul exclaimed over and over: "Christ liveth in me."

How he may live in us

How can Christ live in us? In what part of us? If our thoughts are flooded with him, then he lives in our minds. We need no ghostly theory to prove that much; he is in our thoughts when we think about him. He also lives in our wills if we yield them to him. If he fills our thoughts and controls our wills, he will inevitably mold our acts. When he directs our acts, then he is master of our hands, feet, tongues, and bodies. He does not force our wills. He comes in only where we open the doors of our hearts and give him a cordial welcome. He waits until we say with our whole soul in utter sincerity:

> Take my will and make it thine,
> It shall be no longer mine.
> Take my heart, it is thine own,
> It shall be thy royal throne!

"Behold, I stand at the door, and knock: if any man... open the door, I will come in to him, and will sup with him."

In one of our lovely Christmas hymns we sing:
"O come to my heart, Lord Jesus, there is room in my heart for thee."

Helen Keller is both blind and deaf to this physical world in which we live. Deprived of the senses of sight and hearing, she was nonetheless able to learn much about her physical environment. Under the stimulus of a gifted teacher and faithful companion, she became an educated woman. Today she can write about the unseen world with such sense of beauty and insight that we are amazed. Just as she learned about her unseen physical world, so we can learn about our spiritual world. That world is all about us, but we are blind and deaf to its beauties. Yet our Master, whom we do not see or hear as those others saw and heard him in the days of his flesh, longs to teach us what that unseen spiritual world is, so that, like all spiritual giants, we become citizens of two worlds.

Is he ever visible?

Just before his death, Jesus said: "In a little while the world will not see me any more, but you will still see me, because I shall live on, and you will live on too." Does he mean we shall see him after we die? or while we are still alive? Does he mean to say: "I will reveal myself to those who love me, just as I did to Mary Magdalene, to Peter, to Paul, to the twelve, and to more than five hundred others in the forty days after Easter." Does he mean to say: "Watch carefully, or you shall not know me when you see me, just as Mary Magdalene in the garden and the disciples on the way to Emmaus failed to recognize me. Seek me in the tone of voice, in the breaking of bread, in the burning of your own heart, and in wounded hands." Does he mean that? Yes, he means "always"—both here, now, and there in the hereafter: "Lo, I am with you always, even unto the end of the world."

To be sure, he is unseen. But so are you. People do not see the you. All that they see is your body, your shell, the fleshly house which you occupy. Has it ever occurred to you that we never really see one another with our eyes of flesh? When you look at your photograph you see a picture of what you look like to other people. But you know very well that your photograph is not by any means a picture of what the you, the inner person, really is. Only your best friends ever see that you. Love and faith give them the eyes to see into your soul.

Even so, when the disciples first heard this attractive Jesus call them, and followed him over the country, they did not see him. They saw only the body which he occupied. Very slowly they began to suspect the identity of him who occupied that body; they watched their leader, how he looked and spoke, how he worked, how he served and sacrificed and suffered, until they saw in him the Christ, the Messiah of their prophets. Christ was not his body. He only dwelt in his body, using it as his house, just as we use our bodies.

Is he visible? No and yes. In one sense he never was visible, nor are you! But in another sense he was visible to love just as you are, and he is still visible to love and faith. If he is within us we shall know where to seek him in the world outside us.

Especially we may be sure to find Christ where there is distress, or poverty, or fear, or bereavement, or loneliness, or helplessness, or heartbreaks, or despair, or penitence. Watch for him in a look of pain. Watch for him in the beggars on the roadside. That is where he appeared in Lowell's *The Vision of Sir Launfal*. He is always drawn to the center of every need. There he stands pleading with us to help him as he moves to help others. "I was an hungered... thirsty... a stranger... naked... sick... I was in prison, and you came unto me.... Inasmuch as ye have done it unto one of the least of these my brethren, ye have done it unto me." Those who have not yet grasped this actual visibility of Jesus in people ought to ponder much upon it, for it is a fact and not mere poetry. Spiritual truths are like that; they require time to become real to the mind.

When this presence of Christ becomes a reality to our consciousness, it is the most stimulating and revolutionary experience of our lives. As the realization first crashes in on the understanding of some, it sends them delirious with joy. It did so to the early Christians at Pentecost. They were so full of the reality of Christ that they acted like men intoxicated.

Christ Pursuing Us

The friendship of Jesus is not originally of our choosing, but of his. "Ye have not chosen me, but I have chosen you," he said. This is an amazing thing, the reverse of what one might expect. There is every reason why we should desire him: He is so lovely. But why should he choose us, who are so little and mean? Why should one as pure as he is go about seeking vile bodies like ours for his dwelling place? Why should he submit so meekly to our rebuffs and betrayals, and pursue us with never tiring persistency? What does Jesus find in us to love?

When I think of his love, and of the terrible price he paid for winning my love, and the shameful way in which I have ignored him, I for one, feel like crying: "O Christ, I am not worthy of this. I hate myself for what I have done and for what I am. I do not see how you can love and pursue me thus, for I do not deserve you. If I were in your place, O Christ, I should not waste my love on a worthless fellow like myself." But I know his answer is this: "I love you for what you need, for the fine possibilities imprisoned in you. I love you for what I long to do for you. I cannot give you up. I am determined to win you at last."

That is why he came to the world. He put aside the happiness which rightfully belonged to him from all eternity, and endured the cross and the shame because he saw something worth that much in us. He has joy "over one sinner that repenteth, more than over ninety and nine just persons, which need no repentance." His leading passion is to transform; to go like the roots of the rose down into the vile dirt and draw glorious color and ravishing perfume out of that soil. What the artist loves to do with a shapeless block of granite, Jesus loves to do with our lost and wandering souls. His supreme artistry is to take the very refuse of our evil past and make of it a saint, as he did with Magdalene.

> "The Spirit of the Lord is upon me,
> Because he hath anointed me
> To preach the gospel to the poor;
> He hath sent me to heal the broken hearted,
> To preach deliverance to the captives,
> And recovering of sight to the blind,
> To set at liberty them that are bruised."

From eternity Jesus has had an inveterate, incurable habit of creating and transforming. Because it is his nature to change bad to good, low to high, sorrow to joy, he loves us for our need and our imperfections. He revels in making imperfection perfect. He loves us for our chains because his joy is to break them. He loves us in prison because his joy is to open prison doors. He loves us sick, because his joy is to make us well. If he could not work miracles, it would be intolerable misery for him to look upon suffering, captive mankind. But because he is a creator and miracle worker, he feels sorrow and joy at the same time. He could weep in sympathy with Mary the moment before he raised her brother to life.

His plan for us is far greater than we dream! Far greater than merely to make us well or strong or peaceful or even happy. He aims at nothing less than making us like him, so that we will possess all his insatiable passion for lifting, healing, and transforming. Indeed, in his eyes we are not yet really alive until we yearn to save as he yearns; to share with him in the work of rescuing and transforming all we meet. A father derives some pleasure, to be sure, from giving aid to his son, but genuine joy does not come to the father until he sees that son with nobility of character doing beautiful and creative deeds to bless mankind.

His love is a magnet

We acquire this taste for lifting others by dwelling in Christ's company. The way to educate our growing children in character is to place them with persons of radiantly beautiful character, for we know that character is not taught; it is caught. One burning soul sets another on fire. Thus did the disciples learn from Jesus. "He chose twelve that they might be with him," that they might listen and talk, work and rest, eat and sleep with him for three years until in the end they began to be like him. He transforms by intimate contact.

The magnet that attracted the first disciples and that still attracts us is the mysterious power in Christ's love. We cannot comprehend love as great as his because we do not have it, but in many Biblical scenes we can perceive evidences of its power. "Never man spake like this man," they said. His heart overflowed until love poured from his lips with every word. When he was approaching Jerusalem and when the crowds were shouting his praises on every side, at the moment when other eyes would have gleamed with triumph, his eyes were suddenly blinded into tears. He cried, "Jerusalem, Jerusalem... how often would I have gathered thy children together, as a hen doth gather her brood under her wings, and ye would not." He loved Jerusalem as passionately as David loved his slain son Absalom, when the old King cried: "O my son Absalom, my son, my son Absalom! would God I had died for thee, O Absalom, my son, my son!" You see the same heartbreak in every step Jesus took in the direction of the cross. But there is a difference between David's lament and Jesus' deed. David wished to die. Jesus did die.

This death on the cross and the wonderful all-consuming love that inspired it is what draws men to Jesus. It is a magnet which, alone among all forces that influence the human heart, is powerful enough to call us away from the allurements of this world to the lofty and exacting levels of goodness and purity. Such love "redeems the world."

He made love pure

Jesus achieved a wonderful combination of love and purity. Throughout the heathen world purity was a synonym for coldness, and love was a synonym for sex passion, typified by the poetry of Horace, Catullus, and Sappho. Jesus revealed a pure spiritual love, warmer and more appealing than all the passion of earthly lovers. He has made purity beautiful. He has made love so pure and spiritual, has given it such a devine definition, that his beloved disciple dared to say that "God is love." He has given the word "passion" a new meaning, for he has put a cross in the center of it. He alone has revealed a love, a passion, and a purity so magnetic and appealing that it has lifted millions out of enslavement to lust. His love is the perfect illustration of the "expulsive power of a great affection." He has made pure love of soul for soul more romantic than sex passion. More exquisitely beautiful poetry has been lavished upon Jesus than upon all the women who ever lived. For nineteen centuries tender hymns to his love have been sung by countless millions of his worshipers.

Had we journeyed with him through Galilee we would have seen a charming courtesy, overflowing from the depths of a heart of pure affection. Rudeness and loudness and crudity seemed impossible in his presence. The rough fishermen who followed him absorbed his charm gradually into their own personalities, until they became gentlemen in the best sense of the word.

Love, with the picture of Christ as its center, is the most beautiful thing in the universe. It longs to give and encourage, to lift and comfort, to share and save, to ennoble and transform; love longs to do all this every day of our lives, without thought of rest and without consideration of self. Exquisite poetry and solid truth are blended in the words of a lovely song:

> Let the beauty of Jesus be seen in me,
> All his wonderful love and his purity.

The meek and lowly lover

"They that are whole," Jesus said, "have no need of the physician, but they that are sick.... I came not to call the righteous, but sinners to repentance." He earned a reputation for associating with publicans and sinners. He sympathized especially with weak sinners who had been swept away by temptation and who had suffered for their sins. The dominant passion of his whole life was to lift the fallen; to heal the sick of mind, body, and soul; to change despair to radiance. He went out to seek and save the lost. His sympathies were strongly with the poor. His close companions were from the lower classes of society. Of himself he said, "I am meek and lowly in heart."

Every person who is truly reborn has to adopt Jesus' basis for choosing friends and for loving them. Our instinct is to select friends who are attractive, who are congenial, or who give some social advantage. Jesus gravitated toward men because they were unlovely and because they needed to be transformed.

Rabindranath Tagore had caught the spirit of Christ perfectly when he wrote:

> Pride can never approach to where thou walkest in the clothes of the humble among the poorest, and lowliest, and lost.
> My heart can never find its way to where thou keepest company with the companionless among the poorest, the lowliest, and the lost.

College men and women as a rule are plagued by a pride of education and degree and class, which makes them regard certain tasks as beneath their dignity. They usually find ignorant people uncongenial and unsuitable for close friendships. Thus the educated man must crucify pride of class and position before he can keep company with the very people who need his help most. The love of Jesus for men was so overpowering that it broke all barriers of class, sex, race, language or custom; to be like Christ is to have a love no barrier can resist.

He never gives us up

The terrifying poem "The Hound of Heaven" declares that God cannot and will not let us go, but will at all costs find us and win us at last. If he cannot find us in health, we must suffer. If not in comfort, we must have adversity. If not with friends, we must be left alone. If not in life, we must die.... He pursues us insistently, relentlessly, irresistibly, until our ravished souls at last yield in a heartbreaking and gloriously joyous abandon of surrender.

> O Love that will not let me go,
> I rest my weary soul in thee;
> I give thee back the life I owe.
> That in thine ocean depths its flow
> May richer, fuller be.

In his great picture, "Christ Knocking at the Door," Holman Hunt has painted the door without a latch on the outside. That is like the door of our hearts; the power to open the door rests with the inner man.

God is inviting us to be his sons, and God's first step in making us sons is to entrust us with an immensely important decision. The soul has such amazing freedom that it can say "yes" or "no," even to God who made it! What an astounding conception! What boundless conceit to suppose that our Creator is playing the role of humble petitioner and suitor outside the door of our souls! Yet that is literally what Christ tells us: "Behold, I stand at the door, and knock," says the risen Lord in Revelation 3:20; "if any man hear my voice, and open the door, I will come in to him, and will sup with him."

> O Jesus, thou art standing outside the fast-closed door,
> In lowly patience waiting to pass the threshold o'er:
> Shame on us, Christian brothers, his name and sign who bear,
> O shame, thrice shame upon us, to keep him standing there!

It is not only the so-called "heathen" who reject him. The majority of us who call ourselves Christians also close the door. Time after time we keep him out because we desire to receive through the back door of our lives some evil or selfish thought. We put Jesus out of our minds, for example, if we play with some lascivious thought which we know would sicken Christ's pure soul. Or we plan some advantage over another with a selfish meanness which we dare not ask Christ to bless. When we are done with that vile little morsel of wickedness, we wait a reasonable time and then open the door and invite Jesus to return. He comes back meekly as though he were our servant instead of being God. He told us to forgive others seventy times seven times, but he has forgiven us seven thousand times. He has bowed his head and stepped humbly out of our thoughts; submissively he has returned again when we gave him the invitation. We are like little children abusing their own mother; we are too stupid to see how we hurt and insult. Yet I should not use the word "insult." He loves us too much to allow that word.

Even when we invite him into the main room of our heart, we often keep him out of some hidden little room in the mind's cellar, where we try to hide sly secrets from him and from the world, just as many people hid liquor during Prohibition days. This is why we do not feel the sense of his approval and why we lack power. The pure sincere Christ, who has nothing to hide, cannot give us his perfect friendship so long as we lock him out of dark sinful rooms within the depths of us.

Not our power but his

Many of us are kept away from Jesus by the paralyzing sense of our unworthiness. We feel unclean and unfit even to look into his face. We do not believe he can forgive us, for we cannot forgive ourselves. I for one would never dare to approach the spotless Christ if I depended upon any virtue in my past life. But thank God, I can come to him, bringing nothing save his invitation.

If any of us stay away because we have sinned, we misunderstand Jesus. Our staying away is what torments him, just as it pained the father when the prodigal son was away. Nothing but our coming back to him with all our sin and filth will stop Christ's sorrow. The only thing that ever satisfies his abiding love is for us to come saying:

> Just as I am, without one plea,
> But that thy blood was shed for me,
> And that thou bid'st me come to thee;
> O Lamb of God, I come! I come!

Then he will dip our guilty souls into "the crimson flood" and bring them out cleansed, pure, unashamed, and unspeakably happy. Whatever anybody may think of the theology of bloodshed, the fact it describes is happening somewhere in every province, state, and nation every day, and the bliss felt by released souls is the world's most poignant ecstasy.

A second reason preventing many people from surrendering to Christ is despair: they do not believe they can remain true. They are slaves to mighty urges of the flesh which the Bible condemns. They have tried and failed, risen and fallen, until they feel themselves to be hypocrites if they make any promises, for they know they will fall again. They want at least to be honest with God.

But that is not being honest with God, it is doubting God. Christ's promise is, "My grace is sufficient for you." He does not ask us to guarantee to remain good. He asks us to give him his chance, and he guarantees to give us the victory. If he has full control he can break the chains of any secret vice. He has done it for countless millions. He is now doing it daily.

> Come now, and let us reason together, saith the Lord:
> Though your sins be as scarlet, they shall be as white as snow;
> Though they be red like crimson, they shall be as wool.

"Come unto me, all ye that labour and are heavy laden, and I will give you rest. Take my yoke upon you, and learn of me; for I am meek and lowly in heart: and ye shall find rest unto your souls. For my yoke is easy, and my burden is light."

This is the wistful plea of Jesus. It is a heartbroken call; for like spoiled little children we fail to see how we have hurt him by our refusal. The beautiful words of invitation for the Lord's Supper express the exact truth. "Come, not to testify that you are righteous, but that you sincerely love our Lord Jesus Christ and desire to be his true disciples; come, not because you are strong, but because you are weak; come, not because you have any claim on heaven's reward, but because in your frailty and sin you stand in need of mercy and help... before the throne of the heavenly Father and the cross of the redeemer make your humble confession of sin, and pray for strength to do and to bear the holy and blessed will of God."

If God Is Christ

The person of Christ not only transforms us and our conception of other human beings, but it transforms our idea of God. Through Jesus we see a very intimate and understandable and approachable and magnetic God. If God is as charming as Jesus, then we can "Love him with all our heart, and with all our soul, and with all our might." We can love him with everything we are and have, because we find Jesus so irresistibly loving. The Jews were commanded to love God with all their hearts, souls, minds, and strength—but they could not. The Jewish conception of God was not lovable enough for that much response, at least not for most people. But now we have seen Jesus and we can love God with this reckless abandon.

Someone may ask, "Where can I find God?" Our answer is the answer Jesus gave: "He that hath seen me hath seen the Father.... No man cometh unto the Father, but by me."

I used to deny this. "Surely," I thought, "multitudes of non-Christians know God." Yes, they know God, but not "the Father of Jesus Christ," not this Father with the intense fire of love coursing hotter than the sun. This Father is found only through Jesus.

Christ revealed that side of God's nature, the side which neither science nor history could reveal—God's tenderness, his sympathetic sweetness. Jesus alone was able to reveal "love so amazing, so divine," surpassing everything the world ever supposed possible. The Bible strains at words to help us appreciate this "Father of our Lord Jesus Christ... that ye may be able to comprehend... what is the breadth, and length, and depth, and height; and to know the love of Christ, which passeth knowledge, that ye might be filled with all the fulness of God." Words of inconceivable love.

Jesus is so irresistibly lovable that the masses of mankind need only see him clearly in order to love him passionately. After Christ was here men could feel near to God as we feel near to those of our own blood. Christ's thirty-three years in human form enabled men not only to know God, but as well to surrender to him in utter abandon, as an infant surrenders to its mother's arms and sleeps. Men dared to "let go and love God." They found that they could trust his love unhesitatingly; they discovered that God wants such loving trust. So close your eyes, weary wanderer, and accept these tested truths.

When God's heart broke

In a Filipino home during a funeral, one often hears loud, heart-rending cries of grief. No need to ask whether the weeping comes from one who loves greatly, a father, mother, wife, brother, or child. The greater one's love, the greater is one's grief when one's beloved is lost. God's love is greater than that of any relative. Who then can estimate his grief when his children are lost and dead?

In the eleventh chapter of Hosea we read God's cry, out of a broken heart: "When Israel was a child, then I loved him, and called my son out of Egypt.... I taught Ephraim also to go, taking them by their arms.... I drew them with cords of a man, with bands of love... and I laid meat unto them.... How shall I give thee up, Ephraim? how shall I deliver thee, Israel... mine heart is turned within me, my repentings are kindled together.... I will not return to destroy Ephraim: for I am God, and not man."

"God so loved the world, that he gave his only begotten Son, that whosoever believeth in him should not perish, but have everlasting life."

In the ancient story, when Abraham was about to offer up Isaac as a human sacrifice, God stopped Abraham's hand and gave him a lamb to be sacrificed instead. But when God's turn came to sacrifice his own Son, He stopped not his own hand. God so loved the world that he did not stop! When the world turns away from him and destroys itself in wicked madness as it has been doing during this century, it leaves the Father in anguished disappointment. Has it ever occurred to us to pity God; to reach our arms upward and whisper: "God, I understand a little of thy pain. I have caused much of it. And I offer my sympathy." If he did not love us so much he could forget us, but love like his cannot forget any more than the old father could forget while his prodigal son was away living in debauchery.

It was a custom of the ancient Aztecs to select the most magnificent youth in their land, lay him on an altar, and tear from his breast the still beating heart.

When the Roman soldiers stretched and nailed Christ to the cross and left him there for six terrible hours, they opened the very heart of God, beating and quivering for the sin of the world. That cross is the most terrifying fact in all history; it hangs over the universe holding a bleeding heart that was lacerated for you and me. The only reason our hearts do not quiver with his is because our dull, dead, selfish love cannot comprehend real love. We are not capable of seeing love in others unless we have love ourselves.

God suffers with all the sufferings of the world. No individual person in the world could endure to suffer even an infinitesimal fraction of what God suffers. He and he alone endures all the sufferings of the last tragic creature in his universe.

It is not the pain and sorrow of the world that wounds him most; it is the failure of men to measure up to his high plan for them. If only his expectations for us were not so high, he could more easily endure our terrible failure! When one has a very high dream for the children one loves, and they disappoint that dream, one knows a little of the heartache God must endure.

I recall the gasp with which I first read Lyman Abbott's bold assertion: "God is still suffering." But to ponder upon it deeply, is to see that if God is love, if he has as much love as we saw in Jesus, God must suffer. Jesus said that not a hair falls from our heads without the knowledge of our heavenly Father. If God loves us more than a mother loves her child, then he suffers with us more than a mother suffers when her child is harmed or when it does wrong. His is the torment of frustrated love. We cannot imagine how much God suffers unless we ourselves have seen some relative or friend, in whom we placed enormous hopes, come crashing down in disgrace.

Hosea saw that God resembles a disappointed suitor, for he is seeking to woo fallen and blindly groping men, and God's eternal cross is that men prefer darkness rather than light. Certainly all the great Biblical prophets showed us God who not only created the world, but also felt the world in all the depths of his being. Paul said, "the whole creation groaneth and travaileth in pain together until now with eager longing for the sons of God." Creation for millions of years has been in the pangs of giving birth to sons of God, and God himself feels those birth pangs. Men who have walked the floor for hours while their wives were going through the shadow of the valley of death in childbirth can conceive of God walking the floors of Heaven in eager anxiety during the billions of years in which his creation has been in travail. What science has called "natural selection" is God, trying and trying again through countless quintillions of years until at last he brings forth from the womb of the universe his highest and loftiest creation. God is determined at whatever cost, to have sons like unto himself in holiness and goodness and purity.

This awful conception sets the imagination staggering. Such immense effort, such apparent waste of materials, so many countless trials before the first Son of God could be born! Such agony, such struggle, before other sons of God could come forth! In the magnificent words of Robert Browning, "this we are worth to God!" You and I and our brothers are of enough value to keep God and the whole creation in anguish for billions of years! If our eyes could behold that picture even for a moment, we would go mad if it were not for one fact: Eternal travail and eternal bliss exist in God side by side!

Christ Speaks to Us All

Anything which calls us from wrongdoing, which fires us with his purpose, enkindles love, or whispers peace into the troubled heart, is the voice of Christ—anything with a message for the soul. Kagawa says that he considers books of science letters from God explaining how he manages his universe.

The young people of the church in Dansalan, Lanao, collected about five hundred "words which God uses," and prepared definitions for each word. It may not be a contribution to world literature, but its preparation proved to be an excellent project in learning to see and hear God. Here are a few of the definitions which they wrote in their "Dictionary of God's Language":

Accidents: Most accidents happen because we let go the guiding hand of God to play with Satan, who delights in seeing us suffer and go to destruction. If we are hurt without being killed, that is God's way of saving us from sin before it is too late.

Aspiration: When the soul longs for a higher life, it is the voice of God.

Affection: A person who has love is walking and talking with God, for God is love.

Animals: When an animal like a cat or dog rubs his nose affectionately against us, he is God speaking to us. When we see an animal maltreated and moaning in pain, the pity in us is the groan of God.

Advice: Often God speaks to us through other persons. We must be sure that the person who advises us has the Holy Spirit. Sometimes through such a person we find the answer to our hardest questions.

Births: A baby fills us with joy and reminds us God alone can work such miracles as making a new life.

Bereavement: When we lose a loved one, we always pray and try to be near to God. Sometimes that is the way he draws people away from leading wicked lives.

Birds: The sweet songs of birds carry the messages of God; and they are the symbols of love, peace, and the Holy Spirit.

The art of conversing with Christ

It is important for us to learn the art of conversation with Christ. One good way to cultivate this art is to talk aloud, if we can go where others will not hear us. We can make it a two-way conversation by saying in a distinct voice what we believe the Master would reply to us if he spoke aloud. Both we and he use the same tongue. When we are sure of what he would say, then we may be sure that he does say it. Our conversation resembles the intimate talks one has with his dearest companions. We talk for hours, beginning and ending at any time without formality, while at work, or at leisure.

We need not be deterred by doubts as to whether we are indulging in autosuggestion. Christ can speak to us through autosuggestion as well as through any of his thousand other channels. No religion is possible without a venture of faith. If you were telephoning to a friend, you would not begin by trying to prove that the voice you heard was really that of your friend. The conversation would be self-attesting. You would be sure it was your friend by what he said.

This is equally true of the two-way conversation which uses your own faculty of speech. What Christ says to you should prove whether it is he. And it does! The longer you continue the practice the more unshakably convinced you will be that you have been speaking with the Lord.

Perhaps you may feel most reverent on your knees with your eyes closed. Perhaps you can speak with him best while taking a walk, looking at the green trees and the blue sky. Some of us are tremendously helped by having a picture of Jesus before us. Many people are helped by glancing frequently at an empty chair and endeavoring to visualize Jesus sitting in that chair. Each of us should experiment until he finds which technique helps him most to keep his mind on Christ. The tax on one's powers of concentration is greater than when one is talking to a person whose face is visible, and so, like children learning to walk, we may need aids to which our weak minds may cling.

Sometimes we feel like doing all the talking to him. Sometimes Jesus does all the talking to us. Most often it is a give-and-take conversation, as it is with any other person. But it is on a higher level than any other conversation because the desires of Jesus are higher than those of any other friend.

After a while, when we have learned to hold inner conversations with Jesus, no sound need escape our lips. This is the art which all the great followers of Christ have practiced down through the centuries. It is often called "Interior Prayer." Then we can have the joy of his constant companionship and help, whether we are surrounded by other people or are quite alone. If we persist in this type of conversation, it can grow dearer and warmer each day. Ten or twenty years spent thus in his presence develop an intimacy which defies description.

If prayer is to be wholly satisfying it must take some form. When one has learned a form which affords sweet intimacy with Christ, it becomes for him the most precious discovery in the world. He tends to regard the form itself as devine.

Thus Anglicans find this intimacy with Jesus while using their Prayer Books, a fact which explains the emphasis which they place upon them. Roman Catholics find Christ in the Eucharist. Quakers meet him in silent waiting together. Musicians hear Christ speaking from a violin, a piano, or the human voice. Lovers of art adore him most as they look at some lovely painting in Jesus. Many of us have hanging on the walls or over our desks a picture of Jesus. The same picture gazes up at us from beneath the glass on our tables and from the walls of our dining and living rooms. Whenever we glance at that picture, Christ speaks in our hearts. Now all of us, Catholics, Quakers, musicians, Methodists, have found him in a variety of ways—hence all are equally right.

There are men and women who often forego sleep in order to spend their hours at night in a delightful communion with Jesus. The two or three such hours are so lovely that they are anticipated all day. Some of them bow with eyes closed, but many more sit gazing at some picture or at a cross. The dearest friends of Christ have a closeness with him that no other earthly experience can equal. Every minute may be filled with secret whispers, with questions and answers and words of love and gratitude. Those who attain this intimacy share in the sorrows and joys, in the pities and triumphs of the Lord they adore. Language cannot reveal their inner bliss, nor can words ever hint at the peace and security in their souls. Some at times are "ravished" with his ardent love until they cry: "Dear Christ, please stop. My soul can endure no more."

You Must Be Born Again

When you have a new truth and can find no words to express it, you must either coin new words as scientists do, words which nobody will then understand, or else you must use old words to express new meanings. Jesus chose this latter "old-word" method. He gave new meaning to "light," "water," "bread," "love," "life," and "birth." "Ye must be born again" was a new idea clothed in the oldest of words. Our souls, Jesus saw, are not yet "alive" until this "new birth" occurs. "Let the dead bury their dead," he said to a disciple, and he meant, "Let those with dead souls bury dead bodies."

St. Paul says that when we are born again, the old self dies and Christ enters our bodies to take the place of the self which has just died. "It is no longer I that live," writes Paul, "but Christ who liveth in me."

At Christmas time we sing:

> O holy Child of Bethlehem, descend to us we pray;
> Cast out our sin and enter in, be born in us today."

This new birth means far more than being "intellectually convinced." Even if we say, "Lord, Lord, I accept thee as my Savior," that is not enough. We must make an unconditional surrender all the way down the line. Inside yourself there must take place a transformation in every corner of your intricate and many-sided nature. It is a stupendous achievement for Christ to capture even one soul thus completely. There is a painful and thorough-going operation to be performed which is like death of the self and a new birth of somebody else. When Paul, after his conversion, had his name changed from Saul, it was symbolical of what happened to him. "Saul" was a Jewish name but Paul ceased to be a typical Jew, and he became exactly what a Jew was not, for he lived like Gentiles. His attitude toward other races was changed, his ideals were changed, his life work was changed. Old things had all passed away. Behold, for him all things had become new. He had abandoned everything he held dear "for the excellency of the knowledge of Christ Jesus my Lord: for whom I have suffered the loss of all things, and do count them but refuse."

We Protestants usually do not see as clearly as do the priests and nuns of the Catholic Church what devastating completeness there is to this self-losing. When they break with their old ties to enter a convent or monastery, the roots are supposed to be torn out of almost everything they hold dear. Those who achieve this to the center of their hearts know what Jesus meant when he said that he has "come to set a man at variance against his father, and the daughter against her mother."

Unfortunately, this total unreserved letting-go has been confined too largely to the nuns and monks. The great masses of Catholics as well as the great masses of Protestants live in a world of compromise. As a result our Christianity has been too insipid and paralytic to save the world. There ought not any longer to be two kinds of Christians, those who profess to be Christians and those who make the great renunciation. According to Jesus there is no true disciple who does not leave all and follow him. The rest are hearers only, and not doers of the word.

Yet we cannot blame the masses. They do not know that their profession of religion is paralytic, because the very organization of our church provides for this kind of half adherence, which is not total surrender of all we have, but is merely conformity to the codes of respectability. In this life of compromise people themselves are dissatisfied and hungry for real life. A new Pentecost must come which will tell people that they have been victims of self-deception.

What figure could describe more perfectly than the words "second birth" the change which takes place when Christ controls the life? Appetites and desires for evil melt away, and we begin to love and desire the highest things of the spirit. Old selfish plans go out and a whole new life-program takes their place, a program which helps build up the kingdom of God. Love, love for everybody, even for criminals, even for enemies, and a great pity for the needy, rises in the heart and flows out through the senses. People begin to say: "What has happened to him? He isn't the same person at all. He has lost his temper and his sharp tongue. He has become so kind." The very face loses its old lines of selfishness and worry and cynicism, while new lines of friendliness and peace and joy transform the face until it becomes radiant. "Old things are passed away; behold, all things are become new." This is what happens in a reborn life.

That is what we pray for when we say "Thy Kingdom come, Thy will be done on earth, as it is in heaven." Jesus had "come down out of heaven" where they obey God's will all day every day, to our earth where we ignore God's will almost all day every day. To make the total change from our earth way to his heaven way is to be reborn. It is because we have felt the miracle of rebirth within us that we are so sure that eventually Christ can perform his miracle of rebirth for the world. Indeed the thing that will give the world itself a new birth is an ever-increasing number of reborn people.

The continuous surrender

Let us suppose that you have decided to accept his conditions of friendship and to surrender your life. What is the first step? You simply say earnestly and sincerely to him, believing that he is unseen beside you: "Jesus, I surrender. Here I am, take me. Take all of me. Thou didst say: 'Ye are my friends, if ye do whatsoever I command.' I mean to do what thou commandest. I mean to spend all my hours obeying thy will. I will follow, as the disciples followed, without knowing where thou wilt lead. I repent, because my past has been so full of wrecked resolves, so wicked, and weak, and disappointing. But thou hast called me. Thou art eager to change me. Now I give thee all I know how to give. I am not strong, but I lean on thy promise to give me strength."

That is the beginning. But the surrender is continuous. The rest of your life you will consciously move toward him with a constant gentle pressure of the will. That pressure is not strain; it is rather a letting go and a perfect relaxing. A wise physician advises nervous people: "Lie down and relax every muscle—your forehead, your eyes, your facial muscles, your mouth, your throat, your arms, your chest, your legs, relax, relax...." This requires determined will power, especially if one has been tense and worried. When we surrender to Christ, we must exert this same will to yield; we must let loose and relax the soul. That is what faith and trust mean. Yet this relaxing is not a mere passivity. It is an eager active response to his every whisper. It implies a persistent effort to form a new habit.

The formation of any habit is a painful process at first; it cuts new paths through the gray matter and destroys old channels and old motivation tracks. But the pain does not last long—unless we allow our new grooves to be destroyed before they have depth, by breaking our new resolutions. We must follow those grooves again and again. We must not let up or we shall fail.

Jesus expressed long ago the technique of habit-formation, and the well-known instructions of William James for forming a new habit can be found in the pages of the Gospels. "He that putteth his hand to the plow and turneth back is not worthy of me." Once we have taken the plunge we must succeed! We ought to use reminders and aids to make certain that we shall continue to work on the new shallow habit-grooves until they become so deep that we shall not need to worry about jumping the track. Among these reminders are: Pictures of Christ on the walls, or under the glass of our desk; books revealing Christ, songs that sing him into our minds, friends who know him and share him with us, church services, and, above all, reading daily from the Gospel stories. A practice which some of us find helpful is simply to keep saying as the minutes pass, words like these: "Lord Jesus, thou art here beside me—unseen. Nevertheless thou art just as real as the very walls, as real as my other friends. And I am resolved to listen to thee, to obey thee, to work with thee minute by minute. What art thou saying? I am listening."

The requirements of his friendship

Emerson says, in his famous essay, *Friendship*, that ideal friendships require "natures so rare and costly, so well tempered and so happily adapted to one another" that very seldom can this high level of intimacy be attained. Each party to friendship must pay a supreme price. Each must give to the other the best he has. Perfect friendship is as beautiful and as delicate as a rose. If there be treachery, suspicion, selfishness, irritability, callousness, vulgarity, or low aims in the relationship, perfect friendship is impossible.

If this be true, we may well ask: what high price must be paid for the friendship of Jesus? Jesus himself gives the answer with breath-taking directness: "Ye are my friends, if ye do whatsoever I command." Nothing could be clearer or more final. Surrender, absolute, eager, and continuous, is his price.

Steadiness and dependability are "musts" in the highest friendship. Loyalty cannot go hot and cold, up and down, if it is to be intimate and close. There cannot be disappointments and betrayals. If we are fickle and untrustworthy, both we and Christ face only suffering. We are not to estimate our practice of religion by its high peaks of emotion, but by its steadiness under temptation. When the temperature chart of a patient goes up and down between 98 and 104 we call him very seriously ill. We cannot have a beautiful friendship with Christ if we are like periodical drinkers, good for one week and in a spiritual gutter the next. The Quakers, with their emphasis on steady, quiet, good living, are ideal friends of Christ. A friend who shares our prosperity and joys, but deserts us in trouble, disgrace and poverty, is no real friend. As the cross loomed, the multitudes forsook Jesus. They do the same thing today! Trouble is friendship's acid test. Jesus "humbled himself, and became obedient unto death, even the death of the cross." He asks the same obedience from us.

Christ must be Master

We Americans, saturated as we are with the doctrine of liberty, often suppress this teaching of Jesus. We like to talk of a "democracy of God." Some of us have gone so far as to say that Jesus is "running for election." But the kingdom of God is definitely not a democracy. We do not make its laws nor elect its rulers. God is an absolute monarch. That is precisely why we need democracy in earthly governments; we must obey God rather than men. We cannot let any man command our consciences, because God alone must command them. In the spiritual life no man can serve two masters.

When Jesus demands us to do "whatsoever I command," he is not more absolute than Nature herself. "Obey or perish" is written into the warp and woof of the universe. Nature's laws, which are God's laws, are never broken; the men who fail to obey them are broken. The horrors of our age are the result of the failure of men to apply the Sermon on the Mount to nations and individuals. With perfect accuracy St. Paul said: "Behold therefore the goodness and severity of God: on them which fell severity; but toward thee, goodness, if thou continue in his goodness; otherwise thou also shalt be cut off."

Christ is no temporary or passing acquaintance, but a friend for eternity. As man and wife are married for life, so Christ offers his blood bond of saviour, friend, master for eternity. That or nothing! That high or nothing! That is why the requirements of his friendship are so lofty, because the stakes are so tremendous!

He accepts only crystal-clear sincerity

John declared that "God is love." That declaration is true only if a picture of Christ is in that love, to make it sincere and pure. In all human history there is nothing else as relentless as the love of Jesus, hard, like a diamond and as transparent. It gives all and demands all. Thus Jesus is terrifyingly strict about sin. No suggestion of evil can enter the holy of holies where he abides. Jesus and sin are incompatible, cannot remain together. The sin goes or he goes.

What about the sins of our past? The Master is eager to cover them and to forget them, if we repent and cease to sin; but he will neither forget nor forgive our purpose to do wrong in the future. We cannot share our resentments and malices with Jesus. We can only beg him to remove them from our minds, for he condemns all malice and all ill will. We cannot read books of which Jesus disapproves. Our conversation and even our very thoughts must please him. Our words must be honest. Our dealings must be honest. Our work must be done as honestly as we can do it. He will not tolerate poor work. No demands upon any worker were ever more strict than the demands Jesus makes. "After you have done all," he tells us, "say, 'We are miserable and worthless servants. We have done what it was our duty to do.' "

He expects results rather than mere promises. "Thou wicked and slothful servant.... Take ye away therefore the talent from him, and give it unto him that hath ten talents." That is his attitude now—this Friend who will spur life on to efficient service.

"Not every one that saith unto me, Lord, Lord, shall enter into the kingdom of heaven; but he that doeth the will of my Father which is in heaven. Many will say to me in that day, Lord, Lord, have we not prophesied in thy name? and in thy name have cast out devils? and in thy name done many wonderful works? And then I will profess unto them, I never knew you: depart from me, ye that work iniquity."

Jesus climaxes these uncompromising demands of his with the final words: "Be ye therefore perfect, even as your Father which is in heaven is perfect." And he meant it! He was strict even unto that degree of perfection. It strikes our faces like ice water, and stimulates us like ammonia.

It is said that all great men are paradoxes. Jesus is the best illustration of this truth. He was at once the most tender and the most exacting, the most gentle and the most relentless being who ever walked the earth.

How Christ obeys his Father

Jesus himself had to purchase the complete confidence of God by perfect obedience. He told his disciples that he did nothing from the moment he awoke until he fell asleep, excepting what the Father told him to do. This meant being sinless, of course, but it meant far more than that. It meant that he listened and waited minute by minute for God's instructions, that he did nothing at all until God said: "Do it." Jesus asserted no will of his own, excepting the will to continuous and complete yielding to God's will in every trifle. This seems slavish, extreme, undemocratic. Indeed it is well nigh incredible to us who have not lived that way.

The Gospel of John, as translated by Goodspeed, hurls this into our very faces with stunning directness. What else can you make of the following verses?

"The Son cannot do anything of his own accord, unless he sees the Father doing it. For whatever the Father does, the Son also does." (John 5:19) "I cannot do anything of my own accord... I am not seeking to do what I please, but what pleases him who has sent me." (John 5:30) "I have come down from heaven not to do what I please but what pleases him who has sent me." (John 6:38) "My teaching is not my own; it comes from him who has sent me.... My teaching comes from God." (John 7:16) "I do nothing of my own accord, but speak as the Father has instructed me... for I do always what pleases him." (John 8:28, 29) "I have not come of my own accord, but he has sent me." (John 8:42) "I have not spoken on my account, but the Father who has sent me has himself given me orders what to tell and what to say.... So whatever I say, I say only as the Father has told me." (John 12:40). Only!

Continuous, total, never varying obedience to every whisper of God was what it cost even Jesus to preserve the wonderful confidence of the Father. The rest of us obey when it is not too distasteful or painful. We shrink back when we are confronted with shame or disgrace or extreme suffering. Jesus said "Yes" to his Father when he saw the destined cross on a hill in Jerusalem. He might have stayed in Tyre and Sidon with perfect safety, but "he set his face steadfastly to go to Jerusalem." It was tramp, tramp, tramp to execution between two criminals, because the Father had said "Go." "This is why the Father loves me, because I am giving my life" (John 10:17) "Now is my heart troubled... Father, save me from this trial! And yet it was for this very purpose that I have come to this trial." (John 12:17) "Not my will, but thine, be done." (Luke 22:42) "He carried his obedience so far as to die, and to die upon the cross." (Phil. 2:8, 9)

Obey him today, trust him for tomorrow

The price we pay for entering the Perfect Family of God is the same price Jesus himself pays—perfect obedience. "A disciple is not above his teacher, nor a servant above his lord. It is enough for the disciple that he be as his teacher and the servant as his lord." (Matt. 10:24, 25) "If you keep my commands you will retain my love, just as I have observed the Father's commands and retain his love." (John 15:10)

Our experience reveals several peculiar problems when we try to keep his commands. For one thing it frequently happens that we cannot see his will for the future. We have to walk ahead by faith, not knowing what the next month will bring forth.

A missionary walked for hours on top of a lonely hill, begging heaven to show him what the future held for him; but heaven seemed deaf and silent. After a long struggle there came to his mind an old hymn learned in his childhood: "Trust and obey, for there's no other way, to be happy in Jesus but to trust and obey." In a flash he saw the way out of his trouble. He had wanted to judge God, to decide whether God was planning right. Now for the first time he saw what God asked: "Trust tomorrow to me. I trust today to you." He cried: "Lord, I do trust thee for tomorrow, and I promise to obey thee just for today. I do not ask to see the distant scene. One step enough for me." His heart melted in wonderful peace as he heard Christ's voice whisper into his ear. "Lo, I am with you. Be not afraid." With new meaning the words of John came into his mind: "Anyone who resolves to do his will will know..." (John 7:17, Goodspeed's translation.)

How His Love Enlarges Us

When a youth and a maiden fall in love, their interest in the rest of the human race is likely to diminish. Lovers are eager to get away by themselves and be let alone. To them, engrossment in one another becomes the supreme virtue, and other people are largely forgotten.

To be in love with Jesus has exactly the opposite effect, if one understands Jesus. For scarce does his love suffuse us, but we feel it reaching out from us in an effort to help others to know our Friend. As we come under his spell he stretches our small minds wider and ever wider until at last we shall have a love as wide as the wide world—as wide as his own. All exclusive cliques which ignore others are contrary to Jesus' way of loving. He was and is the supreme breaker-down of the walls which divide us. He aims to remove those walls between nations and classes which have turned our planet into a raving madhouse.

In the sublime 55th chapter of Isaiah God declares: "My thoughts are not your thoughts, neither are your ways my ways, saith the Lord; for as the heavens are higher than the earth, so are my ways higher than your ways, and my thoughts than your thoughts." Isaiah might have added "and my love than your love." His love reaches to the boundaries of the universe. But more important for us than this reach outward, is his reach downward. Not a sparrow "falls on the ground without your Father," and "ye are of more value than many sparrows." He is big enough to be interested in everything we do, however small or insignificant it may appear to be. He is either for it or against it.

He makes our hearts tender

Jesus is never satisfied with our love because it is always too narrow and cold to match his love. He condemned the exceedingly righteous Pharisees because they were callous, exclusive, and self-centered. Hard-heartedness was hideous in his eyes, especially so if he found it in religious leaders. Tender-heartedness was virtue number one. That is why Magdalene was so easily forgiven, so much more easily and readily than respectable, prosperous, pious Pharisees.

Jesus once met a clean-minded, wholesome youth, and the disciples saw that he loved him. He yearned to give to this youth the rich love that he himself had, so he said: "One thing thou lackest: go thy way, sell whatever thou hast, and give to the poor... and come, take up the cross, and follow me."

We can see what might have happened had the rich young man obeyed Jesus; he would have become like Jesus in sacrificial service, and his money could have been invested in a transformed community. He might have become another St. Paul of Christian history. But like most other wealthy young men, he had acquired the habit of refusing appeals for help. He could not break that habit. He went away sadly, his love for money shutting him from a love for humanity. Jesus sighed as he watched the departure of this youth who had saved his money but had lost his life. "How hardly shall they that have riches," he said, "enter into the kingdom of God."

Love because men need us

Walls of money may so easily be built between ourselves and the great mass of the poor and lowly whom Jesus loves. Those who sincerely follow Christ find these walls melting away. Gradually they learn from him to be strangely tender toward the people whom others loathe and have forgotten. Was there ever a Salvation Army, working day and night to help the fallen, until Jesus taught people to love the unlovely? Was there ever a Bowery Mission for inebriates? Did ever a Florence Nightingale minister to the wounded soldiers, friends and foes alike, until Jesus taught us how to love? Did ever a Kagawa leave his wealth to sleep with diseased men in the slums of Kobe until Jesus had taught him how to love? Did ever people pour out their money to meet emergencies and famines in distant countries until Jesus taught them how to love? Did ever a Robert Morrison toil hidden for a lifetime in the cellars of China to help the very people who would have killed him on sight if they had caught him—did ever that happen until Jesus taught men how to love their enemies? Did ever fifty thousand men and women offer their hopes, their pleasures, and their dearest associations, to go as missionaries for life to distant and often dangerous lands to use their splendid energies ministering to need, and telling the good news of a coming kingdom of God, until Jesus had said, "Go ye into all the world"? There are millions of people doing disagreeable, difficult, dangerous tasks for unfortunates whom they would have disdained if Jesus had not shown men a more excellent meaning of the word "noble."

The average "good" man has the words "love" and "desire" hopelessly confused. He says he "loves" a thing when he craves to possess it, as one says, "I love to wear beautiful clothes." This kind of "love" ought to have another name. Love with a picture of Jesus at its center desires only to give. It looks at every individual, asking, "What can I do for him?" never "What can I get out of him for myself?"

We have a thermometer by which we may now judge our likeness to Jesus; this thermometer is the heat of our compassion and the wideness of our love. When we become perfectly Christlike we shall search every face for an opportunity to help and help and help all day long.

Inasmuch as ye have done it to these least

A son asks his father: "What can I do to express my gratitude for all the love you have lavished upon me?" A wise father will reply: "The only way you can repay me is to pass on to others the best you have. What you do for the future, you do for me." This is precisely what Christ says to us, and he says it in vivid and unmistakable language. We cannot fully comprehend the intense passion of his appeal. He loves the countless millions of this earth as much as he loves us; not more, not less. He loves all races and conditions for their own individual needs. He pleads with us to help him reach anybody, anywhere, who has had no opportunity to know him. Other people's needs are Christ's needs. So deep is his affection that he feels their pains, as much as they themselves feel them. In the twenty-fifth chapter of Matthew he says exactly that:

"When I was hungry, you gave me food, when I was thirsty you gave me something to drink; when I was a stranger, you invited me to your homes, when I had no clothes, you gave me clothes, when I was sick, you looked after me, when I was in prison, you came to see me.... I tell you, in so far as you did it to one of the humblest of these brothers of mine, you did it to me."

Now we are face to face with a second mystery of Christ's fathomless love: he is in everybody who has trouble. Not only does he come to accept any invitation, but he comes to meet any need. No faintest shadow of hunger, cold, sickness, pain, loneliness, imprisonment, or any other kind of human suffering is without the presence of Jesus. This was the thought that motivated C. F. Andrews, the saintly friend of Mahatma Gandhi. "Saint" Andrews had caught Christ's superhuman capacity to love the loveless, and so he spent his life going around the world and sharing its darkest tragedies. He had discovered the only way in which men can really make a gift to Christ.

Inasmuch as ye did it not

There is an Indian fable about a man who prayed to be lifted out of hell to heaven. A huge carrot was let down from heaven and the man in hell grasped its leaves. As he began to rise toward heaven other men in torment seized his feet until there began to be a long chain of souls. Fearing that the leaves of the carrot might break under this weight, the man holding the carrot tried to kick off those who clung to him. Instantly the tough leaves tore loose like tissue paper, and everybody dropped back into hell. This tale might have been a parable of Jesus, only he would have it happening on this earth instead of in hell.

Suppose Jesus had said: "I will not receive you into heaven at all unless you have done your best to bring everybody else to me." Would that not give us worry? Well, that is exactly what he meant when he said: "Inasmuch as ye did it not to one of the least of these, ye did it not to me."

We for our age stand where Jesus stood for his age—midway between God and lost men. It is a terrifying thought. We dare kick nobody down. We must reach one hand up and one hand down as he did. "He that findeth his life shall lose it: and he that loseth his life for my sake shall find it." He that loseth his life saving other lives for Christ's sake shall find it.

Loving in spite of

The acid test of Christlikeness is what we do when we encounter unattractive or repulsive people. The natural man allows himself to be moved by winsome personalities; he is neutral or even antagonistic toward those who are without charm or appeal. For example, tattered clothes and wretched homes, illiteracy or the habitual use of incorrect English, lack of manners, disagreeable voices, overtalkativeness, shyness, sadness, conceit, grumbling, silly attempts at humor, ugly faces, blindness in one or in both eyes, skin diseases, disfiguring scars on the face, halitosis, bad teeth, stupidity, palsy, offensive body odor, selfishness, an unsavory reputation, the use of profane or disgusting language, the color of a different race, the profession of a different religion—all these things may be listed among the possibilities that we may not like. It would be easy to extend the list.

As the spirit of Jesus permeates us, we shall be enabled to conquer one antipathy after another until at last nothing can separate us from anybody. Jesus and snobbery are as far apart as Heaven and Hell; indeed one makes heaven and the other makes hell. Yet religious people are tempted by their very love of beauty and virtue to be the most snobbish of all classes.

Even our enemies!

More difficult to love than any others are the people who will not love back, the people who persist in hating us and in trying to injure our reputations or our careers. By some intentional or unintentional insult we may have made them our enemies, or they may have developed a complex because they thought we were in the way of their ambitions. If we espouse any social reform we make enemies of those whose profits grow out of social evil. A man without enemies is a personality dud. "Woe unto you," said Jesus, "when all men shall speak well of you!" Jesus, the world's most wonderful friend maker, made enemies who crucified him after only three years of his public life. St. Paul's footsteps, from the beginning of his missionary career, were dogged by his own hostile countrymen. Yet not a word of resentment has found its way into his writings.

Although to love unreasonable and unforgiving enemies is of all things most difficult, Jesus is adamant in demanding that we do it. His own life was perfect in forgiveness from beginning to end. When Judas led a mob to betray him, his only words were, "Friend, betrayest thou the Son of man with a kiss." On the cross he cried: "Father, forgive them; for they know not what they do."

To be close friends of Christ, we must pass even this test. These are his own words: "Ye have heard that it hath been said, Thou shalt love thy neighbor, and hate thine enemy. But I say unto you, Love your enemies, bless them that curse you, do good to them that hate you, and pray for them which despitefully use you... that ye may be the children of your Father which is in heaven: for he maketh the sun to rise on the evil and on the good, and sendeth rain on the just and on the unjust.... If ye forgive men their trespasses, your heavenly Father will also forgive you: but if ye forgive not men their trespasses, neither will your Father forgive your trespasses.... Ye have heard that it hath been said, An eye for an eye, and a tooth for a tooth: but I say unto you, that ye resist not him that is evil: but whosoever shall smite thee on thy right cheek, turn to him the other also. And if any man will sue thee at law, and take away thy coat, let him have thy cloke also.

"If ye love them which love you, what reward have ye?... If ye salute your brethren only, what do ye more than others?... Be ye therefore perfect, even as your Father which is in heaven is perfect."

If he asked us to be perfect in judgment or power or physical appearance or memory, we should be in despair; but he says, "Be perfect in love, love without boundaries, reaching around the whole world like a perfect circle, perfect in impartiality, perfect in loving those who do not love us." He proved, as Paul proved, that this kind of perfection is altogether possible. Edwin Markham captured Christ's idea in this charming verse:

> He drew a circle which left me out,
> Heretic, rebel, a thing to flout.
> But love and I had the wit to win,
> We drew a circle that took him in.

There have always been two ways of disposing of enemies. One is to get them out of the way by killing them or imprisoning them, or by moving so far away we could never again see them. The other way, which only the very wise understand, is to treat them with such unexpected kindliness that they are at last won over as friends. This is the way of Jesus.

Leading others to our friend

No individual is an absolute terminal of the love of Jesus. He reaches through us toward others. Indeed he is not satisfied with us until he has made us as eager to reach out and help others as he himself is to reach them. When a piece of iron touches a magnet the iron itself becomes a magnet. This is what happens to us when we touch Jesus—we begin to draw men toward him.

The simple program of Christ for winning the whole world is to make each person he touches magnetic enough with love to draw others. This "each-one-catch-one" endless chain, geometrical progression of love would, he believed, at last draw all men into his happy circle.

The thing he has been planning for each of us is to lift us to the point where we, like himself, will find all our joy in saving other people. We are Christlike just in proportion as we possess that passion for souls. It has often been said that we cannot keep Jesus unless we give him away. The truth is, we do not have Jesus at all unless we try to give him away.

Since the one most priceless blessing for everybody in the world would be the friendship of Jesus, the chief occupation of life ought to be to show others how to be his friend. "Follow me, and I will make you fishers of men," he says to all of us. We need to become specialists in witnessing to the friendship of Jesus. If we are to become experts we must study the art of witnessing and practice with the same persistency that a great musician follows in practicing his art.

Selling such a wonderful thing as the friendship of Christ utilizes the same principles as salesmanship in general. One must know the interests of the man one seeks to persuade, and build on them. One must recognize the crucial moment and seize it. Dr. John R. Mott has been called "the master of opportunity." The Greeks had a statue with a forelock but no hair on the back of its head; underneath were the words "I am opportunity. You must grasp me by the forelock, for no man ever seizes me from behind." The first principle in working for Christ is not to allow any opening for witnessing to slip out of one's grasp.

During his incredibly fruitful life. St. Paul said very little about anything excepting his own experience of Jesus. He did not even preach much theology. "I resolved... to forget everything but Jesus Christ and his crucifixion." This is still the best of all ways to witness. Share your own life experience of Christ, even though it may be a humiliating confession, if it will persuade another to surrender to Jesus.

If Jesus were to speak to you he would say: "I love all the people you will meet today. I love them all and will not let them go. I am striving to be their Saviour and Friend. I am depending on you to help me. How shall I reach them but through your willing arm? Who will plead with them but through your willing tongue?"

Love not in word only, but in deed

"It is not enough to be good, we must also be good for something, we must do good." European Christians regard these words as a typical American overemphasis on "activism," yet Jesus himself gave this emphasis. Time after time he repeated: "Not every one that saith unto me Lord, shall enter into the kingdom of heaven; but he that doeth the will of my Father."

Jesus meant this in a positive sense. He meant far more than: "You must not break God's commands. You must not sin." Of course you must not sin, but Jesus had more than this in mind. "Doing the will of God" for Jesus himself was hearing every whisper of God and obeying instantly. "I cannot do anything, unless I see the Father doing it. Whatever the Father does, the Son does." And that is what Jesus meant for us—minute by minute we are to do work for God, just as he did. To the man who is good for nothing in God's work, come these terrible words: "Thou wicked servant... Even that he hath shall be taken away from him."

When we set forth on a high spiritual adventure such as these pages describe, we shall need this warning. We are all tempted to stay away from those who are slow to understand, and to enjoy the friendship of Jesus among kindred spirits who sympathize and who stimulate us. We give up too easily when we see a blank stare or an impatient gesture. We hide too eagerly behind the verse: "Neither cast ye your pearls before swine." Or perhaps we tell ourselves: "I must drink deeper of this water of life, explore further in this glorious universe of the spirit, before I am ready to give anything to others. For one can only help others when one is full." This is the exact opposite of the truth; it is indeed self-deception.

We cannot keep Christ unless we give him away. Spiritual life is like electricity. No current passes through unless the wire is connected at the sending end as well as the receiving end. Christ's way for us is first to get a spiritual truth, and then to give it away. He told all his Father said to him as fast as he heard it if he could find hearers who would comprehend. The educational principle. "No impression without expression," applies to us today in our spiritual lives.

What did Jesus mean by "doing the will of my Father?" It is meeting needs as we find them, especially spiritual needs. Perhaps it will mean for you what it did for C. F. Andrews, seeking the world over for man's worst need, and going there to let Jesus use you as a healing instrument. This is what it means to missionaries. Or it may mean staying where you are and doing your best there. It is learning to hear God and obeying instantly and with zest.

We must habitually assume that every person we meet has been thrown in our way by Christ, who expects us to do something important for the man, or with him, or perhaps to learn something from him. In other words we must refuse to believe that any meeting is a "chance" meeting; we must see Christ at work in every one. Our problem will then be to find what the real need is.

Healing the soul

If a man asks for money, we shall do what we can for that need, but behind the need which he thinks he has there is always a deeper need which we know he has. This deeper need is for him to know Christ and to love him as we do. All our efforts to help people without giving them Christ are like putting salve on sores only to find more sores tomorrow. The disease must be taken out of the blood, or it is not really cured. Jesus not only healed bodies, but he said to those who were healed, "Sin no more." Our clear program for service is: Do everything you can to help any need which people may have. But keep constantly in mind that the one supreme need is to find a way to tie everybody to Jesus Christ. If Christ is to get men, he must reach out and grasp them through your hand, voice, eye, smile. You are the body of Christ in reaching lost men. They must have your friendship, and you must win theirs, before they will become friends of Christ. It is therefore vital that while we give a gift we also give ourselves. James Russell Lowell, in "The Vision of Sir Launfal," makes Christ utter:

> Who gives himself with his gift feeds three,
> Himself, his hungering neighbor, and Me.

To the secret place I go

One of the most puzzling problems an earnest Christian worker has to solve is just how much time he must devote to the games, pleasures, and small talk of those he seeks to win. Unless he puts his heart into these things that others enjoy, he will be a rather poor companion. If he does give them his whole heart, he may grow so engrossed in these pleasures that he will lose something of his passion for Christ. His companions will have dragged him to their level of thinking, instead of being lifted to his. Have you never seen a Y.M.C.A. man who lost the keen edge of his passion for Christ and began to regard recreation as the end which he serves?

Every social contact is a struggle not to lose what we have of Christ but to help others gain it too. A violinist must have a tuning fork or a piano to help him to strike the right pitch. Our task of keeping in tune with Christ when others are so tragically out of tune is harder than that of a musician seeking his pitch.

We must alternate between giving what we have and retreating to be refilled. Jesus himself felt the world sapping his spiritual vitality and habitually escaped from the multitude to some lonely place to pray. We shall be useful spiritually, only if we have a secret place to which we can run frequently for prayer. There we shall be recharged like a battery that has run down; and there we shall receive our instructions from him. We shall stay until he tells us where to go, and the moment we receive his orders clearly we shall issue forth to do our deed.

How we judge ourselves

All the following quotations from Jesus are different ways of saying the same thing: that God allows us to pass judgment upon ourselves. We shall be our own judges on the judgment day. We pass this judgment not with words, but by our treatment of other people. "With what measure ye mete, it shall be measured to you again." Nothing could be clearer, nothing more just.

"Blessed are the merciful: for they shall obtain mercy."

"Forgive us our debts, as we forgive our debtors."

"If you forgive others when they offend you, your heavenly Father will forgive you too. But if you do not forgive others when they offend you, your heavenly Father will not forgive you for your offenses.

"Come, you whom my Father has blessed, take possession of the kingdom... For when I was hungry, you gave me food... In so far as you did it to one of the humblest of these brothers, you did it unto me... Begone, you accursed people, to the everlasting fire... For when I was hungry, you gave me nothing to eat... In so far as you failed to do it for one of these people who are humblest, you failed to do it for me."

"Judge not, that ye be not judged. For with what judgment ye judge, ye shall be judged."

"Then his lord said unto him, O thou wicked servant, I forgave thee all that debt, because thou desiredst me shouldst not thou also have had compassion on thy fellow servant, even as I had pity on thee? And his lord was wroth, and delivered him to the tormentors... So likewise shall my heavenly Father do also unto you, if ye forgive not every one his brother."

"Whoso shall receive one such little child in my name receiveth me. But whoso shall offend one of these little ones which believe in me, it were better for him that a millstone were hanged about his neck, and that he were drowned in the depth of the sea."

"Alas for you, you hypocritical scribes and pharisees, for you pay tithes... and you have let the weightier matters of the Law go—justice, mercy, and integrity."

Shakespeare puts in the mouth of Macbeth these famous words: "This even-handed justice commends the ingredients of our poisoned chalice to our own lips... That we but teach bloody instructions, which, being taught, return to plague the inventor." That is the terrifying side of God's justice. Even if we did not believe in God, we could see that this, in the long run, is true of life. The gunman finally is shot and killed. The thief is betrayed by another thief. The gambler is swindled by another gambler. In the world of nature you ultimately get what you give. Be selfish once and others will treat you like a selfish man the next time. Be snobbish and you are rewarded by glances of loathing.

God's wrath against wrongs done by one man toward another and against neglect of one for another is so strong because God loves everybody. If his love were partial he could forget the neglected little sufferers as we usually do. But his love for all is intense. So his hatred of oppression is intense. Besides this, ill treatment and hatred are directly against his world plan. He is engaged in preparing children for his heaven, and the first law of heaven is limitless thoughtfulness of each for all. That is what makes heaven heavenly. Any lack of love and any symptom of hatred is an assault against the heavenliness of heaven, so God hates it with perfect intolerance.

Working With Him

We pay for the rich friendship of Jesus by doing with him what he is doing, helping him work, sharing his interests, going where he goes. All of us have acquaintances who suddenly become amiable and call us "dear friend" when they want to sell us insurance or an automobile, or stock certificates; but their words sound hollow, for they are not in the least interested in the things which interest us. They share neither our religion, nor our reading, nor our friends, nor our social efforts, nor our hopes. We shake hands with these "friends," listen to their persuasive sales talks, say "No, thank you." We know they are not interested in us, but only in what they can get out of us. That is a very thin and sickly type of friendship. Friends cannot be intimate and constant until they have something in common, until they are doing something important together. Nobody who is merely using Jesus for what he can get out of them (even if what he seeks is eternal life), really understands the friendship of Christ.

Roman Catholic writers discuss at length what they call "spiritual dryness," when Christ seems to have withdrawn himself, and heaven seems not to hear prayer. All prayerful Christians have this same experience at times. The usual explanation is that God tests our faith and perseverance, trying whether we will be faithful in our prayers even when he seems to have withdrawn. This is probably one explanation.

But there is often another, as one can prove by a simple experiment. "Follow me," says Jesus, as he goes on ahead of us to serve some tragic need. But often we drop far behind, or go off in some barren corner alone, while Jesus is hard at work "where cross the crowded ways of life." If our prayer is attended by spiritual dryness we may well ask ourselves whether he has gone ahead and is calling us to work rather than to pray at that moment. Let us go out and help some needy person, and suddenly we shall find Christ by our side, because we have caught up with him.

If we perform some act of kindness, it is often astonishing how quickly the sense of joy and of assurance that he is with us begins to flood our hearts. Many of us have tried the following experiments when our prayers were "dry," and can testify with confidence that they work:

1. Visit a sick person and pray by his bedside. Note the sense of pure joy mixed with the pain of pity that fills your soul. When you feel both joy and anguish at the same moment you understand how Christ feels. It is then that you are most like Christ and that you invariably feel his presence.

2. Try to pray with the poorest people in the slums of your city and to help them until it hurts your pocketbook. You will sense that Unseen Presence beside you, smiling at your deeds of mercy.

3. Go to a prison. Listen to the stories of prisoners, comfort or help them, and tell them the love of Christ. His spirit fills the very prison, and inspires you with the words you should utter.

4. Select an article of clothing which you value highly and give it to some needy person who cannot repay you. You will hear a whisper of approval and you will know that Christ is smiling.

5. Comfort somebody who has just lost a loved one. Tell him the consoling promise of Jesus Christ, "I go to prepare a place for you." Note the strange happiness which comes to you in the very midst of tragedy.

6. Sacrifice all the plans that you have cherished for a successful life, and yield yourself to the cause of bringing Christ into men's lives. Note how his hand seems to be on your shoulder, and how elation floods your heart as you say farewell to earthly ambitions.

7. If you are seated in a crowded bus, offer your seat to a woman, or to an old person, or to one weaker than yourself, and remain standing in an uncomfortable position for a half hour. Even for that trifling courtesy Christ fills your heart with a quiet happiness.

8. Go out of your way to greet strangers, ignore the custom of formal introduction, and help them. Jesus, who is close by, will whisper, "I was a stranger, and ye took me in."

9. Give yourself unhurriedly to be helpful to a child, in some matter which seems important to him.

10. Walk down the street looking for the most unattractive and lonesome person you can find. Humble yourself to chat on wholly equal terms with that person, being extremely careful not to seem condescending. Seek a way to help him out of his sense of friendliness. Suddenly you will know that Jesus is there eager to work for him through you.

11. An experiment which every Christian ought to try is to witness for Christ when he finds it very difficult to witness, and when he does not feel like witnessing.

12. Lead a drunkard home by the arm, feed and comfort him, pray with him, and talk to him about Christ.

Better than books or sermons these experiments demonstrate that there is profound truth in the twenty-fifth chapter of Matthew: "In so far as you did it to one of the humblest of these brothers of mine, you did it to me."

You will discover through these experiments this law of Christ's companionship: We are with him when we face discomfort, unpleasantness, and pain in order to help others. We lose him the moment we try to save ourselves and neglect others. "Whosoever does not bear his cross... cannot be my disciple." "The peace that passeth all understanding" is reserved as a special favor for those who pass through great tribulations or run some great risk for other people. Suffer deeply in sympathy with others and lo, Christ is there!

There are countless similar experiments which people may make in finding the presence of Christ. They all point in the same direction. The thrill in our hearts after we make any sacrifice for others tells us that we have also thrilled the heart of Christ. On the other hand, our sense of self-condemnation when we refuse to help others reflects the disappointment that is in Christ's heart.

Slaves of environment

The hardest thing in the world is to see truly, when the vision of all the people about us is distorted. Entire nations are caught in sinful practices and prejudices which they boast of as though they were virtues. When we refuse to assist real need, we call our refusal "thrift," instead of selfishness. When we mistreat the negroes we are preserving our "racial purity" instead of snobbery.

Nobody has a message for his nation unless he sees more truly than those about him and has torn free from their prejudices. The great social sins are not clearly labeled; they are camouflaged. If we have a hundred shades of color to detect, we shall go wrong unless we have a color card with which to compare them. Christ is our color card, When we spend enough time with Christ alone, these sinful attitudes which we all share without realizing it begin to appear in their true guise.

William James pointed out one of our weaknesses—susceptibility to suggestion. We can hardly prevent ourselves from believing anything, however false or wrong, if we hear it repeated often enough. So current gossip, heard time after time, becomes fixed conviction.

Unfortunately we are all to some degree slaves of our environment. We unconsciously believe what our neighbors and our social set believe, and we doubt what they doubt. The only way to save ourselves from a downward drag is to lift the neighborhood and the social set to a higher level. We might of course move to another neighborhood which would uplift us, and many people have done so. But to do this is the exact opposite of Jesus' way. His practice was to go where he was needed most, and begin to try to transform the neighborhood. If we are his fellow workers we will do as he would do.

We need not wait even one hour to make some changes which are at this instant wholly within our power. For example, we can begin inside our own room. We may glance at our walls and ask whether the message they give us is inspiring. If our favorite picture of Christ does not flash before our eyes we can give our walls far richer meaning by hanging it there; we can also place his picture under the glass on our desk. The experience of many of us has been that a picture of Christ looking directly at us literally transforms our thoughts and our deeds for the whole day. On the other hand, if any pictures or periodicals drag out a train of evil ideas, whether of malice or prejudice or lasciviousness, and thus hour after hour continue to pour suggestion of evil into our minds, they have no place in the same room with us and Christ.

A Christian traveling man once confessed to me that in his early years on the road he had to encounter many difficulties and temptations in hotels. Finally he began to set up a row of pictures of Christ on his table as soon as he engaged his hotel room. Soon he discovered that there were no more tempters to lead him astray, while hotel employees and others seemed hungry to hear him speak of Christ.

Many a picture frame which has been entertaining bad company can be saved by replacing its contents with a scene from the life of Christ, where our eyes will meet it hourly. Our books should undergo the same careful censorship. Do their titles suggest Christ and lead us to speak to him? If not, they need to be changed. Books which suggest cynicism or hatred, or moral degradation must not be allowed to remain before our eyes—not even if they are "best sellers." The borders of our retinas catch words when we are not even aware that we see them. Not only can the portraits on our walls and the titles in our bookcases feed our souls all day but they can bless visitors who enter our rooms. Everybody in our home can be subjected at every glance to continuous uplifting suggestions.

Community service

A second step in making our environment Christlike is to persuade our neighbors to study the community needs with us, and to help them organize as rapidly as possible for this service. Usually the church is the natural place for such planning. The Young People's Christian Endeavor is often hungering for plans to serve. Youth loves crusades, and is much more eager for change than are most adults. We will find these young people cooperative in surveying the community and drawing up their plans for making it an ideal neighborhood. A small determined group hammering away at a few projects until the community is won over, and then crusading for a few other projects in the same manner, will gradually gather a powerful minority into the campaign for a Christlike community.

What social improvements ought to be undertaken is a question which we need not discuss here. Countless books and pamphlets are available on the subject. The group should study some of these, asking which proposals are in line with Christ's "Kingdom of God" purpose, and which ones need to be accomplished in our community.

One common disease of churches should be guarded against—finding an interesting answer and doing nothing about it. Many "social action" study-groups think that they have finished their task as soon as they have discovered what ought to be done by other people, by the President of the United States or by Congress or by Labor or even by the churches and schools. To such study-groups the term "social action" means simply the development of a feeling of horror at the mistakes or the wickedness of others. But this is not "action" until we have done more than thinking. The Quakers have the correct idea of it; when they encounter wretchedness or wrong of any kind they are not happy until they have done what they can to correct it. Social action is neither social nor action until we have found what we can do and have tried to do what we could.

Another common weakness comes from deciding that we are helpless. "With God nothing ever is impossible." If a wrong cries to be righted, and a courageous little group undertakes what seems impossible, friends often begin to appear from unexpected directions, and we soon feel sure God is working miracles.

Charmed circles

Traveling about the world one finds thousands of blessed communities, groups of Christlike people who make one realize what heaven is like. Many Oxford Groups are among these. Christian social centers and Ashrams are often such places. To have lived in the Ashram of Stanley Jones in India, or with Kagawa in Japan, or with Roswell Bates in the slums of New York, or to follow the Salvation Army through the streets of London, or to have lived under the charm of Washington Gladden or the chain of Mission Assemblies in Florida or with the Kellersbergers in the Congo, to visit Glen Clark in the Camp Farthest Out where the atmosphere of love seems to blow in from heaven—this is to have had a foretaste of Paradise.

Mission compounds at their best are of this character. The home for retired missionaries at Claremont, California, is accurately named "Heaven Below," for it is fragrant with heavenly people. Multitudes of church groups of all persuasions form heavens on earth. Many convents and monasteries belong to this class of charmed circles. Hundreds of thousands and probably millions of homes contain such heaven-born groups. They are often to be found among Christian students in schools. Young people's conferences often become temporary heavens. Sunday School Conventions not infrequently reach that high spiritual level. Quaker working camps may be foretastes of paradise.

Evangelistic campaigns often terminate in melting the hearts of those present into a sense of joyous oneness. Eucharistic Congresses give those present a sense of divine blessedness. Prayer meetings at their best and preaching services at their best fuse the hearts of those present so that they feel a new affection for one another. The list is simply endless, of communities which are miniature heavens of beautiful saints. These Christian circles include incomparably the most thrilling people in the world. From the Quaker meeting to the Eucharistic Congress, the same precious experience catches every heart. It is the sense of all present that Christ is there in their midst, and that he is binding their hearts together in a wonderful heavenly love.

How to build heavens

These heavenly experiences, which every Christian has had, can be captured and become a daily possession in our own social group; but there are conditions which must be fulfilled, if we wish to form such a circle:

1. There must be at least one (better, two or more), determined to pay the price of long, earnest, unselfish prayer and preparation for each group gathering. That leader must take time from other occupations to develop fellowship alone with Christ for hours, loving him, looking at him, listening to him, as Mary did when he visited her home in Bethany.

2. There must be regular and frequent occasions when friends pray together. The wise old Catholic Church is right in having mass in the church every morning. Prayers both morning and evening are not too much. Most Protestants do not meet often enough to feed their souls. If they acquire the habit of gathering once or twice a day they will soon feel as hungry if they go a day without these gatherings as though they had missed their dinner.

It is a mistake to strive for large numbers. To warm the heart of a crowd toward Christ is impossible unless the gathering contains a large majority of devout followers of Jesus. Small groups are usually more to be desired than large groups, for each individual feels free to express his personal views.

One can begin such a blessed community anywhere if one has the patience and consecration. Indeed it will emerge almost spontaneously if one or two people begin to give Jesus many hours a week in cultivating his friendship. Other people will unconsciously catch the spiritual fragrance of Jesus after a while, and will grow into his kindliness. There is no more delightful adventure than to set out deliberately to create a small sector of heaven in one's home or social circle, and then to observe the gradual transformation in one selfish person after another. There is ecstasy in watching people actually becoming sons of God.

So if you do not happen to have a charmed circle in your community, make it. By starting a heavenly circle around yourself you can render the mightiest service anybody ever performs for the world. That is how we shall transform the world—by founding spiritual oases in the world's spiritual desert.

Helping Christ in your church

Every man's experience proves that if we do not meet with kindred spirits in worship our own religion becomes pale and sickly. We need to associate with a church or group which keeps the fires of the Holy Spirit burning. How much would we know about Jesus Christ without the teaching and influence of the Church? We must answer, "Almost nothing." The church is the central spiritual fire for the community, and also for each of us.

We must not demand eloquent sermons. It is enough that we hear the gospel, and feel the presence of the Holy Spirit. We can help the service mightily by our own prayers. If we do not receive anything at all from preachers or choir, that in itself is sufficient reason why we need to pray for the church. So there is always one of two reasons why you go to church, to any church. Either that church has what you need, or you have what it needs. In an ideal situation both are true. Your prayer and your eager cooperation will set an example to the other members of the congregation. Their rising zeal and devotion will react upon you.

A deeply earnest and prayerful person can set any church in the world on fire within a few months. It requires only one who has spent so much time in the company of Christ that his very presence speaks louder than words. Almost all of us have seen such people. Alas for anyone who has not! It is possible for every person to possess that subtle charm. Indeed it is inevitable, providing one pays the price; it is a matter of cause and effect. Give to Christ hours and days and weeks of time and obedience, and the same thing will be said of you that was said of the wonder-working early apostles, who, though ignorant men, were so full of the Holy Spirit: "They took knowledge of them that they had been with Jesus."

If we go to the church determined to bring to it at least as much as we receive, we shall receive far more than we give. Indeed, nobody ever really gains anything from the church, until he first pours his best love and prayer and service into it. We make our environment even in church, if we fix our eyes upon Jesus. One listener in prayer helps the service far more than an "intellectual" sermon.

If you wish to try an experiment some Sunday, pray from three o'clock in the morning until time for church, eating breakfast alone or not at all, then pray quietly all during the service. We who have tried it have found that the preacher seems to have new power drawn out of him, and that the church seems fragrant with the presence of Christ.

The Rewards of His Friendship

Although it is true that Christ requires total obedience, yet this obedience turns out, as Paul told the people of Galatia, to be perfect freedom. Indeed eager, glad obedience to duty is the only real liberty in this universe. When we love our Lord enough, we desire above all other things in the world to do what he desires us to do. Then we are free, for we are doing as we please. There is, it is true, a downward pull of desire to do wrong, but it is counterbalanced by the lift of love for him, so that the "resultant of forces" is upward. We have all seen man and wife or two lovers so deeply in love that their only thought was to please each other. They were not doing this because they were compelled to do so but because it was their free choice. When we love Christ like that, nothing matters but to please him. Then we have attained what Paul calls the "glorious liberty of the sons of God." When duty and desire are synchronized, that is freedom, and any other kind is nonsense. This is why Jesus says:

"If ye continue in my word, then are ye my disciples indeed; and ye shall know the truth, and the truth shall make you free." "Love, joy, peace, patience, kindness, goodness, faithfulness, gentleness, self-control—there is no law against such things." These are the things the lovers of Christ love because they love to love what he loves."

Bondage, on the other hand, means having an irrepressible desire to do what you know you ought not to do, what you know will harm you and others. The victim of the opium habit or the liquor habit or any other injurious habit is a slave, not a free man. "Let not sin therefore reign in your mortal body, that ye should obey it in the lusts thereof." But that is exactly what we cannot help doing until Christ comes and breaks the bondage of sin, and we are set free by the "expulsive power of a greater affection." "For the law of the Spirit of life in Christ Jesus hath made me free from the law of sin and death."

How Christ sublimates love

A visiting preacher at a high school convocation had two shocks, one before, and the other after, his sermon. Just before he spoke, two boys sang "The Girl of My Dreams," and when he had ended his sermon, two girls sang "I Am Hungry for Love." It happened that the preacher's sermon was also about love—the love of Christ. The minister and the boys and girls who sang had all responded to the instinct which tugs at human desire more than any other. All of them alike were indeed "hungry for love." This, next to hunger for food, the deepest and most insistent of our innate urges, is the best instinct we have, or the worst, depending upon where it finds its expression.

The fate of every man depends upon what he does with his love instinct. The repression of that instinct is impossible, for they who try to repress it in one direction find it breaking out in another. To leave it undirected is fatal. We must choose the channel through which it shall find a healthy outlet.

Downward there are channels through flesh, and upward there are channels into the world of spirit. If we do not plan at all, love is most likely to rush downward as water follows the law of gravitation, for the low lust of the flesh is its ancient river bed. They who follow this channel until it becomes love's chief expression sink back toward the condition of the brutes. We call them "degenerates." To waste the love instinct in flesh is not only wrong and low; it is tragically foolish. People who do so have bet their lives "on the wrong horse," for the flesh alone reaches its limit quickly and cloys or even disgusts. It is a blind alley and a short one. On the other hand, they who direct love's flow upward into spiritual channels find it driving them on to world service, to religious discovery, or to genius. Choosing a high channel for love is called "sublimation."

One of the chief functions of the religion of Jesus is to cut channels for love which will direct it into magnificent spiritual achievements. From earliest times a major task of the church was to help men repress the low and open the high sluices for love's flow. It would require pages to quote all the verses in the letters of Paul, Peter, James, and John where they warn us that "If you live under the control of the physical you will die, but if, by means of the Spirit, you put the body's doings to death, you will live." This is the theme of Romans, Chapters 6, 7, and 8.

The way to purify love and make it lift the soul constantly higher is to fall in love with Jesus, to lavish one's affections upon him as Mary Magdalene lavished her affections upon him when she knelt weeping at his feet and pouring costly perfumes on him. There need be no restraint with Christ. With the channels toward flesh and lust closed, love has nothing to fear but everything to gain by reaching upward as far as it can with utter abandon. If, as John declares, "God is love," we shall only understand the deepest urge in God's nature as we share those high levels of spiritual love with him. Walt Whitman's magnificent poem "Passage to India" fancies the soul soaring like a balloon into the infinite spaces:

> Sail forth—steer for the deep waters only,
> Reckless O soul, exploring, I with thee, and thou with me,
> For we are bound where mariner has not yet dared to go,
> And we will risk the ship, ourselves and all.

O my brave soul! O farther farther sail!
O daring joy, but safe! are they not all the seas of God?
O farther, farther, farther sail....

As filled with friendship, love complete,
The Elder Brother found,
The Younger melts in fondness in his arms.

There is a universe of the spirit to be discovered, reaching out beyond the galaxies—and it opens its welcoming arms to those who are so wise as to sublimate love.

People differ in their capacity for love. Some natures are cold as a mountain stream, some warm and irrepressible. It has often been noted that they who are tempted most by their hunger for love have the most wonderful mystic experiences with the love of Jesus when he captures them. Mary Magdalene, Peter, John, and Paul, St. Augustine, and John Wesley could understand Jesus best, because they themselves felt enormous longings to love. Let those who have struggled hardest and have perhaps fallen in their fight with the flesh take courage and seek Christ, for it is they whom he can use most wonderfully. Jesus found warmhearted sinners easier to save than men of cold-blooded "virtue."

He rescues us from morbid fixations

One of the commonest of all mental diseases is an unwholesome fixation, which fills the mind in spite of every effort to throw it out. Morbid ideas go round and round, becoming what is called "hysteria," deepening themselves in the mind and becoming ever more exaggerated. For example, a strained relationship between two persons of incompatible temperaments may develop into a strong dislike or even into violent hatred. Envy because of another's success and popularity often becomes an obsession. A great part of the world's trouble today comes from just such dislikes developing into blind hatred. This is, indeed, one of the chief causes of war. Irritation between the peoples of two nations is fanned by propaganda until it develops into a fixed and unreasonable hatred.

There are people who develop a dissatisfaction complex. Dissatisfied with what they have and with where they are, they are unable to get the things they would like to have, or to go to the places where they would like to go. So they ruin their happiness by grumbling about their fate. No one can achieve success or happiness until he learns to adjust himself contentedly to his environment. Paul said, "I have learned, in whatsoever state I am, therewith to be content."

Many people, having failed in some effort dear to their hearts, develop a defeatist complex, which paralyzes their courage and causes them to refuse even to try. They are whipped without a fight. This happens to many of the students who fail to pass grades in high schools and colleges. Our present system in colleges is doing a serious permanent injury to its victims, blasting their confidence almost as disastrously as a prison sentence kills the faith and confidence of convicts.

Or again, a married man or woman frequently develops an infatuation for one of the opposite sex and perhaps struggles against this disloyalty only to find it growing ever more irresistible until it ends in divorce or disgrace. It is this fixation that is leaving a trail of wrecked homes across the world.

There are many other situations in which people become enslaved to fixations, and spoil their happiness or their usefulness. How many people, for example, are slaves of fear!

The way to break free from a harmful fixation is to drive it out of the mind with a beneficial fixation, stronger, more fascinating, and more absorbing than the evil one, to employ "the expulsive power of a greater affection."

In all history nothing else ever known has been able to rescue people from disastrous fixations so well as can the strong intimate friendship of Jesus Christ. If you find yourself nursing a poisonous grudge or resentment at some imagined insult, you can master that damning idea by looking at a picture of Jesus, and repeating a score or a hundred times, with deep feeling, "Dear Christ, I love you, I love you...." You feel the hardness melting until at length your heart holds only love for everybody, even your enemies. If you are utterly discouraged with life and see no hope ahead, fix your eyes upon Jesus and tell him over and over again that you love him and will obey his whisper. Thousands of women, disappointed in love, have entered convents, and have traveled happily on the long narrow way that they believe will make them the brides of Christ. Everybody may seek an intimacy with Christ as close as that which those nuns are seeking. The expulsive power of infatuation for Christ can conquer any illicit infatuation which may have threatened married life. The worst fear complexes, fear of an enemy, fear of failure, fear of losing one's home or money, fear of making mistakes, fear of war, fear of disease and death—they all melt away when one acquires a deep affectionate faith in Jesus. "Perfect love," if it is love for Christ, "casteth out fear."

If you are caught in some harmful fixation you can break free from it by beginning four experiences with Christ: 1. By reading his life in the Gospels for hours at a time and by having a lovely picture of Christ near you, let him conquer your eye. 2. Let him conquer your ear by learning tender love songs about Christ and by listening to him while he whispers in your heart. 3. Serve: go out seeking some work of mercy which you can do with him, whispering to him about it while you work. 4. Witness! Tell all the loveliest things you know about Jesus to anybody who is willing to listen, realizing that the best way to feel anything deeply is to try to convince others. After you do these four things for a few weeks you will begin to realize by sweet experience that Jesus satisfies every longing the human heart ever knew.

Friendship with Christ builds character

One method of building character common in schools is to prepare a list of desirable qualities and ask students to check themselves by that list. The weakness of this process is that it intensifies self-centeredness. If students take the list too seriously and find themselves failing to live up to it, they develop a morbid sense of defeat. Such lists have exactly the same defect as Paul said the Mosaic law had. Either they are easy and therefore inadequate lists, or else they leave one with a keen awareness of moral failure.

We all have known pious people who made themselves unhappy by constant self-examination and penitence about their faults. Self-detraction of this kind is an inverted form of egotism. It does not fight the final and hardest of all battles, which is to kill self. St. John of the Cross says that after we have gone through the first dark night of the soul, killing the mortal and the venial sins, we still have a second and even darker night to go through while destroying self. Now introspection does not kill the self. It exaggerates the self. Down that road we end in that unlovely product: a self-centered man with "faultless" habits but without love, a Pharisee.

The queen of all virtues, the virtue which makes heaven heavenly, is to be a worthy member of a society of selves lost in love like the love of Christ. St. Paul says, "I will show you a more excellent way," and then gives us the most magnificent treatise on love in all literature. "If I have all other virtues," he declares, "and have not love, I am nothing." Probing inside ourselves for sins and weaknesses does not beget love of others, but only self-love.

The "more excellent way" is to fall in love intimately with Jesus. If we do that it will not be necessary for us to worry about our character. If we keep "looking unto Jesus," the change will take place of itself. Our line of action is simple—forget ourselves, let go, focus our attention upon Jesus, and trust everything to him. If we continue to admire him and to imitate him day by day, the change will take place inside us without introspection. Nathaniel Hawthorne has revealed this in that wonderful classic *The Great Stone Face*.

The youth Ernest gazed lovingly day after day at the beautiful stone face against the Vermont mountains until at last he himself caught the purity and serenity and nobility of that lovely visage.

One of the tremendous advantages of forgetting self and of looking away toward Christ is that one forgets to be afraid. One has no more fear of important people, no fear of crowds, no fear of being misunderstood or ridiculed, no fear of college professors, no fear of losing a position or a friend. If we are introverts a good half of our power is paralyzed by fear that we may fail. If we can be like the disciples at the transfiguration when "they saw Jesus only," we shall fear nothing. We shall know what he would like, and we shall plunge into his task, free from the hesitations and inhibitions which kill so many of our best ideas and sometimes make us trembling imbeciles. We shall not have the slightest fear before famous men or kings. That is what this consuming passion for Jesus did for two ignorant fishermen! "Now when they saw the boldness of Peter and John, and perceived that they were unlearned and ignorant men, they marvelled; and they took knowledge of them, that they had been with Jesus," (Acts 4:13)

When a new family enters a house, the furniture is replaced, the books on the shelves and the magazines on the table are different, the pictures on the walls change. The very atmosphere of the house bears a resemblance to the new occupants. So when Jesus enters to occupy a man's personality, the whole appearance begins to reveal his presence. It is always fascinating to search people's eyes and faces and words for the sure marks of his lovely touch. There is a simple humble honesty, a clear unshifting eye, a hard straight loyalty to all that is good; there is that strange, characteristically Christlike intolerance of all sin, combined with tenderness toward all sinners. There is deep pity for all who are in trouble of any kind, whether it be sickness, or poverty, or loneliness, or failure, or shattered nerves.

If we were perfectly Christlike we would search every face and look deep into every eye for signs of need that we could help. We would be enormously interested in people, and we would believe in them more than they believe in themselves. We would grip young boys and girls by the hand and persuade them not to sell themselves for twaddles. Like Jesus we would be a strong tonic, slapping discouraged men on the back, and helping them to see that life has barely begun, because eternity lies ahead! But all this Christlikeness comes to us as a direct result of friendship with Jesus. He gave power to his apostles and told them that they would do even greater things than he himself had done. Equally, in the measure of our friendship with him, he will do unto us.

His friendship gives power

Christ's friendship gives power. But this can be said only with strict reservations. Christ gives us power to carry out his purposes. He does not give us power to carry through our own schemes; those schemes which we had before we surrendered them all to him. We shall not get a sympathetic hearing from Jesus if we ask him to help our selfish ambitions. We are so full of selfish plans that to cut them all out is a major operation, and it will be attended by pain. But until we allow him to perform that operation we shall be weak.

Everything Jesus said proves that he expected his disciples to do "greater things" than he did. He expected all his miracles to be possible for them and more. Whatever they asked in his name, he declared, they should have if they were abiding in him. "Ask, and it shall be given you." Have faith, he told them, and the mountains will melt away.

This power he would give us only if we were safe with it! If Christ could trust us to use his power for wise and purely unselfish purposes, he would send it surging through us, not only willingly, but with tremendous eagerness. Christ needs powerful men today who will never use their power for self.

Yet, much as he needs us strong, he dare not make us strong. Our insane age is a vivid illustration of the fact that we are too heartless, too selfish, too small to be entrusted with extensive power. We learn to harness gasoline, and we use it to drive tanks of death. We learn to fly in the air, and we drop fire to burn whole nations and to drive other people mad with horror and hate. We speak by radio around the world, and we make the ether hideous with lies and propaganda and blind prejudice. With the power we already have, it is a question whether in our selfishness we may not destroy our civilization. God save us from harnessing the awful power stored in atoms until we can safely be entrusted with power!

But when saintly men catch from Jesus the spirit of selfless complete love, there comes an ever-rising power. Wonderful people scattered here and there around the world are living embodiments of this immense soul force now. Some heal physical diseases, some diseases of the soul, and some diseases of society. They whisper their questions to their unseen Companion, and he tells them what to do.

When one is in complete harmony with God's will, God works ahead, preparing the way. When we try experiments in complete surrender, we are overwhelmingly convinced by experience. Coincidences pile upon one another, which we never tell to others for fear of being called superstitious, but which we know are from God.

Complete surrender was the secret of Jesus himself. He said: "He who has sent me is with me; he has not left me alone, for I always do what pleases him." That is why God never left him alone—because he always did what pleased God. In the very next breath Jesus said: "If you abide by what I teach, you are really disciples of mine, and you will know the truth and the truth will set you free."

We need look no further for the secret of power. Jesus has told us clearly and repeatedly that his secret is perfect obedience always. And until we have tried that, we do not, of course, know what power he can pour through us: like an electric arc light melting steel! The fifteenth chapter of John is, I believe, the world's most marvelous secret. "If you abide in me"—if you obey every moment—"you shall ask what you will and it shall be done."

He reveals to us our real self

Every young man and woman asks such questions as: "What am I good for?" "What work shall I do in the world?" "What profession shall I follow?" "What service can I render to humanity?" and "Why am I alive?"

If we accept the Mastership of Jesus, he answers these questions. All of us came into the world to do some particular thing. We shall do that thing if we allow him to tell us what it is. If we miss his plan, our life will be a failure in his eyes. But we shall not miss it if we listen constantly, for he knows how to reveal it.

It is interesting to observe how sure Jesus was of himself and of his destiny. At twelve years of age he was speaking of God as "my Father." We have already seen how sure he was that God told him what to do. It is true that Jesus had to fight against doubt, and even more against his own will. In the wilderness temptations, God's will clashed with Jesus' human inclinations. The habits of a thousand generations cried out for him to use his vast powers for self-satisfactions, to fill his stomach, to win applause, to achieve easy domination of the world. The path which God pointed out before him was a tragic path of renunciation and was, with terrifying vividness, prophesied in Isaiah 53. All the human nature in him cried out to use his powers as other people use their powers, for at least a little self-gratification, or at very least for a little comfort. But he would not even make miraculous bread for himself, though he did that very thing later for nine thousand others.

When Jesus gets inside us he leads us to a conviction about our destiny. He will become our destiny. He was the Son of God, and he had a mission in the world, but so are we sons of God, and so have we missions in the world. We have learned that from him. He had to bear a cross. He convinces us that we also have to bear our cross. He came "to set at liberty them that were bruised" by being "bruised for our iniquities," and he convinces us that we also can only set at liberty them that are bruised, by being willing to be bruised for other men's iniquities.

But what looks like sacrifice turns out after all to be a sledge hammer crashing into a vein of gold. We find that we have let loose the little in order to grasp the big.

Jesus told us, "Lay up for yourselves treasures in heaven." His riches are spiritual. They are inexhaustible because the mind and the heart of Jesus are infinite. With Jesus you burst out into limitless glories of exciting discovery, like looking through a huge telescope and viewing stars and universes. No matter how intimate our friendship with Jesus becomes, there are always rich experiences farther ahead than the eye can reach. Perhaps none of us knows one percent of the glories that have come to Christ's most faithful lovers, because we are not yet able to receive them. But we may have one hundred percent if we try, because Christ is one hundred percent. Only our littleness limits his fullness.

Most of us have seen young men and women, captured by the Master, sweep onward to lives of incredible miracle-working—men like J. R. Mott, E. S. Jones, or Kagawa. If heaven is to be our opportunity to plumb all the high reaches of friendship with Christ and to meet the innumerable host of transformed loving brothers and sisters he is gathering about him, that is exciting! We need eternity for it.

Life, more abundantly

One of the chief rewards of the friendship of Jesus is life, as the Bible constantly reiterates. "You must think of yourselves as dead to sin but alive to God, through union with Christ Jesus." "And this is life eternal, that they might know thee, the only true God, and Jesus Christ, whom thou hast sent."

When a lawyer wanted to know what to do to "inherit eternal life," Jesus' answer contained a significant omission—he left out the word "eternal." The lawyer had asked:

"Master, what shall I do to inherit eternal life?"

Jesus replied: "What is written in the law? How readest thou?"

The lawyer quoted: "Thou shalt love the Lord thy God with all thy heart, and with all thy soul, and with all thy strength, and with all thy mind; and thy neighbor as thyself."

Jesus said: "Thou hast answered right: this do, and thou shalt live." He did not say, "Thou shalt have eternal life," for Jesus did not think the lawyer had ever been alive. Jesus meant, "This do and thou shalt begin to live." That existence which the lawyer called "life" was not in Jesus' opinion worth continuing forever, neither for himself, nor for God. When Nicodemus came to talk one night, Jesus said: "Ye must be born again.... Except a man be born again he cannot enter into the kingdom of God." "I am come," said Jesus at another time, "that they might have life, and... have it more abundantly."

As men grow ill or old their problem is that of Job: "If a man die, shall he live again?" But Jesus was not interested in the length of life so much as he was in the richness and loftiness of life. If it were worthy of eternity God could easily save it. But to make it worthy has always been God's heartache—for men must be willing.

We have all heard some man, distressed by the emptiness of his life and driven by some monotonous and distasteful labor, or perhaps without friends or hope, say in despair, "This is not living; this is only existing." Those words express the vast difference between the life lived richly in the warm friendship of Jesus and the life spent without his friendship. Jesus is ushering those who will follow to a higher plateau of living. We can see this most easily by taking our viewpoint from the bottom, the mineral kingdom. Minerals exist. They do not live, for they have neither growth, feeling, nor motion. Vegetables, in the next stage of life, grow and reproduce; but they cannot move. Next is the animal kingdom, wherein the brutes feel and move; but, as Tennyson tells us, "they nourish a blind life within the brain." Then there is Man, who not only feels but thinks, and has the power of free will and self-determination. But there is a further stage beyond the natural level of Man. It is the stage which we call the spiritual world, which Man in his natural state is incapable of seeing. Only after his second birth in Christ is he able to see with the eyes of the soul the vast spiritual universe to which Christ would lead him. Only then can he hear the rhapsodies of heaven. Only then has his soul found eternal life.

The key which opens the door to this higher life, says Jesus, is "love." This do and thou shalt live, love God and man. How big is a man's life? It is as big as his love. A miser who, like Silas Marner, loves only his money, is as big as his money bag. A woman who loves her children and her husband is as big as her family. The man who lives and dies for his country is as big as his country. The man who loves Christ and his great dream for the oncoming kingdom becomes as big as the Lord's Prayer, as big as the world. He begins to own the world. What we love we possess, and there is no other true possession. No man owns a wife until he loves her. This is the reason for the strange words of Jesus: "Verily I say unto you, there is no man that hath left house, or brethren, or sisters, or father, or mother, or wife, or children, or lands, for my sake, and the gospel's, but he shall receive an hundredfold now in this time, houses and brethren, and sisters, and mothers, and children, and lands, with persecutions; and in the world to come eternal life." We own the world if our love is big enough to reach round it.

Christ's Friendship Is Its Own Reward

If we become infatuated with some friend his presence is more precious to us than any gift he can make. If we had to choose between gift and friend we should say, "Keep the gift and give me yourself." This is supremely true of Jesus. His presence, his whisper of love in our inner hearts, is worth more than anything he could do for us.

Fanny Crosby knew well that Christ himself is the supreme reward when she sang:

> Close to thee, close to thee, close to thee,
> Gladly will I toil and suffer,
> Only let me walk with thee.

It is impossible to tell anybody what these words mean to this blind singer until he has himself felt the pang of intense love for Christ, and then no words in any language can do justice to his experience.

Paul sometimes became entangled in his titanic ideas. The truth is, he was trying to express what was beyond any vocabulary. Read the following phrases from Ephesians 3:17 ff., and imagine the emotion behind them:

"Let Christ in his love make his home in your hearts... So that you... may grasp what breadth, length, height, and depth mean, and understand Christ's love, so far beyond our understanding, so that you may be filled with the very fulness of God. To him who by the exertion of his power within us can do unutterably more than all we ask or imagine, be glory..." "For the sake of Christ I have come to count my former gains as loss. Why, I count everything, and think it rubbish, in order to gain Christ and... be united to him... I want to know him in the power of resurrection, and to share his sufferings and even his death... because I have been captured by Jesus Christ."

It was this marvelous experience that made Paul afraid of nobody, made him desire nothing save to have and to share Christ. A captive in ecstasy! That is why his words tumbled all over the page!

He wants to draw you closer

The friendship of Jesus grows closer as we become more loyal and dependable. We are always the doubtful factor, the "variable function"—to use a mathematical term. He cannot depend upon us. In proportion as we are selfish and untrustworthy, we are like thieves who think everybody is dishonest, and so will not trust even honest men. Because experience and practice teach us not to trust anybody too far we do not entirely trust Christ, although we say he is trustworthy. To be sure we sing, "I'll go where you want me to go, dear Lord," and yet we want to weigh his orders carefully and count the cost. Many of us will confess that all our lives we have been afraid God might ask us to go where we did not want to go, to suffer in a way we did not choose, or to give up some things we like to do. We dare not "let go and let God."

This is why we hold Christ at arm's length while he forever seeks to pull us closer. No song ever pleased him more than that of blind Fanny Crosby:

> Draw me nearer, nearer, blessed Lord,
> To the cross where thou hast died,
> Draw me nearer, nearer, nearer, blessed Lord,
> To thy precious, bleeding side.

Because Fanny Crosby was blind she had fewer of earth's pleasures than the rest of us. She was the opposite of the rich youth who could not give up his wealth to follow Christ. Her misfortune was her good fortune—as all misfortune can become, if it draws us nearer to his precious side. If Christ will save our soul he must tear from us the comforts, the social advantages, the powers we possess, even health itself, until at last we are willing to let go what remains, and can say:

> Nearer, my God, to thee, nearer to thee!
> E'en though it be a cross that raiseth me.

Friendship with Jesus satisfies us long before he is satisfied. We do not realize that any friendship could be closer than this we now have with him, but he sees limitless possibilities down the lovely years that lie ahead. His ambitions to intrigue us into the blessed family which he ever enlarges, while his redeemed friends help him weave a golden web of friendship into the Kingdom of God.

As we read the love experiences of mystics, for example those described by Raymond Lull in his *The Lover and Beloved*, we realize what possibilities of intimacy with Jesus lie ahead for us to explore. When every obstruction between him and us has been removed, each day with him brings fresh happy experiences. What surprises us is their endless variety. One day he is strong and determined, another his love is soft and delicate as gossamer silk, and one fears that it may tear with a breath. One day he is radiant, another day his face is lost in sadness. Always, whatever the mood may be, his face is full of tender love.

When weary or lonesome, we creep to him as young John did; he smiles and puts his hand in our hand. This is what he has been hungry for all the while. His heart is far bigger and warmer than ours. No matter therefore how hungry the heart may be for love, he is ready and eager, and after our weak, fickle love has poured out all it has, Christ is happy but unsatisfied, he wishes it had been more! He satisfies us with love because we do not have enough love to satisfy him.

The world is teeming with lonesome souls who cannot find anybody whom they can trust enough to give all the love that they feel in their hearts. These are the people who need to know that Christ, the insatiable lover, holds out his arms and says, "You can trust me, and I want you close. I want more love than you can give."

The only inseparable friend

The more intensely one loves another, the more one feels the pain of separation. Yet partings are inevitable. All of us have them. We bid farewell to our earthly friends, sometimes for long periods; and finally at the door of death we give them one last look. But friendship with the invisible Christ can be continuous. There need be no pain of separation now nor ever; no last look. "I am with you alway, even to the end of the world." All the time and to the end of time! We have the power to direct our own affections, and if we are so wise as to direct them toward Jesus, then he whom we love above all the world has promised never to leave us, never to leave us alone, and the loss of all other things assumes small importance.

Not only is he always with us, but he always meets our experiences, and more. Others, no matter how wonderful they may be, fail to measure up at some point or another. Nobody excepting Jesus ever quite understands. He never disappoints, the failures, the loneliness, the crashing about our ears of everything we have built for years. That is why Christ's closest friends are absurdly happy in time of trouble.

It is wise to follow Christ's advice and not allow our affections to get themselves rooted too deeply in possessing the things of this earth, "where moth and rust doth corrupt, and where thieves break through and steal." The more we love possessions the harder it is for us when we lose them or leave them, as we all must do in the end. In Jesus' parable, what tormented the rich man in hell more than its fires was all the luxury he had to leave behind him. How stupid it is to seal the one life we have here for baubles, when he, the Prize Gift of the universe, is for us all, and will remain with us through life and straight through death, growing "sweeter as the days go by," as those understand who have taken him to their hearts.

Of course, if this is not true it is maudlin sentimentality. But if it is true it is the most important of all truths. There is no escaping the alternative—either it is one or the other. Only those who have tried know whether it be the truth; and they are unanimous in their verdict that it is of all things most priceless!

Jesus alone has no limitations. All the limitations are ours. He makes none. He grows in stature and lovability as we grow able to understand him better. No place is lonely for those who remain in the secret of his presence all day and all night. The hymn writers have felt this glorious aspect of his friendship. For example, "If Jesus goes with me, I'll go anywhere," "In the secret of his presence, how my soul delights to hide."

This paragraph will be understood only by those who have seen their loved ones in death. Others will not understand—yet. We who have had this experience know how Jesus lifts despair unto peace. We know that they did not really die but are with him, and that through him they and we are still together. If heaven is an unseen world all about us our departed loved ones are near. They see us and speak to us. When the Lord broke through the grave he gave us infinite hope where before we had darkness and infinite despair. Death was horror and hell. With Christ it becomes our open door to boundless hope.

It is a question whether youth can appreciate the finest aspect of Christ's friendship. This finest truth is that all down the years he never disappoints, and at the last he crowns life with the supreme triumph of all. We think more upon this after we reach fifty and realize that physically we have passed the zenith of our powers. The last is best! The friend of Christ welcomes death! He feels like St. Paul when he said: "I am undecided between the two, for I long to depart and be with Christ, for that is far, far better, and yet your needs make it very necessary for me to stay on here." If "our treasure is in heaven" then death is the final shout of victory after the long battle. "O death, where is thy sting, O grave, where is thy victory... Thanks be to God which giveth us the victory through Jesus Christ." "For now we see through a glass, darkly; but then face to face..." "It doth not yet appear what we shall be: but we know that... we shall be like him; for we shall see him as he is.

This is why friendship with Jesus is so much wiser than any other friendship. We walk through life with him safely and happily, and then fall asleep in his arms, and shall awaken to see him as he is.

As Paul thought upon this marvel of the inseparability of Christ, he burst forth into one of the most exalted poems in all literature:

> Who shall separate us from the love of Christ?
> Shall tribulation or distress, or persecution,
> Or famine, or nakedness, or peril, or sword?
> Nay, in all these things we are more than conquerors
> Through him that loved us. For I am persuaded

> That neither death, nor life, nor angels, nor principalities,
> Nor things present, nor things to come,
> Nor height, nor depth, nor any other creature,
> Shall be able to separate us from the love of God,
> Which is in Christ Jesus our Lord.

Inner radiance

When you have learned to recognize the joyous glow in the eyes of those who dwell with Christ, you will never mistake it. There is no other radiance like it. Not membership in any church, but that radiance, is what attests the real friend of Jesus. If you study it, you may know it at a glance. He who has it is joyous without being shallow or silly; fun-loving, perhaps, but never satirical; wistful without the shadow of greed; looks past your face into your eyes with eager sympathy; is anxious to do something to help you if only he can discover how. There is fearless love without a hint of flirtation. There is open honesty because there is nothing to hide. Yet there is something deep and beautiful like the blue clear depths of a glacial lake. There is an instinctive glance upward, tenderness on the lips with no trace of weakness, the clear eye of purity, an atmosphere about this man which makes you feel that he has just been praying, or that he is praying even now inwardly. His eye has the light of one who knows something wonderful which he seems eager to tell you, if only you will listen and understand. When you are with him you find yourself thinking of Jesus, and you know he is thinking of Jesus.

In saintly people the radiance seems to come and go. This is because almost all men who are intimate with Jesus have their hours of close fellowship, and other hours when the cares of this world temporarily push him out of mind. The best are only on the way toward perfection; like St. Paul, they will confess that they "have not yet attained . . . but press toward the mark . . ." It is possible to tell when such men have just been with their Master, and when they have spent hours without him. Fellowship with Christ is like a costly perfume; the fragrance gradually disappears if one is away from him long.

When the disciples were with him they were as radiant as the happiest lovers at a wedding. At Pentecost they acted like men full of new wine. It is a not uncommon experience for people to become "God intoxicated" today. People can experience the same unutterable ectasy now, if they allow him to come closer than hands and feet, if they become servants, friends, companions, lovers—all the words of devotion in the dictionary seem to flounder in trying to reach the supreme fact. When men love him like that, they ask nothing and want nothing save to be near him, and please him and look for approval in his eyes.

He satisfies our infinite longings

Within all of us a tension is set up by the fact that the body is limited, while the soul has limitless longings which cannot be satisifed through the body. We aspire for infinitely more than we can reach. The difference between our reach and our aim is as vast as the difference between the reach of the arm and the reach of vision as it peers into the depths of space. As bodies, we are worms creeping about on the bottom of an ocean of air, more restricted than the fish, for they can soar at will through their atmosphere of water as easily as we walk. The human body quickly strikes its limit. After a few years it shrivels and decays. This creeping, aching, dying machine excites the admiration of physiologists perhaps, but it does not satisfy the human soul. Nothing that earth offers satisfies it permanently.

I daresay some reader of these lines will exclaim:

"Nonsense! I am perfectly satisfied." So you may be at this moment. Wait a month or a year or a decade, and you will find yourself aching with new desires which will surprise you as much as they will surprise others. The soul is growing like a child of eleven, and does not foresee this year what it will demand the next.

This is as true of friendships as of other experiences. A man finds a friend for whom he feels a mighty love, and to whom he writes perhaps songs and sonnets, only to find months or years later that this friendship did not, after all, fill the vacuum of the soul. Fairy tales end by saying: "They lived happily ever after," but they are fairy tales. Experience teaches us at last that the soul's desire for friendship seems, like space, to be boundless. Those who foolishly overstep the bounds prescribed by society in pursuit of love's longings find themselves betrayed by their desires, marked as sinners, yet more unsatisfied than ever.

Nobody knows so well as the clergyman that on every side are souls secretly chafing and complaining because they can find nothing or nobody to satisfy their nameless longings. Not infrequently men say, "I don't know what I want." They are like an airplane in a fog without instruments; they know neither where they are, nor the direction in which they are going. They do not even know which way is up! They suppose themselves to be "getting to the top," like the youth in Longfellow's "Excelsior," when they are only laboring toward death. The fatal mistake of that young man was that he tried to go up into the night without a guide.

Thank God, wise men have found their guide, and their friend, who does satisfy the soul's highest demands. The greatest utterance of a thousand years came from St. Augustine:

> "Thou hast made us for thyself, and our souls are restless until they find their rest in thee."

So it turns out that he satisfies us for the reason that we do not satisfy him. Our wants are not infinite after all, but his are infinite. Is it nobility we seek? He asks more, far more. Is it love we ask? He desires more! Is it power we desire? He demands more, far more! He satisfies us because he is always above us and beyond.

That is why our longings are insatiable in every other direction, because the soul was made for Christ, as the fish for water, the bird for the air, and the flower for sunshine. Countless millions down through twenty centuries, "a great host which no man can number," have discovered after years of futile quest that in Christ they find their soul's hunger satiated—and more!

He is so comfortable and gentle to be with that a child is at home in his arms. "Come unto me, all ye that labour and are heavy laden, and I will give you rest. Take my yoke unto you, and learn of me; for I am meek and lowly in heart: and ye shall find rest unto your souls." Men who toiled, men who walked the streets unable to find work, women whose hearts were broken by disappointed love and broken families, have found in him a "peace that passeth all understanding." It is a peace the world cannot take away because it does not depend upon the world.

A yacht was wrecked on a coral reef; a wife, clinging to a life buoy, was cast ashore alone on what seemed to be a desert island. She was paralyzed with despair, until suddenly her husband appeared over a sand dune. He had been able to get ashore at another point. Her despair turned to joy in an instant. The man she loved was with her and she was home. The world might be lost, but not she. This is precisely the change which takes place in a lost soul when it falls in love with Christ.

It is "rest" that Christ offers the soul, but it is not motionless rest, at least it is not motionless for long. An Indian Christian said, "Christ both satisfies and dissatisfies us, for he fills us with new wants." This is indeed what experience teaches. To have him gives a deep peace, yet to see him in his perfect beauty leaves us dissatisfied; dissatisfied not because of things we do not possess, but with our own selves. We cease to blame the universe, but we do not cease to aspire.

But there is this great difference. Now those nameless, mysterious longings which we had before take definite form. We are sure which way is up. We long to be like him, to help others be like him, to be closer to him, and to help others to be closer to him. We are at peace in his love, yet we long to explore the riches of the spiritual universe with him. We are at rest for we are sure, sure of today, and sure of the more wonderful tomorrow.

This is why you have detected in the eye of one who closely follows Christ, not a stagnant complacency, but the burning gleam of a far vision. He is looking into the future and his soul is pregnant with tomorrow. "Eye hath not seen, nor ear heard, neither have entered into the heart of man, the things which God hath prepared for them that love him."

Mystical Experiences

The Holy Spirit

God is, and always was, a Spirit, "the Holy Spirit." As a Spirit he came upon Mary and she conceived. When Jesus was baptized in the river Jordan he saw the Holy Spirit come upon him as a dove. Christ was God and man, his soul divine, his body human.

After his crucifixion Christ arose with a supernatural body, having power to appear or disappear at will. He had, in his own miraculous way, combined the qualities of both flesh and spirit. He was seen by five hundred persons during forty days, and then he rose into the air and vanished. Just before his departure he said he would return. For ten days after his disappearance the disciples assembled together in Jerusalem daily for prayer and praise, waiting for the promise to be fulfilled. Then on the day of Pentecost there came a mighty blast like wind, which filled their house, and brought thousands of people in Jerusalem running to see what was happening. Something like fire came and separated and stood on every head and "they were filled with the Holy Spirit." Christ had returned as pure Spirit so that he might live in them and in us, and in "as many as would receive him." So Paul could say: "Christ liveth in me." Now, as Holy Spirit, he occupied their bodies, and occupies our bodies just as he had occupied his own body under the name "Jesus."

In many a Pentecost since that day he has come with just such tremendous power to dwell in people who were ready to receive him. It is his will to come to us all in every generation with ever fresh Pentecosts. "Where meek souls will receive him, the dear Lord enters in." God, the Maker of the Worlds, God, who took for himself a human form, God, who comes into us as Holy Spirit, is "the same God yesterday, today, and forever."

Joys of the spirit

All satisfactions may be classified as (1) those which diminish with the passing years, and (2) those which increase with the passing years.

1. Of the first type are many pleasures which tend to destroy the very sense organs upon which they depend. The man who uses alcohol finds his pleasure dying out, and an ever-greater dose of liquor necessary to produce reaction. This is true also of drugs. Opium addicts suffer the tortures of hell if they are deprived of their drug. Those who eat until they ruin their stomachs

or who indulge in physical excesses until their natural powers are injured, belong to this class. All of these are like a fly walking down a large cone only to find it growing smaller until at last the fly is in a trap.

They who depend chiefly upon the flesh for their happiness reach a bitter old age, where everything they have lived for has burned out. Every pleasure which depends purely upon flesh sensations diminishes as the sense organs grow weaker. People who live for sense pleasures are like the fly going down the cone. Perhaps Jesus had just this in mind when he said, "Wide is the gate that leadeth to destruction."

2. The other class of satisfaction may begin much more moderately. "Narrow is the way which leadeth unto life," said Jesus. But these satisfactions train and strengthen the faculties upon which they depend. The art of reading is a good illustration. While we are learning to read there are months of tedium, but reading grows easier and more rewarding as we train our powers and acquire a new habit. This is true of learning to play any musical instrument. The cone starts small and grows wider each month. We enter through the narrow gate of discipline and find the way widening into an ever more abundant life. Even though at last our ears should fail us as they did Beethoven, our minds are stored with rich memories.

Such, but in a far greater degree, are the satisfactions of the spirit. The friendship of Jesus begins by demanding sacrifices. Things which previously gave us satisfaction must be abandoned when we enter the narrow gate which leads to discipleship. Indeed, our very reason for living must be abandoned in favor of a new reason. Every soul which leaves all and follows Jesus is like the nuns who take the vows of renunciation for the sake of becoming brides of Christ. "If any man come to me, and hate not his father, and mother, and wife, and children, and brethren, and sisters, yea, and his own life also, he cannot be my disciple."

It is astonishing that anybody who made the gate that narrow should have had even one disciple. Jesus said that a rich man would find it more difficult to enter the Kingdom of God than a camel finds it to pass through the eye of a needle. It is that narrow! We must lay aside every handicap because, in the words of Hebrews 12:1, we are running a race for life. Look at what the author of the great Epistle says:

> "Let us throw off every impediment and the entanglement of sin and run with determination the race for which we are entered, fixing our eyes upon Jesus, our leader and our example in faith, who in place of the happiness that belonged to him, submitted to a cross, caring nothing for its shame, and has taken his seat at the right hand of the throne of God."

Observe that sentence again. It begins at the cross. It ends beside God. What was true of Jesus is true of his disciples also. Friendship with him begins with renunciation. It ends in "the liberty of the sons of God."

If one has paid the supreme price so that he can say, "Fade, fade, each earthly joy, Jesus is mine," then one begins to explore a new and wonderful world. Our ultimate satisfaction does not depend upon the material things of this world which we inhabit at the moment. Rather it depends upon the training we receive to appreciate the things of the spiritual world. As we learn to love the Master with an ever-deeper devotion, we find an ever-greater joy in his constant presence. "In the secret of his presence, how my soul delights to hide." Our joy is in exact proportion to our love of being with him. He is incomparably more lovable than any other person, and so the delight of his love may become a hundred times more glorious than the pleasure we may derive from any other friendship.

The twofold price we must pay for this "pearl of great price" are: First, to become spiritually minded, with the mind engrossed in the things on the spirit level, not engrossed with material things, and: Second, to love Christ with all the soul and mind and heart and strength.

For perfect friendship with Jesus is a glorious affair. Why does that infatuated youth tingle from head to foot while he is with his sweetheart? Because nature made him to love and every cell in his body responds. That and far more is the ecstasy of those who are infatuated with Jesus. Nature made them for him and every fiber in their bodies responds.

If we abandon "the world, the flesh, and the devil" and fix our affections on Jesus, words fail to express the glory, the rapture of his warm intimacy, the gentle purity of his close love. For hours upon hours there may rest upon our hearts a great bliss that is nearly pain. One feels it in the breast and throat, perhaps because the ganglia there become surcharged with the electric impulses of love opening out to the very throne of God himself. Many a mystic in ecstasy has cried out like St. Theresa, "Oh God! please stop this delicious pain or I shall die of it."

The great Christian mystics

The two billions of people on this globe differ greatly in their tastes, hungers, and needs. To each person Christ offers a type of friendship best suited to his needs. All these types are right, but none can say, "I alone am right."

Millions of people of all churches have had such an intense experience of Christ that they are classified among the mystics. In point of fact, everybody is a mystic, if he believes that God answers back when he prays. Most of us are mystics occasionally, but a true mystic believes that he hears God answering back habitually, and perhaps all the time.

We get our knowledge of God, say the classic writers, through three channels:

1. The world of nature
2. Through revelation (This is to believe that the Bible is full of mysticism.)
3. Through the soul's secret and direct experience (This is to be a mystic.)

Evelyn Underhill calls mysticism the way of "life which aims at communion with God." A mystic "aims," pushes his will toward God, just as all of us do when we experience conversion. He does not differ in essence from the rest of us at our very best; save that he seeks God more continuously than we do, and so finds more of him, for the reason that "he that seeketh findeth."

There is as much variety among mystics as there is among the rest of us. To some of them God's message seems to be intellectual. St. John of the Cross, Eckhart and Dante illustrate this type. To some God comes as intense love. St. Theresa, St. Francis, and Walter Hinton illustrate this type. To some mystics God gives power. St. Augustine, John Wesley, George Fox, and Wordsworth belong here. To be sure the great mystics have had all these experiences—illumination, emotion, and power—but they differed in the emphasis which they placed upon each of these.

Many of the mystics had their intercourse with God (or the Holy Spirit), while others spoke almost exclusively with Christ. They are therefore classified as Theocentric (God-centered) and Christocentric (Christ-centered).

St. Augustine well illustrates the God-centered mystic when he writes: "What do I love when I love thee? It is a certain light and melody, and fragrance, and embrace, that I love when I love thee."

St. Paul was Christocentric, when he said "Christ liveth in me." "For me to live is Christ," he affirmed repeatedly. This type of mystic loves God, but he sees God clearly and loves him most when he sees him in Christ, and so spends little time seeking God elsewhere.

This Christ-centered type of mysticism is the ultimate goal of one who cultivates the friendship of Jesus. It is frequently found in Protestants as well as Catholics. Every hymnbook contains scores of hymns which are Christ-centered mysticism set to music. In many chapters we have been quoting from them. It was this kind of mystical experience that enthralled Charles Wesley as he wrote, "Jesus, lover of my soul," or Fanny Crosby as she wrote, "Close to thee."

The nuns of the Roman Catholic Church renounce all hope of marrying and having a family, but they do hope to become brides of Christ, and are carefully taught how this may be accomplished. This hope is not physical, of course, but spiritual. It is not confined to women, for in the tradition of the Catholic Church our souls are "female" in a spiritual sense, and every soul has the possibility of becoming a "bride of Christ." A spiritual interpretation of the Canticles (Song of Solomon) is a favorite frame in which to portary this experience. The mystical love between Christ and the soul does indeed resemble the love of man and wife at its highest and best. But the highest love-experience with Christ, in its white-hot, crystal-pure intensity, far transcends any other love this world knows.

Words are able to convey little more than a feeble echo of our deepest joys. The friendship of Jesus, when it approaches its true level, is something beyond the power of words to express. But oh, how I hope the reader will end this page with the experience which has just now been mine! Christ spoke to me, using my tongue: "I love you. I am sure of you now, and I am sharing your joy. This friendship is forever, and we are setting forth hand in hand to discover new happy surprises of love every coming day down the long, rich, thrilling years that reach into eternity. I have caught you and I shall not let you go."

He wants to say to you—"I am sure of you now—forever." He wants to say that to you—"We are setting forth hand in hand to discover new happy surprises of love down the long, rich years." Let him say that! Out with your doubt. Out with your fear of being thought queer. Break with the materialism of this blind age. Say, "Go ahead, Lord, I am willing."

Part 4

Game with Minutes

Game with Minutes

This booklet describes the prayer techniques that Laubach found helpful in learning to maintain minute-by-minute contact with God. God is revealed in many different ways, and each person must experiment to find the techniques that fit his or her nature. Laubach offers these techniques as suggestions, with the advice that prayer should be delightful, a game, not a grim duty.

Six editions of the booklet were printed in the Philippines, the last in 1940 by the Lanao Press. It was first printed in the United States in 1953.

Game with Minutes

Christ is the only hope of the world

"Disillusioned by all our other efforts, we now see that the only hope left for the human race is to become like Christ." That is the statement of a famous scientist, and is being repeated among ever more educators, statesmen, and philosophers. Yet Christ has not saved the world from its present terrifying dilemma. The reason is obvious: Few people are getting enough of Christ to save either themselves or the world. Take the United States, for example. Only a third of the population belongs to a Christian church. Less than half of this third attend service regularly. Preachers speak about Christ in perhaps one service in four—thirty minutes a month! Good sermons, many of them excellent, but too infrequent in presenting Christ.

Less than ten minutes a week given to thinking about Christ by one-sixth of the people is not saving our country or our world; for selfishness, greed, and hate are getting a thousand times that much thought. What a nation thinks about, that it is. We shall not become like Christ until we give Him more time. A teachers' college requires students to attend classes for twenty-five hours a week for three years. Could it prepare competent teachers or a law school prepare competent lawyers if they studied only ten minutes a week? Neither can Christ, and He never pretended that He could. To his disciples he said: "Come with me, walk with me, talk and listen to me, work and rest with me, eat and sleep with me, twenty-four hours a day for three years." That was their college course—"He chose them," the Bible says, "that they might be with Him," 168 hours a week!

All who have tried that kind of abiding for a month know the power of it—it is like being born again from center to circumference. It absolutely changes every person who does it. And it will change the world that does it.

How can a man or women take this course with Christ today? The answer is so simple a child can understand it. Indeed unless we "turn and become like children" we shall not succeed.

1. We have a study hour. We read and reread the life of Jesus recorded in the Gospels thoughtfully and prayerfully at least an hour a day. We find fresh ways and new translations, so that this reading will never be dull, but always stimulating and inspiring. Thus we walk with Jesus through Galilee by walking with Him through the pages of His earthly history.

2. We make Him our inseparable chum. We try to call Him to mind at least one second of each minute. We do not need to forget other things nor

stop our work, but we invite Him to share everything we do or say or think. Hundreds of people have experimented until they have found ways to let Him share every minute that they are awake. In fact, it is no harder to learn this new habit than to learn the touch system in typing, and in time one can win one hundred percent of his minutes with as little effort as an expert needs to write a letter.

While these two practices take all our time, yet they do not take it from any good enterprise. They take Christ into that enterprise and make it more resultful. They also keep a man's religion steady. If the temperature of a sick man rises and falls daily the doctor regards him as seriously ill. This is the case with religion. Not spiritual chills and fevers, but an abiding faith which gently presses the will toward Christ all day, is a sign of a healthy religion.

Practicing the presence of God is not on trial. It has already been proven by countless thousands of people. Indeed, the spiritual giants of all ages have known it. Christians who do it today become more fervent and beautiful and are tireless witnesses. Men and women who had been slaves of vices have been set free. Catholics and Protestants find this practicing the presence of God at the heart of their faith. Conservatives and liberals agree that here is a reality they need. People who are grateful for what this booklet has done for them are ordering wholesale quantities to give to friends. Letters from all parts of the world testify that in this game multitudes are turning defeat into victory and despair into joy.

The results of this program begin to show clearly in a month. They grow rich after six months, and glorious after ten years.

Somebody may be saying, "All this is very orthodox and very ancient." It is indeed, the secret of the great saints of all ages. "Pray without ceasing," said Paul, "in everything make your wants known unto God." "As many as are led by the Spirit of God these are the sons of God."

How we win the game with minutes

Nobody is wholly satisfied with himself. Our lives are made up of lights and shadows, of some good days and many unsatisfactory days. We have learned that the good days and hours come when we are very close to Christ, and that the poor days come whenever we push Him out of our thoughts. Clearly, then, the way to a more consistent high level is to take Him into everything we do or say or think.

Experience has told us that good resolutions are not enough. We need to discipline our lives to an ordered regime. The "Game with Minutes" is a rather lighthearted name for such a regime in the realm of the spirit. Many of us have found it to be enormously helpful. It is a new name for something as old as Enoch, who "walked with God." It is a way of living which nearly everybody knows and nearly everybody has ignored. Students will at once recognize it as a fresh approach to Brother Lawrence's "Practicing the Presence of God."

We call this a "game" because it is a delightful experience and an exhilarating spiritual exercise; but we soon discover that it is far more than a game. Perhaps a better name for it would be "an exploratory expedition," because it opens out into what seems at first like a beautiful garden; then the garden widens into a country; and at last we realize that we are exploring a new world. This may sound like poetry, but it is not overstating what experience has shown us. Some people have compared it to getting out of a dark prison and beginning to live. We still see the same world, yet it is not the same, for it has a new glorious color and a far deeper meaning. Thank God, this adventure is free for everybody, rich or poor, wise or ignorant, famous or unknown, with a good past or a bad—"Whosoever will, may come." The greatest thing in the world is for everybody!

You will find this just as easy and just as hard as forming any other habit. You have hitherto thought of God for only a few seconds or minutes a week, and He was out of our mind the rest of the time. Now you are attempting, like Brother Lawrence, to have God in mind each minute you are awake. Such drastic change in habit requires a real effort at the beginning.

Many of us find it very useful to have pictures of Christ where our eyes will fall on them every time we look around. A very happy hobby is to collect the most friendly pictures of Christ, pocket size, so that we can erect our own shrine in a few seconds.

How to begin

Select a favorable hour; try how many minutes of the hour you can remember God at least once each minute; that is to say, bring God to mind at least one second out of every sixty. It is not necessary to remember God every second, for the mind runs along like a rapid stream from one idea to another.

Your score will be low at first, but keep trying, for it constantly becomes easier, and after a while is almost automatic. It follows the well-known laws of habit forming. If you try to write shorthand you are at first very awkward. This is true when you are learning to play a piano, or to ride a bicycle, or to use any new muscles. When you try this "game with minutes" you discover that spiritually you are still a very weak infant. A babe in the crib seizes upon everything at hand to pull himself to his feet, wobbles for a few seconds and falls exhausted. Then he tries again, each time standing a little longer than before. We are like that babe when we begin to try to keep God in mind. We need something to which we can cling. Our minds wobble and fall, then rise for a new effort. Each time we try we shall do better until at last we may be able to remember God as high as ninety percent of the whole day.

How to try the experiment in church

You have a good chance of starting well if you begin in church—provided the sermon is about God. When our congregation first tried it, we distributed slips of paper which read:

GAME WITH MINUTES
Score Card

During this hour I thought of God at least once each minute for _____ different minutes.

Signed

At the opening of the service the pastor made this announcement: "Everybody will be asked to fill this score card at the end of one hour. In order to succeed, you may use any help within reach. You may look at the cross, or you may leaf through your hymn book or Bible, looking for the verses that remind you of God."

The sermon that Sunday explained how to play the game. At the end of the hour, the score cards were collected. The congregation reported scores ranging from five to sixty minutes. The average was forty-four minutes, which meant seventy-three percent of the hour. For beginners this was excellent. Such an experiment, by the way, will encourage the congregation to listen better than usual, and will remind the preacher to keep his sermon close to God.

If you score seventy-five percent in church, you can probably make a rather good score for the rest of the day. It is a question of being master of every new situation.

Never use a score card more than an hour, and not that long if it tires you. This is a new delight you are learning, and it must not be turned into a task.

While going home from church

Can you win your game with minutes while passing people on the street? Yes! Experiments have revealed a sure way to succeed: offer a swift prayer for the people at whom you glance. It is easy to think an instantaneous prayer while looking people straight in the eye, and the way people smile back at you shows that they like it! This practice gives a surprising exhilaration, as you may prove for yourself. A half-hour spent walking and praying for all one meets, instead of tiring one, gives him a sense of ever heightening energy like a battery being charged. It is a tonic, a good way to overcome a tired feeling.

Some of us walk on the right side of the pavement, leaving room for our unseen Friend, whom we visualize walking by our side, and we engage in silent conversations with Him about the people we meet. For example, we may say: "Dear Companion, what can we do together for this man whom we are passing?" Then we whisper what we believe Christ would answer.

Where to look for Christ

We have a right to use any aid that proves useful. One such aid is to think of Christ as in a definite location. To be sure, He is a spirit, everywhere at once—and therefore anywhere we realize Him to be. Many of us win our game nearly all of some days by realizing His unseen presence sitting in a chair or walking beside us. Some of us have gazed at our favorite picture of Him until it floats before our memories whenever we glance at His unseen presence, and we almost see Him. Indeed, many of us do see Him in our dreams. Others, like St. Paul, like to feel Him within the breast; many, like St. Patrick, feel Him all around us, above, below, before, behind, as though we walked in His kindly halo. We may have our secret ways of helping us to realize that He is very near and very dear.

On a train or in a crowd

We whisper "God" or "Jesus" or "Christ" constantly as we glance at every person near us. We try to see double, as Christ does—we see the person as he is and the person Christ longs to make of him. Remarkable things happen, until those in tune look around as though you spoke—especially children. The atmosphere of a room changes when a few people keep whispering to Him about all the rest. Perhaps there is no finer ministry than just to be in meetings or crowds, whispering "Jesus," and then helping people whenever you see an opportunity. When Dr. Chalmers answers the telephone he whispers: "A child of God will now speak to me." We can do that when anybody speaks to us.

If everybody in America would do the things just described above, we should have a "heaven below." This is not pious poetry. We have seen what happens. Try it during all this week, until a strange power develops within you. As messages from England are broadcast in Long Island for all America, so we can become spiritual broadcasters for Christ. Every cell in our brain is an electric battery which He can use to intensify what He longs to say to people who are spiritually too deaf to hear Him without our help.

While in conversation

Suppose when you reach home you find a group of friends engaged in ordinary conversation. Can you remember God at least once every minute? This is hard but we have found that we can be successful if we employ some reminders. Here are aids which have proven useful:

1. Have a picture of Christ in front of you where you can glance at it frequently.

2. Have an empty chair beside you and imagine that your Unseen Master is sitting in it; if possible reach your hand and touch that chair, as though holding His hand. He is there, for He said: "Lo, I am with you always."

3. Keep humming to yourself a favorite prayer hymn—for example, "Have Thine Own Way, Lord, Have Thine Own Way."

4. Silently pray for each person in the circle.

5. Keep whispering inside: "Lord, put Thy thoughts in my mind. Tell me what to say."

6. Best of all, tell your companions about the "Game with Minutes." If they are interested, you will have no more trouble. You cannot keep God unless you give Him to others.

When at the table

All the previous suggestions are useful at mealtime. If possible, have an empty chair for your Invisible Guest, who said, "Wherever two or three are gathered together, I am in the midst." Another useful aid is to recall what the Quakers believe about every meal. Jesus told us: "Eat this in remembrance of me." They think that He meant, not only consecrated bread, but all food, so that every mouthful is His "body broken for you."

You might read and discuss this booklet. It helps immediately if others at the table agree to try to win this mealtime together.

While reading a book

When we are reading a newspaper or magazine or book, we read it to Him! We often glance at the empty chair where we visualize Him or at His picture and continue a running conversation with Him inwardly about the pages we are reading. Kagawa says scientific books are letters from God telling how He runs His universe.

Have you ever opened a letter and read it with Jesus, realizing that He smiles with us at the fun, rejoices with us in the successes, and weeps with us at life's tragedies? If not, you have missed one of life's sweetest experiences.

When thinking

If you lean back and think about some problem deeply, how can you remember God? You can do it by forming a new habit. All thought employs silent words and is really conversation with your inner self. Instead of talking to yourself, you will now form the habit of talking to Christ. Many of us who have tried this have found that we think so much better that we never want to try to think without Him again. We are helped if we imagine Him sitting in a chair besides us, talking with us. We say with our tongue what we think Christ might say in reply to our questions.

No practice we have ever found has held our thinking so uniformly high and wholesome as this making all thought a conversation with God. When evil thoughts of any kind come, we say, "Lord, these thoughts are not fit to discuss with Thee. Think Thy thoughts in my mind." The result is an instantaneous purification.

When walking alone

If you are strolling out of doors alone, you can recall God at least once every minute with no effort, if you remember that "beauty is the voice of God." Every flower and tree, river and lake, mountain and sunset, is God speaking, "This is my Father's world, and to my listening ears all nature sings...." So as you look at each lovely thing, you may keep asking: "Dear Father, what are you telling me through this, and this, and this?"

If you have wandered to a place where you can talk aloud without being overheard, you may speak to the Invisible Companion beside you. Ask Him what is most on His heart and then answer back aloud with your voice what you believe God would reply to you.

Of course we are not always sure whether we have guessed God's answer right, but it is surprising how much of the time we are very certain. It really is not necessary to be sure that our answer is right, for the answer is not the great thing—He is! God is infinitely more important than His advice or His gifts; indeed, He, Himself, is the great gift. The youth in love does not so much prize what his sweetheart may say or may give him, as the fact that she is his and that she is here. The most precious privilege in talking with God is this intimacy which we can have with Him. We may have a glorious succession of heavenly minutes. How foolish people are to lose life's most poignant joy, seeing it may be had while taking a walk alone!

Some of us walk on one side, leaving a place for the invisible Christ. We glance at Him as we walk and let our tongues hold a two-way conversation about everybody we meet.

Be my last thought

We make sure that there is a picture of Christ, or a Bible, or a cross or some other object where it will greet our closing eyes as we fall asleep. We continue to whisper any words of endearment our hearts suggest. If all day long we have been walking with Him, we shall find Him the dear companion of our dreams. Sometimes after such a day, we have fallen asleep with our pillows wet from tears of joy, feeling His tender touch on our foreheads. Usually we feel no deep emotion, but always we have a "peace that passeth all understanding." This is the end of a perfect day.

Monday morning

If on Sunday we have rated over fifty per cent in our game with minutes, we shall be eager to try the experiment during a busy Monday. As we open our eyes and see a picture of Christ on the wall, we may ask: "Now, Master, shall we get up?" Some of us whisper to Him our every thought about washing and dressing in the morning, about brushing our shoes and choosing our clothes. Christ is interested in every trifle, because He loves us more intimately than a mother loves her babe, or a lover his sweetheart, and is happy only when we share every question with Him.

Men at work

Countless thousands of men keep God in mind while engaged in all types of work, mental or manual, and find that they are happier and get better results. Those who endure the most intolerable ordeals gain new strength when they realize that their Unseen Comrade is by their side. To be sure, no man whose business is harmful or whose methods are dishonest, can expect God's partnership. But if an enterprise is useful, God eagerly shares in its real progress. The carpenter can do better work if he talks quietly to God about each task, as Jesus certainly did when He was a carpenter. Many of us have found that we can compose a letter or write a book better when we say: "God, think Thy thoughts in my mind. What dost Thou desire written?

Here is my hand; use it. Pour Thy wisdom through my hand." Our thoughts flow faster, and what we write is better. God loves to be a co-author!

Merchants and bankers

A merchant who waits on his customers and prays for them at the same time, wins their affection and their business. A salesman who prays for those with whom he is dealing has far more likelihood of making a sale. A bookkeeper or banker can whisper to God about every column of figures and be certain that God is even more interested in the figures than he is. The famous astronomer, Sir James Jeans, calls God the "super mathematician of the universe, making constant use of mathematical formulae than would drive Einstein mad."

In the home

Many women cultivate Christ's companionship while cooking, washing dishes, sweeping, sewing, and caring for children. Aids which they find helpful are:

1. Whispering to God about each small matter, knowing that He loves to help.
2. Humming or singing a favorite prayer hymn.
3. Showing the children how to play the game with minutes, and asking them to share in playing it. Children love this game and develop an inner control when they play it which renders discipline almost needless.
4. Having pictures of Christ about the house, as a constant reminder.
5. Saying to God, "Think Thy thoughts in my mind."

When in school

An increasing army of students in school who are winning this game, tell us how they do it. Here is their secret:

When in study period, say, "God, I have just forty precious minutes. Help my wavering thoughts to concentrate so that I may not waste a moment. Show me what is worth remembering in this first paragraph"—then read the lesson to God, instead of reading it to yourself.

When going to recitation, whisper: "Make my mind clear, so that I will be able to recall all I have studied. Take away fear."

When rising to recite before a group say: "God, speak through my lips."

When taking an examination, say all during the hour, "Father, keep my mind clear, and help me to remember all that I have learned. How shall we answer this next question?" Visualize Him looking over your shoulder every minute you are writing. God will not tell you what you have never studied but He does sharpen your memory and take away your stage fright when you ask Him. Have you not discovered that when you pray about some forgotten name it often flashes into your memory?

To be sure, this prevents us from being dishonest or cheating, for if we are not honest we cannot expect His help. But that is a good reason for playing the game with minutes. Character is a hundred times more valuable than knowledge or high grades.

To be popular with the other students, acquire the habit of breathing a momentary prayer for each student you meet, and while you are in conversation with him. Some instinct tells him you are interested in his welfare and he likes you for it.

Praying horseshoes

A very powerful way to pray is for a group of friends to join hands while seated in the shape of a horseshoe. Some of us have an altar at the open end of the horseshoe, with a cross or a picture of Jesus, or a Bible, or a globe of the world. The horseshoe opens toward the cities, countries, and people most in need of prayer.

This horseshoe of prayer reminds us of the great magnets which can lift a locomotive when the electric power is turned on. We are seeking to be used by the inpouring Holy Spirit to lift the world, and to draw all men to Christ.

It also reminds us of the radio broadcast which, when the power is on, leaps around the world. We offer ourselves as God's broadcasting station.

The gentle tingle which we usually feel reminds us of the glow and soft purr in the tubes of a radio when the power is on.

Every Christian family at mealtime may form a prayer radio broadcast by joining hands. Young people's societies will love it. It will vitalize every Sunday School class to spend ten minutes in broadcasting. Defunct prayer meetings will come to life when they become horseshoe magnets of prayer. Schools and colleges, public or private, will find prayer horseshoes popular with the students. Here is something that Christians and Jews can do together. Worship can thus be made the most thrilling experience of their lives.

The group may prepare a list of the most urgent world needs and of key persons. An excellent plan at breakfast is for someone to read from the newspaper the issues; and persons which are most in need of prayer that morning.

The leader may say words like these: "Lord, in this terribly critical hour we want to do everything we can. We pray Thee, use us to help the President to be hungry for Thee, to listen and hear and obey Thee. We lift President Eisenhower into Thy presence."

Then all may raise their clasped hands toward heaven. And so with the entire list.

After the prayer list is completed, the globe of the world may be lifted toward God while somebody prays the Lord's Prayer.

During play hours

God is interested in our fun as much as we are. Many of us talk to him during our games. Some of the famous football players long ago discovered that they played better if they prayed all during the game. Some of the famous runners pray during races. If a thing brings health and joy and friendship and a fresh mind, God is keenly interested, because he is interested in us.

While on the playground, do not ask to win, but whisper: "God, get Thy will done exactly.

"Help us all to do our best. Give us what is far more important than defeating our opponents—make us clean sportsmen and make us good friends."

God and love

Sweethearts who have been wise enough to share their love with God have found it incomparably more wonderful. Since "God is Love" He is in deepest sympathy with every fond whisper and look. Husbands and wives, too, give rapturous testimony of homes transformed by praying silently when together. In some cases where they had begun to give each other "nerves," they have found, after playing this game when they are alone together by day or by night, that their love grew strangely fresh, rich, beautiful, "Like a new honeymoon." God is the maker of all true marriages, and He gives His highest joy to a man and wife who share their love for each other with Him, who pray inwardly each for the other when they are together looking into one another's eyes. Married love becomes infinitely more wonderful when Christ is the bond every minute and it grows sweeter as the years go by to the very last day. Imagine, too, what this does for the children!

Troubles

Troubles and pain come to those who practice God's presence, as they came to Jesus, but these seem trivial as compared to their new joyous experience. If we have spent our days with Him, we find that when earthquakes, fires, famines or other catastrophes threaten us, we are not terrified any more than Paul was in time of shipwreck. "Perfect love casteth out fear."

This booklet on the Game with Minutes is good for people suffering from illness at home or in hospitals. Nurses remind us that the thoughts of people turn toward God when sick as at no other time. Patients who are convalescing have many idle hours when their minds reach up toward God. Playing this game produces a perfect mental state for rapid recovery.

Those who are seeking to be aware of God constantly have found that their former horror at death has vanished. We may have a new mystic intimacy with our departed loved ones, for though unseen to us they are with Christ and since He is with us they are with us as well.

Some prices we must pay to win this game

The first price is pressure of our wills, gentle but constant. What game is ever won without effort and concentration?

The second price is perseverance. A low score at the outset is not the least reason for discouragement; everybody gets a low score for a long while. Each week grows better and requires less strain.

The third price is perfect surrender. We lose Christ the moment our wills rebel. If we try to keep even a remote corner of life for self or evil, and refuse to let God rule us wholly, that small worm will spoil the entire fruit. We must be utterly sincere.

The fourth price is tell others. When anybody complains that he is losing the game, we flash this question back at him: "Are you telling your friends about it?" For you cannot keep Christ unless you give Him away.

The fifth price is to be in a group. We need the stimulus of a few intimate friends who exchange their experiences with us.

The prizes we win

It is obvious that this is unlike other games in many respects. One difference is that we all win. We may not win all or even half of our minutes but we do win a richer life, which is all that really matters. There are no losers excepting those who quit. Let us consider some of those prizes:

1. We develop what Thomas à Kempis calls a "familiar friendship with Jesus." Our Unseen Friend becomes dearer, closer and more wonderful every day until at last we know Him as "Jesus, lover of our souls" not only in songs, but in blissful experience. Doubts vanish, we are more sure of Him being with us than of anybody else. This warm, ardent friendship ripens rapidly until people see its glory shining in our eyes—and it keeps on growing richer and more radiant every month.

2. All we undertake is done better and more smoothly. We have daily evidence that God helps our work, piling one proof upon another until we are sure of God, not from books or preachers, but from our own experience.

3. Our minds are pure as a mountain stream every moment when we are playing the game.

4. The Bible and Christian hymns seem like different books, for they begin to sparkle with the beautiful thoughts of saints who have had glorious experience with God. We begin to understand their bliss for we share it with them.

5. All day long we are contented, whatever our lot may be, for He is with us. "When Jesus goes with me, I'll go anywhere."

6. It becomes easy to tell others about Christ because our minds are flooded with Him. "Out of the fullness of the heart the mouth speaketh."

7. Grudges, jealousies, hatred, and prejudices melt away. Little hells turn into little heavens. Communities have been transformed where this game was introduced. Love rises like a kindly sea and at last drowns all the demons of malice and selfishness. Then we see that the only hope for this insane world is to persuade people to "practice the presence of God."

8. "Genius is ninety percent concentration." This game, like all concentration upon one objective, eventually results in flashes of new brilliant thought which astonish us, and keep us tiptoe with expectancy for the next vision which God will give us.

Infinite variety

The notion that religion is dull, stupid and sleepy is adherent to God, for He has created infinite variety and He loves to surprise us. If you are weary of some sleepy form of devotion, probably God is as weary of it as you are. Shake out of it, and approach Him in one of the countless fresh directions. When our minds lose the edge of their zest, let us shift to another form of fellowship as we turn the dial of a radio. Every tree, every cloud, every bird, every orchestra, every child, every city, every soap bubble is alive with God to those who know his language.

It is for anybody

Humble folk often believe that walking with God is above their heads, or that they may "lose a good time" if they share all their joys with God. What tragic misunderstanding, to regard Him as a killer of happiness! A growing chorus of joyous voices round the world fairly sing that spending their hours with God is the most thrilling joy ever known, and that beside it a baseball game or a horse race is stupid.

Radiant religion

This game is not a grim duty. Nobody need play it unless he seeks richer life. It is a delightful privilege. If you forget to play it for minutes or hours, or days do not groan or repent, but begin anew with a smile. It is a thrilling joy—don't turn it into a sourfaced penance. With God, every minute can be a fresh beginning. Ahead of you lie limitless anticipations. Walt Whitman looked up into the starry skies and fairly shouted

> "Away, O Soul, hoist instantly the Sail!
> O daring joy but safe!
> Are they not all the seas of God?
> O farther, farther, farther sail!"

What is meant by winning

You win your minute if, during that minute you either:

1. Pray
2. Recall God
3. Sing or hum a devotional hymn
4. Talk or write about God
5. Seek to relieve suffering of any kind in a prayerful spirit
6. Work with the consciousness of God's presence
7. Whisper to God
8. Feel yourself encompassed by God
9. Look at a picture or a symbol of Christ
10. Read a scripture verse or poem about God
11. Give somebody a helping hand for the Lord's sake
12. Breathe a prayer for the people you meet
13. Follow the leading of the Inner Voice
14. Plan or work for the Kingdom of God
15. Testify to others about God, the church, or this game

16. Share suffering or sorrow with another
17. Hear God and see Him in flowers, trees, water, hills, sky

We never attempt to keep a minute-by-minute record (excepting perhaps occasionally for an hour), since such a record would interfere with normal life. We are practicing a new freedom, not a new bondage. We must not get so tied down to score keeping that we lose the glory of it, and its spontaneity. We fix our eyes upon Jesus, not upon a clock.

Part 5

Prayer: The Mightiest Force in the World

Prayer: The Mightiest Force in the World

This book, which was published in 1946, alerts war-weary Americans that the war is not yet over, for the conditions that breed war have not been conquered. Chief among the problems are the poor nations, whose people are struggling for mere survival while the rich nations are vying for positions of power in the world community. Prayer is the one force that can reconcile conflicting interests, according to Laubach. Through prayer, all people, especially those who feel most powerless to affect change, can make a significant contribution to winning permanent peace.

In this book Laubach explains his rationale for prayer and his emphasis on intercession. The prayer techniques described in this volume are offered with the plea for prayer practitioners to research the effectiveness of prayer in their own souls and keep notes on the results for others.

More than 200,000 copies of this book reached an American audience eager to gain confidence in praying for their war-shattered world. The following excerpts, contain the major themes that inspired Frank Laubach's first audience.

Pray for World Leaders

This war isn't over

"Let's pray hard, you guys, or this ship's goin' to blow up." That American sailor told the truth about the "good ship earth," as well as about his own carrier. For our wounded world is full of holes and fires. One more global war and we shall all be destroyed. "Pray hard, you guys, or this ship's goin' to blow up."

It helped those gobs to keep cool heads, so that they did the right thing to put out the fires—their ship still floats. Prayer will do the same thing for us. We need cool heads to do the right thing—to put out the fires of hate and prejudice, if our ship earth is to survive—and prayer will quench hate, fear and panic when nothing else will do it.

We now know that V-Day did not mark the end of the war, but only the end of one early battle. This war will not be over in twenty years. The war is not won until we win the peace. Thank God for the San Francisco Conference, but that was only a first step toward peace, for the fires of hate are burning all over the world more fiercely than ever in history. The racial hatred in South Africa, or in our own South, has in it a possibility of bloodshed as hideous as the Nazi massacres of the Jews, as every wise person sees. India, China, Argentina, and all the countries of Europe are full of dynamite which could blow up the world.

We need to mobilize a new army of ten million and train them to use a weapon as powerful for peace as rocket bombs were for destruction. Other weapons converted enemies into skeletons. This weapon must convert enemies into friends. It must heal the horrid open wound which bombs have left across the face of the world. Only prayer, which releases the infinite might of God, can win this final battle for men's minds and hearts—this battle against hate, this battle for "one world."

Today few educated men doubt the power of prayer. Millions of people, however, are haunted with a guilty sense that while we have pursued scientific inquiry in other directions with enormous results, we have failed to investigate and use the mighty energies which prayer can release. Especially in this the most crucial hour in all history, when we need to employ every resource there is, we are afraid that we have overlooked the greatest resource of all.

We had better not neglect prayer now! As Cordell Hull solemnly warned us, "The human race is confronted with the gravest crisis in its experience.

We who are on the scene of action have to say which way it is going." We are, in fact, in a terrifying dilemma. Science has been developing robots which travel 3500 miles an hour, and superexplosives so diabolically efficient in wholesale killings that all scientists agree with Anthony Eden and General Eisenhower that "we cannot survive a third world war." But we have never yet had permanent peace. That is our dilemma. We must now find and follow some straight and narrow path never before trodden. If we do not find it, we shall perish.

The way to peace is an untrodden path, but it is not unknown. It is the way Jesus gave us.

"Love thy neighbor as thyself," not in word but in deed.

Let all men spend their lives, as Jesus did, helping others.

Let strong men sacrifice their personal advantage so that all may have equal opportunities.

Jesus' way would be peace itself if we followed it. But men don't want to change as radically as that! They are still trying to make selfish greed work. In the peace negotiations, nations have jostled for special privilege, and selfish business interests have tried to grab advantages that would be sure to make other men hate them. Senator Vandenberg wrote before the San Francisco Conference that nations were striving for "America first," "England first," "Russia first,"—the very attitude which has caused all wars. Peace cannot be permanent until we put "the whole world first." No part of the world, whether America or England or Russia, or any business enterprise, is as important as the welfare of all. "Thy kingdom come on earth" is not only Christian, it is the only possible roadway to lasting peace.

We are still in the heat of a crucial battle between the way of Jesus and the way of greed. The Allies have cut a cancer out of Italy, Germany, and Japan; but the cancer still poisons the bloodstream of the world, and will break out again and kill us unless we get the cancer tissue out of our system. Nobody but God can cleanse tissue out of our system. Nobody but God can cleanse our bloodstream, and even God can remove it only if He has full gangway. We must pray for God's miracle or perish. For if we refuse to yield to God, His only recourse is to sweep us off the earth and start over.

So this is not a time for confidence, nor is it a time for despair; it is the time to turn to God. It is the time for humility, penitence, desperate resolve, rectitude, obedience to the will of God all-out sincerity!

Everybody is important now, all of us, young and old alike, whether in public life or in private. The future of the world depends upon whether you and enough others like you pray widely enough and often enough.

A small group of men are making the plans for world peace, plus a few hundred others who can reach their ears. All the rest of us, the hundreds of millions of us are unable to offer our views. We must be silent, but we need not be helpless. For the humblest of us can pray. Millions of us ordinary people must pour an incessant white light of prayer upon world leaders day after day. We must lift the heads of those leaders toward God so that they will hear Him and will obey His will. Enough people praying enough will release into the human bloodstream the mightiest medicine in the universe, for we shall be the channels through whom God can exert His infinite power. Prayer is to the world of human relations what white corpuscles are to the human body. If enough of us pray enough, there will be permanent peace. If we do not pray, and enough like us, hell will break loose again in twenty-five years, and we and our homes will all be sucked into the bloody maelstrom of a third world war and perish. All of us are needed to save the world from the world's mightiest enemy, which is war itself.

"Prayer alone will not be enough," you say. "We need right deeds." Precisely! But prayer is the door that opens our minds and the minds of our leaders to God, so that we and they may know what deeds are right.

We need a river, not a trickle

"If prayers can save the world," asked a friend, "why haven't the prayers of the devout done it already?"

Because their prayers have been a trickle, when we needed a river. The world at this moment is the resultant of the total thought forces which have struggled for supremacy. We had these world wars because wills all over the world have been at cross-purposes with the will of God and with other wills. The people who were working and planning with God were fewer than those at cross-purposes with God's will. Hundreds were praying, when we needed hundreds of millions. People prayed for a few minutes a week when they should have been praying all week, all year "without ceasing."

The might of mass prayer

We do not "persuade God to try harder" when we pray; it is our world leaders, our statesmen and church men whom we persuade to try harder. We help God when we pray. When great numbers of us pray for leaders, a mighty invisible spiritual force lifts our minds and eyes toward God. His Spirit flows through our prayer to them, and He can speak to them directly.

We can do more for the world with prayer than if we could walk into Whitehall, London, or the Kremlin in Moscow, and tell those men what to do—far more! If they listened to our suggestions, we would probably be more or less wrong. But what God tells them, when they listen to Him, must be right. It is infinitely better for world leaders to listen to God than for them to listen to us.

Most of us can never enter the White House and offer advice to the President. Probably he will never have time to read our letters. But we can give him what is far more important than advice. We can give him a lift into the presence of God, make him hungry for divine wisdom, which is the grandest thing one man ever does for another. We can visit the White House with prayer as many times a day as we think of it, and every such visit makes us a channel between God and the President.

The mightiest power on earth

This idea struck one minister like a thunderbolt:

"Man," he exclaimed, "if this is true at all, it is the mightiest truth in the universe! It means that enough of us praying often enough could make everybody in the whole world look up and listen to God. We could transform the world."

He was right. Prayer is the mightiest power on earth. Prayer's power has been proven many millions of times. Enough of us, if we prayed enough, could save the world—if we prayed enough!

But the clergyman, in his enthusiasm, then went too far:

"If we could get Christians to stop and pray one minute a day, they could save the world."

I do not think that would be enough. The sun could keep nothing alive shining one minute a day. Life itself is dependent on the sun's rays, yet not one ray of light in a million produces life. Not one raindrop in a million finds its way to the roots of a tree. Not a seed in a million germinates. Not a shovelful of dirt in a million turns up a diamond in Kimberley. It is said that if all the eggs of the conger eel produced eels—and if they could find food—they would fill the space from here to the sun in two years. Nature is that extravagant! A very small proportion of our written or spoken words inspire men to deeds. So if we should find that our prayers do not always reach those for whom they are intended, but that every prayer probably reaches somebody somewhere, that is all we can ask, and more! Indeed, that fact is so powerful that if we of the Christian world pray persistently, and "faint not," as Jesus commanded, we shall transform the world. But occasional feeble doubting prayers will get only feeble results. One minute a day will not save us!

No easy victory

So we must guard against expecting an easy victory. Prayer is powerful, but it is not the power of a sledge hammer that crushes with one blow. It is the power of sun rays and rain drops which bless, because there are so many of them. Instead of a minute a day, we Christians must learn to flash hundreds of instantaneous prayers at people near and far, knowing that many prayers may show no visible results, but that at least some of them will hit their mark. When you fill a swamp with stones, a hundred loads may disappear under the water before a stone appears on the surface, but all of them are necessary.

If ten million praying people in the United States stopped for a few seconds several times every day to flash a prayer at the President or our Senators, they would feel a gentle spiritual power almost lifting them out of their chairs. Let's get ten million to try it. We might tell these leaders by post card or telegram that we are praying, and so help them tune in to God.

"But," said a friend, "would you find ten million who are willing to pray? Isn't that fantastic?"

Five hundred million people to mobilize

We did some figuring. We did not depend upon church membership. We looked for people who really have a reason to pray. All who have lost their sons, those separated from their loved ones, the wives, the sweethearts of men in the armed forces, their fathers, mothers, brothers, sisters, cousins and bosom friends, every young mother with her first born in her arms and her husband gone. All these are looking up to God in prayer. So are the boys who have faced death. So are the boys who have been wounded and maimed for life. Those boys without eyes or arms or legs must pray. They will grow bitter or go stark mad if they do not feel necessary, if they must only look on in helpless despair.

In this praying army belong old people who thought they were "has beens." Many people whose lives were irreligious in youth turn to God as they grow old and useless and lonesome, perhaps feeling themselves a burden on society. A husband or wife dead, and the young folks married and moved away, leaving widowed mothers or fathers alone. These lonesome old people are eager to pray if they are convinced prayer will make any difference.

There are millions of other lonesome people, for example, single men and women who sleep in furnished rooms and eat in cafeterias or restaurants. There are traveling men and women who seldom become intimately acquainted with the people they meet and never speak to the throngs of strangers whom they pass on the streets. They would pray. There are laboratory workers, scientists, men and women whose tasks keep them over noisy machinery where they are really alone, even when surrounded by people, for they are unable to talk. They could pray.

There are millions of men and women who do routine work with their hands while their minds are idling. Their work prevents them from reading, but they could pray. What is more, when they see that their prayers are important to save the world, they will pay. While sewing, sweeping, cooking, washing dishes, making beds, watching their children, women will pray, as Brother Lawrence did in his kitchen, if they believe that their prayers will help mold the future of their children and of their children's children.

All these named above total more than one hundred million. All of them could give hours upon hours to prayer. Their minds are empty a large part of the time, their hearts are lonesome, and they yearn to feel necessary and to belong. They want to feel they are doing something really helpful to the world. They will rise to the challenge if they believe that the future of the world depends upon their prayers.

In Europe and Asia there are millions upon millions of others who have been in the horrors of hell, with lost homes, lost families, lost careers, lost hopes, who have nowhere to look save toward heaven. Four hundred million are war victims, wretched, stunned, sickened, blasted, grasping for some way, and will pray with eager desperation, if only praying will bring a different world.

But what of the active men and women whose minds "are very busy streets," people so busy they will hop, skip, and jump across these pages—if they see them at all. They are thronged by people, by problems, and by ideas. They think there is no time to pray. But they are mistaken. There are a hundred chinks of time every day in the busiest lives, and into these chinks they could shoot flash prayers for the builders of the new world. Even when surrounded by family or business associates they could flash momentary secret messages to God.

Out of this enormous reservoir of "man power" can be recruited an army of ten million—as many as we had in the Armed Forces of the United States during this World War. Some of them will fill a hundred chinks a day with prayer and some ten. One hundred million prayers falling upon our world leaders every day will grip these men with a sense of sacred responsibility, a divine love for humanity, and a great hunger and thirst to look up to God and receive His plan.

And when ten million of us pray for our world leaders, think what that will do to us, as well as to them. It will make us larger, more interested in the great world issues, more likely to read carefully all the facts that will enable us to pray intelligently. Thousands of ideas will come to us of ways to help our world.

Silence is more powerful than noise

Prayer is likely to be undervalued by all but wise people because it is so silent and so secret. We are often deceived into thinking that noise is more important than silence. War sounds far more important than the noiseless growing of a crop of wheat, yet the silent wheat feeds millions, while war destroys them. Nobody but God knows how often prayers have changed the course of history. Many a man who prayed received no credit excepting in heaven. We are tempted to turn from prayer to something more noisy like speeches or guns, because our motives are mixed. We are interested in the making of a better world, of course, but we also want people to give us credit for what we have done.

Secret prayer for others all during the day is an acid test of our unselfishness. Our little selves must fade out, leaving a self-forgetting channel, through which God's warmth flows unhindered in lovely unending prayer. The highest form of communion is not asking God for things for ourselves, but letting Him flow down through us, out over the world—in endless benediction. In the old Hebrew story Sodom needed ten good men to be saved. Now the world needs ten million. Anybody Christian enough to have read this far must be one of that ten million or there will not be enough to save our age.

Pray for the Church

The world cannot be saved by three men, or by five hundred around peace tables, even though their plans come out of heaven. Their work is vital, but it is not nearly enough. They draw the blue-prints of peace; but treaties become scraps of paper when men and nations hate or rankle under the sense of injustice, as four men out of five in this world are doing now. In Africa, Asia, the East Indies and Latin America the illiterate three-fifths of the human race are slaves, penniless, hungry, sick, engulfed in hopeless debts, driven to grinding toil from dawn to darkness. Three-fifths of the human race are in deeper poverty, hunger, depravity, ignorance, fear, and despair than any slum in the United States. This war has plunged Europe into that condition, and now misery covers four-fifths of the world. In these wretched areas of hate and resentment new Hitlers will find eager ears.

Bombing these victims of despair if they attempt to revolt against the status quo will not prevent a third world war. A police force cannot keep a billion and a quarter starving victims down with tanks and bombs. They outnumber the people with plenty, five to one. To defeat them we should have to annihilate so many millions that Hitler would seem a saint by comparison with us. We would not defeat them. God has been with us in this last war, but He would be on the side of the oppressed if we fought against them. It is we who would be destroyed by Him and by them. The crux of the peace problem is not the power to frighten suffering men into submission, but the power to heal their misery: this is the way of the Good Samaritan, the way of Jesus, and it is the only way out.

We must heal this festering area of misery as swiftly as possible. By 1965 we shall know whether we are headed towards permanent peace or towards another worse hell. We must labor with loving service, and it will require devoted men and billions of dollars, for this is a large world. Who will do it?

The Christian Church of America not only has the financial resources adequate to save the world, but she has her vast missionary network over the world. This is the arm with which the Church can reach out and rid the world of the dangerous festering areas of despair where the next wars are breeding. Missionaries are better prepared than government diplomats to meet and lift the neediest people. Wendell Willkie reported after his trip around the world that he found the missionaries were the most popular foreigners in every country. Our ambassadors and consuls mingle with the officials and the elite of other countries. Missionaries work in the hovels of poverty with the sick, the lepers, with the dirtiest and most illiterate. They are the diplomats to the masses. They work for the love of Christ at a mere subsistence wage. In turning hatred into love, vice into virtue, and ignorance into light they can achieve more with ten dollars than governments can achieve with one hundred.

Therefore pray for Christians

Pray that American Christians may become large-visioned enough soon enough to pour out their prayers, their money, their love, and their youth over all the world.

Pray that people with war bonds may convert them into Peace Bonds by giving them to Mission Boards, enough bonds to meet the emergency.

Pray that the white race may become color blind.

Pray for missionaries! Every missionary needs ten thousand praying backers.

"But," asked a friend, "do you think American Christians would be that idealistic, that Christian?"

Many would not, at their present low spiritual temperature— not until the Church experiences a mighty spiritual awakening. Cold Christians will not give their lives and will give little money to missions. But when Christians are full of Christ, they will give life and money until they feel the ecstasy of sacrifice. Therefore, one thing upon which the fate of the world hangs is a Pentecostal awakening of our American churches. Prayer is the power which always turns dead churches alive, and makes small Christians big—prayer plus a tremendous sense of being needed, a gripping cause. We have the cause. We do not yet have enough prayer.

The first place for us to center our prayer is upon our own congregation, to say: "Lord, save the world and begin right with us." How, then, can we start a Pentecost in our church?

How Pentecosts begin

When a congregation prays in solid array, we have the same conditions as they had at Pentecost, when, the Book of Acts says, "These all continued with one accord [unanimously] in prayer and supplication.... When the day of Pentecost was come, they were all with one accord in one place.... And they, continuing daily with one accord in the temple, and breaking bread from house to house, did eat their meat with gladness and singleness of heart." Somebody could make a wonderful study of the manifestations of the Holy Spirit in the last two thousand years of the Christian Church. He would, I think, find this statement to be true: "The Holy Spirit is ever eager to break through, but fails, except where He finds loving, joyous, unity in prayer."

The first Pentecost shows us also what to expect when the Holy Spirit comes. We may expect the unexpected—perhaps outward evidences like tongues of fire, or a shaking house, or prison doors opened. But Pentecost also wrought results in people: "All that believed were together and had all things in common, and sold all their possessions and goods, and parted them to all men, as every man had need." Selfishness, the most common of all sins against Christ, melted into generosity. There were also results in people of the surrounding community. "The same day there were added unto them about three thousand souls." The greatest of the results of Pentecost was a spiritual explosion. Christ-filled men and women went all over the world to tell the glad news.

It has been the vogue among us educated people to look down upon the ignorant congregations among whom manifestations of the Spirit are most common. But it will do us no harm to ask ourselves (at least once in a lifetime) this question: "Do the simple people perhaps fulfill the conditions of the coming of a Pentecost better than we do? Does a Negro camp meeting have a oneness of spirit, an utter surrender, a sharing of all they possess with one another, such as we seldom achieve among all the members of a well-to-do or sophisticated congregation?"

We think these "manifestations of the Spirit" are produced by ignorance; whereas, perhaps they really depend upon surrender, faith, unity of spirit, generosity, utter penitence, and humility.

Some of us are seeing unexpected and marvelous visitations of the Holy Spirit among highly educated people whenever they become as humble and full of love and united into "one accord."

The effect of prayer is like genius—fresh, surprising, astounding—but safe, utterly safe! So my fellow minister who may be reading these pages, if your cultured leaders sit back in judgment every Sunday while you preach, don't let them defeat you any longer. Teach them to stop leaning back in judgment and to lean forward in prayer. Then expect the impossible!

Make prayer the climax of the service

The Roman Catholic church secures the united and intense prayer of all present at the moment of the elevation of the host. Protestants need to achieve a sublime climax in the prayer period as unifying and stirring as the Catholic mass. This will come only when minister and people are sure of this, that every prayer we utter from the heart begins to change history at once.

Most prayers of intercession one hears in church are tragic disappointments, meager, vague, half-hearted, powerless, small. People seldom pray as if they realized that prayer changes the world.

Evangelical Christianity is lost unless it discovers that the center and power of its divine service is prayer, not sermons; God, not the preacher. This does not mean that more time must be spent in preparing written prayers, it does mean that minister and people need to spend more time preparing themselves for the service by prayer at home. In order that they may be alone in prayer, some ministers do not have breakfast with their families on Sunday morning.

An inner circle of prayer

A small group of praying people need not wait for an invitation from the pastor or for the rest of the congregation. They can band themselves together in prayer, and if they persist long enough and earnestly enough, they will set a church on fire. It is hard work, but the reward is wonderful. The commonest of all methods of bringing a dead church back to life is to form an inner prayer circle.

One praying person in church

Even one person praying alone in a church can do a great deal toward raising the spiritual thermometer. We who travel much among strangers have many opportunities to try this. Often we sit in the back of the church incognito and pray for the service. When we enter the church we may sense that the congregation is listless and the preacher is defeated by their dullness of soul. It is a hard fight to pray against such a frozen current, but the harder it is, the more it is needed. So we literally fight for God. We pray for everybody, as well as for the pastor. While we are praying with intense concentration, we feel the Holy Spirit moving the speaker; his voice takes on a new timbre, his face a new radiance. He leaves the written sermon, which becomes too cold for him, and utters inspired words which come to him.

Several years ago, in St. Petersburg, Florida, my eyes were caught by a white-haired woman, dressed all in white, with a pale, sympathetic face, and I talked, looking straight at her. She seemed to be drawing from me better than my best, and I felt inspired. At the end of the meeting she came to the platform, and I told her how she had helped me. "That was because I prayed while you talked," she said. "I know what that can do for a preacher; my husband was a minister."

One Easter morning I entered a church in Bombay, India, a total stranger, and sat in the rear pew. The sermon was hopelessly bad, and I, who had come to receive an Easter blessing, was exasperated. I said to God, "I at least will help these cheated people." I began to pray in silence at the backs of their heads, one at a time. To my astonished joy every person, almost the moment I prayed, either turned, or bowed his head, or looked toward the ceiling, or shook his head, or passed his hand over the back of his head. I have never before nor since experienced such a one hundred percent response.

Before some of us speak in a church we close our eyes or look at a favorite picture of Christ and try to raise the spiritual temperature by praying hard for one pew and then another. We imagine Christ descending from above upon the people or walking down the aisle with tearful wistfulness, touching one after the other. It is so hard to fight the "secular" atmosphere of many churches that every nerve aches. But the effort is infinitely rewarding. One's own soul catches fire, and after nearly every such service people say, "We felt Christ," or "The Holy Spirit was powerful today."

It is more important for a preacher to have himself and his congregation ready than to have his sermon ready.

How Prayer Helps God

An honest clergyman confessed that he was baffled by a problem which puzzles many people. "I do not believe that prayer for other people does them any good unless they hear me praying," he said. "When I pray with my congregation before me, they hear what I say, and I open their minds toward God. That is understandable. But when I pray for a Russian leader ten thousand miles away, what happens? I surely cannot persuade God to try harder to help Stalin, for God is like Christ, always doing His best. So what's the use?"

This is how I answered him:

"You can't escape facts. The fact is that thousands upon thousands of people are being helped by intercessory prayer even when they are beyond the range of our voices. Missionaries beg people on the other side of the world to pray hard for them. They feel power when others pray, and are weak when others stop praying.

"Ten thousand people in America promised to pray for our literacy work. Their prayers have opened the doors of men's hearts around the whole world like an invisible love force, and have made impossible obstacles melt away like steel before a blow torch. The enormous results which appear when many people pray is what makes me sure we can do any good thing if enough of us pray enough. Intercessory prayer is as irresistible as Jesus declared it was—'Whatsoever ye ask in my name believing it shall be done' He said that a dozen different ways.

"But you ask why, and the answer is not easy. You are right when you say that God always does His best, and that we do not persuade God to try harder. There is another explanation—that we persuade people to listen to God. That is what you do when you pray in front of your congregation, persuade them to pray with you and to listen to God."

"Persuade them? How could we, when they are far away and don't hear us?"

"Perhaps they do hear us," I told him. "Their subconscious minds might hear us with that sixth sense called telepathy. That is a possible explanation, and recent experiments make it reasonable. Every mind, it now seems probable, unconsciously receives more or less messages from other minds. We all know people who felt intuitively when their loved ones at a distance went through peril or pain or death. The British and American Annals of Psychic Research contain thousands of these instances. Recent experiments, especially those of Professor Rhine of Duke University, have silenced the majority of doubters concerning extrasensory perception.

"Like radios, we seem to be tuned in to each other a part of the time, and turned off at other times. Our tuning-in buttons seem to be in the unconscious mind and nearly out of conscious control, just as the heartbeat is nearly out of our control. It is likely that every time we think intensely, some people near and far who happen to be tuned into us get our thoughts all day long without knowing where their ideas come from. It is likely that we are catching other people's thoughts. A broadcasting center never knows who may be tuned in. New discoveries in electronics are being made every month. Possibly telepathy employs electronic energy as the radio does, but on the other hand telepathy may be 'pure mind' or 'purely spiritual,' for all we yet know."

"I believe in telepathy. In fact, I have experienced it. Who hasn't?" said the clergyman. "But how does telepathy help God?"

How we unlock the door

I replied:

"Christ says, 'Behold I stand at the door and knock.' But God cannot get in, for most men have their doors closed toward Him nearly all the time, and many have 'lost the key'; they never talk to God. People listen to each other a million times before they listen to God once. Their thoughts are turned outward, not upward. If you pray for a man a thousand miles away, his unconscious mind may at that very moment be attuned outward toward you. If so, he will get your prayer, and that may start in him a desire for God. Desire is what tunes men in to God. If you thus help turn a man toward God, you perform the service of a telephone operator, you connect the man with God. That helps God to speak to him directly.

"Suppose, for example, a hundred people are praying for the President of the United States, 'Lord, help the President to feel hungry and thirsty for Thy wisdom,' and the President is tuned in to some or many of that hundred. If so, he will get their prayer subconsciously and will feel a desire to look up, listening to God; then God can tell the President directly the right answer to his problems.

"Thus, by praying, people help God reach the President just as you help God reach your congregation when they hear you preach or pray in church. The President hears them by mental radio."

A dozen of us had an electrifying demonstration of this at a retreat in Washington January 2, 1945. We felt that President Roosevelt needed our prayers because the future so greatly hinged upon his doing God's will. So we decided to send Walter Judd and Rufus Jones to see the President, but, first, we all prayed. Here is the secretary's report of what happened:

"Somebody placed a picture of President Roosevelt on the mantle beside a picture of Christ. 'Let us try to see Christ speaking to Roosevelt,' he said. After a long silence, a wonderful thing happened. I never before saw a Quaker kneel, but Rufus Jones knelt and offered a powerful prayer for Franklin Roosevelt. As this great man knelt, I saw him lifted so far above Roosevelt that I felt the very heavens pouring down through him and flooding Roosevelt with light and love and humility. In another room the phone rang, and the Secretary of Roosevelt, Miss Tumulty, gave a long personal message to our hostess, Marion Johnson, from her cousin, Franklin Roosevelt. When the news of that message at that moment came, Glenn Clark said, 'This was a ribbon of love between the White House and us. I know our prayer was "on the beam." ' "

"Prayer," said Walter Judd, "can reach Roosevelt through the ether better than a visit of Rufus Jones and me to him in body. Let us not attempt to give any resolutions to the President, but let the prayer alone do the job."

There is nothing unorthodox in this supposition. When telepathy is finally proven, it will be a scientific reason for being orthodox. It will mean that telepathy and answered intercessory prayer both employ a sixth sense, just as praying aloud and conversation use the vocal cords and ear drums, and just as the radio is often employed to preach through the ether.

Certainly there is nothing ethically wrong in telepathy. God hears our silent prayers and we hear His silent answer from mind to mind, or, in other words, telepathically. If telepathy operates between God and man it is just as right to use telepathy for drawing others to God as it is to preach to them in church. It is not a question of right or wrong. Nor is it a question of taste or distaste. It is only a question of fact. Is it a fact or isn't it?

Prayers are never lost

"But," asked a minister, "if the other man is not tuned in to me when I pray, is my prayer lost?"

"That," I replied, "is one more thing we do not know yet. When you pray in church, what percentage of your congregation really are listening to you? You might be horrified if you knew. But even if the people we pray for are not tuned in, somebody somewhere in the world is tuned in and catches our prayer. Every prayer is a world broadcast, and somebody always is listening in. So your prayers are never wasted. No prayer ends with your congregation. Even if your flock are not listening, your prayer reaches an audience thousands of miles beyond the reach of your voice. It goes around the world!"

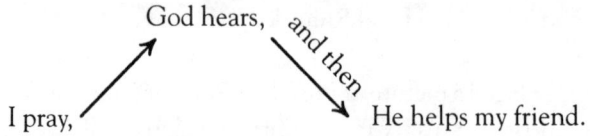

But the formula which would express "our helping God" is this:
My friend is closed toward God but open toward me.
By prayer for him I open toward Him and God.
Then God speaks to him through me.
My friend feels a desire for God and opens toward Him.
The diagram would be like this:

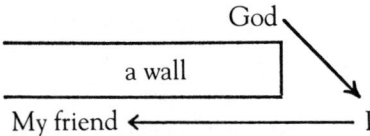

This is exactly what we do when we talk to our friend about God, or preach at him from a pulpit, or talk to him over the radio, or write him a letter about God, or send him a Bible. The same things happen when we pray, because the mind is a "mental radio." Many of us, because we believe this, pray with great faith—and when there is great faith there are great results.

This idea of helping God fits in perfectly with His loving nature, with man's stubborn nature, and with what the Bible tells us.

Helping the unbeliever

A prominent Christian leader recommends leaving this idea out of this book because it might prove objectionable to some devout persons who are rooted and grounded in the other idea. On the other hand, many college teachers and students who have never prayed much for others insist that this is the most valuable contribution to the modern man's faith in the entire book. Scores have testified that it has given them a new reason to pray and a new experience of God. A college professor is now writing a book to show that it has an even scientific basis.

So here was the choice: to risk losing either the complete endorsement of some grand old saints or those who want to believe in prayer yet have no logical basis for their faith. There can be no doubt which choice Jesus would make: "They that are whole need no physician, but they that are sick." He said, "I came not to call the righteous but sinners to repentance." There are multitudes of sinners against prayer, by their own confession. "I, a minister, don't pray," writes a man in today's mail, "and how can I teach others to pray?" There are multitudes whose prayers are wholly adoration and submission—never intercession. Here before me are three large volumes on the subject of prayer—but intercession is dismissed with a few sentences. Those who need no physician for their prayer life are very few, compared with the multitudes who are spiritually drowning and reaching for help.

This explanation is left because it is helping many troubled souls. There is no choice.

Separating telepathy from bad company

Some people dislike associating prayer with telepathy, because telepathy has been associated in their minds with sleight-of-hand and gypsy fortune-tellers. Well, so has prayer been associated with voodoo. And so have medicine and chemistry been mixed with alchemy until recent years, and there are still some "quack doctors" to be found.

Telepathy has come into very respectable company since the invention of the radio. Some universities are studying it in parapsychology classes. Its most recent triumph is with the blind.

At Old Farms, Connecticut, scores of war-blinded veterans are learning "how to see without eyes."

"Call it 'sixth sense,' " says Dr. Levine. "Call it 'human radar' or what you will. I cannot explain its mechanics—but I do know it works.

"Roughly, 'human radar' or 'facial sight,' as it may also be called, is based on the proposition that the human body emits tiny but definite rays of energy of some mysterious variety. These, on coming in contact with a house, wall, car, or any other object are 'bounced back.' A person taught to be attuned to those messages receives them, in some little-understood manner, through the skin or facial nerves. With training, their meaning can be interpreted by the brain—much as sights, sounds, or feelings are interpreted through their own organs. Distance, size, shape and texture can be determined with remarkable accuracy. What happens is that the face, and in some degree the whole body, is converted into a supplementary organ of sense."

An influential psychologist who had been concerned over his barren spiritual life was led into a new very vital religious experience through the following train of reasoning, which may appeal to other scientific minds.

What science knows

Our two billion nerve and brain cells are all miniature electric batteries. Together they produce a magnetic field which we have instruments to measure. Our brains are broadcasting faint radio waves with every thought. Do we also possess receiving sets? Can these be tuned in and can they interpret ideas through radio waves from other brains? Yes, this is within the range of possibility. Gray matter under the cortex of the brain is the most sensitive matter known to science, for it is delicate enough to be the home of thoughts. It might just as easily receive messages too delicate for any radio instrument to detect, probably using wave lengths still unexplored by science. Our knowledge of radio activity is still new and meager. Wave lengths could be used all the way down to electronic waves 1/100,000 as long as light waves.

So there is no reason why the brain's radio waves could not be picked up and correctly interpreted: but are they? This is merely a question of cumulative evidence. Telepathy is unquestionably gaining headway, though there are eminent psychologists who regard it as unproven. The experiments of Professor Rhine at Duke University, after the most rigid scrutiny, stand unshaken.

Experimenters ought to pray

On the other hand, psychologists who call telepathy unproven have tried experiments with negative results. Perhaps these psychologists omit a factor which Professor Rhine manages to capture—emotional sympathy. His most successful associates are students for the ministry, religiously inclined persons, with complete confidence in one another and unity of spirit. Sympathy and confidence seem to be the radio dials which attune minds to one another. Many laboratory tests which get negative results may be too cold or monotonous for the subconscious minds to make the effort to tune in—just as we turn off radio broadcasts which weary us. Thousands upon thousands of telepathy cases reported by the societies for psychic research are, ninety-nine times out of a hundred, charged with deep feeling between mother and son, man and wife, dear friends.

If sympathy and confidence are the "catalytic agencies" necessary for subconscious minds to venture to tune in, then prayer experiments ought to be far superior to those in a laboratory with cards or other apparatus. People would certainly feel more confidence and eagerness to "turn on their mental receiving sets" if we were praying for their welfare than if we were using them as guinea pigs. Prayer would be the best imaginable key to unlock the defensive suspicion with which people shut themselves from others who are not very near and dear to them. One reason Professor Rhine has succeeded is that he has secured the requisite emotional conditioning in the subconscious minds of his associates.

These considerations led the psychologist to begin praying experimentally. He got the same results as we have here described. But what is even more important, his own relationship with God was transformed. He wrote exultantly: "It is surprising how God can be a reality in one's life and how it is possible to have Him in the background of one's thinking and acting all the time."

The hypotheses about prayer using the same channels as telepathy may turn out to be only half of the truth. Glenn Clark believes that prayer operates at a deeper level than telepathy, at that deepest level where we all flow into God, our great Father. If he is right, then our experiments are at least headed in the right direction.

We have landed on a new continent

Explorers in the realm of the spirit are like Columbus when he landed on a new continent and did not know what lay beyond. We probably have only just reached the beach-heads of prayer. A vast unknown continent lies beyond us to be explored, conquered and cultivated. Nothing is so thrilling as discovery. Every Christian can and should join in the highest of all adventures in the most wonderful of all worlds, the world of the spirit. Nobody need leave home nor give up his work, for he has his mind with him every minute, and it is in the mind that this exploration is carried on.

Those closing lines of Walt Whitman, in his poem "Passage to India," can be true of us all as we make this fascinating spiritual voyage of discovery:

"Sail forth, steer for the deep waters only,
Reckless, O soul, exploring,
I with thee and thou with me.
For we are bound where mariner has
not yet dared to go,
And we will risk the ship, ourselves and all.

"O my brave soul!
O farther, farther sail!
O daring joy but safe!
Are they not all the seas of God,
O farther, farther, farther sail!"

Prayer Experiments

Spiritual explorers

The electrical wizard Steinmetz said the greatest discoveries of the twentieth century would be in the realm of the spirit. He is right—and only those who pray will make these discoveries. Heaven knows that we need these discoveries now, for we are in the midst of a war to control men's minds. Some of us are tingling with the zest of adventure, for over every hill and around every corner new breathtaking surprises greet our eyes. Adventuring in prayer is exciting fun. God is there ahead of us when we walk out in His direction, and God loves surprises and endless variety.

In the alchemy stage

In the realm of the spirit it is not easy to determine what is truth and what is superstition, because spiritual facts are more difficult to count and hold steady than most physical phenomena. Much of our data concerning spiritual matters is in the same stage as chemistry and medicine were when they were still called "alchemy." Three centuries ago the technique of checking and cross checking physical phenomena had not been developed, and so truth and error were intertangled. We are in that stage yet in many matters of religious experience. Our checking and rechecking of spiritual data is still crude. These data need tests all their own. You cannot put a pin through prayers nor hold them under a microscope, nor dissect them on an operating table. Each of us must go into the laboratory of his own soul, try most of his experiments alone, and exchange notes with other men who are trying similar experiments. Since there is but one witness to the inner experiment, it is liable to faulty observation, faulty memory and unconscious distortion. Words may not mean to the reader what they meant to the writer of the experience.

What results are visible

Some results can be seen by all men. If prayers are miraculously answered, if divided wills become integrated, if bad men become saints, if the lame walk, or the blind see, we have external evidence which is plain to us all. We need to devise better tests to show what results come from praying for others at a distance. The evidence on this question is verifiable. All doubts will be ended not by argument but by experimentation under test conditions. The next few pages suggest some fresh ways of testing intercessory prayer.

More trained experimenters needed

A larger number of the men who have been trained in scientific method, and who are experimenting with intercessory prayer, must exchange their findings. Only so can we sift the true from the false, and at last describe the laws of prayer for others with greater accuracy. That this field is too sacred to be subjected to experimentation is untrue. The opposite is the truth. Is prayer as vital as the Bible and the church say it is? If so, then everybody needs to be made sure beyond the shadow of doubt. Prayer is too sacred not to be given to the entire human race.

New names for new facts

Like all discoverers of new things, we shall have to name what we discover. In one of the Camps Farthest Out we had great fun suggesting names for the golden bath of love and prayer which surrounded us all week. "You have been swishing prayers at one another and the world all day," the leader said. "You know how it feels; now let us name it!" They made many suggestions like these:

"Flash prayers, scatter prayers; let prayers flow around people or through them; whisper prayers, throw a halo of prayer or a prayer cloak around people; envelop them in prayer, help Christ inside people, hold people and Christ together."

Many people think Glenn Clark's *Broadcasting Prayer and Love* is the truest description of the beautiful experience.

The camp broadcasts

Under the leadership of Glenn Clark a hundred or more people form circles, or horseshoes, or a V, like the outstretched arms of Christ, and hold hands while they "broadcast." Dramatizing prayer in this fashion induces everybody to participate and stimulates imagination. They imagine their circle transferred to Washington, where it encircles the White House, with the President seated in the center. Then the leader says:

"Lord, use this circle as a great funnel through which Thy love can flow to the President. Use us to make him hungry and thirsty for Thy guidance in the vast problems he confronts. Use us to help him hear Thee and do Thy will for the world. We lift him with our hands to Thee and leave him there in Thy presence."

The big circle is then taken in imagination across the Atlantic, to London, and thrown around the Prime Minister of England, where the same prayer is repeated; then to Moscow, and thrown around the Premier of Russia; then to China, to India, to Japan, to Germany, and so on to the men and the countries which seem most in need of God's wisdom and help.

Glenn Clark's camps have seen miraculous happenings during and immediately following their prayer broadcasts, and have been convinced that mass broadcasting changes the very course of history.

Objects for which to pray

There are prayer priorities with which we must enlarge our prayers while we continue to pray for our friends, our relatives, and ourselves.

All the following people need to be floodlighted with prayer: The President of the United States and Congress, especially the Senate; the Prime Minister and Parliament of England, Russia's Premier and leaders, China's leaders, delegates at every peace conference, Japanese, Germans, church members and the clergy of Christians and Jews, the missionaries, motion picture leaders, radio broadcasters, all kinds of slaves and oppressed, Negroes, Americans of Japanese ancestry. We must pray that whites may become color blind, pray for illiterates, for all teachers, mothers and fathers, for understanding between capital and labor, for human brotherhood, for cooperatives, for the enlargement of people's minds to world vision, for business ethics and for a Christian economic system, for returned soldiers, for children and youth, for wholesome literature, for victims of liquor, drugs and vices of all kinds; for educators and better education. We must pray for hatred to vanish and love to rule the world; we must pray for more prayer, for it is the world's mightiest healing force. Doubtless, this long list omits some of your own prayer priorities. Each of us must pray about the themes which he considers most vital, for prayer is valueless unless heart and faith are in it.

Pray with pencil and paper at hand. When God sends a thought, write it down and keep it visible until it can be carried into action. Pray for individuals by name. Vital prayers always suggest things to be done. Indeed, prayer and action must be mates, or both are weak. The mightiest men and women on earth are strong in prayer and strong in deeds. These are the only unbeatable combination.

Glenn Clark, in his *I Will Lift Up Mine Eyes*, tells us how to write out thoughtfully our deepest soul's desires and offer them up to God, and make them a burnt offering in a fireplace. Many who do this say it is uncanny how exactly and completely God answers those prayers. This technique has no magic influence with God, but it does aid our own thinking to be more definite and careful. Many of us are not sure what we think until we have written it down. Most people do not think complete thoughts, but have their heads full of splinters and slivers of thought—broken like a shattered pane of glass. Their prayers, like their thoughts, are usually in splinters. Writing out our thoughts forces us to make them more complete. This does not mean they should be complicated. The clearest thoughts are often written so tersely they snap like a whip. Many perfect prayers can be flashed in ten seconds.

Flash prayers

To join in the "Praying Ten Million" one need not leave home nor neglect his business. Everybody in every ordinary day has hundreds of chinks of idle wasted time which may be filled with flash prayers ten seconds or a minute long. Here are illustrations of such moments:
Upon awakening in the morning
In the bath
Dressing
Walking down stairs
Asking the blessing at table
Leaving the house
Riding or walking to work
Entering the elevator
Between interviews
Preparing for lunch
And a hundred more chinks all day long until crawling into bed and
Falling asleep...

Experiments in trains and restaurants

Some of us who travel have hundreds of days when we can sit behind people in street cars, trains, stations, restaurants, concerts or lectures, and pray at the backs of their heads with our eyes open to see how many of them show signs of being aware.

At this instant I was looking at a man sitting by an open window half a block away. I shot a rapid fire of prayer at him, saying three or four times a second: "Jesus, friend,— Jesus is coming to you." In thirty seconds that man put his head in his hands and bent down over his desk, as though in prayer. Flashing hard and straight prayers in a street car while repeating "Jesus,

Jesus, Jesus" usually makes some of the people near you act as though they had been spoken to. If they do not respond the first time, you can return again and again, until they show signs of being "tuned in." They look at you curiously, often smile, and frequently say something. All Christians should acquire this habit. I will try to describe how it feels. It seems to me I am pushing these prayers from my breast and fingers, as well as from my brain—from my whole nervous system. I find myself exhaling a little through my nose with each pressure. After a while, the car or room seems gently "excited," like the magnetic field around a magnet. Everybody behaves like an old friend. People seem to like us to pray for them.

People who are busy reading or talking seem not to respond. That is understandable. All of us have seen how two broadcasting stations, having the same wave length, interfere in our radios. Thoughts can do the same. It is the people whose minds are unoccupied and who are asking, "What next?" who will respond, and often with a quick sharp look of recognition or curiosity.

Far from making one tired, this prayer for others is the finest tonic I know. When you are utterly tired from work or study, walk out into the street and flash prayers at people. Your nerves will tingle with the inflow from heaven. Prayer "is twice blest. It blesses him that gives and him that receives." If you want an experience full of profit and stimulus, take a day off and ride incognito in the buses or street cars of your city, flashing strong, fast prayers at people one by one, and noting results. Do this hundreds—if possible, thousands—of times, observing what percentage of them get your broadcast.

Some startling answers

I was on a Pennsylvania train praying at the back of a woman's head with a picture of Hoffman's "Boy Christ" in my hand, when she suddenly turned around and said, "What the world needs is more religion."

"Are you a missionary?" I asked her.

"No," she said, "my husband is the conductor."

"You must be a very religious woman," I said.

"No," she replied, "I am a Methodist, but I don't do much at it."

"Then why," I asked, "did you say the world needs more religion?"

"I don't know," she replied, "but I just felt like talking about it."

Something of this kind is an everyday occurrence with us who pray for everybody we meet. It never happens unless we are praying.

How to know when they hear you

If people reveal no response we cannot conclude that they are unaware. It may be because they repress their impulse to respond. All of us are aware of being gazed at but repress any response unless we are definitely interested, or unless we trust the person gazing at us. We instinctively "play safe." This is why people often do not speak to us when we pray for them (or for that matter, when we say good morning to them). Frequently they betray their awareness by some such response as putting their heads in their hands as in prayer, looking upward and closing their eyes, sighing, looking around, rubbing the back of their heads with their hands, getting up and walking about, shaking their heads sidewise or up and down, a sudden quick jerk as if they had been spoken to.

A railroad station is one of the best places in which to experiment if you have minutes or hours to wait for trains. Fix your eyes on any object you choose, and from that still position try to send a "mental radio field" around in all directions. One seems to "warm up" and gather strength exactly as a radio does when we turn it on. Some of us talk to God about the hopes He has for all the people about us. We send the "still, small" pressure of prayer toward one person at a time, whispering to God or to them, and watching to see who seems to hear and to respond. Only those who try such experiments ever faintly imagine what good prayer in a railroad station can do. At this moment in this station the man opposite me keeps looking at me intently as I write, as though he would ask, "Did you speak to me?" The young woman near me whispered to her soldier friend, and he replied to her aloud, "You're just psychic, that's all." And they both are looking hard at me.

It must be the prayer that does it, for when I do not pray for people they show neither interest nor friendliness. I am personality zero when I do not pray. The moment the prayer pressure starts, the strange, sweet kindliness begins to appear on people's faces and they look at me, ready to talk. If hundreds or thousands of Christian people tried this experiment of "turning on" and "turning off" prayer for those near them, our knowledge of this important matter would vastly increase. And until they do try prayer for others, they miss one of life's richest joys.

All of us have sensed in certain rare persons the strange sense of something we call vaguely "a saintly personality." It develops only in men and women of prayer. Science knows little about it, but that proves nothing. Science knows nothing about the nature of such a simple thing as fluorescence, yet many of us have seen it. When we experiment with prayer, we become scientists in the most important and least understood of all fields.

It is time to stop our "conspiracy of silence" about intercessory prayer. "Educated" people have as many taboos as the Hottentots, and this is one of them. Scientific investigation is hampered by the fear of being called a "mystic." For example, not many people would confess the following in public—yet what could be more Christlike?

Loud silence

The praying—and thinking—of nine people out of ten is too feeble, like a very low-grade broadcasting station. By persistent training we can make our thoughts and prayers louder and to reach much farther. Nobody, I think, has yet described any special technique for making our thoughts shout and our prayers broadcast far. That there is a direct relation between intensity and outreach is suggested by the fact that so many people get messages at a great distance when their dear ones are frightened or in an accident.

Some of us, while in a car or bus, fancy our spirits walking over to others and touching them on the shoulder, making some such speech as this: "Christ is in this car. He walks down the aisle to you—and you—and you. He is saying:

" 'I see in you hidden powers for greater usefulness, personality, happiness, friendship. These beautiful qualities are still in the bud; I will unfold them if you will say yes. I will make a wonderful person of you, a blessing to all the world.' "

The subconscious minds of people appear to be eager to hear about Christ's wonderful plans for their future. When one silently whispers to them about Christ's hope for them, they sigh and look happy.

Throwing a cloak of prayer over people

When we pray thus toward a man or a group, it feels as though we had thrown a spiritual cloak around our man. When another person is praying for me, I can feel the same spiritual cloak very distinctly enveloping me. I often check this feeling by turning to people and asking, "Did you start to pray for me just then?" and I always have found that I had guessed right. I like the thrill of being prayed for better than anything in the world. If you pray for people, they like it, and so does God like it; for you are helping Him reach them.

On the other hand, all of us dislike being stared at to make us turn around. We may refuse to turn because we are annoyed. It is too much like trying to invade another man's will, and nobody likes to be made a slave.

Moreover, people do not like to be reproved in prayer. If others fail in this experiment, possibly one reason may be that they try to convey ideas disagreeable or irrelevant to the receiver. So if you want your prayers to get by the suspicious guards of other men's unconscious minds, pray for the highest dream you have, and leave out the negatives. Jesus' prayers were all positive.

Pray while you read

Some of us, while reading newspapers, pause for a second over the names of world leaders in print and whisper, "Lord, may this man be hungry for Thee." Or we simply breathe the word "Jesus" and the man's name together. This will not delay our reading more than a second, and we may be doing great good by holding Jesus and that man together in prayer, even for one second. When this becomes a habit, we shall spread countless thousands of secret blessings over the world, and when millions pray over their newspapers the world may be saved by it.

Pray while listening to radio music

When listening to radio music, one may enjoy a very fruitful quarter or half hour, sitting with open or closed eyes and saying silently:

"What wilt Thou have me share with Thee now? Think Thy thoughts in my mind. Use me as a channel to make those on the radio hunger and thirst to be closer to Thee, to hear Thee speak, to do Thy will."

Pray for all whom we remember

It is beautiful to acquire the habit of whispering "Jesus" at every person who comes to memory. This has a splendid retroactive effect upon ourselves, for it begets love instead of the spirit of criticism. It is a good corrective for that unlovely tendency we have to disapprove of others. The more unattractive people are, the more we need to love them and pray for the ideal they can, by God's help, become. Forget the man as he is, and think vividly of the man he ought to be—and your thought at once begins to force itself into reality.

At last we shall reach a point where only sleep itself interrupts the day full of prayer—sleep, prayer's sunset; awakening, prayer's new sunrise. Then we shall see answers coming in ever-increasing wonder. One's heart aches to find so few who share this ecstasy.

Pray when awakening and when falling asleep

The moments of falling asleep and awakening are beautiful if they are filled with prayer. We can easily develop the habit, so that closing the eyes at night or opening them at dawn automatically reminds us to pray. "When I awaken I am still with Thee."

When people are unable to sleep at night, they waste millions of hours. We can put these sleepless hours to wonderful usefulness for a better world by praying for every person who comes to mind. For example, "Lord, use my prayer to help Stalin to feel hungry and thirsty for Thee; may he hear Thy still, small voice, and obey Thy will."

And so on, and on, perhaps for an hour—turning those fleeting fragments of thought which come when we are half asleep into prayers. The sum total of our prayers, if millions of us learn to do this, will be immense beyond all computation, and their influence incalculable.

Precede, enfold, and follow all deeds with prayer

Prayer and action should be wedded. Just as a great surgeon does his best work when praying while he works, so all of us do our best work. Have you not found that when you precede your efforts with prayer, and immerse them in prayer, and follow them with prayer, they always succeed beyond all your expectations? Prayer is four-fifths of the deed. When, for any reason, we forget to pray, our efforts are a dud. On the other hand, prayer is weak until we do all we know to help in other ways.

E. Harold Bredesen has a clock which his brother rescued from a sinking ship during the war. It strikes every fifteen minutes. Each time it strikes, Bredeson looks at a card on which he has written some cause for which he is praying, and, after a flash prayer, puts the card on the bottom of the pack of prayer cards. His pack of prayer cards keeps growing as he finds new causes for which he desires to pray. This is playing a game with quarter hours!

Another man put more than a thousand photographs of friends on his wall and prayed for them in the darkness throwing a flashlight on each one. There were extraordinary coincidences of friends writing him at the very hour he was praying. Cures of minor illnesses and sharp turns for the better were reported.

Some of us have written to the senators of our own state and to the representative of our own district, telling each of them that we desire to pray for him and asking him if he has a photograph which he will autograph and send us, to help us pray more realistically. Nearly every senator and representative will welcome such a letter and will be helped in his fight with subtle, endless temptations to yield to selfish lobbyists if he realizes that we are praying for him. Enough of us might mold the very course of history by this simple act.

Position of your body does not matter

Some people fail to make full use of prayer opportunities because they think they must assume a special position. It is not essential in praying to close or raise the eyes, to kneel or stand, to fold the hands or lower the head, nor to make the slightest change of position. However, these customs are all helpful if one is accustomed to them. Some positions are valuable for relaxation of mind and body. But you must never postpone flash prayers until you can find a prayer stool or a chance to close your eyes. You can pray wonderfully while driving an automobile, with your eye on the road every instant.

Rev. Calixto Sanidad, a Filipino saint, wrote: "I used to farm with my hand on the plow, my eyes on the furrow, but my mind on God." That was real. Prayer and work were wedded!

Praying with the body

Some of us who attend Glenn Clark's Camps know how powerful calisthenics can be as an aid to prayer. While pushing our arms full length out, up, front, down, we can repeat rhythmically:

"Lord... use—my body—and my—mind—and my—emotions—to help—the President—to hunger—and thirst—to hear—Thee speak—and to—do Thy will."

Glenn Clark writes:

> "We discovered that to pray truly, to pray with the greatest abandon and with all of one's power, one should pray with all one's being. It must be a technique that would include one's body as well as one's mind and one's soul."

Pray while taking a walk

One of the best ways to pray is to take a vigorous walk, talking to God in rhythm with the steps, thus:

"Lord, use my prayer—to help these people I am passing— to look up to Thee—to be hungry for Thy voice—to long to do Thy will—to hear Thee speak—to obey Thy voice—to do Thy will."

There is no more exhilarating way of taking exercise than a walking prayer. When your brain is weary, go out into a crowd and waft prayers in all directions; let them trail like a bridal veil, after people as they pass you. You will get the sense that something delicately gauzy, like soft morning light, floats after those for whom you pray. If your experience duplicates mine, you will feel a strange power developing like some long unused muscle. You will be strengthening your soul, just as victims of infantile paralysis strengthen their weak muscles.

If you feel you have cheated yourself in the past by not having a technique in prayer, and if you wish to discipline yourself to this form of prayer, it is simple—so simple that a child can do it. You may say silently with each breath, "Jesus," while you look at the people you meet, trying to help Him reach them. If you think of something else important enough, say it, but if not, the word "Jesus" with every breath is enough. There will never be a more blessed, higher thought to broadcast over the world. Do not strain, for that produces discord.

Then have a notebook to record the instances of observed results.

Practice makes perfect

Time and again, as you have read these pages, you have probably stopped and prayed. From now on, you must never fail to pray whenever you think of it, if only for a second. Habit building is a process of starting and sticking to it. If you begin to refuse, refusal becomes habitual, and soon checkmates the habit of prayer. Then you become the victim of an inner conflict between two impulses. The habit of praying is simple and unstrained, unless you allow it to be complicated by exceptions and refusals. If you keep sending flash prayers every time you think about it, without ever an exception, after a while you will find it is second nature. Any normal person can develop a habit of making every glance at another a gentle pressure of prayer, until, at last, the whole day is as full of little prayers as the sky is full of stars. There develops a sweet flowing into us from God, and an endless flowing out toward humanity. The quiet rhythm of heaven can be ours in the midst of a crowded, troubled, and desperate world. And the terrible world itself gradually changes around us when we live in His peace.

Our prayer may seem to be weak at first, but as we practice with thousands upon thousands of these flash prayers, we feel them grow in power, we feel them come back to us like radar. When that happens our hearts skip a beat with the thrill of it, for we know that we are learning to be channels for God, and, what is more, that we are children of God, working with Him for His Kingdom plan.

The blinding realization that by letting Him use us we can help save the world forces upon us an all-demanding challenge. It presses upon our time, every moment of it, as the air presses every moment against the wings of a plane, holding it to its high course.

Teach youth to pray frequently

A progressive American educator said: "Instead of teaching young people to listen to long prayers and longer sermons on Sunday morning, teach them to make brief sentence prayers many times a day; teach them that prayer is the best way to meet every need and every task."

Youth has a thousand times more mental and physical energy than Protestant churches have helped them use creatively. If high school boys and girls are taught that by praying for leaders they actually mold world history, they pray with all the reckless abandon of youth. This sense that they can do something vital rescues them from cynicism, enlarges their worldview, creates interest in really important affairs, keeps them close to God, makes them ambitious to serve, gives them a sense of mission, and saves them from throwing their lives away in cheap sin. American youth need a powerful Cause and a program they can undertake at once. Prayer for everybody is one such program, and saving our age is the Cause!

And we adults need that Cause just as much as youth, especially people over sixty. On every hand, one sees elderly people resigning from their work in order to "enjoy life during my last years." Most of them are lost and unhappy and in a few months they are likely to pine away and die. Joining the prayer army is their best hope, and if they know how prayer changes the world they will tingle with the sense of helping God.

Christ—The Answer

Modern psychology bears out every word Jesus said about thoughts, with sledgehammer emphasis. Every man's thinking takes on worldwide importance. Every evil thought not only contaminates the man himself, but makes the world worse, pushes it toward hell. Every good thought not only blesses the man himself but also pushes the entire world up toward heaven.

So Jesus plunges deep into the mind, the source of all action. "You have heard that it was said by them of old times Thou shalt not commit adultery, but I say unto you do not lust. Ye have heard do not kill, but I say do not hate." Because every theft, every lie, every vulgar word, and every murder comes from evil ideas.

To the Pharisees Jesus said: "You wash the exterior of the cup and saucer, but inside you are full of licentiousness and rapine. You are like white tombs, outside lovely, but inside full of bones of death and filth. Outside you appear just, but inside you are full of hypocrisy and wickedness." This is what Jesus was saying to the Pharisees. His words are just as true for our day. "These people," he said, "honor me with their lips, but their minds are far from me and in vain they worship me."

The Jews of his day supposed that eating pork poisoned the soul and the body, but Jesus told them: "Nothing that enters the mouth contaminates a man, but what comes out contaminates the man; because from the mind proceed bad thoughts, murders, adulteries, fornications, thefts, false testimonies, blasphemies. These are the things which defile a man."

Several times Jesus repeated these words: "A good man out of the good treasure of his heart bringeth forth good things; and an evil man out of the evil treasure bringeth forth evil things."

A clean mind is good but not good enough

It isn't enough to cleanse the mind of evil thoughts, though that is essential. An empty mind will not stay empty, or clean! Jesus' strange parable about a devil which left a man's mind and came back with seven more devils was exactly to the point. The demons found the man's mind cleansed and a vacuum, so they rushed in. The only way to keep out demonic ideas is to have the mind full of "a good treasure" of thoughts, vital, burning thoughts, big enough to fill the mind and heart.

Moreover, a clean empty mind is purely negative and useless to others. It does nothing to fight or cancel out the active burning hate—thoughts which curse our world.

That is why Paul was speaking a truth he got straight from Jesus when he said:

> "Whatsoever things are true, whatsoever things are honest, whatsoever things are just, whatsoever things are pure, whatsoever things are lovely, whatsoever things are of good report, if there be any virtue, and if there be any praise, think on these things."

If people have any virtue, praise it, says Paul rightly, and forget their weaknesses. For whatever we think about we fan into a flame, whether we think for it or against it.

No new brilliant thoughts are needed

It is not necessary for our thoughts to be new thoughts. Indeed, new ideas are not what we need at this moment, not even new good ones! Decades would pass before our new ideas would be accepted by the multitudes and before we could find out whether they were really workable. We cannot wait for decades. now is when our world needs help—now!

Besides, most new ideas prove to be wrong. They are like the "sports" in the plant world which appear in such profusion when electricity is applied to plants—only one new mutation in a million is a real improvement. The rest are inferior or monstrosities. Machiavelli and Nietzsche had an idea. When Hitler tried it on the world he dragged it into its present horror. We must suspect all new thoughts until they have been tested in the light of the life and teachings of Jesus. He and His way must become master of the Kingdom, and every thought must come into harmony with Christ.

Christ's teaching is the world's hope

Fortunately, the knowledge that can save the world is already ours. It is the way of Jesus Christ, what He is, what He teaches, and how He transforms men. When we join our thoughts to Him we are in an immense river, pouring through every race and every nation. Jesus has already proven to be the world's greatest blessing. He has not yet been able to save it from its present state, because not enough of us are thinking and acting upon His ideals. You and I and all true Christians confess that we have done far below our best. When we get behind the stupendous ongoing Christian current, we aid the only program which has any hope of saving our generation.

Christ is not only the most powerful person the world has known; He is the noblest. All the highest ideals since His day, as H. G. Wells declares, have sprung from His teachings. What is more, Jesus himself lived His ideals even better than He could find words to express them. Nine-tenths of the human race would follow Christ if they knew what He is, when they would not follow an abstract truth.

Becoming Christ-saturated

But how shall we help all men to know Him? That was Paul's question, and it still is ours. The greatest way to help Christ conquer the world is to saturate our own minds with Him. We do this by thinking about Christ and His Kingdom as much as we can. If we think about Him we shall inevitably witness for Him and work for Him. Other people will catch Him from us by our deeds and words. "Out of the fullness of the heart the mouth speaketh." But, equally important, they will catch our thoughts telepathically, just as advertisers send their messages out over the radio, in the knowledge that tens of thousands of people will tune in sooner or later. If we keep Him in our thoughts persistently all day, every day, we shall radio thoughts of Christ to the minds of countless millions all over the world.

His life in the Gospels

How can we saturate our minds with Christ? There is but one way to get a true picture of Him. This is to read His life in the four Gospels so often that we know it by heart. We who wish to be Christlike ought never to allow a day to pass without reading at least a chapter of the Gospels. We get the best results if we take a definite hour (and a fresh hour) every day. The last hour before going to bed is poor, especially after a hard day's work, for we are likely to fall asleep half way through a chapter. Many of the spiritual giants read their Bibles at four or five every morning, before others can disturb them.

To prevent this reading from becoming tedious, many of us, after finishing the Gospels in the familiar text, use fresh translations—The New American Revised, Goodspeed, Moffatt, Weymouth. After we have these Gospels practically memorized in English, a good way to learn a new language, like Spanish, French, or Chinese, is to read the Gospels in that language. Lord Macaulay read the Hindu New Testament while on the way to India, and surprised the Indians by speaking and reading their language upon his arrival.

We need determined wills to protect this hour with Christ from competing interests. Busy people are under constant temptation to allow Bible reading to be crowded out every other day, until omission becomes a habit. Then they find the edge of their interest dulling and their attention wavering. The only protection we have is to consider this hour of devotions a sacred engagement with God, and to decline all interrupting invitations. Even better is family Bible reading and prayer as a solemn daily engagement.

Having our shrines at home

Many of us, like the Roman Catholics, can pray better if we look at a shrine. Most Protestants churches are now using altars.

If we ought to "pray without ceasing," then we need shrines to remind us of Christ wherever we spend our time. We can construct little shrines for ourselves instantly at home or in a hotel room by placing a cross or the open Bible in front of our favorite picture of Christ. Some of us travelers have a picture folder containing pictures of Christ which we unfold and stretch across our dressers whenever we reach a new city. One Christian leader has a large globe, with an electric light inside, to represent "The Light of the World."

Many Christians have pictures of a friendly Christ in every room in the house, including the bathroom, to serve as reminders for their treacherous memories. The Catholics, with a cross around their necks to remind them of Christ, are using better psychology than those of us who use no helps and who never pray. Better to walk with crutches than not at all.

Filling the chinks of time

While a daily devotional hour is vital for saturating our minds with Christ, it is not enough. All during the day, in the chinks of time between the things we find ourselves obliged to do, there are moments when our minds ask: "What next?" In these chinks of time, ask Him:

"Lord, think Thy thoughts in my mind. What is on Thy mind for me to do now?"

When we ask Christ, "What next?" we tune in and give Him a chance to pour His ideas through our enkindled imagination. If we persist, it becomes a habit. It takes some effort, but it is worth a million times what it costs. It is possible for everybody, everywhere. Even if we are surrounded by throngs of people we can continue to talk silently with our invisible Friend. We need not close our eyes nor change our position nor move our lips.

How we think Christ's thoughts

Thinking about Christ constantly is easy to understand. It is not easy to do. Yet there is a way to do it without stopping our other occupations. It is to acquire a new way of thinking. Thinking is a process of talking to your "inner self." Instead of talking to yourself, talk to the Invisible Christ. If you do that all day every day, then your thoughts are spreading Christ all over the planet wherever other minds are tuned in to yours. Hundreds of thousands, or perhaps millions, of minds will be better. You become what George Eliot described in her "Choir Invisible":

> "The sweet presence of a good diffused,
> And in diffusion even more intense!
> So shall I join the choir invisible
> Whose music is the gladness of the world."

How to hold a conversation with Christ

Prayer at its highest is a two-way conversation. You may say silently or aloud, "Lord, what are Thou saying to me?" Then let your imagination perfectly loose while you reply to yourself what you suppose He would answer. You may imagine Him saying:

"This is for you and for everybody. I have been waiting for this moment all your life, waiting until you opened the channel so that I could speak. I have wonderful plans for you which cannot be realized until you listen as you are listening now. The trouble with all the world is that people do not stop to listen while I speak...."

Thought transformed into conversation with Christ becomes large, more unselfish, more worthwhile, purer, more noble. Try it!

When tired

When the mind is too weary to do hard thinking or praying, the loveliest word we can allow to float through our thoughts is "Jesus, Jesus, Jesus. Sweetest name on mortal tongue, sweetest name by angels sung, Jesus, precious Jesus." Many a dear mother of mediocre ability, walking through life, whispering, "Jesus" every moment will do more to sweeten and save humanity than all the cunning schemes of diplomats or the fine-spun guesses of philosophers who leave Jesus out. Just to think of others and whisper, "Jesus," is the noblest contribution most of us can ever make to other lives as well as our own. The spiritual life is a true democracy, for it is as freely given to the humble and unlearned as to the scholar!

Making it a habit

If we have had a lifetime habit of thinking with Christ left out we shall find the old habit stubborn. It is as difficult to learn the new way to think as it is to learn to typewrite or to play a piano or to learn a new language. We do it haltingly and rather feebly the very first time, like taking the first lessons in any high art. We must not underestimate the time required to become proficient, or we may say impatiently, "it can't be done," which is sheer nonsense. It can't be done well in a day. It can't be nonsense. It can't be learned perfectly in a year. But it can become nearly perfect in ten years. Meanwhile, the progress from day to day is so thrilling, and the satisfactions so wonderful, that every day is a joy. Perhaps we do other people more good while we are still learners than after we have become perfect, for we understand their difficulties and they understand ours. "The best teacher is he who is also a learner."

Even after a lifetime of prayer, the saints realize that they do not fully attain the perfect surrender of Christ to the thought of God. There will always be heights for us to attain—and that adds to the zest of living.

Jesus kept his mind in perfect surrender

Forty-seven times in the Gospel of John, Jesus said He was under God's orders, and that He never did anything, never said anything, until His Father gave the command. He was listening every moment of the day to His invisible companion and saying, "Yes." This perfect obedience was what made Him one with His Father and what gave the Father perfect confidence in the Son. It is the reason the Father loves his Son so fondly. This is exactly what the Gospel of John declares that Jesus said over and over and over. Here are typical passages:

John 5:19: "The Son can do nothing of himself [nothing!] but what he seeth the Father do; for what things soever the Father doeth, these also doeth the Son likewise."

5:30: "I can of mine own self do nothing:... I seek not mine own will, but the will of the Father which hath sent me."

7:16: "My doctrine is not mine, but his that sent me.... (28) And I am not come of myself: (29)... for I am from him, and he hath sent me.... (33) And I go unto him that sent me."

8:16: "I am not alone, but I and the Father that sent me.... (26) And I speak to the world those things which I have heard of him.... (28) I do nothing of myself.... (29) He is with me: the Father hath not left me alone; for I do always those things that please him."

10:17: "Therefore doth the Father love me, because I lay down my life.... (18) No man taketh it from me, but I lay it down of myself. This commandment have I received of my Father."

10:38: "The Father is in me, and I in him. (30) I and my Father are one."

At the heart of the universe is this wonderful, never-ending harmony, this incredible love between Father and Son. "I have kept my Father's commands and abide in his love. All things that the Father hath are mine." Jesus had earned the confidence and love of His Father, and so the world could be entrusted to Him as His responsibility.

We are invited to join them

Into that wonderful loving family we are invited, not as servants but as brothers of Christ, as sons of God. This is what Jesus says over and over in many ways. It is what He came for.

John 13:15: "I have given you an example, that ye should do as I have done."

14:24: "If a man love me, he will keep my words; and my Father will love him, and we will come unto him, and make our abode with him."

15:14: "Ye are my friends, if ye do whatsoever I command you. (10) If ye keep my commandments, ye shall abide in my love; even as I have kept my Father's commandments, and abide in his love.... (16) I have chosen you, that ye should bring forth fruit, and that whatsoever ye shall ask of the Father in my name, he may give it to you."

Sons of God

This incredible invitation to be more than an angel, to be a son along with Christ the Son, a member of the Holy Family, is all summed up in a few verses (Jesus is praying to His Father)—John 17:21: "That they all may be one, as thou, Father, art in me, and I in thee, that they also may be one in us:... (23) I in them and thou in me, that they may be made perfect in one.... Thou has loved them, as thou hast loved me. (24) Father, I will that they also, whom thou hast given me, be with me where I am (26),... that the love wherewith thou hast loved me may be in them, and I in them."

We are invited to the center of the wonderful love at the heart of the universe, not merely as an onlooker but as a "son." Words could not be plainer. This is what Jesus came down from heaven for, "that we may have power to become sons of God." That is the most audacious conception that ever entered the human mind. "I," said Christ, "am God's son, but so are you!"

After the resurrection He said (John 20:17): "I ascend unto my Father, and your Father, and to my God, and your God." He invites us to his side. It is a family, a father and his children—we are God's family.

That is all one can make of these startling words which Jesus quoted when they accused Him of blasphemy for calling himself the "Son of God." John 10:34,35: "Is it not written in your law, I said, Ye are gods? He called them gods, unto whom the word of God came." Then Jesus added: "Why then call me blasphemous when I say I am the Son of God?" This could mean but one thing: so are you a son of God if you obey the Father perfectly, as Jesus did!

How we earn sonship

We earn this inner place with Father and Son at the center of the universe, the same way Jesus earned it. We earn it by perfect obedience, the kind Jesus gave His Father every minute and every second. But for us this is the obstacle in Jesus' invitation—and it is a very formidable hurdle. For when one undertakes to listen and obey as incessantly as Jesus listened and obeyed, one finds it almost impossible. We can go through the better part of some days perfectly surrendered, but eventually we forget or politely bow Christ and the Father out, while we indulge in some useless nonsense, perhaps something we know He would not tell us to do. We use our time one way, while, if we were listening to Him, He would tell us to use it differently. This is unlike Jesus who said: "I do nothing of myself." It is the difference between an utterly dependable character and a wobbly character.

Nearly all of our lapses are pure forgetfulness. Often our subconscious minds play us a trick and make us forget intentionally. This inconstancy of ours is the chief reason why the promises of Jesus are untrue to our experience, why we ask for so much that does not happen. Of course, it doesn't happen when we are apart from Christ. "Apart from me," He said, "ye can do nothing." His incredibly sweeping promises depend upon our staying with Him as a branch stays with the vine. "As a branch cannot bear fruit of itself unless it abides in the vine, no more can ye, except ye abide in me. If ye abide in me and my words abide in you, ye shall ask what ye will and it shall be done unto you." You who read this know that our failure is at this point—our minds are busy with many other things, and we pull loose from the vine many times, probably most of the time every day. What branch grafted on a tree could flourish if we pulled it loose every day to see whether it was growing? It would soon be dead!

Don't stop to regret

Several persons who have read my booklet, *The Game with Minutes*, advocating an attempt to think of God at least one second in each minute, have written that they found it so beyond them that they gave up trying and decided that they were not "built to be saints." A few, given to taking life very seriously, were inclined to be self-condemnatory. Several persons say that it saved them from insanity. Others say it saved them from being introverts. The "game with minutes" is well named a game, a game which practically nobody wins all the time.

Yet everybody really wins it who tries, for he does better than he would have done without a trial. James Russell Lowell said: "Not failure but low aim is crime." When we fail to make a high score, let us laugh and start all over afresh—for, you see, we have eternity, so long as we are headed in the right direction, and a few hours lost does not mean that we are lost. It means that we are building spiritual muscle, that we are trying something worthy of our best possibilities. We grow to the stature of our goals. Without a goal to keep us trying our souls atrophy like unused muscles.

Begin over instantly!

God forgives us instantly and eagerly. Let's forgive ourselves! To "repent" does not mean to "repine," but to "right about face and start moving in the right direction." Christ's joy is in helping men make new beginnings. He finds no pleasure in condemning. He delights only in helping us rise higher. No matter what the last hour may have been, it is past, and we live in this moment, to make it as fine as we can in thought and deed. Never let the sins or errors of the last hour poison this! "Snap out of it" instantly, and, lo, a new fresh page is turned. He who adopts the philosophy of instantaneous new beginnings has the secret of peace.

The most subtle of all forms of selfishness is over-anxiety for ourselves to be more perfect than other people; not desiring that our neighbor shall be as perfect as we are. The quest for self-perfection is often sanctified introversion. The ideal is to forget self as Mary did, sitting at the feet of Jesus, and to gaze enraptured "full in His glorious face," listening for His whisper and doing all He asks. This is what Jesus does with His Father every moment.

Playing life's game with a smile

American leaders are nearly always photographed with a smile on their faces. That is the way to greet every day, with a smiling face and a shining heart. Life is our great game, and it's fun to play it the best we can. Temporary defeats never matter unless we fret about them, unless they keep us down!

Robert Browning struck the brave, healthy note:

> "One who never turned his back
> But marched breast forward:
> Never doubted clouds would break;
> Never dreamed—though right were worsted,
> Wrong would triumph.
> Held, we fall to rise;
> Are baffled to fight better.
> Sleep to wake....
> For we have eternity!

If we can't play any game for the sheer fun of it, we ought not to play it all. But we must all play this game with life, so let's do it with a light in our eyes and a song on our lips. We have every good reason to be radiant. We are undefeatable—unless we defeat ourselves. And even then we can begin all over in an instant—this instant!

Thank God, one needs no unusual ability to be full of Christ, one need not profess unusual goodness, nor worthiness, nor an unusual past, nor blue blood, nor social connections, nor money. The Gospel is for everybody, and "no questions asked."

Listen and say, "Yes." Enter God's open doors unafraid. He is there waiting. "Down God's street there are always green lights." What an undefeatable Gospel!

A friend remonstrated, "You make it altogether too easy. This is the hardest achievement on earth and your light-hearted promises will deceive people."

Very well, then, let us say plainly it does cost. You have got to stop loving things and yourself. There is no substitute for that. Worshiping mammon and self is of all ways of living the most wretched. Let go courageously of self and things, and, lo! it is as easy to begin living with Him as breathing. The final goal is far, far away, but every step with Him toward that goal is heavenly!

Our Appalling Power

Every thought is a deed

When Roosevelt, Churchill, and Stalin were holding their fateful conferences during the Second World War they must have had an overwhelming sense of their responsibility to bless or curse the entire world. If mental radio operates between people, it means that everybody has an overwhelming responsibility for good and evil. It means that every thought we think is helping or harming other people. If you shout, your voice carries barely fifty yards. But when you think, your thoughts go around the world, as far and as fast as the radio. The thoughts of a single day pour blessings or cursings into the great river of world opinion. Every man, in the course of a lifetime, pours so many million thoughts for good or ill into the ever-moving stream of human history that he leaves his impress upon the world as long as time lasts. This is literally and terribly true if thoughts do leap from one mind to another.

If you and I are convinced that we are so connected, we must never harbor a thought that would poison others; we must try to think.

> "Thoughts sublime that pierce the sky like stars
> And by their mild persistence urge men on
> To vaster issues."

The ordinary thoughts of good men are good little thoughts. The extemporaneous prayers one hears in public are like most thinking, full of "miserable aims that end in self."

The most acute need of our age is for global-minded people who "think the world thought, do the world deed, and pray the world prayer."

Co-creators with God

Since every thought is creative, we are creators of the world—we, along with God. He began the world well without us, but we help Him now—and that is the trouble! We humans helped create the world of 1944 by what we thought and planned since World War I. Our end of creation has been pretty bad—that is the reason we have been through this war. The warped little thoughts of selfish, contemptible men from 1918 to 1940 made World War II—and not all of them were on the Axis side. Nothing brought us to the brink of hell but warped, prejudiced, greedy little thoughts.

And now, in 1945, our thoughts, large and small, are at work making the world of 1960. There are two reasons for this:

1. Every thought tends to become true in proportion as it is intense and as it is long dwelt upon. Thoughts result in deeds and deeds make history.

2. Our thoughts leap across space and appear again in other minds, in proportion as they are intense and long dwelt upon. Thoughts are contagious. "What you whisper in secret," said Jesus, "shall be shouted from the housetops." Yes, even your thoughts shout, though others may not know it is you who are shouting!

"I said ye are gods"

The Greeks believed that the gods were on Olympus, but if Jesus is correct, then God has set millions of little gods free on this earth to help create whatever we think about. We are "sons of God" with a vengeance. Our thoughts are the threads weaving the garment which the world tomorrow will wear. You and I created a piece of tomorrow in our thoughts today. We cannot help ourselves. We are gods without knowing it—even if we refuse to believe it. There is no escape from this responsibility; we have got to measure up.

Right and wrong are nearly balanced

You and I need to ask: "When my thoughts come true, and when they leap around the world to start the same thoughts moving in other minds, are my thoughts making the kind of world we really want? I am only one of two billion of the world's population to be sure, but my thoughts are as creative as any of the others, and so are yours. The human race—if we may judge by what people read and say and do—are a mixture of good and evil thoughts, large and little thoughts. If they could be checked over against each other they might pretty much cancel out. One may "guestimate" that the sum total of right and wrong thinking is nearly in balance, like a balloon suspended in air, hesitating whether to rise or fall. Our world seems to rise for a period, then to fall, then to rise again. It has been in a tailspin during these war years. If a few millions of us determine to keep our thoughts right all the time, we can, I believe, tip the balances the other way, and, by God's help, start our bad old globe rising instead of falling. If this earth is indeed in a state of near balance, then your thinking and mine may be decisive, may save the world from a worse hell. We don't know how much good we may be able to do by keeping our thoughts high and large and creative—we do know that all of us are important. God only knows how important we are.

We have delayed God

That excellent anonymous book, *God Calling*, puts in the mouth of Christ these words:

> "I do not delay my second coming, my followers delay it.... The world would be brought to me soon if only all who acknowledge me as Lord and Christ gave themselves unreservedly to be used by me.... I could use each human body as a channel for divine love and power."

The same picture fills the Bible, the picture of God, heart-broken and delayed by man's disobedience. This is the eternal meaning of Adam thrown out of Eden. This is what the flood at the time of Noah means, when "God repented him that he had made man." The story of the forty years in the wilderness says plainly God was delayed. The captivity in Babylon means a delayed and disappointed God. The story is written on nearly every page of the prophets. Christ spoke for the God of the whole Bible when he wept over Jerusalem: "How oft would I have gathered you as a hen gathers her chicks under her wings and ye would not; so now your house will be left desolate."

Is our world headed for destruction, or can it be saved? Perhaps God has not yet made up His mind; perhaps He lets our actions decide, perhaps His plan is to let us make up our minds. This is what He does with individuals—"Whosoever will may come." It may be that this is His way with nations and eras—to let us pronounce our own judgment. It looks as though He will allow this generation to destroy itself if we cannot join hands in brotherly co- operation. It would be easy to quote fifty pages from the prophets, who, like Ezekiel 18, says exactly that. They say it, not only about individuals, but also about their nation Israel. The whole Bible plays around the word "if," and the doubtful element is what men will at last do. If, if, if!!! Unless, unless, unless!!! God's will is clear—man's will hangs in the balance, and man's decision in this generation decides this generation's fate. That is precisely the message of the Bible, and it is most certainly the message of science. God's laws are immutable. Obey and live, or disobey and be ground to powder.

This judgment does not depend upon outward deeds alone. It plunges into the depths of the mind: "For the word of God, is quick and powerful and sharper than a two-edged sword, piercing even to the dividing asunder of soul and spirit, and of the joints and marrow, and is a discerner of the thoughts and intents of the heart.... All things are naked and open unto the eyes of him with whom we have had to do." (Hebrews 4:12, 13).

Somebody cringes at this terrible responsibility. "You are saying that I help decide my world's fate. But I'm powerless to do anything about it." Powerless? On the contrary, you are enormously powerful. Your thinking this very day has helped make the world what it is. When you think in perfect harmony with God, the titanic forces of the universe bend like gravity to pull things and people in your direction, because you are going in God's direction. One man with God shall be stronger than ten thousand!

The greatest truth in the world

You and I will be responsible for 1965, and even though we deny our blame, that does not change the facts. There is but one escape, not to dodge, but to rise to the challenge. If this is true at all, it becomes the most vital truth in the universe for us and for everybody. What could be more awe inspiring, more heart gripping, more overmastering, more terrifying? The universe pays the price if you and I fail to measure up to our highest!

The sheer responsibility of this realization might drive one mad if it were not for the one redeeming fact that by the help of Christ we can think His thoughts. When we share our thoughts with Him, the enormous responsibility for the future of the world rolls over on His shoulders. He carries what is too big for us, and He supplies the power. St. Paul's marvelous words, as translated by Goodspeed, are true: "God working through us is able to do unutterably more."

Whenever man opens the windows of his mind toward God, then God tells him what to do, and helps him to do it. That man thinks and does "unutterably more."

We can! Enough of us can!

We can! We don't need to wait! It's in our power now! We can have a world of peace, justice, happiness, the Kingdom of God as soon as we want it. Every new scientific discovery can bend to aid humanity if people will love Christ and one another. But we must pay a price, just as soldiers must give up all they cherish. We must give up most of our ordinary little thinking for the world's sake.

Non-Christians constitute no more than half of God's problem. Christians who sit on the sidelines and who do not help, are the other half of His problem. It isn't that they can't, it isn't that they won't, it is just that they don't, because they don't know how. Many more of us would "get into the game" if we saw how important, how terrifyingly important, each of us is for the saving of our generation; if we saw how easy it would be for us to help tip the scales toward the Kingdom of God; if we saw that all the time, no matter where we are, our right thinking builds a bridge between God and other men—the bridge that God needs if His will is to be done on earth and if this generation is to be saved from destroying itself.

Enough of us could transform the world right now

We have enough Christian people to transform the world right now, if only their thoughts were always on Christ's side. But they suppose their thoughts are their own, and so a large part of their thinking cancels out the rest of their thinking. Many people enjoy dreaming about the wicked deeds they are condemning in other people; that is why scandal is so popular! If our postulate is correct, we help evil even when we roll it around under our tongues in delicious hypocritical disapproval of others. We need to mobilize the minds of the men of good will so that they will form a mighty mass attack of good thoughts. Then we all together will tip the scales the other way, will lift the world upward to a new high, in spite of the selfish little thoughts of mean people.

Here is a principle most people need:

Fix your thoughts upon what ought to come to pass, and not upon the things you dislike. Let the things we oppose die of neglect. For we help everything we think about—even when we are thinking against it!

The reaction of good thoughts upon ourselves

Some readers of this book may be murmuring: "There is scarcely a word about what prayer and right thinking will do for me! It is all about what I can do for others." That omission was deliberate. There are enough books already on helping yourself through prayer—on how to get what you want, how to acquire riches, how to find health, how to be famous, how to go to heaven. But in this era, when our bleeding world faces the worst crisis in history, when it calls like a drowning man, it is contemptibly selfish to ask what advantage will come to us if we go to her rescue.

Nevertheless, this much may be said. The habit of praying for others makes you noble.

Your thoughts grow wider and higher, your selfishness melts away.

You become Christlike.

You bless mankind.

You are loved by all who know you.

People think you are beautiful, for you become radiant with the smile of Christ.

Your joy comes from what you give, not from what you accumulate.

"He that loseth his life shall find it."

Take no thought for your own life, what you shall eat and wear. "Seek ye first the Kingdom of God and his righteousness, and all these things shall be added unto you."

Let us dismiss these personal considerations with a paragraph and train our sights once more upon helping others. We are needed as channels between God's power and the world's need. The more we think about self, the more we block the channel between God and His world. The more we eliminate self, the wider becomes our channel of blessing to others. Men's refusal to help others unless they get praise or profit is God's "bottleneck"' as He strives to bring in the Kingdom. God's greatest need is more than unselfishness, it is selflessness, wide open channels for His love.

There is a well-known fable of heaven and hell. In hell they sit on both sides of a table, but their arms are straight and stiff, so that they cannot get the food to their mouths. In heaven they sit around the same kind of table with the same straight arms, but with one difference—they feed one another across the table. That fable is not true of heaven and hell, but it is true of our earth now. All hunger is because we are too selfish to feed one another. Our thoughts and even our prayers have been too self-centered.

God has permitted science to unlock the ultimate forces locked in the atom, thirty million times as powerful as dynamite. Now scientists are frightened lest men may use this awful power to destroy the world. Prayer will enable God to unlock in the spiritual realm the only power that can save the human race from destroying itself. This is the one and only great contribution most of us can make, and it is enough.

This is the untried way

Your contribution can be titanic beyond all imagination. It depends upon one thing only—how much time and heart and mind and soul and strength and prayer you give to God's world task.

If true at all, the truth in this book is the most important of all thoughts. God's thoughts, plus ours, create the future! Even fools dare not turn their backs on this terrific challenge. All of us must stop being vindictive, stop being prejudiced, stop being little; for our folly, our spite, our prejudice, our narrowness are poisoning the universe. We must think thoughts worthy of the sons of God, worthy of creators of the world of 1965, and beyond.

Well, then, let us pray:

God, use my prayer to help the delegates and officials of the United Nations to feel a sense of awful need for Thy wisdom. May they pray, listen to Thee intently, hear Thee correctly, and obey Thee perfectly. Use my prayer to give Christians everywhere a sense of awful responsibility to pray, to listen to Thee and hear Thee right, and obey Thee fully. Use me as an open channel for an outpouring of the Holy Spirit upon mankind.

Part 6
Channels of Spiritual Power

Channels of Spiritual Power

This book was published in 1954 in the midst of a religious revival, a time when Americans, increasingly afraid of nuclear holocaust, were crowding their churches hoping to allay their fears. Laubach invited his readers to cease searching for a false sense of security and to respond, through prayer and action, to God's plea: "I need your help to save the world."

In the chapters selected for reprinting, the reader finds a summative statement of how to address the needs of the world through profound devotion, and the deeds to which that devotion gives rise. The book struck a new note of urgency. Laubach saw the fear of war as a goad to action on behalf of the world's poor. But he was afraid that the American people would become accustomed to their fear before they could act to alleviate the worldwide suffering that he had witnessed firsthand.

The Only Way Out

History will record that from 1950 onward America began to have her greatest religious revival. There is reason to hope that this is the beginning of the greatest revival of all time, not only in the United States but throughout the whole world. The latest statistics available show that the churches gained more than twice as many members in 1952 as they had gained in any previous year. The churches grew 2 1/2 times faster than the population. The report of the National Council of Churches called this "a whopping gain of 3,604,124 over the count of 1951." Two thirds of these new members were Protestants and one third were Catholics.

Norman Vincent Peale says that there is a revival among businessmen. His own astonishing audience, said to be as much as thirty million a week through his radio, television, syndicated newspapers, magazine articles, books and sermons, seems to support his statement. Evangelist Billy Graham has bigger crowds and more penitents than Billy Sunday had in his most impressive years. Bishop Sheen is equally effective in the Roman Catholic Church.

But this American revival is not confined to a few preachers or even to a few hundred preachers. Preaching is not the cause of this revival; the preachers whose churches are crowded have merely responded to the real cause. This revival is not produced by men preaching hellfire as Jonathan Edwards and Billy Sunday preached it; a future hell does not scare many people today. But people are scared about their own world here and now.

The scientists started this revival, not with sermons but with atom and hydrogen bombs and guided missiles. Newspapers and magazines have stimulated it to the point where they have Americans thoroughly scared about a future war that can destroy every human being in any large city in the world in a matter of seconds. Most of the people of the United States feel like the characters in a murder story when hidden death creeps upon them. This apprehension affects them in a variety of ways. It has driven some people to heavier drinking in an attempt to forget it. And, on the other hand, it is driving millions of others to God and to church.

The popular preachers seldom mention war or bombs; that is the last thing people want to hear in church. They want sermons on "How to get rid of fear and worry." "How to emphasize the positive and eliminate the negative." People are crowding the churches, hoping that somehow their courage and faith and peace of mind may find new support.

This is of tremendous value, but it has one defect. The bomb and the threat still remain, while the "spiritual" tonic wears off in the course of a week. Monday morning's newspaper again confronts us with the statement of some military expert that neither the United States nor Russia has found any defense. In two or three years, perhaps in less time than that, Russia will be able to annihilate the greater part of the people of America within twenty-four hours. We can retaliate and convert most of Russia into a vast Hiroshima. Then some meek little neutral country could have what was left of the world. The scientists and the military men do not want us to learn how to live in peace with the hydrogen bomb. Einstein says:

> I think the most dangerous thing for us would be to get accustomed to this new danger and try to live along as usual. To live in an armed camp where each threatens to annihilate the other, is simply intolerable.

This bomb hanging over our heads is producing another type of revival among many thousands of our people. When they turn to God they seem to hear Him say: "You ask me to save the world from catastrophe. I need your help! You must help me to change those evil men who have power to destroy you and your world. I am ready to pour heaven's help on the world, but I need you and multitudes like you to be my channels."

The best measure of the power of this revival lies in determining how many men and women answer "yes" to this call of God, and how many are willing to sacrifice their own plans and interests in order to help. Jesus called on His disciples to take up their cross and follow Him. Swelling church rolls may or may not represent the religion of Jesus.

I crossed the United States during the past few months, asking for men and money to reach out a helping hand to the world's unfortunates. After the services, men and women, young and old, came forward and offered to give all of their lives and all of their money.

One of these came to see me. He is president of a prosperous engineering company. This is what he said:

> I heard you say that in America men and women of large talents devote their efforts to selling gadgets to people who already have too much. This struck home. I have been doing that, and I'm sick of selling people what they do not need when the world is so desperately hungry. I want to devote my engineering skills to helping real need. I do not need any salary; I can support myself.

Hundreds of men and women like this man have become disgusted with wasting their talents on tasks that leave the world no better, and in many cases leave it even worse. They want to consecrate their talents to God and human need. They want to become God's channels.

If this peril continues, the revival will continue, and as it grows, an ever-swelling army of our finest men and women will be increasingly disgusted with prostituting their talents on baubles and will offer themselves to help save the world. Two things will continue to stand out high above all others. First, the unthinkable peril for the world. Second, the uncompromising demand of Jesus Christ to sacrifice self for the cause.

Already the men and women who have offered their all to save their world are giving this revival a nobler quality than any previous revival has ever had. These are the people who are following Christ, not for what they can get here or hereafter, but for what they can do for the world. These are really taking up their cross; they are the true successors of Paul.

But men who have made this great decision find that their problem is not ended the moment they decide. It is only just begun. We are always tempted, as Jesus was, to try some surface shortcut cure which will leave our way of life as little disturbed as possible. But, alas, no surface cure is going to be enough. This world has a deep soul disease, and nothing short of a drastic change in our human nature will save us. We are too human to be trusted with atom bombs. We must rise to a new level, or we shall destroy one another.

So long as little boys have cap pistols and popguns they do no harm in shooting at one another, but with real guns those children can be dangerous. Today we are confronted with the horrible realization that the people in power on this earth are not spiritually mature enough to be safe with hydrogen bombs. The bomb itself is perfectly safe; it will not go off accidentally. But the men who can explode it are not safe. As Einstein put it, living in this armed camp has become intolerable. We must stop it. How?

One way would be to try a surprise attack and destroy the enemy while he is still unable to retaliate. But there is no sense in considering that possibility. The conscience of the American people would not tolerate so monstrous a crime. We are too Christian for that.

If we cannot tolerate this armed camp, and yet are too decent to destroy the enemy and try to rule the world ourselves, then what is there left for us to try? Just one thing. We can try to turn our enemies into friends, to change evil men into good men, to remove the causes which produce enemies, to have a world-wide religious revival.

Many will reply that this cannot be done. Maybe not. But at least it can be tried. It must be tried, for a Christ-like God wants it done this way.

I do not share the pessimism of many people. My work has taken me all over the world, and I have had a chance to see how miraculously whole nations can be changed from enemies to friends within one year when we go all-out to win their friendship. I know, too, that we can make evil human nature good, for I have seen that happen, too.

In his book, *Human Nature and Its Remaking*, Ernest Hocking says that the gray matter in our brain is the easiest stuff in the world to change.

Indeed, every sense impression from outside keeps changing it every second. He proves not only that human nature can be changed, but that it is being changed everywhere all over the world, all the time.

But we don't need a philosopher to prove this. Hitler proved it when he changed the youth of Germany in the wrong direction! Stalin proved it when he changed the entire viewpoint of the people of Russia in the wrong direction.

We could change the world in the right direction if we would work as zealously for right as these men worked for wrong! We know what the right direction is. It is the way of Jesus Christ. We could make the whole world right if we joined in an all-out crusade for the way of Christ.

But before we can change the world like that, we American Christians must first change ourselves. We are sixty percent sham in our following of Jesus today. That is all too easy to prove. Christ told us, "Love your neighbor as yourself." He did that. If we did it, we could save the world. But we are counterfeit Christians. We do not love our competitors in business as we love ourselves. Or do we? Still less do we love the people of other countries as we love our own people. The very idea of doing that sounds unpatriotic—or like a violation of our Constitution! But until we do love our neighbor-nations as we love ourselves, we can neither win them as friends nor change their ways.

We must prove that love with unselfish deeds. Communism began because the masses of Russia were in poverty and the Communists promised to give them something better. Communism breeds today wherever people are hungry and dissatisfied. Who will deny that? About fifteen hundred million people, two thirds of the world, who are hungry and unhappy today hear the promises of the Communists, and they will go Communist unless they are assured that we will help them out of their misery.

The answer to the promises of the Communists is clear; it is to go with a compassionate program of helping needy people to help themselves, and so prove that we are their friends. If we did enough of that we could make those fifteen hundred millions our firm friends. One of two things would happen. Their governments would change, or the people would overthrow them. The issue is very clear. Lift those fifteen hundred millions out of the pit of want or they will hate us and our system.

When we in America place personal profit above our country we are hurting democracy. The rising prices all over the United States in the midst of plenty—we have so much abundance we don't know what to do with it!—is due to selfish desire for gain. The President has rightly said that profiteers are willing to jeopardize the nation for their own gain. We used to believe in the law of supply and demand, but producers have learned the trick of holding back or even destroying supplies so that there will be less supply than demand. This is so common that we call it legitimate.

People would not do that if they placed the welfare of their country above their own profit. We have inflation for no other reason than that so many of us are engaged in profiteering at the expense of the rest of us. For example, when the bread makers of America agreed to raise the price, the only reason they gave was that they feared the Government would freeze the price; so they raised it while they could—and not because they needed more money.

When, inspired by Moral Rearmament, a public-spirited man in Canada named Cecil Morrison set out to keep down the price of bread by introducing economies and taking a small profit, his praises were sung throughout Canada and the United States as though he were doing something extraordinary and patriotic. You know and I know that that is the way every one of us ought to be. And that is the way only the minority are. This old way of selfishness could exist in past years. It jeopardizes our country and freedom now.

People will say, "What do you expect? Isn't this the American way of life? Rugged individualism! America is so strong that she can take it!" The answer is that she could take it before, but she can't risk it in this new age.

The soldiers who were captured in Korea and who, under pitiless brain washing and torture, "confessed" that America used germ warfare, are now being tried for betraying their country. Yet they did not endanger our country one ten thousandth as much as the profiteers who are sacrificing the people to gain selfish profit. Why, I ask, do we not demand that the standard for business shall be as high as the standard for soldiers?

Where there is no true religion there is no educated conscience. Where there is no conscience there can be no democracy. This is why Governor Martin of Pennsylvania was right when he said: "Gentlemen, the trouble with our country is not our laws. It is the lack of true religion. We have often said, 'Eternal vigilance is the price of freedom.' But we should write that in another way. 'Eternal fanning of the flames of true religion is the price of freedom.' "

But what do we mean by "true" religion? It is not enough for it to be "true." It must have power. It must have the vitality to arouse a vast world compassion.

Edward Barrett advocates a "Crusade of all Faiths." He points out that the Golden Rule is to be found in all the six major religions. This is a happy discovery. But all rules and laws, including the Golden Rule, have one defect: they lack vitality. They are not alive.

St. Paul discovered this in his own experience. He saw that the Jewish law told people what was right, but it lacked the vital power to make people want to do right. He found that power only in the risen, living Christ. When Christ came to live in Paul, He drove Paul out across the world in unconquerable zeal to save other men. When He lives in any man He sets that man's heart aflame with compassion.

Compassion for the multitudes burned strongly in Christ. You seldom find it on the pages of history, except where it was started through Jesus Christ. The other great religions contain the Golden Rule, but that rule lacks the power to drive men to compassionate service.

So if Barrett means that we are to ignore the living Jesus, out of deference for other religions, that kind of syncretism will not produce the thing most needed. All religions accept Jesus as a man who once lived and gave us the Golden Rule. But a dead Jesus is not enough. The power of Jesus lies in His presence here now as risen Lord.

We can, and we must, work with people who do not believe this, but our hope must lie in those who have a far more profound experience of Him as the living Christ. Compassion will flow from the hearts of those who have Christ in their own lives.

Before 1930 I held what many people call "the university man's religion." I believe that Jesus was probably the best man who had ever lived. But that beautiful memory of Jesus lacked power. I was a failure in my spiritual life.

Then I had a personal experience of Christ in Mindanao, Philippine Islands, which left me sure that He not only lives, but lives in my heart. When He entered my heart, He brought to me a tender compassion for the multitudes which has been the driving power of my life ever since. The living Christ put it there.

The only hope of this evil, selfish world is for the living Christ to abide in enough of us to change the spiritual climate of the world. He alone is able to change greed to compassion, fear to faith, and hate to love.

But that is only half of the story. When He enters into us we become a part of the way. God's highway runs straight through us! We become His physical bodies. That was the meaning of Paul when he wrote in Ephesians 3:19,20 "I pray that you may be filled full of God." When His power works in us He is able to do far more than we dare to ask or even think.

Now I am sure that Christ came and must live in everybody.

Becoming Sons of God

When a spoiled child fights and shrieks for something he desires, as though his life depended on securing that thing, he does not understand that in a week or a year that thing will mean nothing to him. All of us are like that. We cling to the advantages of this moment because, like little children, we are shortsighted.

We need the long view. Indeed, we are not mature Christians until our point of reference is in eternity. We need to see the summit of the mountain we are climbing. When a man gets a vision far up into eternity, as Paul did, then no loss on this earth, however big, can shake his peace or his faith. His religion will not depend on what he has here. He will be undefeatable. St. Paul, looking into the teeth of death, saw not death at all, but only real life: "For me to live is Christ, but to die is to gain more of Christ."

Moreover, if we can look into eternity, we will never hesitate to be unselfish. We will see that we never can give anything away, that… what we give away here may or may not come back to us in this life, but it is sure to return to us manyfold in a future life.

There are people who advocate a completely selfless life which asks for nothing in this life or the next. I think that is unnatural. Such selflessness kills one of our two greatest driving instincts. Buddhism asks us to kill all desire. But Jesus does not ask us to desire nothing. He asked us to take the long view and to find our highest self-realization in eternity. "Great is your reward in heaven." Christ does not ask us to be selfless. He asks us to be big and to take a long view.

If we follow Jesus, then we will live a life of self-giving to the end of our earthly days, with no regret, no self-pity and no self-praise. We will not even call ourselves noble. We will just be wise and far-sighted. We will treat every other person with infinite reverence, for he is eternal. All these things above, below, around us decay. Even our granite monuments at last will wear out, or some irreverent person will destroy them. The mummies of Egypt are falling to pieces. But the soul of a man is eternal. We shall meet him again. We will be reverent, therefore, if we meet him now.

If God has His way in each of us, our future is so dazzling that the imagination reels to contemplate it. Paul saw this, and he cried, "Eye has not seen nor ear heard, nor has it ever entered into the heart of man what God is preparing for those who love him."

When I was in the "know-it-all" stage common to heedless youth I discredited the first chapter of Genesis as a figment of the imagination. But science does not know as much now as it did at the beginning of the twentieth century. Today both the astronomer and the physicist have come back to the first chapter of Genesis, and they admit that it is the best description of creation that ever has been written. They say that between two and three billion years ago God gathered or created energy in one incomprehensibly dense ball, and then in an awful moment cried, "Let there be light!" And the ball exploded and flew out through interminable space to form the suns and the galaxies of suns and planets, so far apart now that it takes a light ray hundreds of millions of years to come from the most distant stars to our earth. Even the Hale 200-inch telescope on Mt. Palomar California, cannot see the farthest stars. The most distant stars are traveling fastest, just as would be the case if there had been a terrific explosion. The astronomers know where in space that ball of energy must have exploded when God first hurled his cosmic thunderbolt. And they can tell that it was three billion years ago from the distance which those pieces, which we call suns or stars, have traveled.

Therefore, if we interpret the "days" in the first chapter of Genesis as periods, then the scientists verify the Bible account. Many Christians do so interpret the "days," because the Bible says, "A thousand years to God are as a day."

One of the wholesome facts about the scientists of our age is that they are humble, not "know-it-all," as they were when Herbert Spencer started to write a complete explanation of the universe. And they stand in open-mouthed awe at the power and wisdom of the God who is behind the world we see.

But I think the eighth chapter of Romans is even greater than the first chapter of Genesis, because here Paul tells, for the first time in history, why God made the universe. Now we step out beyond science. Why did the Creator hurl those myriads of suns into space in that first superb hour when He created the universe? Paul says he knows. He says that God's purpose was to create sons of God, to beget us and to train us to grow at last into the full stature of His Son. And we know what that means because we have seen His Son Christ.

All that we see with a 200-inch telescope, Paul says, has that divine purpose. Is it a purpose just for this one little earth? No one can answer that question. No one can even dare to try. We do not know how many planets like ours there may be. That makes no difference. But what does make a difference is that we shall treat each other more reverently when we realize that three billion years of time and more than a billion light years of space measure God's incomprehensible effort to bring us forth.

We shall realize then that we are employing sons of God in our factories and on our farms. We shall stand aghast at the thought of measuring God's sons against so many productive "work hours." We shall appraise everything we undertake, not by what we can accumulate or gain from it, but by what it does to the souls of those who are working with us and for us. We shall some day consider it the most heinous of all sins to cramp or stultify the growth of a soul in the interest of selfish gain.

Now let us look straight into this dazzling, breathtaking conception of the universe and of what it was made for, and of what man is destined to become. Paul must have got this when he was caught up into the third heaven and heard things that mortal tongue cannot utter. He said, "The whole creation has been groaning in the pains of childbirth until now, and the creation waits with eager longing for the birth of the sons of God. When they appear, then the creation itself will be set free from decay." So this universe is a delivery room for the sons of God! It is more than that; it is the kindergarten for the sons of God. We are born here, and here we get our first training for eternity.

This planet is our school; it is also a series of examinations. Day by day we are trained, and day by day we are tested to see how far we have advanced. "This," says Paul, "is the meaning of trouble." Trouble in our life here is like problems in mathematics to a student. The tests which help us grow are temptations, pains, disappointments, and struggles. These are our spiritual muscle-builders.

If we are on the way toward "that far-off divine event toward which the whole creation moves," we can judge how marvelous that end must be by the type of training which God gives us. I cannot understand why He subjects other people to the miseries which they suffer or allows them to suffer as they do, because I cannot see inside them. The only person I can study from the inside is myself. I want to testify that, as I look back over my life, those periods which looked the hardest to me, those when I suffered the most, have turned out to be the periods in which I grew the most. And those periods in life which were easy and pleasant and free from struggle turn out now, as I look back, to be the periods of coasting, not of rising. For the soul, as for mountain climbers, rising is work. Life is easy only when we are on a level or going downhill.

"Well, then," I say to myself, to my soul, "stop grumbling. God let this happen, and He is the perfect teacher."'

One of the great values of athletic training is that it disciplines us to be good losers, never to grumble and never to lose patience.

Now the wise man learns to look on life as the athlete looks on a game. He may lose today and tomorrow, but he knows that he will not lose the war, even though he loses many a battle. He knows that all things, easy and difficult alike, are working together for ultimate good to those who love God. He doesn't rebel against God's arrangements today, against God's textbooks, or God's curriculum, or God's difficult problems, or His high goals. He is in training for the incomprehensibly wonderful life that lies ahead.

I suppose that this eternal life will not be the same for all of us. I don't believe that all this grooming and enduring hardships, this being buffeted about, is getting me ready to wear a white robe and to play a harp. If God intended us to play a harp through eternity I would rather spend my life here taking music lessons. Perhaps God is preparing the music lovers for that. We can infer what He is going to do with us in eternity from the training that we get here. I think He plans for many of us to continue in the conquests of seeming difficulties, in cosmic achievements of creation.

One of the most interesting statements of Jesus was made when His foes took up stones to kill Him because he said He was the Son of God. If we understood this statement of His, it would throw light on who we are and where we are going. They said to Him, "You are only a man, but you make yourself God."

And Jesus answered, "is it not written in your law, 'I said you are gods?' If those to whom the word of God came are called gods, do you say, 'You are blaspheming' when I say I am the Son of God?"

What does this mean? It means that Jesus is what we are to become. He said the same thing in His prayer in John 17. "The glory which you gave me, I am giving to them. They shall be with me where I am; the love which you have for me will be in them, and I will be with them." I could quote many other passages that mean the same thing. Here is the key to the mystery of the universe, according to Jesus and according to Paul.

The world around us is God's best idea for helping us grow into His sons. It isn't perfect because it needed to be imperfect so that we would have something to work on. Its imperfection makes it a perfect place as a gymnasium in which to develop our muscles and to become strong sons of God.

Now, in this last half of the twentieth century, God seems to have taken another very long chance with us humans. He revealed to us one of the ultimate secrets of His creation—the incredible power imprisoned in an atom. He is letting us human beings know how to destroy ourselves and our race and perhaps our planet. He is saying to us, "I trust you with this. But you will destroy yourselves with it unless you can treat one another with the reverence that belongs to eternal sons of God, not like powers in a selfish game, not like expendable cannon fodder." It seems as though God were issuing an ultimatum to the human race: "Rise to a new level, or perish by your own hand." Of course, ultimately, God Himself cannot be harmed if we fail Him and destroy ourselves. Yet if we fail God, it is God's failure, too. It is His disappointment as well as ours. He must begin all over again and develop a new human race, as He did in the days of Noah.

There are deeper truths than we have been able to see in this chapter. God's mind is infinitely beyond ours. I suppose that Paul had his finger on a truth when he said, "What if it is necessary for evil to exist in order to bring out the goodness of God, as a black background is necessary for a picture?" And I suppose some day, perhaps at the end of some eternity, every one of us will gasp as we behold the utter wisdom and goodness of God's total plan.

But in our day, knowing so little, like a fly on the edge of a great painting, we cannot begin to comprehend the total plan. All we can do is to trust. We have seen enough of God to know that He is good, and we can wait until we know it all. It is not necessary for us to know all about God. Our part is to be sure that we are dependable.

While we must try to understand God, we must never forget this: God is not on trial. Once a man visited the Louvre in Paris, which contains the world's greatest collection of art. As he came out he said to the guard, "Your pictures are no good. I am disappointed." The guard replied, "Sir, those pictures are not on trial; you are!" We must never forget that God is not on trial, but that we are. One thing we can understand about God is this: God waits! He waits from century to century until He finds men and women whose hearts are so open to Him and to their fellow men that His love can flow through them as it flowed through Jesus Christ. There is always a limitless reservoir of His love. But the world remains thirsty for love because too few of us are pipelines from heaven to the thirsty world.

We have been too much like Adam. We have gone against the will of God. And then we have hidden from Him. Alas, it is easy to hide from God—or to think we are hiding. All we need to do is to forget Him. God's voice is so still, so small, and the other voices around us are so loud. So you and I ignore God's voice. Especially in this noisy age our minds are like radios which let trivial messages from some nearby station drown out some great message from afar.

As we become wiser we shall realize the infinite importance of the infinitesimal. All of the achievements of science today are the result of paying more attention to the smallest detail. Gasoline could be harnessed only when cylinders could be ground down to a millionth of an inch. The camera and the motion picture are triumphs of infinite accuracy, and the radio and the television are even greater results of the mastery of even the most delicate light waves. Atomic energy and the atom bomb itself are results of understanding and mastering the smallest things in the universe.

Becoming dependable, grown-up sons of God is a matter of learning to give attention to the still small voice of God. His voice is more delicate and refined than the smallest physical thing in the universe. Hearing the whisper of the Spirit, as Jesus heard it every instant, and obeying every whisper that comes from the Father—this is the perfection for which the school of life must train us.

I close this chapter with one more thought. There was one step God had to take which was the most dangerous thing, I think, He ever did. He is bent on making us sons, not robots, not automations, not work animals, and so He had to give us freedom to obey. He seems to be saying to us: "I must allow you to try every way until you learn that all ways except my way are disaster. I must take this long chance with you, and it may be very long, indeed. I will let you wander through millennia, if you want, but I will follow you to the end and in some future aeon I will have my prodigal son back home."

Christ Opens the Way

Becoming sons of God is our goal. This means that we are to become like God's Son, Jesus Christ. Then our question becomes: "What is Christ like? How does He behave toward His Father, and toward His Father's work?"

The first thing we notice about Jesus is His everlasting obedience to the Father's will. The Gospel of John says forty-nine times in forty-nine different ways, words that mean simply that the Son can do nothing of Himself, and that He does only what He sees the Father doing. "I have come down out of heaven not to do my will, but the will of him who sent me."

So to become perfectly Christlike means to become perfectly obedient to the will of God.

This is what Christ asks us to do. "If you keep my commandments, just as I keep my Father's commandments, you will abide in my love as I abide in his love.... You are my friends if you do what I command you."

Experience has taught us that such total obedience is impossible if we have to do it in our strength. If that is the price of sonship we are defeated from the start. Much of the time our wills refuse even to want to be that submissive. If we force our wills to a reluctant obedience we shall be far below the obedience of Jesus. So, at first glance, there seems to be an impossible gulf fixed between us and Jesus.

But Jesus promises that His Holy Spirit will enter us and give us the will to do God's will. Then we will obey, not because duty is the "stern daughter of the Voice of God," but because there is nothing in the universe we want so much to do. When we love somebody enough, our supreme joy is to do what he wants done. So the Holy Spirit makes us love God so much that we yearn with one supreme desire to please Him. Such perfect love transforms every hard task and even death itself into joy.

Jesus' incredible, never-ending listening and saying, "Yes," made it possible for God to trust Him with literally everything. The Bible says that God has "put everything into His hands, everything in the universe," because He found that He could depend on Him so completely. It is not sacrilegious to say that Jesus earned the confidence of the Father by being trustworthy every moment, under every trial, in every detail. The Son and the Father have no disputes, because the Son never disagrees. The Son knows that the Father is always right. The Father never finds it necessary to persuade a reluctant Son.

We, too, are becoming sons of God, and we must learn this unflinching loyalty that never falters when a cross lies ahead. This is the first Christlike quality.

But even if we are willing to obey God every instant, as Jesus did, how are we to know God's will? Jesus knew it because He heard God speaking all the time. Can we hear God like that? Or must we always be as we now are? Must we be forever wondering what God's will is, but hearing no answer to our question? Millions of people are desperate to know what God wants them to do. Perhaps half the human race hesitates between two courses of action at this very hour.

That is the reason why *In His Steps or What Would Jesus Do?* by Charles Sheldon, sold nearly thirty million volumes; next to the Bible it is still the world's largest seller, because so many people hoped that in that book they would find the answer to the question: "How do I know what God wants?"

Is there a great gulf fixed between Jesus and us, so that He, coming down out of heaven, could know everything, while we, living on this earth, must be satisfied to know only a little? Is the song, "Teach me the patience of unanswered prayer," the best we can do?

You want a straight answer to that question. Here it is. I believe we often do get God's answer almost the instant we ask for it, but we do not like God's answer, and so we persist in asking, hoping that God will answer otherwise. I believe we should ask God for an answer; I also believe that when we get a reasonable thought or course of action, we should believe that God gave it to us, and act on it. We must accept it as an act of faith.

But you reply, "It is so easy to deceive yourself!" That is true. It is easy to think we are wholly open toward God, and our minds may be tricking us. It is the easiest thing in the world to mistake our own wishes for the call of God. How, then, can we know when it is God and when it is wishful thinking?

The answer is that we must spend more time listening to God. We forget to listen nine-tenths of the time. We suppose that if we listen for a few minutes God ought to be prompt and answer us then. I want to testify that in my life at least I can never accuse God of not answering my prayer, but it took time! If you have a wet shirt, and put it out in the sun to be dried and it isn't dried in two minutes, you know better than to be angry because it is not dry. It takes more time than that. And so does prayer.

If you want a college education, you can't walk through the college campus and then say you have "gone through college." It isn't done that way. We must be there when the knowledge is made available. The perfect student misses nothing.

Jesus was always listening for God. He was always there with His ear to the phone when God was ready to speak, so He never missed a word.

But all of us listen to God so seldom! We would blush to have anybody know how much we neglect God's voice.

Suppose you make up your mind to listen more constantly. Then you want a straight answer to the question "How shall I listen?"

Jesus said, "He that is willing to do his will shall know." The first condition of knowing is being willing to hear the truth. Many of us are afraid of what God will answer, and so we dismiss that still, small Voice because we do not want what we fear we will hear. As a matter of fact, we are often pretty sure that God will disagree with our own will.

Jesus' answer is, "If you want to do God's will, he will speak."

I have never met anyone who persisted lovingly in the quest of God's will who did not find it.

The second supreme quality in Jesus Christ, was that He was perfect in love. In what way was He perfect in love? I think, in the first place, that His love reached out further than ours. We love our family most, then our intimate friends, and then our school, then our club, and then our nation. The further from ourselves we go, the weaker becomes our love. But Christ's love reaches all the way around the world. In the second place, it is a warm love, always warm, no matter how far it reaches. It is like the sun. Compared to His bright sun, our love is like twinkling stars. His healing power was so much greater than ours because His love was so much greater than ours, and what we find impossible He found easy.

Jesus' love had a healing quality. It healed and cured instantly all that is touched. It turned disease into health and sin into saintliness.

His love was contagious. It flowed into others and then flowed out from others who came under His spell. Indeed, it was so contagious that you can see it in people's eyes and faces and hear it in their voices today, after two thousand years. People of every climate and of every tongue fall under His spell and catch that strange kind of love that He had. It was a compassionate love, which reached down to the depths.

It was not an easygoing affability. It was a mighty force. It wasn't a gentle breeze; it was a terrific, powerful wind. When He was around, one felt that love. The sick, the weak, the despairing felt His love pulling them, and rushed to Him as a piece of iron rushes to a magnet. Rulers and oppressors felt it and trembled with fear. It wasn't personal magnetism. It wasn't will power. It was pure, strong, resistless love.

The cross is the great symbol of the extent to which Christ will go in His love for us. "No man has greater love than this, that he lay down his life for his friends." But on the cross He went further than dying for His friends. "God showed his great love for us in that while we were yet sinners, Christ died for us." He did not die for good people; He died for people who did not deserve it and did not appreciate His death. His passion to help was so powerful that He died for us, not because we were lovable, but because we were hateful. Every angel in the universe would loathe such creatures as we were, so he died to change our hatefulness into lovableness. We were helplessly caught in sin. He helped us because we could not help ourselves. He died, not only for the sinners, but for His enemies. He died to save those who crucified Him. On the cross He could cry, "Father, forgive them, for they know not what they do."

This kind of love, so intense and so selfless, is what He depends on to save the world. There are three ways to treat enemies that we find advocated in the world today: First, kill them! Second, get as far away from them as you can. Third, try to make them your friends. But Jesus went beyond all three of these. He tried a fourth way. His plan was, "Let them kill you and keep on loving them. After you are dead they will realize how much you loved them and it will break their hearts and redeem them." He could have killed His enemies, but He let them kill Him.

Jesus expected that such love, set free in deeds of compassion and self-sacrifice, could save the world. I think that here we see behind the veil into the very heart of God. Here we catch, for a moment, the stupendous adventure on which God has started. He has let us try every other method under the sun of making a good world. At last we discover that love as selfless and as intense as the love of Jesus is our only hope of saving the world.

If Jesus loves like that, then we, as other sons of God, are to love like that.

We see, then, that to become like Jesus our present nature must be transformed by Him into an intense passion to help those in need. This is what He means when He says, "You, therefore, must be perfect as your heavenly Father is perfect" (Matt. 5:48).

In the third place, Jesus was perfect in faith. This is extremely difficult for an educated man to understand. Our scientific training insists upon testing everything, not in believing what we cannot prove. The Christian life takes the opposite view, emphasizing that we believe the best about God even when we cannot prove it.

Jesus had to fight a terrific battle for His faith. There had come to Him an inner conviction that He was the Son of God. He felt it, but He also pondered: "I am the only one who feels this way about myself. Am I right?" He struggled 40 days in the wilderness with that question, and when He was very hungry the voice of Satan said, "if you are the Son of God, then turn that stone into bread and eat it. If..."

And again the voice of Satan said, "If you are the Son of God go and jump off the pinnacle and land among the people. If..."

Again the voice of Satan said: "If you are the Son of God, compromise and you can have the world." It would have been a short cut to world conquest. He could have done it. He had powers above any civil official or any military commander of His time. He could have overthrown Caesar. Compromise would have been a good short cut. But it would have been the devil's victory over faith.

Our age and every age before us has been caught in the great doubt; we are in the midst of it now. Our nation is caught in it. We are saying, "Trust God and pile up your hydrogen bombs." We trust love and hate at the same time. We are compromisers. We can't trust love and we do not trust God alone as Jesus did. We believe (more or less) in Jesus, but we cannot be uncompromising in following love as He followed it.

The temptation of Jesus to compromise was sharpened by the fact that the Old Testament had prophesied two kinds of messiahs. One was to suffer like the Messiah of Isaiah 53; the other was to become like King David. David trusted God and killed his enemies. Jesus trusted God and refused to lift a finger to harm anybody. He suffered but He never made others suffer.

To be a son of God involves faith in love and goodness. To be like Jesus we, too, will have to refuse to compromise with the idea of killing our enemies. We, too, must put our faith wholly in love, the kind of love Christ had.

At once you and I begin to rebel against this idea. We feel like the minister who said, "If a man came in to molest my wife and children I would kill him. That is my duty. And therefore," he said, "when enemies threaten my country, they are threatening my wife and children, and I must kill them."

That is what we all feel like saying. But it reveals a lack of faith. It is not measuring up to the stature of sons of God. All of us see that the devil leers at us in the atom bomb we have begotten. We are seeing, to our dismay, that "they that take up the sword will perish by the sword."

And yet mere refusal to fight with swords or guns is infinitely below the level of Christ's faith. Mere refusal to fight would never save the world. I have been a pacifist all my life, but a very uneasy one. To allow people to go and get killed to protect me seems like a very cowardly thing. I must earn my right to be a pacifist by fighting as hard as I can all the greed and misery and hate that breed wars. I must work for my country with the weapon of love as hard as others do by military means. I believe that we who put our faith in the love of Christ have not only got to be willing to fight with the love of Christ, and to sacrifice for it; I believe we must go out and find a place to sacrifice for it. We must not wait for need to come to us, but we must go out and find it!

The Gospel of John is to me the most precious book in the world. To me it reveals better than all the other books the intimate family relationship of

Jesus and His Father. As we see that tender family tie we begin to realize what an incredible glory it will be to become a son of God. It will mean that we too are to join that household of the Father and the Son.

If we are becoming sons of God, then the most beautiful thing through all eternity will be to share the living, loving intimacy which the Father and the Son have. They live in perfect harmony, two wills as one, in a relationship that no words can describe: they have perfect faith in each other, perfect love for one another, such a oneness in their planning that Jesus could say. "I and the Father are one." Into that wonderful family He invites us. Jesus prays this wonderful prayer:

"Father, I desire that they also may be with me where I am, and that as thou art in me, and I am in thee, that they may be one in us."

The religion of the Old Testament and all the other religions kept God at a distance. He was holy, and dangerous; the people trembled in His presence; they could not look into His face. "The fear of God is the beginning of wisdom." But when at last we achieve sonship and become sons of God, "we shall be like him"—intimate with the Father, and members of His family.

For that we are being prepared. We must become spiritually ready to respond to that perfection. We cannot spoil it by any whimsicalities, by being opinionated and stubborn and self-willed. To be in a perfect place, like the family of God, means that in love and responsiveness we, too, must be perfect. Otherwise we would spoil it. It is going to be a big family, and unless that family is harmonious and loving, free from criticism and from sharp, ungenerous, cutting remarks, heaven will cease to be heaven. So this long period of life that we are living on earth is mellowing us and sweetening us, and preparing us to be worthy so that we will not spoil heaven.

God the Bridge Builder

Dr. D. B. Steinman is one of the world's most famous bridge builders; he has received at least eleven honorary doctor's degrees for his services, and he makes his friends as fanatically devoted to bridge building as he is himself. His bridges are things of beauty. They are meant to be admired and loved as well as used.

Dr. Steinman has gone beyond his own field of bridging rivers and gulfs and canyons. Now he is trying to build bridges between people and nations. He sees that bridge building is the chief unfinished task in human relations. How right he is!

Why is the brain the most marvelous machine in the universe? Because it has such a great, complex system of bridges—interconnections from one cell to another that can store up and transmit and transform and reorganize thoughts. I think no one has yet calculated how many thousand miles of such connections there are in one man.

Around the world our new miracle inventions—radio, television, telephone, motion pictures, airplanes, newspapers—are building fantastic bridges between one country and another. No one sees this more vividly than the radio and television and visual education pioneers. A leader in visual education said: "The big problem for God and for man is communication. It is a matter of getting ideas from where they are to where they are needed. God has the ideas; men need them." And today God is at work night and day weaving the intricate connections necessary for a "world mind."

The longer you think about that, the more certain it becomes. At last you see that bridges of one kind or another are necessary for every step in the long road of progress. The way is blocked without them. It is true that bridges are not everything, but they are a vital part of everything. Indeed, they are so much a part of everything that not even an atom can exist without bridges to hold its parts together. And that is not an exaggeration!

There are bridges between wishes and fulfillments. To us in this world, life seems to be a ceaseless rhythm of wishes and fulfillments. Wish long enough and, lo, it is done! Plato was the first great thinker to see this in his philosophy of "architectonic ideas." These ideas are first in the mind of God the Architect, and then they come into being.

God puts His ideas into our minds, and our ideas create telephones, radios, airplanes, the United Nations! Here is one respect in which we are truly "sons of God" even now. I think our chief joy in all eternity will be to be co-creators with God. And half of this creation will be a matter of bridge building.

Lecomte du Nouy, in his tremendous *Human Destiny*, has accumulated evidence from modern biology that there is a master mind hidden deep within every living thing. The single cell, whether of a tree or a butterfly or a bird, starts life as an embryo. No life could ever unfold, the biologist now sees clearly, without a master mind inside developing the various parts and breathing life into them.

This master mind not only works within every living thing, it works among them, keeping all living things in perfect balance with all others. It builds bridges between all living things.

It was not until this century that scientists discovered this amazing balance of bridges throughout the universe, because we little men have looked at everything from our own short-sighted viewpoint. We knew that the bee needed the flower, because we wanted the honey, but it was a long while before we realized that the flower needed the bee before it can produce other flowers. But today the scientist sees a vast exquisitely balanced world at work in every clod of soil. Now he realizes that the fish worms are boring air holes and the tireless bacteria are all working together to make the soil digestible for the plant. God is there working before man comes with his plow and his seed.

God has His finger in the unfolding of not only every tiny cell but of every atom and every electron. What a finger it must be!

It makes one dizzy to think of this capacity of God to handle everything, everywhere, every minute. The more we know about this bewildering universe, the more amazed we become at God.

God has built countless bridges to men's minds, but He has placed one limitation on Himself: He does not cross the last drawbridge into our minds until we invite Him. It is a drawbridge which we open and close from within the castle of our souls. Don't ask me why; I don't know. I suppose it is because He wants His sons to have free wills. Whatever the reason, God's final problem in bridge building is to get past the portal of our own minds.

The statement of the risen Christ in Revelation, "Behold, I stand at the door and knock; if any man hear my voice and open the door, I will come in to him," is one of the strangest paradoxes in the universe. God made us, but He fashioned us so that He could enter our hearts only when we invite Him. We are invited to be sons, but we make the decision ourselves whether to be in God's family or not. We are free. God will wait, if He has to wait, a year, a decade, a century, or a thousand years. Why it is that way I do not know; but it is that way, as we know from our own experience.

In fact, there are two drawbridges in the castle of our soul, and the man within has control of both. One opens up toward God, and the other opens out toward our fellow men. If we open both our drawbridges we become God's highway.

This is what Luke calls John the Baptist: "The voice of one crying in the wilderness." Isaiah had prophesied:

> Make ready the way of the Lord;
> Make straight through the desert a highway for our God.
> Fill up every valley and lay low every mountain.
> Make every crooked road straight;
> Make every rough place smooth,
> Because all mankind is about to see the salvation of God.
> Luke 3:4-6.

John the Baptist was himself that "highway for our God." He was open at both ends. That was why he had power.

I saw this truth illustrated in Liberia. The social director of the Firestone plantation took me to see their great hydroelectric plant which runs their mill and supplies their light. I had never seen the inside of a hydroelectric plant before. There was a huge pipe, and four great turbine wheels. The water was open above them, but they were standing still. I said, "Why don't these turbines run?" He said, "Because the pipe is closed down at the outlet. If that were open, the water could flow through. The turbines can't run unless both the inlet and the outlet are open."

I said to this man, "That is the way our lives are. The pipe must be open up toward God and open down toward man. And then currents flow through and the wheels go round and we work with the power of God."

He said, "I never thought of that. I wonder where my pipeline is closed."

Many people who have opened themselves toward God have had a marvelous experience for a few minutes or a few hours, but because the pipe was closed at the bottom the spirit's flow came to a stop, and they wondered what was the matter. That has been the experience of many Christian people ever since Christ came. They have opened, they have received a great blessing, and then their Christian life has come to a standstill, and they wondered why! Their little bucket could hold only a small amount, and it was soon full. The infinite resources of heaven were awaiting them; all they had to do was to open the gate at the bottom—to kick the bottom out of their buckets—and to let God flow through. It doesn't matter how big heaven is; it matters how big our pipe is and whether it is open. The bottleneck is never God; it is always ourselves.

In one respect, however, we are different from a pipe. A pipe cannot decide how big it will be, and we can. We can grow. We are small pipes at first, but if we keep open all the time the total flow for a day and a month will be great and, as the flow continues, we will become bigger pipes.

How shall we keep open toward people? There are two ways. The first is by prayer. That prayer of intercession connects God and other people; it is one of the purest forms of service, the mightiest single power on earth. When we pray for others we open the pipeline at both ends, and God flows through to bless those for whom we pray.

The second great outlet to people is by deeds of kindness. It may be through talking to people. It may be through feeding them. It may be through healing them. Jesus spent His life in prayer for others, and in loving deeds. Any man who spends his life that way can forget all about himself, for he will be the most blest of all. The spirit pouring through him will make his soul sing, and everybody will see the glory shining through. The glory and the power are not his own. He is only the pipeline through whom the infinite power of God pours down to meet the infinite need of humanity.

We become channels like that simply by being willing and unselfish. But the moment we desire to keep any of the power for ourselves we cease to flow. If we strut and say, "Look at me," as the spirit passes through, that "me" obstructs the passage. The Spirit of God doesn't flow until the "me" is washed out and only the pipeline is left. That is the meaning of the paradoxical saying of Jesus, "Whosoever would save his life shall lose it: and whosoever shall lose his life for my sake shall find it."

Stop being a terminus and become a bridge! Stop being a bucket and become a pipe! That is the secret of receiving the power of God.

Saints Get Blocked, Too!

Many people tell us of sharp disappointment soon after they have had a great spiritual experience. This happens after revival meetings so often that some people are bitterly opposed to all revivals. They say that the reaction is bad.

The trouble is not with the revival, but with something else. I believe it is because our bucket is filled up, and there is no room for more. We begin to coast along on the memory of a wonderful experience, and it turns bad, like manna in the wilderness or like milk left in a pail.

The Spirit of God is like gasoline in a tank of an automobile or an airplane. It is of no use unless it is harnessed to accomplish something. If you have had a spiritual experience and it is slipping from your grasp, if you look up toward heaven and heaven seems deaf, then stop looking toward heaven and look toward humanity. You can't have a great spiritual experience again until you have given the one you do have to someone else. That may mean sacrifice. It may mean moving out of your comfortable home. It may mean going where there is great need. Many a man who had been going dry spiritually has gone down to the slums and found Christ waiting for him there, and his soul has soared once more.

In the Roman Catholic Church and in all the literature of mysticism one of the most common phrases we find is "spiritual dryness." Pious people prayed to heaven, and heaven seemed deaf and dumb. The literature of piety is full of explanations of this; it says that even Jesus on the cross cried, "My God, my God, why hast thou forsaken me?" and that God forsakes us as a sort of spiritual discipline.

I think that is not the real reason. I believe it is because people forgot human need and so had stopped the flow downward. I believe it is because buckets cannot contain the Holy Spirit. Only pipelines open at both ends can hold the Spirit. Any man to whom heaven seems deaf and dumb should not look toward heaven, but toward the bottom of his bucket; then kick the bottom out! The pipeline is not wide open until the opening out toward humanity is as big as the opening up toward God. The pipeline is as large as its smallest diameter.

Heaven is neither deaf nor empty. All the resources of the universe are there, ready to be poured on the world. But we hold the faucet in our hands. God says: "Ho, every one that thirsteth, come..." We decide, and yet the law of God's giving is that "you cannot have it unless you give it away." This is the meaning of so many of the sayings of Jesus: "Give, and it shall be given running over...."

The water of life will flow to us only if it flows through us. You can't keep it unless you give it away. You can't even have it. The greatest thing in the world changes color and taste even while you hold it. Let go of it quickly—pass it on. God is love, and love is what pours through. Love does not mean self-love. The moment a man tries to keep God to himself he ceases to have love; he has only self-love. Love is love only if it passes on. So all any saint who is suffering from spiritual dryness needs is to open a wide outlet of self-giving service.

The Salvation Army lassies never write books about spiritual dryness, for they reach downward as well as upward. They are radiant as the glory of God passes through them to where it is needed. "He that receives the water that I shall give him will be a well of water.... Out of him shall flow rivers of living water."

It is easier to love God than to love people. The God we see in Jesus Christ is the most lovable person in the universe—but people are often contemptible. We must school ourselves to love people because they need love and not because they are attractive. As a matter of fact, the people who need us most are those whom others do not love at all. They are likely to be irritating. They are often bad mannered and bad tempered. They may be dirty and bad smelling. In my own work among illiterates I have learned that one must forget dirty clothes and bad smells and rough manners and see only the soul, with its pathetic need, behind the repulsive and sometimes bestial human facade.

One of the problems of those who seek the good life is that the closer they draw to God, the more clearly they see the sins and weaknesses of human nature. And the greatest temptation of one who is trying to be a Christian is to be critical of those who do not share his Christian ideals. So it is often said that the hardest man to live with is a saint! The fault of a saint is his unforgiving and critical nature, sometimes his cruel tongue. How to hate wrong, yet feel love and tolerance for one who does wrong is a problem every Christian must face. This problem does not grow less; it grows greater as one's dedication to God increases.

A great many saints are blocked also because they try to hold God to only one channel. For example, the Roman Catholic Church seldom appreciates any saint except one who has been canonized by the Catholic Church.

My Baptist friends have admitted that they appreciate and talk about the achievements of Baptists more than those of other denominations. This goes to a greater or lesser extent for every denomination.

We all tend to shut ourselves out from God's myriad channels because we insist on God flowing down through our particular denominational or social or political channel. The dryness of many a saint has resulted from his closing off every pipeline except one. It is dreadful how sectarianism makes men consider goodness sinful unless it flows down their own ecclesiastical ditch! To be perfectly fair, I suppose I am as prejudiced as others, unconsciously. We are all plagued with blind areas. We can see the specks in other eyes but not in our own. We do not see our own sins.

And inability to discriminate between what is good and what is just narrow prejudice is the block of many saints. Jesus said it was a sin to put up barriers of custom and make them more sacred than the laws of God.

> The love of God is broader
> Than the measure of man's mind
> And the heart of the eternal
> Is most wonderfully kind.

The little "I don't like this!" whispered in every direction frustrates God, and He must discover some way—if He can—to get past us to get His will done in spite of our silent rebellion. We start by not liking the weather, and that is the one thing for which God is solely responsible.

Glenn Clark's little pamphlet, *The Divine Plan*, is so good that every saint ought to memorize it. Dr. Clark believes that every instant of the day every incident that arises is God's best answer to our need at that particular moment. He who is willing to listen to God, no matter from what direction God speaks, will never know spiritual dryness. The greatest and highest lesson to learn is to say yes to the God who is speaking forever and forever in six billion ways!

One reason it is so difficult to say yes is that God's voice upsets our own previous intentions. You and I struggle between two things, both of which are right—the right which we had planned to do and the right which it seems to us God is telling us to do now. We plan a morning in which to do very important work, and a stranger interrupts us. He needs help; and need is the voice of God. But you and I are tempted to get rid of him as quickly as possible, so that we can carry out our plans.

These are not the sins and trials of bad people. They are the sins and trials of the best people. The more conscientious we are, the more we struggle between the better and the best. The saints are constantly plagued by the question, "How do I know this voice is God's? How do I know that this idea at this present moment is not a device of the devil to block the work that needs to be done?" How do I know that the devil has not blocked this book month after month because he wants it frustrated? What is the answer to that question?

Is this the answer: that God gives us judgment and expects us to use our judgment to decide when the devil tempts us? Are we to use our best judgment and then have faith that that is His Voice? The commonest of all questions that we ask ourselves is, "How can I know, so that I will not make a mistake?" I suspect that these questions remain unanswered in order that we may be trained in judgment. For we are being trained to be sons of God, and good sense is a characteristic of the good son of God.

You can't be sure all the time; you have to guess. But in my own life and experience I find that if I guess while praying, my guess is usually right. I believe it is a pretty safe policy to say, "God help me to guess right," and then to go ahead. Men and women who have big responsibilities in this world have to make decisions and stand by them.

There is one thing that we are not free to do. We are not free to decide whether to do God's will or disobey it. After the decision to join the family of God has been made, the only question we have to answer is, "What is God's will?" He doesn't always tell us, at least not at the time we want to be told. He waits while we ponder and weigh, and the very pondering and weighing, if we are praying at the same moment, makes us stronger Christians, just as a hard problem helps a boy in school to become a better mathematician.

There is a deep reason why many of our questions remain unanswered for some time. The greatest and wisest thing any human being ever does is to pray to God. When you are talking to God you are doing the last supreme thing God wants of you. In eternity we shall be talking with God all the time. So God leaves us groping for answers because God wants us to keep on praying. The prayer is far more important than the answer.

In a Camp Farthest Out a woman told me that there was just one request she had to make of God, and then she would be satisfied. That was that she might actually see Jesus. I thought this request would have been more beautiful if she had longed for all the world to see Jesus. Wanting more for yourself than you want for others may be "human," but it is not divine. One finds people forever longing for some more wonderful experience for their own satisfaction; they thoughtlessly assume that God will reward them with blessings others cannot have.

From beginning to end, Jesus rejected the temptation to use His gifts for Himself. In the wilderness when He was tempted to take things for Himself He said no three times. "Make bread for yourself," was the temptation to seek His own comfort. No! "Jump from the pinnacle of the temple," was the temptation to become prominent. No! "All the nations will be given you if you compromise," was the temptation to use His power. No! There in the wilderness Jesus decided that He did not live to satisfy self. He had one obligation: endless compassionate service. He hewed to that line all the rest of His life.

If He turned water into wine, it was to serve. If He calmed the storm, it was to serve. If He made five loaves feed five thousand, it was to serve. If He opened blind eyes or raised the dead, it was always the measureless love of God in service. He never did anything to amaze people nor to frighten them, nor to serve Himself. On the cross His enemies wagged their fingers at Him and said, "He saved others; himself He cannot save." That was one of the truest things ever spoken about Jesus. Those men had seen in Him just what He had wanted them to see. He had revealed that side of God which no one else would ever have thought of revealing. God stays out of sight while He saves others; He hides Himself and gets His joy out of seeing people unfold the best they have in them. God loves to save others; He has no interest in saving Himself.

The saint is not a saint until he ceases to desire comfort or notoriety or power. And one of the blockages of many a person who is saintly in other regards may be his desire to bask in the limelight.

The ultimate test of a saint is his willingness voluntarily to take up a cross and suffer and die, just as Jesus did.

"Why," you ask, "was it necessary for Jesus to endure that agony?" Perhaps it was necessary in order that all of us might be sure that Jesus understands how we suffer. He was made perfect in understanding of human misery through His own suffering.

I Peter 3:19 says that right after the crucifixion Jesus "went and preached unto the spirits in prison." Perhaps Jesus had to go through hell to understand what hell is. Hell is separation from God. When Jesus cried "My God, My God, why has thou forsaken me?" He experienced hell. Most of us in this world are so accustomed to hell that we don't know we are in hell until heaven pours in and pushes hell out. Hell and heaven are both inside of us before we are inside of them. Hell is inside of us when Christ is outside of us.

I met a beautiful, saintly woman who was bedridden. She was a very rich woman. Her faith in God was serene on the surface. And yet she had doctors to treat her for a dozen diseases. I suspected that the best way for her to be cured was to forget herself and think of other people in need. I talked to her about the millions who were worse off than she was, both sick and miserably poor. But she became impatient with me, and immediately returned to her own troubles. I believe if that woman had been able to give away her wealth and to think about other people, she would have been made well. With all her piety she was selfish; she wanted God to make her well, while she remained completely indifferent to a world in agony.

I know another woman with a like saintly face, but she was different. Her thought and effort are directed toward helping people in need. She works hard all the time, and travels everywhere; she uses her talents and her money for other people, and she is radiantly healthy. The Spirit of God pours in and through and out, unhindered and in perfect rhythm. It never makes her ill. It makes her gloriously beautiful and well. Many who read this page will guess her name—Mrs. Harper Sibley.

So here is a law for the saints: Don't open the gate too wide toward heaven unless it is opened equally wide toward the lowliest and the neediest. Where the Spirit of God is blocked, it becomes spiritual indigestion; it ceases to be real love and becomes conflict. Never ask God to give you more than you want Him to give to others.

I realize that this is not the writing of our "sweetness and light" school. It sounds more like the ancient prophets. Too many false modern prophets are saying, "God is good to us, no matter what we do with His goodness." But I think we need to go back to the plain realism of the ancient prophets: "It is an awful thing to fall into the hands of the Living God," as you do when you try to keep Him for yourself. God cannot stomach luxurious religiosity. If you really want to find God give everything away, and give yourself away. That is exactly what Jesus said.

Success is dangerous for saints, because success always tempts them to self-esteem, which leads to hypocrisy. Many a man, in what he supposes to be a higher office, softens his message. He finds reasons for living in luxury; he becomes an unconscious sincere hypocrite. Few are the preachers in the United States who do not have to fight that battle. More money, more popularity, more success—these are the rewards they get for toning down and sweetening the Gospel. I think the hardest thing in the world is to keep utterly free from unconscious hypocrisy.

One last blockage of the saint is that often he doesn't feel in the mood to seek God. He would prefer for a time not to be bothered with religion. All of us are swept back and forth by our moods. We feel like reading something serious at times; at other times we may crave a mystery story. Sometimes it isn't quite that simple. We may claim that it is just a desire for variety when it is actually yielding to an impulse in our lives that we know He would condemn, if we were to ask Him. If we turn to Him and place the thought honestly before Him, He might require something less congenial of us, and so we do not raise the question we conveniently forget! We agree that Jesus listened to God all the time, but we just don't want to be quite that perfect.

What are we to do with these "out-of-the-mood" periods? Can't we let up just once in a while? To put it sharply, should we pray when we don't feel like it?

Of course, if we ask God that question, He will answer us quickly. We need prayer most when we feel the least like it. Feeling that we are not "in the mood" is not an excuse.

All of us know that when we start a new habit we don't like it at first. But if we persevere, we will at last enjoy what at first we disliked. The lack of an inclination toward God is not a misfortune to which we must surrender; it is a misfortune which we must remedy. It is like a lesson in school. Rather, it is a lesson in school, preparing us for membership in the Divine family.

One of the lessons that we all have to learn is to do the thing that at times we don't like to do, and to reject the thing we want to do. Paul put it this way: "Evil is close at hand. I do what I do not want. I do the very thing I hate."

And all of us in our secret hearts know that no matter how we have disciplined ourselves, we must admit that "evil is close at hand." Paul cried, "Wretched man that I am, who will deliver me?" And there came the only answer there is: "Thanks be to God through Jesus Christ our Lord!"—He forgives and He delivers.

So we all need to pray: "Lord, I depend entirely on Thy saving grace to forgive me. I have found out that I cannot do right without Thy help."

"Just as I am without one plea,
But that Thy blood was shed for me,
And that Thou bid'st me come to Thee
O Lamb of God, I come."

The purpose of this chapter was to discuss the blockages of saints, but at the end of it we find that there are no saints. All of us alike are sinners. As Reinhold Neibuhr said, "Nobody but sinners can get into the Kingdom of Heaven. The 'righteous' cannot get in."

How to Be a River

In John 7:38, Jesus said, "He who believes in me, out of his heart shall flow rivers of living water." And again in John 4:14, He said, "Whoever drinks of the water that I shall give him will never thirst; the water that I shall give him shall become in him a spring of water welling up to eternal life." It is not by measure that He gives His spirit. He doesn't measure it out in a bushel basket. It flows in and flows out, like rivers—not even like one river. The way it operates reminds one of a huge river that flows into a delta: it flows in through one channel and flows out across the world in as many channels as there are people needing it.

This thought is also expressed by Paul when he says, "God's love has been poured into our hearts through the Holy Spirit." The chapter which precedes this helps us to realize how tremendous this concept can be.

There are three questions in connection with such a river. The first one is its source, and how much water is there to feed it? The second is: How big is the channel, and how wide is the valley through which it is to pour at the narrowest point? The third is: Where will it go? Is it free from dams and blockages so that it can flow out unimpeded?

Let us consider first the source of the river. The year 1949 was unusually dry in eastern United States, and our water supply in New York City was dangerously low. Everyone was warned to conserve water, and for some weeks men conserved it by observing a shaveless Friday. But wearing a beard was hardly the right answer to the water supply of New York. The permanent solution was far up in the mountains. It was to find and channel to New York a far greater water supply. In the Hudson and Delaware rivers there is enough for New York City and to spare, and if they ever went dry New York could tap the Great Lakes.

But the supply of the Holy Spirit is infinitely greater than this. It is as great as the heavens above us—but we are just like the people of New York: we have to have our pipelines reaching to the source. So the Christian answer to a weak spiritual life and to religious ineffectiveness is a wider intake, not a smaller outflow. The entire world now waits for men and women who are large enough rivers of the Spirit to encircle the globe.

Keep the connection open! New York offers us another illustration here. One morning the *New York Times* ran big headlines: "Twelve Hour Black-Out in New York City!" The main connections were broken with the main city powerhouse, and all subways, street cars, etc. were halted. Millions of dollars were lost in one day. Here the largest city in the world had lost connection with its powerhouse. It is far more serious when the world itself blacks out and breaks connection with the Powerhouse. And that is what happens when people are out of contact with God.

Even if we spend a few hours or minutes a day with God, we do something, just as a turbine wheel does during that period. But it is only exercising a fraction of our total possibilities. If the connection is constant, then we are able to say with Paul, "I can do all things through Him who gives me strength."

We know now much more about bodily health than did people in the days of Jesus. When a body is weak, the germs which were always present and ready to attack multiply at our weakest point and may result in death. When the body lies dead, it is again attacked by millions of phagocytes, which were there all our lives but kept quite harmless while our tissues were alive. Indeed, this is so true that Jesus said, "If you are in full contact with God, not even a viper can harm you."

But the pipeline from heaven must also be wide open toward the world. It must have no blockages to prevent the free flow of the Holy Spirit. If all the blockages are gone and the channel is wide open to heaven like the wide open mouth of the young robin which is fed by its mother, if it is wide open like an airplane sowing rice across a field in California, if it is wide open in the middle like the great current in the Mississippi, then the rivers of living water pour through us and they pour out across the world. Those rivers of living water carry everything with them. They sweep away obstructions; they break dams. They keep on rising to cover and to heal and bless the world. If a man can be wide open so that he himself no longer blocks God, then all the power and love of God's infinite heart can flow through and out in every direction. One sees a few such men and women who are uninhibited channels in every generation.

Some days there comes a sigh, a longing: "Oh, I wish I had more of God and more of Christ!" That is the key that throws the doors open for Him to enter our souls. If the longing is strong enough the doors fly open and we feel a Divine invasion. He enters when we feel like that, no matter whether we call Him "Christ" or "Father" or "Holy Spirit." He enters because we have invited Him in. Then we feel a quiet joy or a deep ecstasy.

I have just talked with a young woman this morning who, after years of resisting God, threw her doors open. The disease which had plagued her for many years and which, I have no doubt, was the result of her resisting God, had disappeared. She was in such a state of ecstasy that she didn't want to eat her breakfast.

This young woman was afraid the new glow might leave her. She had reason for that fear. It would indeed leave her unless she began to give it away at once. I had to tell that released woman: "This new wonderful something must now be channeled into rivers flowing out to the world." She has fallen in love with her Lord, and now she must go with Him into His work in the world. For elation and peace and contentment are all good, but they are all only temporary. They are like the tingle of the wire when the electric current flows through, or like the vibrating of the pipe when rivers are rushing through. And they will stop unless the river goes on flowing. It is a wonderful experience while it lasts. This young woman felt that she had at last arrived, that this was what she was born for. She was having her second birth. It was to her soul what mutation is to plants and animals when suddenly a new variety or species appears far in advance of anything that had appeared before. When that entrance of God into her soul took place, it was the most precious thing that ever happened to her or that can ever happen to any human being.

If you have had this Divine love experience, you know what I am talking about without any further description. If you have not had it, no description will explain it. A man who is blind to red or blue can never be told what they look like. No words can explain it. He has to experience those colors to know. And so I realize that I am now talking only to those that have had the experience and do not need to have it explained. Nobody can explain it to those who have not had it.

We can't keep Him unless we give Him away. First, there is no room in our very little souls for so much of Him as He has to give. He has got to pour in and then pour out to others. Just as the rushing in of electricity demands that it shall pour on through, so it is with Christ.

Another reason we must give Him away, is that if we really have Him like this, it is the most important thing in the world for other people to share.

Many people's consciences plague them because they have not been doing their duty in telling other people about Jesus Christ. They are bothered because they are not soul savers. All of this becomes meaningless the moment you get an invasion like this dear girl experienced this morning. She won't be able to keep it back. She won't need to think about sharing it, because what is uppermost in her thoughts is the thing she will want to talk about. Out of the fullness of her heart her mouth will tell the story, her face will shine, and she will tell what her heart cannot contain. So, effectual witnessing is a matter of having something which it is impossible to conceal.

I started to write on a piece of paper this morning with my pen. But I couldn't make a mark; the pen was dry. It didn't matter how often I tried to shake or to coax the pen along. It had to be filled up. But then after it was filled up, it had to be used before I could put any more ink in it.

Just so, life is a balance of receiving and giving. But it is not rhythm. They both happen at once. And the peculiar thing about the Spirit is that it is inexhaustible. You get it by giving it, and the more you give, the more you get, provided your gates are open upward and open outward. You can't give it without getting it, and you can't get it without giving it.

The nearest analogy to this is knowledge. The man who tries to accumulate knowledge for his own sake as a rule gets bored to death by the process. He cannot remember it unless he keeps repeating it. But the moment he begins to share it with other people, if they are interested and receptive, it stays with him, and he enjoys it.

In my own business in working with languages I find that I must use the new words that I get, or I lose them in a very short time. The secret of learning a new language is to use it before you lose it! The same thing obtains in the spirit world. The law of that world is: "You get by giving, and you lose by failing to give. You lose when you stop giving, and you gain the moment you start giving.

This morning after an "All Night of Prayer" at the Camp Farthest Out people came to a number of us for a blessing. As I put my hands on their heads I asked myself, "Is this soul wide open for everything that God offers? Is she wide open toward His community and toward His world? Can God give her what He wants to give and flow through her to touch those who need?" And I seemed to sense that some of them were eager to be channels, while others, for some unknown reason, were blocking God. Being God's channel to bless others is a strange and wonderful experience. I at least had been richly blessed. And as I left that service, I said, "God, I myself henceforth will have one hand lifted toward the sky to let Thee pour in, and the other hand of my soul reaching out toward the world to let Thee pour on to them." It seemed to me this blessed morning that the only thing I needed to do in this world was to get started that right way every day.

I have never seen anything that quite illustrates what I mean so well as these lawn sprays that throw water on the grass in all directions as they go round. The water flows through and spreads out in a big circle to make everything grow. He that is open to God and men is like that: out of him flow, not drops of water, but rivers of living water.

The Holy Spirit is more light than water. It isn't a liquid; it is an energy. One cannot write on this subject except when his own soul is vibrating and bursting with the joy of Christ's tingling presence. Or if he did write about it, it would be dead stuff. This water that we are talking about is the liveliest thing in the universe because it flows straight from the heart of God, straight through the heart of man, straight out to meet the need of the world.

The spiritual folk in many a frozen pew will call this "crackpot," but down in their hearts they know that it is true. I say this not as a rebuke, but in great sorrow, for they know not what they are missing. When Jesus was with His disciples, people said, "Why don't you fast and weep as other people do over your religion?" He answered, "The bridegroom is with them; they can't weep nor fast." What Jesus gave His disciples was radiant. And it was still radiant in the early Church. The saddest thing that has happened to the Church of Christ is that it has lost its radiance.

I believe it is the universal experience that the things we desire in this earth are more or less disappointing when we get them. In addition, we always get something we hadn't expected. Suppose you inherit a million dollars. You have a headache with it because you are worried about where to invest it safely and worried as to how you are to keep away from people who want to steal or beg it from you. Your million dollars becomes your prison; it makes you afraid of the world. Or suppose you try drinking. Judging from the way some people behave, they get a tremendous temporary stimulus from liquor. But each day they have to take more and more liquor to get the same effect, and finally it becomes, as the Bible says, "a mocker" that ruins their lives.

But I am not referring now just to things that are wrong. Take eating, for example. We get satisfaction out of food, but if we live to eat, we get less and less satisfaction from life. If we eat too much, we are soon plagued by a "bay window" and the fear of heart disease, and we are obsessed with the problem of how to slenderize without eating less. Our very pleasure becomes our master.

The athlete who lives for the fun of games faces the inevitable law of diminishing returns. His athletic life is short. The baseball player has to retire while still in his prime. He is soon incapacitated to compete with younger men. I do not know any exception to this rule in the world or in the realm of matter. But in the spiritual world it is exactly the opposite. The satisfactions may be small at the start, but they grow greater. It is as the song says, "sweeter as the years go by." Those saintly old men and women, with their radiant smiles, are reflecting a life experience which grew more beautiful every year. There is nothing to compare to the blessing and peace of one who has walked with Christ for a lifetime.

St. Augustine told us the reason for this. He said, speaking to God, "Thou hast made us for Thyself, and our souls are restless until they find their rest in Thee." There is a great vacuum in every soul. We try to fill it with all sorts of things on this earth, and they all fail. But when we turn to Christ and let Him fill it, He satisfies.

Our dissatisfactions are our growing pains. We are made to be unhappy with our present state because we are meant to grow into the sons of God. Without those dissatisfactions we would settle back in sleepy contentment long before we began to be the sons of God. So the Christian life is a strange combination of joy and discontent. We are happy to be on the way, but always longing to go further. We are satisfied, and yet we hunger and thirst. It will be that way all our lives, and it should be. We are like Paul, who said, "I have not already attained, but I press on toward the high mark to which I am called by Jesus Christ."

When Peter was preaching his great sermon at Pentecost, he was marvelously inspired. This uneducated fisherman who had his only schooling with Jesus Christ for three years, poured forth this wonderful vision: "Jesus, being ascended to the right hand of God and having received from the Father the promise of the Holy Spirit, has poured this out which you see and hear." That is what was happening at that Pentecost and it happens in every Pentecost.

The Father pours the Spirit out through Jesus, then through His disciples out to others and on and on through the world. On the first Pentecost day, the Spirit reached three thousand people.

So today you and I have only one responsibility. We must go forth with the flood gates wide open upward and wide open outward and let the rivers of living water flow from God to men. We must forget about ourselves. Our business is to keep open, and He will do the rest. We must forget about whether our words or acts are the best they might have been. All that is God's responsibility. Ours is to keep wide open upward and outward. God will come in; He will go through. He will reach the rest of the world through you.

Many people who are called geniuses feel that the music or the poetry or the vision does not come from them at all; it comes from above them, from behind them, gushing and rushing through like a stream of water bursting from a rock. Emerson said in his *Oversoul:* "From within or from behind, a Light shines through us upon things and makes us aware that we are nothing, but the Light is all. The little eating, sleeping, counting man we do not admire, but when the Light shines through him, then every knee bends."

Emerson was right, but he did not tell us the secret. He told us what we need—not how to get it. The secret is that the way to receive heaven and to let it pour through us is to be open above, in the center, and outward.

But just how do we keep open outward and upward? Is it a question of the will? Is it faith? Is it desperate effort? No, it is none of these things. The secret is in the great Commandment, "Love God and love your fellow men." It is easy to love God because He is lovable. But it is more difficult to love people. Indeed, much of the world is very unlovable, and yet that part of the world which is unlovable is the desert. There is where the land is bitter with alkali and dry and hard. And there is where we are to reach with the water of life.

So we are not to measure our love by other people's love, but rather the reverse. The less they are lovable, the more we should love them. If they don't love at all, we have to reach the whole way. We sing a simple little song in the Camp Farthest Out: "It's love, it's love, it's love that makes the world go around." Indeed, it is!

I still shudder at the memory of a municipal hospital I once visited. I went there full of eager expectations. At the door I was greeted with a hostile scowl. It gave me a sickening feeling. I wouldn't have been a patient in that hospital for a million dollars! One might better commit suicide some other way than breathe the poisoned atmosphere of that hospital. Until recently, most mental hospitals were fatal. The patient may have entered temporarily insane, but he was soon driven permanently insane. The attendants in these hospitals were mad, too, in every sense of the word. Love alone works in a medical hospital or a mental hospital or a pulpit or an office. There are just two alternatives that we face in this world—love or hell. For love is the absence of hell, and hell is the absence of love.

And so the living water is the water of love, and it expresses itself in our prayers, in our words, in our deeds. The more love you give, the more you have. The more love you give people, the more love they give back to you in return.

I suspect that some people reading these words will say, "I wish I could experience that condition, but I can't." And yet nothing is in your way except yourself. Do you the moment any situation arises instinctively ask, "What will I get out of this?" or "How does this person treat me?" If so, self is blocking that way. Try to cancel out every question about yourself. We keep blocking God by our sense of insecurity, and we are distressing God because we have that fear. Let Him sweep you out into the sea of His love. Forget yourself, your little self, in the glory of this larger Self. The self that reaches up to God and reaches around the world is the only real You. The little self isn't worth worrying about.

The trouble with so many of us is that we strut and show off, trying to "make good" or to "be important," as are other people. We need, therefore, to become like little children, pretending to be nothing, and able to sing a little song as elementary as this:

> This little light of mine,
> I'm going to let it shine;
> This little light of mine,

I'm going to let it shine,
Let it shine, let it shine!

Immanuel Kant, who is considered by many to be the world's greatest philosopher, laid down as a principle of life: "So live that if everybody else lived that way, it would bring the greatest good to the greatest number." We are sure that being a radiant channel for God is the best way for other people to live. We are sure it is the best way for us.

The tragedy of our world is that so few will open themselves at both ends so that the infinite abundance of God can pour down and out to meet the infinite need of the world. But we need not mope nor mourn over that tragedy. We can begin and discover that it doesn't take as many people as we thought to transform the world. When Divine yearning took hold of MacArthur when he was appointed to rebuild Japan, he worked a miracle. And I think that if we knew the truth underneath, we should see that it was the prayers of Kagawa that had reached through MacArthur to save Japan.

One of the most wonderful poems in the world is George Eliot's, O May I Join the Choir Invisible. It isn't as popular as it ought to be, perhaps, because it isn't popular in our day to be invisible. Perhaps you imagine you have to die before you can belong to that choir invisible? But you don't! It is a marvelous prayer for you and me here and now, as well as for those who are dead. I suggest that you read that little poem, in one sitting, before going to the next chapter!

God Speaks

The most important discovery a human being ever makes is that God can speak to him. When one makes this discovery it reorganizes his entire life. If he can hear God he can tap the source of all truth and all wisdom. God did speak to the characters in the Bible; that is the reason that we look on the Bible as an authority. All of us need to develop the spiritual ear that will enable us to hear God's voice. We also need to learn His language so that we will know what He is saying when we hear Him. He doesn't speak the English language all the time. He doesn't even use words all the time when He speaks to us. As a matter of fact, His vocabulary is quite large. He uses sights, sounds, smells, tastes, thoughts, beauty, sorrow, friends, indeed, every incident in life to speak to those who are able to understand His language.

And yet I have never found a book which tells you the language of God. You must learn it for yourself, just as an infant must learn how to use his own muscles by trial and error.

The Journal of the National Education Association, in December of 1945, printed a story about some children who learned to listen to God in a school in Massachusetts. Vera E. Smith, a lovely Christian teacher, was confronted by a very dull looking class. She determined to try the experiment of having them listen to God. She told them that "God is broadcasting all the time. Any boy or girl can pick up a message from God if he will put his receiving set in order. George Washington listened to God at a time of conflict; Abraham Lincoln listened at a time of crisis; I should like to begin with you this morning and have a listening period." Then all the children bowed their heads reverently and were absolutely quiet. After a few minutes Miss Smith asked the children if they wanted to say anything. There was no response. Two days later she tried it again with the children. She said, "When you want a program on the radio from a certain station, what do you do?" They responded, "Turn to the number of the station broadcasting that program." Miss Smith said, "In other words, you have to tune in your radio to receive that program. God is broadcasting all the time, and if we tune in to Him we shall hear what He says. This morning, will each one of you turn on your radio and listen to God broadcasting? Everyone ready now, to turn on your radio!" They bowed their heads and closed their eyes. One child twisted his nose and another his ear, another his lip, as though he were turning on a real radio.

Then Miss Smith asked, "Who wishes to tell me what he heard?" Many hands were raised. One little boy, who had been doing very poor work in school, said, "God told me to work harder and get better marks." Another, who was in the giggling stage, said, "He told me not to be so silly." Another boy said, "God told me not to cheat when I correct my arithmetic papers." A girl said, "God told me that I should not whisper so much." Miss Smith says that the ability of the pupils improved until they were able to read six months earlier than the normal time required; one boy improved two years ahead of time. One of the children said, "We are an entirely different class from what we were last fall. Our minds are more alert and we are doing much better work in all of our lessons."

After several months the teacher asked the children what their parents thought, and one boy said, "My mother thinks that listening to God is a very good idea. She thinks that she will try it." Miss Smith says, "Toward the end of the year the pupils wrote a summary of what listening had done for them. They recognized what a slow class they had been when they entered the fifth grade and what a change had come in them both in their work at school and at home. So eager were they to let the other children in the school know what they were doing that they gave a play called "The Thinking Schoolroom," and presented it to the entire school of some five hundred pupils. In the audience were many parents and the school superintendent, all of whom made enthusiastic comments. One boy wrote enthusiastically of what had happened to him. He said, "Listening to God has made a change in me at school, at home and in my play. When I am home I do things more cheerfully. I used to whine and quarrel. At school I attend to my work better. I used to sit and daydream. At play I try to be a good sport. I have found that listening to God has made a great change in me."

Miss Smith also testifies what happened to her that year when she and her pupils were listening to God. This is what she says:

> For several years I had been losing my earlier zest for teaching. It was becoming more and more a matter of routine.... Then came this new experience, and I found that not only the class but the teacher needed changing. God had several suggestions to make to me and I took them. Now my whole attitude is different. I am convinced that teaching is a most challenging opportunity.... I am finding that there is a power outside myself which gives me a plan for living... and gives me the strength, the wisdom, and the grace to live that plan.

Many of us wish we could have been in a school like that! But it is never too late to begin. Children learn everything more quickly than do we who are older, but if we persevere we can learn too.

I suggest that we try listening to God on the borderlines of sleep. There are two such borderlines: just before we fall asleep at night or after we begin to awake in the morning. At those times we are passive, and nearly free from outside distractions and noises. Then God can speak to us with His still, small voice. All you need to do in order to start Him speaking is to fix your attention on Him, look up at the ceiling where you lie, or close your eyes and say, "Lord, speak, for I am listening." If your own noisy, feverish ideas have subsided enough, there often begins to flow a gentle train of ideas, fresh with the clean flavor of heaven. These lovely ideas rise out of the deep unconscious. Many writers have a pen and paper ready at their bedside to record their inspirations before their treacherous memories lose what comes to them.

This unconscious mind seems to have several windows open. It is opened toward the spirit world, both the good spirit world and the bad. It is open toward other minds. It is also open toward our own conscious mind. But the conscious mind can be the master of those windows, and it ought to be master.

Hypnotism reveals how credulous and impressionable the subconscious mind can be. Under favorable conditions, every suggestion determines the direction the subconscious will follow. It is pathetically gullible! The hypnotist can make the unconscious mind entirely oblivious to pain. Your own conscious mind has the same control over your unconscious. You can tell your subconscious mind whether it is to be open to the voice of God or to the voice of the devil. Indeed, we are always doing this, even though we do not know it. What havoc we play with God's growing wayward sons when we open to the devil! Jesus might very well say to the way we treat our unconscious minds, "Father, forgive them, for they know not what they do."

If we are open toward heaven, we cannot tell what ideas will flow into the unconscious mind. If we could do that the ideas would not be fresh from heaven! There is always the glory of surprise in messages from heaven.

To hear God we must do two things, not just one. The first is to spend our days with our attention and our interest fastened on things that are good. That is why Paul was so wise when he said, "Whatsoever things are true, whatsoever things are honest, whatsoever things are just, whatsoever things are pure, whatsoever things are lovely, whatsoever things are of good report, if there be any virtue, if there be any praise, think on these things." For thinking much upon these things plants seeds in the subconscious mind, and opens the subconscious mind toward God.

The second thing we must do is to take time to listen to those voices which come up from the subconscious.

Our minds are beaten and wounded by the pitiless sounds and sights that crowd in from the outside world. We are defeated, terribly defeated by our own world. The radio, the noises that swirl about us, our social engagements, our work, all crowd out our own thinking, crowd out any chance of listening to our own deeper, subconscious mind. That is why the Quakers are very wise when they go to their meetinghouses and sit in complete silence for an hour every week. Moral Rearmament varies this by listening in silence with pencil in hand.

It is difficult to become calm and receptive to God. But the more difficult it is, the more necessary it is for us to discipline ourselves. If our minds refuse to become still it may prove that "the cares of this world and the deceitfulness of riches are choking the word."

The pursuit of riches chokes the word just as much as their possession. We must not expect that we can turn from a day of crass materialism, where we were seeking advantages for ourselves, and expect thoughts to flow freely from heaven into our feverish brains. The occupation of the day cannot contradict what God tells us at night; we cannot live double lives. Many a business man, if he reads this paragraph, will feel like hurling this book out of the window in desperation. He knows that he has got to think about his business; in other words, he must be materialistic during the day. Therefore he will conclude that listening to God is not for him!

But there is a better way: That is to take listening to God into his business. He can secretly commune with God all day. To hear God properly requires the whole day, not just five minutes early in the morning.

Genius in any field is rightly called "the power of intense, continuous concentration." This is as true of genius in religion as it is true in art and science. Our minds work all day in deciding what we should ask for, and what we should get. We do not "create" our ideas. They come from somewhere—up from memory or from other minds or from God, or possibly from the evil spirits in the air, as Paul said. Our thoughts do not originate with us. There are two entrances to the mind, and we allow thoughts to come in by one or the other of those two entrances. They come down through the conscious mind, which acts as a guard, or they come straight through the ether from other minds, or straight from God. If ideas come to our conscious mind from other people, we accept or reject them according as we find them palatable or not. The subconscious mind tries to take the impressions it receives through the conscious mind or directly through the ether, and make them orderly, for the subconscious mind wants everything to be reasonable. This is why we can solve mathematical problems in our sleep if we have given enough attention to those problems in our waking hours. We give them to the unconscious mind and that mind goes to work on them during the night. It is in this attempt of the subconscious to organize all the facts into a reasonable whole that makes us create.

Hearing God speak is, as we have said in a previous chapter, not a matter for a few minutes but a matter for all day every day. We shall grow better and better at it. We must look for God and listen for God in every transaction and pleasure and problem of the whole day.

A few years ago it dawned on me that the language of God is infinitely greater than all the words of all the languages in the world put together. The large dictionaries have about six hundred thousand English words; it is said that the Oxford unexpurgated dictionary has three million English words. But the vocabulary of God is far greater than that! He uses all the words of every language, and yet most of His language is not spoken words at all. It is written into His universe for those who can read. For example, when one takes a walk alone God speaks from every direction to those who can hear and those who can see.

Twenty years ago on the island of Mindanao in the Philippines, the high school students in our church began to write a dictionary of God's language. They never finished it—indeed, nobody ever will finish it. The world would hardly contain the volumes such an unexpurgated dictionary would fill. For the very universe is God's language. "The heavens declare the glory of God and the earth revealeth His handiwork."

These high school students began by taking the words in Webster's dictionary, trying to imagine what God is saying through each word. They found it to be a most fascinating game. I too was fascinated when I saw how fertile was the imagination of these young people. They would take a walk through the fields and forests, or out under the night sky, and ask what each thing that met their eye or ear said about God. What does a tree say about God? What is God saying through the flowers? What is He saying through the quiet sky? What is He saying through the people we meet? What is He saying through the ground on which we walk? What is He saying through the birds who fly over our heads?

God is encompassing you and me and everybody every instant with His best training for sonship. A deeper insight would reveal that He cares for every human being, not only for some of us but for all of us; not only in some countries, but in all countries; not only for the literate but for the illiterate; not only for some colors but for every color, not only for those of one religion but of every religion. We would see the whole human race marching toward "that far off divine event toward which the whole creation moves."

I realize that this statement is a venture of faith. It appears to fly directly against the evidence of one's eyes, especially among the lower three-fourths of the human race, among whom I work. Everything that happens to everybody is certainly not good. Much if not most is wicked. This is the testimony of our eyes and of the Bible. And yet, what is wicked in the world is not what God does or what He neglects to do; it is what man does. Even when the courts call an accident "an act of God," it is often true that someone in that accident had deliberately or recklessly placed himself where that accident could take place.

I have just been reading the thrilling book called *Annapurna*, by Maurice Herzog, about how the frost froze off the fingers and toes of the men who climbed to the top of the mountain. Nature did that, and yet these men put themselves where nature would do it, and they expected to be treated roughly. The spiritual experience which came to Herzog, he would testify, justified his agony a million times.

I think in the next life God will gather up the sufferings of the whole human race for the blessing of them all. I think this universe had to be "made perfect through suffering." Physical pain has been the watchdog protecting life, pushing life higher. Somebody should write a book on "The Values of Pain." Mental suffering is in most cases a part of our spiritual "growing pains." When the present seems intolerable and we reach for that which we have not yet attained, we are struggling in the travail of childbirth toward something which God is still creating. As Paul puts it, the whole world is in the pains of childbirth bringing forth the sons of God.

We complain constantly about our suffering, as though it were our worst enemy. Though we would not dare to say it, we feel like saying that God deserves our censure for that! But I think if we understood everything we would realize that pain is always remedial, physically or spiritually. Without pain children would burn off their fingers, or cut them off. Man is forever beginning to destroy his eyes, his stomach, his feet, until pain comes and stops him. If God can be criticized at all on the score of pain, He could be criticized because, in some cases, He doesn't send it soon enough. I cannot think of a single instance where pain came too soon.

The trouble with cancer is that it does not hurt soon enough. If it did hurt badly enough and soon enough, we should have it treated or cut out in time. You may ask me, Why does it hurt at all, then, if it is too late? Frankly, I don't know. I think that the chief riddle of pain is that it often comes too late.

But I do know what cancer has done to many people. I know a woman who never had the slightest use for religion until she spent months of pain with cancer, and then she began to have wonderful experiences with Christ. As she was about to die she cried in glory, "Oh, I see heaven, and Jesus there waiting for me." She died with the smile of a saint. It looks as though that cancer had saved her soul. She had been made perfect through suffering. So, when we cannot see the physical reason for suffering, the spiritual purpose in the mind of God is often, though not always, clear. It is often pushing us from behind like the stubborn donkeys that we are.

Of course, it is obvious that that does not explain all pain. I am sure we do not know enough to explain all pain, but it does justify most of it.

You probably know that it has protected you and often pushed you higher. As for me, I must confess that I have made my greatest spiritual growth in those weeks and months when I was suffering the most with social or mental or spiritual pain.

I believe that when we face God on the Last Day we shall praise Him not for the ice cream and cake we enjoyed on this earth but for the spiritual growth which came in pain and anguish. That is eternal.

> And from the ground there blossoms red
> Life that shall endless be.

God has infinite variety at His command. This may be seen in any bush or book. But those of us who seek Him directly in prayer find that same riot of variety. This is the reason why the witness of the saints seems so conflicting. God comes to each of us in ways never predictable. This is one of the things that the sticklers for orthodoxy overlook—that just because God came to one man in a certain way is no evidence at all that He will come to everybody else in the same way. I think He may come to people in about as many ways as there are people, just because God abhors monotony and loves variety. Don't listen to those stuffy little men who not only try to cramp other people but to cramp as well their own capacity to experience God. God wants to come to them with surprises, but they reject surprises because they are not found on "the approved list." They try to whittle God down to their own finite image. All they do is shut out God; as Emerson said, "The exclusive in religion exclude only themselves."

Those who think God must obey man's scientific laws are just as stuffy in the realm of science. The true scientist and the true saint walk in humility, admitting that they know little, and are eager to discover new truth. When God breaks through He plays havoc with our little rituals and restrictions.

One night not long ago I was sleepless. I saw a long room, in the center of which sat God with Christ beside Him. It wasn't necessary for me to examine whether this was orthodox or whether it was a picture out of Revelation or Ezekiel. It was God coming to me in one of His fresh ways. All I needed was to believe and to be glad. The Lord Jesus Christ and I spent hours in conversation; I no longer remember it all, but bits of it come back to me. Jesus said:

Here is where the Father and I spend our time in secret interviews. I ask the Father about everything before I say it or do it or even think it. And so now when I speak the Father speaks just as much as I do. My deed is His and His is mine, since I forever and forever obey Him.

The Father and I have invited you to come in and have your secret interview with us tonight, here in this long room. It is the perfect time, for there is no other sound or sight to distract you. In this world of the Spirit it is not rough and crude and loud, as it is in the material world. Compared to those noises you hear all day outside, our voices are very still and very gentle. The Father and I want you to learn to obey constantly, just as I do. Before you can do that you must learn to hear, because if you cannot hear you cannot obey. So tonight you are taking a long stride toward becoming a full-grown son of God. To be fully grown means only to spend your life, day and night, with the door wide open into the secret audience room with us.

Your best thoughts have been flowing from us, the thoughts which had power to transform other people. In those fleeting moments when you whispered for help you opened the door to this audience room and we could give our instant answer.

Tonight the Father and I are helping you with a clearer vision of our secret interview chamber, so that you may glance up into it at every moment when you are hesitating and get our perfect answers. This room is in the front of your head, although it extends out wide beyond your own body. When you wish to consult us, lift your eyes a little and there we are.

Your game with minutes was in the right direction, but tonight you are going to step beyond that game into the game with moments. One of the songs which best expresses the goal for you all in your world is:

"Moment by moment
I'm lost in His love.
Moment by moment
I've power from above."

That word 'above' is not beyond the stars but just over your own eyes. In the secret audience chamber, where the Father and I want to meet you moment by moment and enrich you from our limitless variety, fear will go when you learn to look up, even when the world swirls about you, for the Father and I are ruling the universe. Life experiences will test your faith, but they will never harm you.

Not only is God speaking to us every moment and everywhere, but He is also doing everything He can to help us. In Romans 8:28 St. Paul says, "We know that in everything God works for good for those who love him." And I think Paul might have ended his sentence more quickly, "In everything God works with good," not only in those who love Him but ultimately in those who do not. If they are not following His will He works to bring them back to follow His will, and if that involves suffering on their part so that they will turn away from wrong, that will prove to be a benediction to them also. To say that God always does good and never does bad is an understatement. He always does all the good that needs to be done.

If we could get hold of that truth clearly, all fear would be taken out of our hearts. "If God be for us, who can be against us?" That means us.

But, you might add, does this not paralyze our passion for right? If everything is as right as the Christian Scientists believe, why try to improve anything or anybody? I think the answer to that is easy. Sufferings of all kinds are real, and they reveal a real injury or disease or danger to be removed. Pains should stir us to compassionate service like that which we see in Jesus. Suffering is not what God wants in the world. He uses suffering only to help us to what He does want, which is to bring His children back to Him and to help them grow. Men are not right. Suffering reveals that men are not right. God is always right, but men are mostly wrong. The things which cause us to cringe and to weep in the world are symptoms of the deep wrong which is in men themselves.

I realize that it is impossible to throw the blame for all the suffering of the world on the wickedness of men. Can we blame the savagery of lions and rattlesnakes and sharks or dinosaurs on the wickedness of men? They were here long before men came on the scene. You can say that ninety-nine percent of the world's pain occurs without any man knowing it. But we do not know how much pain there is when a lion breaks the neck of a zebra or a big fish swallows a small one. Is there any? All I am saying is that we do not know how much needless suffering goes on in the jungle or the sea.

Sin is very deep. Curing surface troubles like hunger and disease is not curing the deep, hidden trouble; it is only curing the symptoms. God is unsatisfied until the worst of all diseases is cured. That disease is separation from God. When we get back into God so that His Spirit has a perfect channel through us we have abounding health of soul and body.

We are prodigals. We arrive home only when we learn to live every second with our heads pressed up against the breath of God whispering, "Father, what next? What shall you and I together think, say, write, hear, see, and do? What next?"

Perhaps one should not say, "What next?" but "Who next?" for it is persons that really count with God. Things do not count at all, except as they help or harm people. And so at last we would be saying most of all, "Father, who next? For whom shall I pray? Of whom shall we think together, to whom shall we listen or speak or write, whom shall we help, to whom shall we bear witness, whom shall we praise and love and guide? Father who next?"

Asking that question in all its infinite varieties all our waking hours and hearing His answer would be the perfect life which Jesus lived and asks us to live. We would be asking it not only when beginning or finishing a task but all the time that we were performing our tasks, just as Brother Lawrence did while he wiped his dishes. It would become more than a habit, it would become an invariable way of life, and at last it would become involuntary.

We must not understate its difficulty. It is as exacting as learning to become a master on the piano. I suppose it is easier for some people than for others, but it is an arduous road for everybody. It is not as arduous, however, as the way of the transgressor, for every step of this way toward Christ is a joy and a glory. At its highest it means that instead of thinking alone you listen to God; you think by listening to Him. Instead of talking to ourselves (as we do if we have not learned this new art), we talk to God in an endless, quiet fellowship, never hurried, never worried, never tense, but always aspiring for a somewhat closer walk with Him. For the goal which is the fullness of the stature of Christ is far beyond our sight. Like Longfellow's youth in Switzerland, we are forever saying, "Excelsior!"

The attainment of constant communion seems to be high and hard to those of us who have not yet attained it. We are still spiritual children all the weeks and months and years that follow our first resolves to follow Christ. I suppose only those who have gone up ahead of us on that high road hand in hand with God can ever know what it is like. There are no words to express the experience, so those who have never been on that highway can understand it. It needs a vocabulary of its own, and when that vocabulary is spoken nobody but saints in heaven understand it. To try to transcribe it into man's speech has been difficult for all the prophets of all ages. They were trying to describe in words that did not exist that which others never even glimpse. But this much I believe we all can understand. One can ask God questions and hear God's answers. Sometimes that conversation is aloud, sometimes it is silent. We need no carefully thought-out questions; we need only to wait. As the Psalmist says,

> Wait thou for God,
> Wait patiently for Him.

Wait, listening for him to speak. Do not crowd God; do not wait in eager impatience, but in patience, to hear Him and to do what He tells you to do. It is impossible to record what comes to you, just as it would be to record all the thoughts that crowd into the mind in a day. God talks just as fast and just as naturally as we think.

We who have tried both ways of thinking—one with and the other without sharing it with God—know that there is as much difference in the two levels of mind as there is between heaven and hell. Without communion of this kind with God, the mind runs along much like a popular weekly magazine, if indeed it does not even sink below that low level! But when one is "en rapport" with God, listening and answering, then one's thoughts are wide and pure and selfless and creative. It is the difference between the worm in the ground and the airplane soaring thirty thousand feet above the ground. The worm sees a few inches ahead; the other sees far around on every side and into the future. The worm is interested in himself and the seer is interested in the whole world. And the soul in constant contact with God is far more than thirty thousand feet high. He is God's bridge from heaven to earth. He is like a tall tree with its head in the clouds and its roots in the soil. Through that soul God walks among human beings as He did in and with Jesus.

There is a warning needed, however, at this point. We must forever be on our guard against cocksureness that what we heard was really the voice of God. We have a very subtle and dangerous tendency to mix His pure message with wishful thinking. We instinctively hope that God will talk to us about ourselves. We pander to our desire for comfort or enjoyment, or flattery, and unless we understand our mental processes we are likely to expect only messages that please us and only messages about ourselves. You have read all through the pages of this book that God is forever seeking to carry us past ourselves. We, on the other hand, are forever seeking to drag God down to ourselves. The contest goes on between us and God all day every day. It is a war between the little life which we inherited from the millions of years that have gone before us and that larger life to which we are called in the eternity that lies ahead of us. We are going to find the larger life by losing the little life—the little life which seeks self. God calls us to pour ourselves into world need. He asks us, when need be, to lose our physical lives in that.

We are therefore able, as Paul says, to "test the spirits." When we receive messages from some secret source, we have a measuring stick to test whether those messages come from below or from above. The messages from below pander to our little selves; the messages from above call us out of our little selves to a larger self. This needs to be said very, very often! Even among Christian people there is a sanctified selfishness that differs from other kinds of selfishness only in that the satisfactions which it seeks to achieve are "spiritual." He who struggles only to save this own soul does not get that message from God. If he does not want to carry other souls with him he has not yet touched God.

There is a very widespread religiosity which begins and ends with self. Men belong to church for what they can get out of it for themselves here, and perhaps they look upon it as a sacred life insurance policy for a possible future life. This is the devil's counterfeit. This is not the religion of Jesus Christ. Our religion does not even begin to be Christlike until we reach out to save the whole world.

So, if you wish to test the voice of God, ask yourself whether your thoughts reach beyond yourself to help other people.

John learned from Jesus to declare: "God is love." Love does not mean self-love. John also says, "Beloved, if God so loved us, we ought also to love one another." That is the authentic word of God. John says again, "We love Him because He first loved us." That is authentic. It reaches outward. John says again, "He who does not love does not know God." That is authentic. It reaches outward. He says, "Let us not love in word or in speech but in deed and in truth." That sounds like the voice of God because it reaches outward. John says again, "This is the message that we have heard from the beginning, that we should love one another." That sounds like the voice of God. Again John says, "If we love one another, God abides in us and His love is perfect in us." That is the voice of God. It reaches outward. John says again, "If a man says 'I love God' and hates his brother, he is a liar. For he who does not love his brother whom he has seen cannot love God whom he has not seen." That is the way God talks.

The spiritualists insist that the earthbound spirits are trying to invade our minds constantly. Maybe they are. One does not need to believe that if he does not like it. But one thing on which everybody does agree is that very "earthbound" ideas keep invading the mind all the time, and to discriminate between those and the ideas of God is far from simple.

One ought not only to read the Sermon on the Mount over and over and over, but he also ought to memorize every word of it. For example, if the impulse comes to judge somebody else, to criticize or punish or hate or defeat or to surpass another person, it is very human, but it does not come from God. It will not stand the test beside the criterion of "God is love." It is wholly contrary to what Jesus said, "Judge not, that ye be not judged.... Love your enemy, do good to those who hate you, pray for those who despitefully treat you." Anything that is contrary to that does not come down from God.

> God speaks when love speaks.
> What love can do God can do.
> Where love is God is.

But even that alone is not safe. For the word "love" is one of the most vague and ambiguous words in the whole English language. It is more ambiguous than it is in the ancient Greek in which there were two words, agape and eros. Our English word "love" covers romantic love, the love of material things, and the "love" of St. John. The love which is God is love with the picture of Christ in the center.

We have been talking about how God speaks. We need also to ask ourselves, "How do we hear?" How do we use that key that opens the floodgates heavenward? We do it in prayer, and it is much simpler than we usually think. It does not require some erudite supermind like that of Gerald Heard to tell us how to do it. A little old woman in a rocking chair, if she knows her Lord, can understand it just as well as some spiritual or intellectual giant. We need not strain, we need not use exactly the right words, we need not put our bodies in the right posture. Indeed, paying much attention to form deadens our ear to God. All we need is faith. We believe, then we simply say to the Unseen whom we expect to be near us and to answer us, "Lord, what have you to say to me?" And He answers. At first His answer may not be very clear. That is because we are not yet familiar with God's voice and do not know whether it is God speaking. When God spoke to the boy Samuel he thought it was Eli speaking! The great mistake we make is to give up too soon. It is the experience of the saints that they often have to wait an hour or two before they are sure that they hear God. "Take time to be holy," applies when we are trying to hear God. Remember, He is in you. Or, if you prefer, the Holy Spirit is in you, and you and He are listening to the Father.

Jesus said, "Without me you can do nothing." He might well have said, "Without me you can think nothing, and without me you can hear nothing." Unless we open our ears and eyes to God, and go hand in hand with Jesus, we shall neither think anything nor say anything worth saying or thinking.

It is a misfortune to be too brilliant. Some people think such brilliant nothingness that they never feel the need of Jesus. Lucky is the man whose brain stands still unless he prays!

How We Can Help God

If our homes and our education were right, every young American would ask before choosing his life work, "Where am I needed most, and what is the best way in which I can help the world?" The influence of the church and of my home was so strong in my own life that I did ask that question; for me the answer was, "Go to Mindanao, Philippines, as a missionary."

But where I was needed most was far from easy. In disappointment and distress I was driven back to God until I was close enough to Him to learn how to be directed by His will. This happened on Signal Hill, Lanao, Philippines.

Alas, I have vacillated since then between the God-directed hours and the hours in which I forgot God or even refused to hear Him. Now I know by long, often bitter, experience what happens to me when I neglect or refuse to let God lead. Without God every plan fails.

When I keep saying to God, "I want to do your will," and I keep listening and saying yes to Him, then everything comes out right. If I forget about God and begin to think again that I can go it alone, things go wrong. If I remember Him and try to keep following His will, and whisper to Him, "What next, Father?" just trying to follow, then He opens doors. I believe He does that for everybody. In other words, we must look toward God, listening and saying yes, and then toward others' needs and saying yes to their needs.

If I were a young man again I would choose my career where the world needs me most. There is an idealism in youth which rises to the challenge of need. Every college should have a good course in geography taught from the point of view of world need; then college students could find out where they are going to fit in by studying this world need. Our unfortunate sectarianism prevents schools and colleges from teaching young people what they most need to know. The young man needs to learn the importance of being God's channel, until it is as natural to him as breathing.

Everybody realizes that at times we are definitely helping God, but few realize how much God depends on us to help Him. Many people help God without ever thinking about Him. The Bible says that God used Cyrus, the ancient Babylonian king, although Cyrus knew nothing of God. God is using the Communists today to make us examine ourselves and see whether we deserve the friendship of the world. We are working harder to help the world because of their threat, yet they deny that there is a God.

Two verses in the 9th and 10th chapters of Mark are richer in meaning than appears at first glance. When Jesus was coming down the mountain from His transfiguration, He found at the foot of the mountain the disciples whom He had left behind, and a boy with an epileptic fit. The father of the boy said to Jesus, "If you can do anything for my boy, have pity on us." And Jesus answered, "Did you say: 'If you can?' All things are possible to him who believes.' Then He cured the boy. The disciples asked Jesus why they had failed to cure the boy, and He said, "This kind can not be driven out by anything but prayer and fasting."

Those disciples had been praying. What, then, did He mean? He meant, "Let your whole time be dedicated to prayer." The capacity to channel enough of the power of God to cure that boy had to grow and grow day by day as people prayed and allowed God to make their pipelines bigger. Some things can be driven out by nothing but perhaps years of prayer. If, therefore, we fail to accomplish something difficult, like curing an epileptic, here is our straight answer: We need to devote more time to prayer to God in order to help Him do the hard things.

In the 10th chapter of Mark, Jesus was talking about rich people. He said, "It is easier for a camel to go through the eye of the needle than for a rich man to go into the kingdom of heaven." That sounded impossible. The disciples asked in amazement, "Who then can be saved?" And Jesus replied—these are words we must memorize—"With men it is impossible, but not with God. All things are possible with God."

They are possible with God, but not for us alone. When we try for a little while a day to become channels of God we are unable to see much result. The reason is obvious, so obvious that perhaps we miss it. If a boy saw a champion weight lifter lifting a four hundred pound dumbbell, and the boy tried to lift it and failed, he would hardly be silly enough to say, "If he could do it, why can't I?" That champion weight lifter had been in training for years.

Examine that sentence again: "All things are possible with God." It doesn't say, "All things are possible for God." It means that God exerts more power when you work with Him. Jesus may have implied, "when you help God." The scripture does not make it clear whether the word "with" means "if you are with God," or whether we can read it, "All things are possible if you and God work together." Evidently God is not doing all things that need to be done in the world by Himself. Could He if He wanted to? Everybody asks that question; nobody has ever answered it. All we know is that He doesn't. But may I venture a guess at the answer? I think that He has made the world so that He needs us, so that while helping Him we can become His cooperating sons. I think that is it, although there may be a deeper reason than any of us can fathom. At any rate, all we know is that God waits until we help Him.

A vast number of people are kept from Christ because they cannot throw off their past. The past doesn't prevent Him from using us in the present. But that is what the cross means. Jesus on the cross threw off our past. When Zaccheus the tax gatherer followed Jesus his past was wiped out. So was the past of Mary Magdalene. That is the greatest glory of the cross for us. It has crossed out our past. If we turn and let God have the present, He can make the present and the future victorious.

This needs to be said because so many people are defeated by their past. They are afraid to face God because of their past and, therefore, they are useless in the present.

Thank God, what I have just said of a man is also true of a nation and of the world. Civilization has had a very ugly past. We had just better not try to defend it! Our Western civilization has been living the way that leads to destruction. It is all the more ugly because we have so often talked in a sanctimonious manner about being a "Christian civilization." We have been like the devil wearing the mask of Christ. But if we turn, and repent, and begin to help the world in the Spirit of Jesus, it is astounding how quickly things will change. In my own experience around the world I have seen how many nations have been changed from hate to love. It can be done in a year if we go at it seriously.

Is God, then, defeated until we work with Him? A part of that answer is so easy that it seems ridiculous even to mention it. You can't defeat God or enslave Him. All of us might be defeated, but He will survive. In His vast universe the defeat of the human race is but the failure of a tiny little speck in space. God can do all this again if He wishes. A thousand years with Him are as a day. So we can say that He is delayed, and that He will wait. God has been thought of as "playing a chess game" with the universe, and with no time limit for his moves.

It is also true that the gates of the Kingdom of Heaven cannot be blown open by hydrogen bombs. But that fact does not satisfy God, and it does not satisfy us. He loves us and has set out to save us here. Jesus told us to pray. "Thy Kingdom come on earth as it is in heaven." Another way of saying this is, "He wants us to annex the world to heaven." Every man, woman, and child in the world who is lost or who has hate in his heart is a failure for God. No, he is a delay for God.

Now we are ready to see why God left His world imperfect, unfinished until we are ready to help Him: it is because we are being trained in this school of life to become not only sons but also fellow creators with God. This part of His universe is a joint program in which His perfection is combined with our imperfection until we learn to work with Him as members of His divine family.

So the words of Jesus, "All things are possible to him who believes," are true if we believe long enough, intensively enough, and if we carry that belief to the limit and do something about it. I think the type of religion that says, "All I have to do is pray and God will do all the rest," is wrong. He would do it all without us, if that were true.

But an opposite mistake would be to try to do it alone without God. Working with God, all things are possible. Working without God, nothing will come out right. This general truth is not enough. We need to know how to put it into practice here and now.

Here is how it can be applied. Suppose that we are to have an interview with an important person. Let us try to cooperate with God. We may say:

"Lord, I am to see this man today. You have a plan in your mind for our conversation which is beyond my present understanding. Please prepare us both, prepare him and prepare me so that both of us will be following Thee. May we both agree with Thy plan. Then we will agree with one another. May we both see the importance of what we are doing as Thou dost see it. Help us to see what can be omitted. Now, Lord, I am going. Come with me, and while we are on the way, I want to do nothing, say nothing, think nothing but what Thou wantest. I want what Thou wantest. I am listening hard to hear what Thou art whispering. Speak, for Thy servant heareth."

Have you tried that? Whether it works or not depends of course on whether there is a God who answers back. Millions of people who have tried calling on Him say that He does answer. I am one of them. I witness, as millions of others do, that it makes every contact with important people better. It works so well that we are sure God was there preparing the way before us. Our experience assures us that God goes ahead and sets the stage. He is the unseen companion during the interview.

We are helping God, and He is helping us, and the two of us together are helping the world. Thus it becomes literally working with God.

In the last terrible week in Jesus' life He wept over Jerusalem and said, "Oh, Jerusalem, if only you knew the conditions of peace, but they are hidden from your eyes. There shall not be left one stone upon another that shall not be thrown down because you did not know the time of your visitation." God in Christ was there to save them, but they crucified Him. If Jesus wept then, He weeps now. I think we have not yet seen or followed the conditions of peace. We have thought our salvation lay in the philosophy which says, "In time of peace prepare for war." And then we got too strong or else our opponent got too strong, or we became so afraid that one of us started war. Each side is always sure that it was his enemy who started it.

Will God permit another world war? Nobody knows. We have seen that God set us free because our free cooperation with Him was necessary before we could become the sons of God. God took a chance when He set us free. We could go to the devil instead of going to God. Thus far God has taken the risk and stayed by His daring experiment on this planet. I often wonder if He has tried this experiment and finally wiped it out in some other parts of the universe. Will He stand by it here to the point of allowing us to destroy ourselves on this planet with the Frankenstein which we have created? We just do not know. We may pray that He will intervene before we annihilate ourselves. Many Christians do pray for that, but I do not think it is what we should pray for. I think we should pray that all of us may see before it is too late that the pathway to peace is through the love of Christ expressed in surprising kindness.

Helping God means that we must understand Him, what He is doing, what He likes, what He dislikes, what He is. And that means that we must walk and talk and live with Jesus daily because, as Jesus said, "He who has seen me has seen the Father."

No man ever really sees the Father except in the life of Jesus. This is exactly what Jesus said Himself, and it is true. We have seen gods, but we have not seen the Father of Love except in the face of Jesus Christ.

So we help God, first, by understanding Jesus Christ, and we help Him, second, by praying and listening.

The third way in which we help God is by helping others, asking nothing in return. The man who is helping others for a price may get the price, but he spoils the gratitude and love which would come if he had not driven his bargain. This applies to the nation as well as to the individual. America and the United Nations are launched upon a great program of helping the world. The danger is not that we shall stop. The constant temptation is that we shall ask people to pay us back by granting us special privileges. The proposal to withhold money from India because she will not join a military pact with us is bad from every viewpoint. It will punish hungry people who knew nothing about a military alliance.

There is a world of difference between those who help when their attention is called to need, and those who go out to find need.

Most people will help if a need is called to their attention. They let God come to them and do the asking. But the New Testament does not teach that. It says: "Go ye into all the world and preach the gospel to every creature." We must "go and teach all nations." "You shall be my witnesses to the uttermost parts of the earth." "It is not the will of my Father that one should perish."

"God desires that all men shall be saved and come to a knowledge of the truth." No man can find a word in the teachings of Jesus to agree with the motto, "All things come to those who wait," or "Serene, I fold my hands and wait." It just isn't there!

One of the most startling things Jesus ever said was said to Peter: "I give you the keys to the kingdom. Whatever you loose on earth will be loosed in heaven. Whatever you bind on earth will be bound in heaven."

That is a terrifying responsibility when you understand it. It applies to us just as it did to Peter. Everyone who is exposed to the truth of Christ holds the key for other people. The more you think about it, the more alarming it becomes. We have to bring the truth to them or they will never get it.

I think there is nothing in the world that bothers me more than this. I am just not worthy to be trusted with that key. I am afraid to go to the Judgment Day and have people point accusing fingers at me and say, "You held the key, and you failed to open the door for God." That is a terrifying thought! I wish there were some way to escape it, but it seems to be what the Bible says. If we could feel that only Peter had the keys, we might let Peter take the blame. It is too obvious when you think about it that it applies to us. Even if our door is open toward heaven, but closed toward people, then we have shut them out. Jesus put it positively, as well as negatively, in the end of the 25th chapter of Matthew:

"Inasmuch as ye did it to the least of these you did it to me, and inasmuch as you failed to do it to them, you failed to do it to me." And that is terrifying. But He also said this:

"Whatever measure you use for others shall be used to measure yourself."

In India there is an ancient parable which might easily have been in the Bible. A man in hell held up his hands to God and implored Him to lift him out. So God let down a huge carrot out of heaven to hell. The man grasped the leaves, but as he was being pulled out of hell people grabbed his feet and held on. A great pyramid of people was building up below him. The man looked down and was terrified. He said, "This carrot will break if these people hang on to me." He gave a vicious kick, and the carrot broke. He and all the other people fell back into hell.

If you feel as I do as you face this uncomfortable thought, you will want to say with me, "God, be merciful to me a sinner. I have failed to open the door for others. I have lacked zeal for others. I have been concerned mostly about not getting lost myself." This points the fact that the gravest sins we ever have committed are sins of omission—of what we did not do, of what we left undone for others.

By this measure of what we didn't do we are deep-dyed, terrible, hopeless sinners, and we must throw ourselves on the mercy of God.

In this life we are very inefficient apprentices. We are being trained to become master workmen and fellow workers with Christ in His vast enterprise. Our obligation is to do every task before us as well as we can. There used to be a settlement house called "Do Ye the Next Thing." If we do the next thing well and unselfishly, that is all God expects of us. In fact, our work with God is extremely simple. It is hard, but it is simple. It is keeping open toward God and keeping open toward people and doing the next thing that comes to be done, not worrying about the distant scene but happily doing what we can do for others every day. We should not care whether our work gets publicity or not. Every kindness is important, and everyone who does a kindness is important, because at that moment he is doing what God most wants him to do. It would be better for us to throw away ninety-nine per cent of our learning and our tangled philosophy and stick to just one simple thing for our daily life—to keep asking God, "Who needs me next, Father?" It is not necessary to look too far ahead. God is there waiting for us, and we can trust His wisdom. If we are doing something that helps people, it helps and pleases God.

We cannot keep Christ unless we give Him away. Alcoholics Anonymous know that. They are so weak that they dare not allow themselves to lose even a little ground. They keep their victory by starting at once to save other alcoholics. When the rest of us fall, our fall is not so obvious to other people as when a man gets drunk. In that respect the alcoholic has the advantage. He knows when he is lost, for he falls all the way to the bottom of the stairs. We lose our battle with the devil, and often nobody knows we lost. We can lose all our religion without going to jail or without even being censured by our neighbors. Our sin can be like a hidden, inactive cancer. It may not hurt for the moment. When it does cause us pain, it may be too late.

Many Christians are suffering from slow death of the soul because they are not helping God reach others. In non-Christian areas it is easier for the ordinary Christian to perform some kind of service than it is in this country, because in those areas the people are illiterate and eager to learn to read. They are hungry and very eager to be helped. So the Christians can teach them or help them to feed their families and thus witness at the same time.

We are not going to win this world for Christ until our clergymen get the church members out of the bleachers and into the game. You cannot have the glory until you become a channel.

It is harder to witness for Christ in America than it is in non-Christian countries. At least it was, until recently. It was not considered good taste to talk about religion, much less about Jesus Christ. But I think this has changed in the past few years, in many areas.

Many people are troubled because they do not know how to witness. They cannot use the language that the minister uses. Never mind; the greatest witness is kindness and helpfulness. If you pray for others enough and love them enough they will not need words. In the heart of every man and woman there is some need, a longing to be understood, or some other need. It would be good for every Christian to read Dale Carnegie's *How to Win Friends and Influence People*. We might also study the techniques of Alcoholics Anonymous, for they have learned how to win their man. They wait patiently for months, until some day, when their man is thoroughly disgusted with this debauchery and, like the Prodigal Son, is ready to go home, they come and lead him by the hand back to the Father. So if any man tells you he is miserable and wants the secret of the happy life, say to him, "Start today saying silently, 'God, I want to help You. What can I do for You? Whom can I help You with?' "

Isaiah 6 records a wonderful vision in which he saw the Lord "high and lifted up on a throne." And He heard a voice saying, "Whom shall I send? Who will go for us?" And Isaiah answered, "Here am I; send me."

That is what God is looking for—people who will pray until God speaks and then will say, "Here am I; send me."

People who say that they have not studied the science of reaching people and do not know the techniques about "saying the right words" need not worry. The right words do not matter; it is the right spirit that counts. Even if you stumble and stammer and don't say anything that is persuasive, those in need will catch your spirit. Love will convince them far more than a thousand words or even a thousand pages. If we have all the techniques in the world but lack love, we are like a cracked bell. And people see through the imitation; they see the crack.

The viewpoint in this chapter and in this book is high and beautiful, but it is not easy to hold. There is a constant downward drag by the practices and the viewpoints of people in our selfish world. In every situation in which we try to be different from others there is a spiritual warfare between us and them. Either we lift them up, or they drag us down.

And so this practice of lifting people to God has got to be intense and energetic and constant. If we have one hundred friends who are hostile to it, that means that our zeal must be one hundred times as great for our way of life as theirs. And it must have no exception. When we are in God's service, it is fatal for us to allow ourselves to be frustrated by one little weakness or by one little failure of others to return our love.

Above all, we must be interested in the whole of a man's life. We dare not say, "I am interested in your soul, but not in the rest of you." We must be interested in all that everybody is doing, is saying, is hoping, or our negatives will cancel out all the good that we are trying to do.

How We Can Save the World

We used to be told that ostriches hide their heads in the sand when they hear the lions roar. It is now denied that ostriches ever really did this. But many human ostriches hide their heads when danger is near, and just try to forget it! They are foolish.

Equally foolish are those who wring their hands in despair.

It is terribly wrong for us to think we have nothing to do—no part to play.

It is also wrong to say that "somehow" everything is sure to come out all right. I say it is not sure to come out all right. I say it depends on what we (all of us) do about it.

Preachers always have been tempted to say, "Peace, peace," when there was no peace. Their congregations want a sense of security. Never in history has a nation made creature comfort its passion as much as we do now in the U.S.A. And preachers today find that the temptation to keep their congregations comfortable is stronger than ever before. Today it is the scientists and the military men who are sounding the prophetic warnings.

When the atom bomb first appeared, and our great scientists told us what an appalling threat hung over our heads, we were really frightened. Then we all asked, "What can we do?" Among most people that terror is beginning to disappear. We are getting accustomed to peril as people become accustomed to living near a volcano. Perhaps the most dangerous state of mind is that in which we are plunged right now: "Nothing has happened so far, so perhaps it won't."

I think it would be a tragedy for the human race to get over its fear of the atom bomb and settle back into the old rut. For that old rut can lead our world to annihilation. The thoughts and plans of men around the world are at cross-purposes with the plans of God. Men have turned God's gifts into poison. The threat of immediate conflict seems not to be as great as it was four years ago, yet doom hangs over us just as truly as it did then. That doom will come sooner or later unless we can lift our low standards of social morality. We have got to find a new rut, and fast!

Opposition to such reform does not come entirely from evil men. Some very devout people find this threat of doom corroborating their theology. Some even say that the worse we get, the sooner Christ will return. They wait for Christ to appear on the clouds in the air when things get bad enough!

Others think that "it is all in the hands of God." They can look on calmly while He saves His world or destroys it, as He desires.

One man told me he had made his peace with God—"So let it come."

Still others are whistling in an attempt to conceal their secret fear.

But the largest number have put their faith in "meeting force with force, and gun with gun, and bomb with bomb." "An eye for an eye and a tooth for a tooth," the Old Testament called it. The theory is that if we have a larger pile of bombs than the enemy we shall frighten them into refraining from attack.

None of these points of view will save the world. The only people who can do anything for our age are those who know what to do and do it.

Do we know what to do? We have seen that the cause of our present peril is a far deeper fear than is commonly supposed. No one is more zealous than I to accomplish political and social reforms, and yet I know perfectly well that this alone will not solve our problems. I think social reforms are necessary, but I am sure they are not enough.

You may set up a perfect political system in any country, but if the people are unworthy the system breaks down. Our democracy is unquestionably the best government in the world if it is carried on by good people, but it is far and away the most difficult system in the world to work successfully—because every man must rule. A helicopter gets us around much more rapidly and efficiently than walking, but if we do not know how to run it, the helicopter is a menace instead of help. Democracy is like that. It is a good thing if the people are ready for it, but most democracies around the world have been failing: they have failed because their people lacked character and public spirit and education.

If we are to survive with our inconceivably dangerous atomic power we have got to change the thought, and will and character of the world. It isn't enough to change the wills and thoughts of Americans. We have got to work all over the planet with the entire human race. If we can't do that we are doomed. At best, we shall only postpone doomsday. Meanwhile we must tremble under an armed, uneasy truce.

A generation ago, people were saying, "You can't change human nature." But now we know better. It can be changed. Thank God, that is easier to change than anything else in the universe, because it is so incredibly impressionable. Infinitesimal electric currents which the most delicate machines can barely detect are impressing and changing the cortex of our brains all the time. If our brains required as much energy as ordinary telephone wires, it would take more energy to run one brain than to supply all the electrical energy used in New York City. The brain is that delicate. Evil men made use of that fact first. They did it with scientific propaganda. I have heard good Christians oppose propaganda on the ground that it "invaded personality." But what is the Gospel if it is not propaganda?

One thing is clear that we must do. We must release a sufficient volume of the right kind of propaganda not only to counteract the evil propaganda all about us, but to build up a great reservoir of good thinking and of good will. Only thus can the world be saved.

We could have done this sooner if we had been interested. But we did not realize how important it was. We were not earnest enough about saving the world; we were obsessed with making money. We Christians today must therefore confess our responsibility for the world's failure. While we slumbered, other people were hard at work. While we failed to go all out in spreading the Christian Gospel, energetic evangelists of a false materialistic gospel have gone all out to sow their ideas everywhere. Not only did we not sow our ideas; we failed also to live up to them.

Our sin has found us out. It is time for us to repent. But repentance merely in words is a fraud. Repentance really means turning around and going the other way. That would be sufficient if we went the other way fast enough.

What is the matter with our Christianity? We have watered down the high summons of Jesus until it sounds like a lazy, good-natured, but utterly selfish, philosophy of "Mind your own business." We were able to do this because a large section of the churches came to believe that only a part of the Bible was true, and we chose the part that suited our own predilection! Many of us doubted that there was a future life, and many, many doubted that the way of salvation described in the Bible was true.

So we became obsessed with our own salvation and with our own comfort here, and we gave little thought for the salvation of the rest of the world, either here or hereafter.

We must change before it is too late. Fortunately, the world was never in such a state of receptivity to the idea of change as it is now. A hundred factors have all pulled the world together and made it think as one world. It is becoming one world, in spite of the iron curtain. The airplane and the radio, the steamship, the automobile, the motion picture, the tourists, perhaps above all the soldiers who have gone into all the countries where wars have taken place, have helped in this.

The world is like an overripe fruit. It is going to be evangelized to something. If Christianity is not energetic enough and virile enough to capture the world, something else will be. It may be Communism. And if all the Communists were destroyed some other idea would come to take Communism's place, because these multitudes of the people around the world, who up to this time have been asleep in despair, are reaching up their hands for somebody to help them. Whoever helps them can win their hearts. Our hydrogen bombs and atom bombs cannot prevent these nations from voting Communist, but whoever convinces them that he is their friend can win their hearts. The new nationalist countries are suspicious of people who spend their time only on evangelism, but they are very enthusiastic about men who help them with their great needs—food, health and literacy. If the Christians do help them adequately there will be little or no need for propaganda for Christianity. The people will want to be Christians because Christianity does so much for them. They will be seekers; it will not be necessary to pursue them.

You and I as Christians need some simple formula for daily living that will hold us to our task within our community and also around the world. Is there such a formula? After a lifetime of labor, Einstein has formulated an equation which describes the behavior of all our physical world. Can we write a formula which will describe our best way of living day by day as a Christian?

I propose this. It is so simple that a little child can understand it and do it. Its only defect is that it is so simple that educated people may think it is beneath their dignity. Here is the formula: The soul will have one hand reaching to the sky asking: "Father, how can I help you help your world?" and will listen for His reply. The other hand will reach down and out to humanity all around the world, asking, "Everybody, everywhere, how can I help you?" Wide open, upward all the time—and wide open outward all the time. It is allowing ourselves to be a wide open channel, ever widening as God stretches us. Minute by minute we do the thing that comes to us, not worrying about the future.

If we live this way, the sum total of our years will be enormously beneficial, and we shall be happy because we shall be free from worry. We throw away the multitudinous, useless, and often harmful habits that would encumber us, and live a simple life—simple as a pipeline between God and the world.

Part 7

Two Articles on Prayer

Two Articles on Prayer

These two brief articles: "Meditation on the Lord's Prayer" and "What Kind of Prayer Abides?" help to summarize Frank Laubach's life-long teaching about prayer. Of the Lord's Prayer, Laubach said, "I have become an internationalist so much that patriotism means the Lord's Prayer for the whole world, and especially for those who are being forgotten or oppressed."

The second article contains the warm, calm reflections of a man toward the end of his life offering his most precious insights.

Meditation on the Lord's Prayer

More people repeat the Lord's Prayer than all other prayers put together. It is the prayer most used and least understood. People think they are asking God for something. They are not—they are offering God something.

In the first place, this is a world prayer. The "O" which begins the word "our" is the whole wide world. This is clear by the time we finish the first paragraph, which ends "Thy Kingdom come on earth, as it is in Heaven." It might have been called the "Lord's World Prayer."

In the second place, the Lord's Prayer is not a prayer to God to do something we want done. it is more nearly God's prayer to us, to help Him do what He wants done. For example, "Hallowed be thy Name" means "may thy Name be honored and loved on earth as it is in Heaven." That is what God wants, and when we say it we mean, "I will help your Name to be loved down on this earth, as it is in Heaven." We are saying, "I am back of You, Lord. I want what You want. I enlist."

This is still more obvious in the next phrase. "Thy will be done." It is asking God nothing. It is offering God everything. It is giving Him our will. It is saying, "I will help Your will to be done." It is enlisting.

The next phrase shows this perfectly: "Thy kingdom come on earth, as it is in Heaven." It is what God sent Christ for. This is what He asks us to help Him accomplish. It is saying, "I join Christ's army. I enlist to help thy Kingdom come."

But what of the next phrase. "Give us this day our daily bread"? That sounds like a request; but if it is, we in America can cut it out. Our problem today in America is not to find enough food. It is to have willpower to stop eating before we eat too much. Half of us die of heart disease, which is caused chiefly by over-eating. If this were a petition, we would say, "Lord help us to stop before we eat too much!"

But if the Lord's Prayer is the world's prayer, then "Give us this day our daily bread" has tremendous meaning. Half the world goes to bed every night hungry, because they do not have enough bread. Little children moan all night from the gnawings of hunger. Half the world has too much, and half the world is hungry. And all God needs is for the people who have to help those who do not have.

So when we pray, "Give us this day our daily bread," we are saying, "I will get back of Your desire for all men to have food, and I will help persuade those who have to share with those who have not. I enlist!"

"Forgive us our trespasses as we forgive those who trespass against us"—this is not necessary, if it only means God. He is all too eager to forgive us. That's what Christ came for! Our trouble is that men hate, and refuse to forgive one another. If we would wipe out the past and start all over, as God wants us to do, we could have His Kingdom on earth. So this phrase means, "I will forgive those who have trespassed against me, and I will try to persuade all men to forgive their brothers. I enlist!"

"Lead us not into temptation"—this is not a prayer to God. James says, "God never tempts anybody." We tempt one another. Or we shut our eyes and keep silent while others spread temptations before our youth. For example, our magazines are full of lies about liquor, which is rapidly becoming America's worst killer. This would not be so if Christian people insisted upon laws forbidding magazines and radio from telling lies to our young people. When we pray, "Lead us not into temptation," we mean, "We will get back of You, Lord. We enlist in helping You stop temptations to those who are young and foolish." We enlist!

"Deliver us from evil"—this is not begging God; it is offering to help God, for this is exactly what He wants. His Kingdom cannot come until we enlist to help Him get rid of evil of every kind. The reason that evil is everywhere around the world is because not enough people have enlisted with God. We enlist!

So the next time we pray, "Our Father," remember that "O" is about the whole planet, and remember that we are offering to help God. He wanted that entire prayer answered before we prayed it. We didn't. At least, we didn't want it hard enough to work for it.

The Lord's Prayer is not intercession. It is enlistment. It is saying, "God, You can count on me. I want what You want. I promise."

What Kind of Prayer Abides?

In writing about prayer one ought to be practical and not just theoretical. It is not enough to tell people how necessary it is to pray. They want to know how they can pray. Praying is the most difficult thing in the world for most people most of the time. They may start a method of praying for a while, but they give it up after a brief effort. People need to know what kind of prayer can last through a lifetime. Some kinds of prayer will work when we are in the mood, or when we are in a foxhole. But a real Christian will not be satisfied to pray only on such occasions. You and I want a type of prayer that stays with us and is as workable on ordinary days as it is in the depths of despair. We are sure that prayer ought to be as much a common day-by-day practice as eating or breathing. We all believe that. But for most people it is for emergencies or church services only. They do not like it to be that way and they do not admit it to others but they know it deep down in their souls. They want the answer to this question: "Have I missed a kind of prayer that goes with me all day every day for a lifetime."

The only person who can speak with authority is one who has gone through a lifetime and found that there is a prayer life that goes right on to the end. You cannot ask young people this question. They know what looks attractive but they do not know what has staying power. Only an older person who has passed through the stages of life can speak from experience and say "This prayer worked with me, that did not." He can speak only for himself, it is true, but that is better than nothing.

I have tried many kinds of prayer, and hope that it may interest some other people to know which stayed with me and which I dropped either because they bored me or because they were too difficult. This is like the report of a chemist in a laboratory. It is laying the experiments of a lifetime on the table for others to see. In the realm of the spirit the only thing we can do is to report what happened to us and exchange notes with the findings of others who have tried the same experiments. I am going to be ruthlessly honest even though the truth is not at all flattering to me.

The only form of prayer that came down from my childhood was the fund of prayer hymns that I learned in Methodist prayer meetings and class meetings. Those prayer hymns have stuck and keep returning daily. Singing or humming these tunes is one form of prayer which millions of us practice all our lives.

It was not until 1930 that I had any other great prayer experience. I was alone in Mindanao so far as religion was concerned, and desperately lonesome. I spent every evening on "Signal Hill" talking with God and trying to see Him in the marvelous cloud shapes of the sunset. One night began the most important event of my life. I talked to God and He talked back to me, both of us using my lips. That two way kind of prayer has stuck. I never am out of hearing of others in a bathroom or out of doors without immediately starting off on a conversation with God. This has stood the test of over twenty years. I recommend it.

But there are obstacles to trying this experiment. I find one must exert a little effort of the imagination. He must throw his gear into "idle," and let words and thoughts come as they will, trusting that they are from God—not of course knowing they are. In our critical age it is especially difficult for educated people, for they begin to call up the phrases they learned in psychology and to ask whether they are practicing self-deception and wishful thinking. Some people have such profound reverence for supposed discoveries of psychology that it becomes their slave driver. Many books of psychology now on the market make us pure atheists if we believe them. I don't believe them. But are we guilty of self-deception and wishful thinking when we practice the two-way conversation with God. If there is no God, of course that settles the question. But if there is a God like the Father of our Lord Jesus Christ then He is trying to converse with us as He did with Christ all the time. If God tries He can. Perhaps I distort and emphasize some things to agree with my predilections. But all of us do that all day in every situation. I think I do less of it when I try to talk two ways with God than at any other time, for I try to say what I believe God would say, knowing full well that "God is not mocked." This prayer of listening is more honest than when one tells God what he desires, hoping God will agree. I do not see how one could find a better way than this to try to find the mind of God. I shall not insist that we succeed, but we run a better chance of succeeding than though we never tried.

A great many people are challenged by Brother Lawrence and wistfully long to practice the presence of God every moment as he did. Brother Lawrence was in a monastery with the minimum of outer distractions. Is his achievement possible for us outside a monastery with the insistent pressure of distractions which the modern man faces all day long?

I wrote a booklet called *Game with Minutes* telling many methods which we found successful for remembering God in Mindanao. It worked there. But many people in the United States have written that they lost the "game with minutes" every day and at last gave it up. I too failed to a great extent in America. The pressure proved too great. "The cares of this world," if not "the deceitfulness of riches choked the word." Some people have asked whether it is good to urge people to try the impossible. That is indeed a debatable question. If anybody is overconscientious and lacks a sense of humor, constant failure might make him morbid and discouraged, though as yet I have heard of nobody who ended in nervous prostration or became a mental case. People who try and fail at least do more praying than they would do without the trials. This is one instance of that long debated question whether one should reach for the unattainable or be satisfied with what he can grasp. There is no doubt what St. Paul and Robert Browning would answer. Heaven is for those who have such a high goal they cannot reach it here. So as for me I expect to keep on trying the "game with minutes" even if I fail on the last day of my life. But even that is not the highest form of praying.

Prayer for others is the noblest type. One way to do this is to use a list of names; for example the list of the members of the United Nations which the Laymen's Movement distributes for people to use. I have used the list and believe in it, though experience shows that any list can be a drudgery and put one to sleep.

There is another way of praying for people which not only keeps one awake but gives him new life. Take a prayer attitude toward every person we meet, every person whose name we see in the newspaper, every person whose name comes to memory. By prayer attitude I mean reaching out toward people with a desire to help them. It is inwardly asking God how we can help people. The mind reaches out not to get anything but to give all it can. One feels generous love toward other people and a yearning to understand and meet their needs.

This kind of prayer builds a mental bridge between God and man. I am holding some person close to God. They come face to face in my mind. I see God reaching out toward that person. I become a channel from God to that person. Experimenting with that form of prayer grows more and more fascinating. One is forced to the conclusion that it actually influences people to turn to God, as though one talked to them about God. Intercessory prayer seems not only to talk to God about people but to tell people about God. It does if there is enough love.

The new word "CIHU" "Can I help you" expresses this "prayer attitude." If one practices CIHU he looks at people habitually asking "Can I help you." One speaks to God and man at the same moment asking "Can I help you get together." There is no higher prayer than that, because "getting together" is the greatest need of man and the greatest desire of God. The noblest prayer and the noblest deed and thought is a universal CIHU in every direction, outward to everybody, upward to God. And I must especially stress downward, because it is more than human to reach downward to the underdog, especially if he is ill mannered and uncouth. The more they need us down there the more we naturally dislike them. But CIHU means to love the unlovable. In the beautiful words of Rabindranath Tagore it means to reach down and help the poorest and the lowliest and the lost.

This kind of universal CIHU prayer is possible. It is not easy. But it can be cultivated. It does not come by drifting. It is not natural, it is rather supernatural. At every encounter there is a brief struggle within our minds between the desire to help the man and the impulse to judge and reject him. We must exert a gentle and sometimes a rather heavy pressure to love those we naturally dislike. We must learn to like people not for what they are but for what they need. The more they lack the more we need to love. So we do not ask: "Do I like you," or "Do I need you," or "Do I despise you," but only "Can I help you" and "Can I help you find God."

This state of mind is not only possible. It is also the happiest state of mind as well as the noblest any man can have. It is worth all the effort and sacrifice involved in achieving it. If we could say to God and all mankind every minute "CIHU" and live it, we should be exactly like Jesus Christ in our spirit. We shall not end with the wistful word "should." I know after a long trial that we can live the CIHU prayer, and until we do so we have not lived at all.